87-1073

P9-DUT-768

THE PRESIDENCY AND THE MASS MEDIA IN THE AGE OF TELEVISION

William C. Spragens

WITHDRAWN

Shambaugh Library

UNIVERSITY
PRESS OF
AMERICA

LANHAM • NEW YORK • LONDON

JK
518
.S673
X

Copyright © 1979 by

University Press of America,™ Inc.

4720 Boston Way
Lanham, MD 20706

3 Henrietta Street
London WC2E 8LU England

All rights reserved

Printed in the United States of America

ISBN (Perfect): 0-8191-0476-0
LCN: 78-51149

TO MY MOTHER

EDNA CLARK SPRAGENS

5/14/87

TABLE OF CONTENTS

ACKNOWLEDGEMENTS

This book grew out of the author's conviction that there was no up-to-date work available which analyzed in depth the important relationship between the Presidency and the mass media in an age when television and "image" politics have come to dominate nearly all political relationships.

The analytic framework is essentially an approach of institutional analysis of both the Presidency and the mass media in the overall context of the American political system. Both the media and the Presidency are analyzed as institutions; then the relationship between them is examined in depth, with emphasis on the actual linkages between the two which focuses special attention on the White House press secretaries and the White House press office, as well as the way in which television networks, metropolitan daily newspapers, wire services, magazines, and other components of the mass media handle news about the President and the Presidency. The emphasis has been on recent administrations, with particular attention paid to those since Franklin D. Roosevelt's time.

It is important to note that my analysis concludes with a look at the future of the relationship between the Presidency and the mass media, and the present state of affairs.

I am particularly indebted to Jody Powell, press secretary to the President, for making possible some of my research. A special acknowledgement is also due to Barry Jagoda, special assistant to the President for mass media and public affairs, for an interview which allowed me to investigate this relationship in depth. I am also indebted to the staffs of the Dwight D. Eisenhower Library, Abilene, Kansas; the John F. Kennedy Library, Waltham, Massachusetts, and the Lyndon B. Johnson Library, Austin, Texas, for their assistance. I wish particularly to thank Sylvie Turner of the Kennedy Library and Tina Lawson of the Johnson Library for their aid, and I am grateful to the following who granted permission to use their materials or to quote from their papers and documents: James C. Hagerty, George Reedy, George Christian, Tom Johnson. I wish also to acknowledge the access I had to the John F. Kennedy Library oral history interviews and to the Columbia University oral history interviews regarding the Eisenhower Administration, as well as to the Lyndon B. Johnson oral history interviews. Special acknowledgement is due to David Powers, curator of the Kennedy collection; Donald Wilson, director of the Eisenhower Library, and Louis M. Starr, director of the Columbia University Oral History Project. If there have been any omissions I wish to thank any others whose names may not have been specifically mentioned. I am of course solely responsible for any errors of content or interpretation.

I am also grateful to the various representatives of the University Press of America, including my editor, James E. Lyons, as well as Vesta Koehler and Carol Pierson. I wish also to thank Dr. Harold Fisher of the Bowling Green State University School of Journalism for his reading of chapter drafts and his suggestions. In addition I wish to acknowledge the cooperation of Dr. R. Gordon Hoxie, president of the Center for the Study of the Presidency, New York, in granting permission to reprint material from my article on executive branch reform, published in the Spring-Summer 1977 Presidential Studies Quarterly. I also acknowledge a grant from the Bowling Green State University Faculty Research Committee which enabled me to complete work at Austin and Abilene, as well as the assistance of Dean John G. Eriksen of the B.G.S.U. College of Arts and Sciences and the Department of Political Science in approving an adjusted quarter for Spring 1976 so that the manuscript work could be pursued uninterruptedly. I am pleased to acknowledge the assistance of Karen Rogers and Amy VanVoorhis, draft typists; Becky Rogero, who handled correspondence; Susan Schwarz, manuscript typist, and Carol Terwoord, who prepared the Index. Last but not least, I am indebted to my wife, Elaine J. Spragens, for her patience and for her valued assistance.

W. C. S.
January 1978
Bowling Green, Ohio

CHAPTER ONE

THE PRESIDENCY'S LINKAGE WITH THE PUBLIC IN AN

AGE OF MEDIA-DOMINATED POLITICS

Richard Nixon never came to terms with the
fact of a free press. When it was on his side--
which was most of the time--he took it for
granted as just another campaign tool. When it
wasn't, he and his people treated it like an
enemy. Thus, one of the enduring myths of the
Nixon years is that the press was somehow out
to "get" Nixon, and finally succeeded. . . .

--Frank Mankiewicz in U.S. v. Richard M.
Nixon: The Final Crisis (p. 81)

The Nixonites envied JFK for the way he was
able to manipulate the media, and profoundly
respected the Kennedy apparatchiks for the
ruthless way they play the game.

--William Safire in Before the Fall (p. 312)

* * * *

Introduction: Mass Media as the Vital Linkage for Public Officials With the Public

Television's rise and political leaders' recognition of the key news media role in reporting political events, have left Presidents and would-be Presidents preoccupied with seeking a positive image for
themselves and their governmental programs through the
media. This has been especially true of television,
but radio and newspapers, especially their syndicated
columns, remain important also.

This development has not necessarily made all
existing analyses of the Presidency obsolete. But it
necessitates analysis of the Presidency in the light
of the terrific impact which the national news media
have on the Presidency and on the political system.

In this book I propose to analyze the relationship of the Presidency to the other elements of the
governing system and to the public. Analysis will be

1

through the prism of media coverage which influences public perceptions too strongly to be ignored.

This chapter, as an introduction, will spotlight the important linkage between Presidents and the public through the national news media. This linkage occurs in the context of the general linkage which the media provide between the public and all the basic institutions of federal government--including the President, Congress, the court system, the political parties, and the related institutions of interest groups and political movements. Parties, interest groups and movements are not a direct part of government itself, but they interact so closely with government that a systematic understanding of the whole requires familiarity with them.

With a solid understanding of the linkage relationship between government and public through the mass media, this chapter's focus will shift to linkage between the President and the public. I emphasize ways in which the news media help shape the public's perception of the President and his White House establishment.

A final concern in this chapter is the linkage between the President and other parts of the political system in terms of media reportage's impact on public perception of White House-public relationships.

Next I look at the dynamics of the relationship from the viewpoint of the media themselves, analyzing the question of how and why television has revolutionized these relationships. I conclude with the plan for the remainder of the book, and outline subjects detailed in later chapters.

Linkage Between Government and the Public

The national news media's function in providing a linkage between government and the public may once have been taken for granted in quieter times. But recent events such as Vietnam and Watergate have so undermined public trust and belief in the efficacy of democratic government that in the 1970's we must take a close look at this linkage to determine its nature. Another concern is what its nature and functions should be in the future.

2

"Linkage" is a relationship in which the news media convey to the mass public various perceptions, impressions and images of governmental institutions and leaders which in turn affect the public's response to government. Although individual citizens get their impressions of government from talking with friends and from direct observation of elected leaders, the size of the nation today--both in area and in population--practically guarantees that the average American citizen will rely heavily on mass media accounts for information about government and public officials. This makes it important that the media perform their functions responsibly and that leaders be able to employ the media effectively to get their message across without developing a corroding public cynicism in the process. This state of affairs indicates that both public officials and public events reporters and editors need to re-examine this relationship from the viewpoint of today's public.

A key element in linkage between government and public is government officials' perceptions of the mass public; they follow public opinion polls, seek the advice of staff people on whom they rely, and absorb contents of the mass media. To take a readily understandable example from the 1976 presidential campaign, when former President Ford decided how he would answer former Governor Ronald Reagan's charges about Ford Administration policy on negotiations with Panama over the Panama Canal, he must have first learned about the Reagan attacks through news media reports. He then must have discussed his possible reaction with his personal and political staff, and in particular with Ron Nessen, the White House press secretary. After these various consultations, the President formed a notion about the public reaction to Reagan's charges, and then formulated a counter-charge that Reagan's policy was irresponsible. (Reagan said, "We bought it, we paid for it, it's ours," regarding the Panama Canal.) Ford argued this would be bound to result in hostilities and would complicate the task of defending the canal.

Thus public officials develop perceptions of the mass public and its attitudes. They frequently commission public opinion polls to indicate public attitudes on issues which they may deem crucial during an election period or during a crisis period when decision-making processes are at work. At a critical juncture such as the Cuban missile crisis of 1962, or the oil embargo of 1973 and 1974, Presidents and other

3

decision-makers may factor in many other variables in their decisional processes but they always find public opinion to be an important element; they neglect it only at their own peril.

A second significant factor in linkage between the government and the public is the public's perception of government officials. This is exemplified by the public opinion polls taken by Gallup, Harris, Yankelovich and other polling organizations. These indicate what percentage of the public thinks the incumbent President is doing a good job, and are a measure of public perceptions of the President as one key leader.

At least two reasons for government officials' preoccupation with public perceptions and reactions to their decisions exist: (1) officials feel they will find it difficult to make new policy departures without substantial public support; (2) elected officials are aware they stand or fall before the public in elections on the basis of how good a job the voting public perceives them as doing or having done during their most recent term.

Content of the news media in covering governmental affairs, obviously is an important point in shaping the perceptions of both government officials and the public they serve.

It is possible for the news media to convey either a positive or negative image of newsmakers. The sophistication and the skepticism of the public should not be overlooked. Despite this, the reporting of a critical comment about a public figure may be damaging to that official's public image. Conversely, the publication of a positive comment might help to buttress that official's image with the public. As the Watergate scandals proved, mere mention of derogatory information in the news media alone may not be enough per se to damage a public official's standing, but the media content does constitute one of the relevant variables. If one analyzes Watergate, public knowledge of wrongdoing in the Nixon Administration may first have been brought to public attention by reporting in the news media, but it was not until Judge Sirica, members of Congress and others in official positions began to show credence in these media reports that the President's position with public opinion really began to hurt.

Impact of the news media in covering public
affairs is the result of media content. The content
conveys impressions either favorable, unfavorable or
neutral about public figures. But the news media's
impact depends in large measure on credibility (does
the public believe what the media are reporting about
public officials?). Credibility makes not only reporting in the media important, but it also makes interpretation, news analysis and comment very important.
Thus television commentators, syndicated columnists
commenting on government affairs, and others who interpret events for the public may have a more lasting
impact than reporters who simply convey facts.

However, there has been a controversy in recent
years about interpretive and investigative reporting.
Critics have suggested this brand of reporting strays
too far from the facts. Newspaper and television
reporters, not content with merely reporting bits of
information or unrelated facts, have made a stronger
effort in recent years, to provide analysis and interpretation along with the reporting of the news. Some
government officials say this function belongs on the
editorial page and in commentators' columns, but the
fact remains that reporters have found it necessary to
provide background for news developments.

Controversy has arisen when those who are
described in the news find themselves portrayed in a
negative fashion. Criticism of news leaks and negative coverage usually comes when a political figure is
under attack; when positive things are being reported
about that political figure in the news media, there
is normally no complaint. This is true even though
the public figure may not give the news media credit
for reporting positive things about him or her. But
the whole matter of interpretation or analysis becomes
closely tied up with public perceptions gained through
the media.

Several case studies can be presented to give
an idea of the impact which news media have on the public and its view of government. Here is a case study
of the events of Vietnam between 1961 and 1969.

When the Kennedy Administration came into power
in 1961, insurgent activity had been going on in Vietnam at least since 1959, although there was a period
between 1954 at the advent of the Diem regime in South
Vietnam and the late 1950's when this activity was
relatively slight. By 1961, terrorist activities and

assassinations of village chiefs in Vietnam had so
increased that the Kennedy Administration stepped up
support for the Diem regime, even though it had mis-
givings about some of the Diem policies. The strategic hamlets program was developed, and various kinds
of counter-insurgency training were undertaken.

Americans then were still serving as advisers
to South Vietnamese military men. But the Diem regime
was becoming unpopular with the Buddhists and other
non-Communist neutral elements in the country. Prior
to his death in 1963, President Kennedy had ordered
combat Marines into South Vietnam and the American
presence had turned into actual military involvement,
even though this was on a relatively small scale. But
the American public was still relatively favorably
disposed to these official government policies; the
public, or at least a majority of it, appeared to feel
that the policy of opposing Communist infiltration was
wise and desirable. As the repressive nature of the
Diem government became more clear, American public
opinion became less supportive, but it was long after
the Johnson Administration began in 1963 when public
opinion turned around on this issue. The Gulf of Tonkin incident was reported in the press in 1964, then
the escalation of the war which occurred in 1965 and
1966. But it was not until the public began to perceive policy failure because of news media reports in
the late 1960's that the public mood changed. At the
same time, Senators Fulbright, Morse, McGovern and
others were voicing opposition to Administration policies. In the late 1960's the public began to feel
that while it was desirable to stop the spread of Communist influence in Southeast Asia, the cost in lives
and treasure was too great for a country like South
Vietnam--not perceived as strategically vital for the
United States. Thus the Johnson "credibility gap"
began to develop, and finally the President reversed
the policy of escalation in the spring of 1968 and did
move toward negotiation with the Viet Cong and the
North Vietnamese in Paris. Public opposition to the
war by that time had grown to the point that two Democratic presidential candidates, Robert Kennedy and
Eugene McCarthy, had based their campaigns largely on
opposition to the war in Vietnam. The eventual winner,
Richard Nixon, felt he had to obligate himself to a
policy of at least gradual withdrawal from South Vietnam. After his election in 1969, Nixon began to carry

6

out this policy.[1]

It should not be overlooked that the news media impact alone, despite its significance, alone, did not bring about the turnaround in Vietnam policy. This policy shift was also closely related to the shift in public opinion, and the fact that many leaders such as Robert Kennedy and McCarthy and others were now speaking out against the war and calling for an early settlement of the hostilities.

For a second example of media impact, consider Vietnam policy during the Nixon and Ford years between 1969 and 1975. All during the Nixon Administration (1969-1974) the Administration's foreign policy aimed at achieving a negotiated truce and withdrawal of American troops from Vietnam. The truce was actually achieved in the early part of 1973, after an election-eve statement in 1972 by Secretary of State Henry Kissinger that "peace is at hand" proved to be premature. All through this period, the Nixon Administration

---

[1]See, for example: David Halberstam, The Best and the Brightest (Greenwich, Conn.: Fawcett Crest Books, 1973); Bernard B. Fall, The Two Vietnams: A Political and Military Analysis, Revised Edition (New York: Frederick A. Praeger, Publishers, 1965); Bernard B. Fall, Last Reflections on a War (Garden City, New York: Doubleday & Co., 1967); Robert Shaplen, The Lost Revolution: The U.S. in Vietnam, 1946-1966 (New York: Harper Colophon Books, 1966); Robert Shaplen, The Road From War: Vietnam 1965-1970 (New York: Harper & Row, 1970); Robert S. McNamara, The Essence of Security: Reflections in Office (New York: Harper & Row, 1968), especially pp. 22-24; Lyndon B. Johnson, The Vantage Point, Perspectives on the Presidency, 1963-1969 (New York: Holt, Rinehart and Winston, 1971), especially pp. 42-68, 112-153, 232-264, 365-424, 493-531, 605; Doris Kearns, Lyndon Johnson and the American Dream (New York: Harper & Row, 1976), especially pp. 251-285, 335-352; Joseph A. Califano, Jr., A Presidential Nation (New York: W. W. Norton & Co., 1975), especially pp. 100-121; J. William Fulbright, The Arrogance of Power (New York: Vintage Books, 1966); Chester L. Cooper, The Lost Crusade: America in Vietnam (Greenwich, Conn.: Fawcett Premier Books, 1972); Robert Metz, CBS: Reflections in a Bloodshot Eye (Chicago: Playboy Press, 1975), especially pp. 351-354.

attempted to sell its position of gradual withdrawal and Vietnamization of the war as a strong anti-Communistic stand.

However, the political right was always dubious of the Administration's position; when it became clear that the truce was one in name only and largely a cover for allowing graceful withdrawal of the United States from the war, many erstwhile supporters of Nixon's foreign policy began to turn against him independently of the events of the Watergate scandal. Again, this perception was aided by news media accounts of what was occurring, but it could not have become so widespread had there not been political leaders and others actively promoting this viewpoint.

For the left, the war had remained politically unpopular ever since the 1968 campaign, when leftwing defections from the Democratic campaign had caused the defeat of Hubert Humphrey, the Democratic presidential nominee. This anti-war sentiment, found in large measure in the domestic peace movement, furnished one of the basic constituencies for the McGovern campaign of 1972. It was not McGovern's view on the war which defeated him in 1972 so much as the public's perception that Nixon was ending American involvement in the war and that McGovern had committed other errors in his campaign--regarding the $1,000 "demogrant" program[2] and the controversy over whether Senator Thomas Eagleton should be his running-mate. In this instance, Nixon benefited all during the 1972 campaign by the media's focus of attention on the weaknesses of McGovern. It

---

[2]See Gordon L. Weil, The Long Shot: George McGovern Runs for President (New York: W. W. Norton & Co., 1973), pp. 69-89 ("The Controversy over $1,000"). "Under the demogrant idea, each person would receive a given sum of money from the government. (McGovern suggested $1,000.) For middle income people, part of the demogrant would be taxed back. For upper income people, the entire demogrant would be returned in taxes and the program itself would be financed by higher taxes on the wealthy. . . . The demogrant actually would act as a strong work incentive to the poor to seek jobs because they would not lose their full payment when they began to earn income. . . ." (p. 75). McGovern was never able to explain the plan satisfactorily to the electorate. See also Theodore H. White, The Making of the President 1972 (New York: Bantam

8

was only after the election was over and the James
McCord disclosures put Nixon in an embarrassing light
that the public began to see the true nature of the
Nixon Administration and the men who led it. Again
events outside the media made the real difference but
the media provided the catalytic agent for change.[3]

The final phase of this review of Vietnam
policy covers the period between the Nixon-Kissinger
truce of early 1973 and the collapse of South Vietnam
in early 1975. It was becoming apparent to most Americans that, because of the essential corruptness of the
Thieu government, South Vietnam was destined to fall
to the Communists despite what was done in the way of
economic and military aid by the United States. This
both explains why near the end of the long Vietnam
ordeal, Congress refused to supply further aid, and
why this position appeared to reflect the dominant
public opinion of the time. The public appeared to
feel the entire venture had been a mistake and it
would be a mistake to throw good money after bad.[4]

Another example of the news media impact is
found in the tragedy of Watergate and the scandals
between 1972 and 1974 which led to the ultimate downfall of the Nixon Administration.

Books, 1973); ". . . Quite simply, the demogrant program promised $1,000 a year to every man, woman and
child in America from Henry Ford and Jean Paul Getty
to each unwed mother with her out-of-wedlock children
in the city slum. . . . The $1,000-a-head demogrant
program is not nearly as bizarre as it was later made
to seem. . . . Everyone would get a minimum $1,000 a
year from the federal government--and then the government would tax back enough from the comfortable above
a certain gross income to make up for what it paid to
the poor. So far, so good. But what kind of new
taxes? On whom would they fall?. . . . The trouble
was that no one on McGovern's staff knew. . . ." --pp.
156, 157.

[3]See Nicholas Katzenbach, "Foreign Policy, Public Opinion, and Secrecy," Foreign Affairs, October
1973, Vol. 52, No. 1, pp. 1-19.

[4]See Congressional Quarterly, Presidency 1975
(Washington: Congressional Quarterly, 1976), pp. 3, 4.

The Nixon Administration's connection with the spring 1972 break-in at the Democratic National Committee headquarters in Washington's Watergate Hotel complex had been known prior to the 1972 election. But the news media were preoccupied with the McGovern campaign, except for fairly accurate reporting by Woodward and Bernstein in the Washington _Post_, and some election eve reporting by Walter Cronkite on CBS News, and in the New York _Times_. Thus the public believed that the press did not take the anti-Nixon charges seriously and that routine partisan activities were involved. The true nature of the scandals became known only when the media reported the cover-up connected with the trial of McCord and other defendants and the allegations made by McCord in his famous letter to Judge Sirica led to the Senate Watergate Committee investigation. Even then, it was not until the media had extensively reported this and other wrongdoing by Nixon and associates that the 1974 move toward the impeachment of Nixon actually got underway in earnest. At this point the news media probably hastened the end of the Nixon regime by pointing out the possibility that money contributed by Howard Hughes had been used illegally by Bebe Rebozo to make purchases of jewelry for Mrs. Nixon, that the President was delinquent in payment of his income taxes, and many other disclosures. But opinion in the nation really had turned against Nixon, as measured in the public opinion polls, before Congress appeared ready to take decisive action.[5] After three impeachment articles were voted by the House Judiciary Committee in the summer of 1974, following a Supreme Court ruling on release of the tapes, and after the White House finally disclosed a tape which indicated that the President did indeed become involved in the obstruction of justice, Nixon was finally forced to resign or face impeachment. But in this case at least, public opinion led congressional opinion, and public

[5]Anthony Lukas, _Nightmare_ (New York: Viking Press, 1976); Theodore H. White, _Breach of Faith: The Fall of Richard Nixon_ (New York: Dell, 1975); William Safire, _Before the Fall: An Inside View of the Pre-Watergate White House_ (New York: Belmont Tower Books, 1975); Jonathan Schell, _The Time of Illusion_ (New York: Vintage Books, 1975); Elizabeth Drew, _Washington Journal: The Events of 1973-1974_ (New York: Vintage Books, 1976).

opinion was mobilized or at least in part catalyzed by media disclosures about Nixon's wrongdoing. Later disclosures brought out information about still more things that had occurred but by this time the real outcome had been largely determined. A major turning point was the "Saturday Night Massacre" of October 1973 which rapidly weakened public support for Nixon.

As for the linkage role of the news media between government and the public, the mass media represent a two-edged sword. They cannot long get away with the publication of fabricated or exaggerated material because of the intense public scrutiny to which they are exposed. The media can provide a public relations "buildup" and contribute to positive public images of political leaders and institutions, when good things are said or reported about them.

Alternatively, as the Vietnam and Watergate experience shows, the media can also be an element in destroying the reputations of Presidents and other public leaders when derogatory information is brought out about them. However, it is clear that the media do not do these things alone; they basically must report the actions of politicians, and the public reacts to this.

Linkage Between President and Public

To analyze the linkage provided by the mass media between the President and the public, let us examine a special case of the general phenomenon of linkage between government and the public. Statements from the 1976 presidential campaign would lead one to believe that this linkage is tenuous at best.

Realistically, it is difficult to describe the perception of the public by the President and the White House staff, because very few persons have served as President and almost as few have held key White House staff positions. But we do have some evidence that a President typically feels himself responsible to the public. He feels he must be responsive to the public in order to retain the kind of support that will make it politically possible for him to do his job. In two recent cases where Presidents lost that kind of public support, involving Lyndon Johnson and Vietnam and Richard Nixon and Watergate, both men lost their effective power to govern, with crippling effects on the Presidency.

To the degree that Kennedy and Ford were able to elicit this kind of support, and to the degree that Johnson was able to elicit it during the Great Society period of his administration (approximately the first two or three years), we have a pattern of a working relationship between President and public which can sustain White House programs and help an incumbent President build a successful record. This will be discussed later in terms of specifics.

After each President takes office, he usually has perhaps two years during his first term when he has, or can build, fairly solid support. During that time he must try to achieve his controversial legislation (if he has any), as it will normally become more difficult for him the longer he has been in office. There are of course exceptions to this pattern. President Kennedy was elected by a very close margin, and he spent a good part of his first two years building a supportive coalition which would sustain his policy initiatives. He never got the backing of foreign-policy hard-liners nor much of the business community; yet he was quite popular with the mass public at the time of his death, and was in a firmer position with Congress then than he had been before. He did, however, face a Congress dominated by the conservative coalition, and his legislative victories were hard-won and dearly bought. He was rallying public opinion on several key issues--civil rights, the test-ban treaty, the tax cut bill--at the time of his death, but of course the achievements had to take place in the Johnson years. And Lyndon Johnson was typical in that much of the movement during his administration did come during those first two or three years. Toward the end of his term, he became almost entirely absorbed in the crises of Vietnam and domestic problems, such as riots in Detroit, Newark and other major cities.

As for the view of these events from the White House staff, some of the best testimony has come from former White House staffers, who have written memoirs about their experiences. Jack Valenti and Bill Moyers, who served Johnson well, and Ted Sorensen and Kenneth O'Donnell, who served Kennedy well, all preserved their

views in memoirs.[6] From the staff aide's point of
view, all is subordinated to the success of the man on
whose staff the aide serves. This is true to a considerable degree for senators and congressmen, but it
is vitally true for a President, who has a great deal
more at stake in his every move. The staff aides
follow polling results and the national news media to
keep up with the public pulse, and they may at times
propose an over-cautious course for the Presidents
they serve, but they do it in ways they perceive to be
in the President's best interest.

White House staffers may do a disservice to
their President, by keeping important information from
him or by overshielding him from unpleasant news.
This was true in the case of Richard Nixon and the
Watergate scandals, but it is doubtless also true to
some extent in each Administration.

As far as public information is concerned, the
key White House staff position is that of press secretary. Jody Powell, a veteran of the Carter gubernatorial term in Atlanta, holds that position in the
Carter Administration.[7] Ron Nessen, a former correspondent for the National Broadcasting Company, has
served in this position for President Ford. His
immediate predecessor was Herald ter Horst, veteran
correspondent for the Detroit News, who served Gerald
Ford as press secretary during the first month of his

---

[6]See Jack Valenti, A Very Human President (New
York: Pocket Books, 1977); Bill Moyers, Listening to
America: A Traveler Rediscovers His Country (New York:
Harper's Magazine Press, 1971); Theodore C. Sorensen,
Kennedy (New York: Harper & Row, 1965); Theodore C.
Sorensen, The Kennedy Legacy: A Peaceful Revolution
for the Seventies (New York: New American Library,
1969); Kenneth P. O'Donnell and David F. Powers with
Joe McCarthy, "Johnny, We Hardly Knew Ye": Memories of
John Fitzgerald Kennedy (New York: Pocket Books, 1973).

[7]See Kandy Stroud, How Jimmy Won (New York:
William Morrow & Co., 1977), especially Chapter 18,
"Jody Powell, Press Secretary," pp. 217-227. Powell
was a political science major at Georgia State Uni-
versity and did graduate work in political science at
Emory University in Atlanta before joining the 1970
Carter gubernatorial campaign. He has been with Carter
ever since.

Administration before resigning in protest over the pardon of former President Richard Nixon.

Among the best known press secretaries in previous administrations have been Bill Moyers (Johnson), Pierre Salinger (Kennedy), and James C. Hagerty (Eisenhower). Hagerty was considered perhaps the most professional of these men, but Salinger and Moyers were held in relatively high regard by the news media.

The press secretary who had the most difficult press relations in recent years was Ron Ziegler, press secretary to President Nixon. Ziegler was unpopular with the news media because he reflected the Nixon Administration's dislike for much of the press, and he sometimes operated in a high-handed way. He also had a problem which has been true to a lesser degree for Nessen--he was not always informed about important stories. Lack of information puts a press secretary in a difficult position with the news media, even though the latter are aware the secretary's first loyalty is to the President rather than to the press. Press secretaries perceive the public primarily from the viewpoint of the President and the administration and only secondarily from the viewpoint of what they believe the news media want for news dissemination. But some have handled this role better than others, and the most successful ones, such as Hagerty, Salinger, Moyers, and for a time George Reedy, have been successful because they viewed the mass media as representing a channel to the public through which favorable views of the Administration in power could be funneled.

Perception of the President and his White House staff by the public depends in large measure on the reportage in the mass media, including television (especially network coverage), radio (primarily the networks), and newspapers (wire services and large daily newspapers such as the New York _Times_ and Washington _Post_ are especially important in this category).

Even during presidential campaigns when most of the public gets an opportunity to see a traveling incumbent President if it wishes, most citizens get only a fleeting glimpse of the President. And then he is usually surrounded by Secret Service security

agents.[8] President Carter has tried to develop a more
extensive relationship with the public, including his
"inaugural walk" in January 1977, a "town meeting" and
a "phone-in" as well as an FDR-style "fireside chat."

For this reason--limited personal exposure of
Presidents to the public--most of the impressions
which the American public develops about an American
President grow out of coverage of his activities in
the mass media, especially television. The President's activities are covered daily on network television, including filmed and taped coverage and on
some special occasions, such as the State of the Union
message to Congress, live coverage. Thus, the mass
media perform the important role of surrogate witness
to presidential activities for the mass public most of
the time. It is chiefly from the media and their
coverage and commentaries that the public forms its
impressions of the President. A typical citizen may
see the President in person only once or twice or less
during a single Administration--and that perhaps at
campaign time--but he or she will probably see the
President daily if he or she so wishes by television.
Prior to television, citizens occasionally would see
their President in newsreels shown on local movie
theater screens. This aspect of the public's perception of the President in modern America makes possible
the phenomenon known as "image politics".

Perception of presidential candidates also
comes largely through the news media, although they
may be somewhat more open to direct personal exposure
to the public. The media's crucial role can be seen
in the part played by the media in building up to
celebrity status such men as John F. Kennedy, George
McGovern and Jimmy Carter--and in earlier days when
radio exposure was what counted, men like Wendell
Willkie. Television has made it possible for a relatively obscure and unknown politician to become--in
Spiro Agnew's phrase--"a household word" within a
matter of days or weeks.

_____

[8]Each President gets a considerable amount of
threatening mail, and two attempts on President Ford's
life were made within a span of about 15 days in California in September of 1975. An unarmed woman got
inside the grounds of the Carter White House in March
1977.

The public's perception of the President is also magnified by the President's nearly unlimited access to the news media. When President Johnson or President Nixon wanted to appear on network television, they normally had merely to life a phone to make a request to the network presidents and they were soon on the air. President Ford was sometimes denied this privilege, but in practice he too could get national network exposure on short notice, while Ronald Reagan, Frank Church, "Mo" Udall, and other presidential candidates usually had to purchase time or do something especially newsworthy to achieve the same kind of exposure. During the "honeymoon" Carter never failed to get exposure when he wanted it.

Congress can in no way match the President's exposure in prime time, for even when the opposition is given time it does not achieve the ratings scored by the President. Apparently Congress can do little about this, although by 1977 it was moving toward limited telecasting of floor debates or important committee sessions. A large audience was obtained by the Ervin Committee during the Senate Watergate hearings, and by the Fulbright Committee during the Senate Vietnam hearings, but normally such media popularity is a transitory phenomenon. Thus the President can expect to dominate the media if he knows how to use them properly.

The public's perception of White House aides is normally rather dim because aides purposely leave the limelight to the President. President Carter does not have a chief of staff, but the two most prominent aides of his administration are Hamilton Jordan and Jody Powell. Richard Cheney, President Ford's "chief of staff", was probably known to only a handful of people outside of Washington who normally follow national politics closely. The one exception to this in most administrations is the press secretary or news secretary, who is fairly well-known, as is the case with Ron Nessen.

In extraordinary circumstances, such as the Watergate notoriety, aides such as John Dean, H. R. Haldeman and John Ehrlichman may receive widespread publicity and become quite well-known to the public. During the Nixon Administration, Haldeman and Ehrlichman were probably better known than many cabinet members. During the Johnson Administration, McGeorge Bundy was probably better known than many of the Johnson cabinet officers. The visibility of his staff to

16

the public will depend to some extent on how visible
the President wishes them to be. Sometimes, Presidents become resentful when staff members get too much
of the limelight. It is seldom, however, that a President will publicly rebuke a press secretary the way
Richard Nixon did in New Orleans when he bodily turned
Ron Ziegler around and ordered him to take the press--
which had been following Nixon by mistake--elsewhere.
The original White House aides under Franklin D.
Roosevelt had a "passion for anonymity" although some
such as Tommy Corcoran became well-known; there was no
one on FDR's staff with the visibility of a Kissinger,
a Sorensen, or a Bundy. The importance of the White
House staff had grown considerably since Kennedy's
time and it was probably this growth in importance of
the staff which led to its getting broader publicity,
and to the public's greater awareness of it. The
Watergate affair no doubt did some short-range damage
to the standing of the White House staff with the public, as Dean, Haldeman and Ehrlichman among others
were discredited by the scandals. However, in the
long run, the trend toward greater public visibility of
White House staff personnel can be expected to continue.

An important mass media linkage function
between President and public is the content of news
media coverage of White House actions. Coverage may
give favorable or unfavorable connotations to the public, and this may be related to some extent to the
kinds of events which the news media select to cover.
The President has some control over this, since it is
the President and his press secretary who determine
what events the press will be notified about in
advance; but the President's control is partial,
because, with our free press, the news media select
those events to which they will give coverage.

During the Kennedy Administration, favorable
coverage was given by the majority of newspapers and
television reporters to the President and his family,
as well as the White House staff. Both President Kennedy and his aides cultivated the news media in an
effort to receive favorable coverage. Certain pro-
Administration newsmen were given an opportunity for
exclusive interviews; this brought criticism from
their disappointed competitors, but the one-on-one
interviews were widespread enough that the criticism
was muted when they got their opportunity to interview
the President. Pierre Salinger also was gifted at cultivating good will among the working press, and his

sense of humor, as well as that of the President, often paid off handsomely in good treatment in news media.[9] President Kennedy sometimes bantered at news conferences with well-known news media people such as May Craig, of the Portland (Me.) _Press-Herald,_ and these witty exchanges were a popular feature of his news conferences. Kennedy's press relations were not always satisfactory, however. He got bad publicity when in a fit of pique he cancelled the White House subscription to the Republican New York _Herald-Tribune._ He also earned bad publicity when it became known that he had tried to persuade the editor of the New York _Times_ to recall David Halberstam from South Vietnam after Halberstam had written critically of Administration policy in Vietnam. Nonetheless, Kennedy in general had a good press and his high popularity rating with the public reflected this.

When Lyndon Johnson came into office, he had good media coverage for a time. But eventually his penchant for secrecy and what came to be known as the "credibility gap" on Vietnam policy began to undermine his press relations which were at least fairly good at the start. The Eastern press began to see Johnson's cowboy style and lack of Kennedy grace as flaws in his performance in office, and the departure of Bill Moyers from LBJ's staff presaged a worsening of Johnson's relations with the news media. By the end of his Administration, LBJ was getting a poor press partly simply because he no longer cultivated the news media, as he had done in the early part of his tenure. Indeed, he showed real resentment at some of the coverage he received.

But the most exacerbated relationship between news media and a modern President was that of the press corps and President Richard M. Nixon, especially in his final months. Nixon was particularly bitter toward the newspaper press, which he felt had misrepresented his campaign statements and had helped to cause his defeat in the 1960 presidential election and the 1962 California gubernatorial election. When he ran for the Presidency again in 1968, he made very few public appearances at news conferences, and instead used the media in a tightly controlled manner with the so-called "Hillsboro format" similar to the Reagan

---

[9]Pierre Salinger, _With Kennedy_ (Garden City, New York: Doubleday & Co., 1966).

"citizen press conferences" of the 1976 campaign.
Nixon only appeared on one open-answer television
interview program during the campaign, and that was
on NBC's "Meet the Press" the Sunday before the election.

As President, Nixon held few general news conferences but made extensive direct use of television
in broadcasting directly to the nation. He used TV
for a widely applauded speech on Vietnam policy in
November 1969, and he used it increasingly during the
remainder of his term. He always felt direct use of
"live" TV made it impossible for newspaper correspondents to distort his words for the public. He even
encouraged Vice President Spiro T. Agnew to attack the
television networks and the newspaper press in
speeches in Des Moines and Montgomery after Nixon's
November 1969 Vietnam speech. In these diatribes,
Agnew (on cue from the White House) attacked "instant
analysis" and "querulous criticism" of the President's
speeches. For a time Agnew even bluffed CBS News into
dropping its "instant analysis" comments by Eric
Sevareid and others. Agnew was angry over the CBS use
of Averell Harriman, who had been Johnson's ambassador
to the Paris peace talks from 1968 until 1969.

The fight between the White House and the news
media for control of the content of news coverage and
the related problem of official and unofficial "leaks"
led to several controversies, the most noted of which
was that over the so-called Pentagon Papers. In 1971,
Dr. Daniel Ellsberg, a Marine veteran and former
research political scientist with the RAND Corp., a
Santa Monica, Calif., "think tank", had gone to
Senator McGovern and Senator Fulbright with copies of
a Pentagon report on the causes of U.S. involvement in
Vietnam. Ellsberg had wanted McGovern or Fulbright to
release these still secret papers, but they refused
because they knew this might cause them to lose their
access to secret Pentagon documents. So Ellsberg
released the report to the New York _Times_, which carefully edited the material to remove anything considered by the editors to be dangerous to national
security. Neil Sheehan and others began writing
reports on the Pentagon Papers for the _Times_ and they
began to appear in mid-1971. After the first such
report, Attorney General John Mitchell asked the _Times_
to cease publishing the documents, which he maintained
endangered national security. The _Times_ refused, and
continued publication the following day, after which

19

Mitchell secured a subpoena to order the _Times_ to cease publication. The _Times_ did temporarily cease publication of the secret material, an action which marked the first instance in American journalistic history of prior restraint of newspaper publication. But the _Times_ passed the material on to the Washington _Post_, which published the next installment. The _Post_ too was subpoenaed; it also complied but it passed the material on to other newspapers, and succeeding installments appeared in such newspapers as the Boston _Globe_, St. Louis _Post_-Dispatch, and the _Christian Science_ Monitor. The matter was taken to the district court, where the newspapers won their case, to the circuit court of appeals, where the newspapers won by a 3-2 vote, and finally to the U.S. Supreme Court, where the newspapers won by a 6-3 vote. But the Supreme Court decision was not a complete victory for the press, since the Court upheld the principle of prior restraint as a temporary matter, and indicated there might be cases in which the press could be legally restrained from publishing "leaked" material. Ironically, not long after the Pentagon Papers case, a book entitled _Cold Dawn_ was published in which material leaked by Henry Kissinger to John Newhouse, the author, was published even though it had been classified. But the Administration wanted to be its own judge of "leaks" and not some unauthorized person such as Ellsberg, who expected to go to Jail but escaped as the result of some bungling by the White House "plumbers" during the break-in at Ellsberg's psychiatrist's office.

Discussion of the content of the news media and its impact on the linkage between the President and the public leads naturally to a consideration of problems of access to news for media in the White House. In the first place, news media have little trouble gaining access to White House news when this puts the President, his staff, and his Administration in a favorable light. Indeed, the press secretary has a considerable staff working with him on cultivating favorable images for the President and his official family.

But when there is information damaging or derogatory to the President and the Administration, or which for whatever reason the President wants to keep secret, it may prove difficult even for White House regulars to get access to such news. Thus, the President can keep the press from getting official news reports and in some situations can prevent "leaks"

20

from his own staff, but he cannot in all cases prevent the news media from learning about this information elsewhere. For example, President Ford did not release very much information about his reorganization of the intelligence community, but some of the information about intelligence reforms was "leaked". Whether it was leaked by Senate staff members working on the committee investigation or whether it was leaked by the Central Intelligence Agency to embarrass the Church investigation, is not as important as the fact that some of this information was leaked. The Ford Administration used these leaks in an apparently successful effort to turn public opinion around to favor the CIA after a period when the public had been very critical of the CIA.

President Carter, who spoke as a candidate in 1976 in favor of more openness about intelligence, complained as President in 1977 that too many persons had access to intelligence secrets. He ordered the list of those with clearance further restricted.

The foregoing example has shown that the White House frequently can affect public reaction to the news through its control of access to details of the news. But the Nixon Administration's experience shows this control over access is not total and, indeed, when the news media learn information from non-Administration sources, it can be very damaging indeed to the President and his White House aides. Most of the Watergate disclosures, those from James McCord in Judge Sirica's courtroom, those emanating from the Ervin Committee hearing, came despite the original cover-up and the efforts of the White House to put the whole Watergate affair in a more favorable light for the President. Eventually Nixon's deceptions caught up with him, just as some of Johnson's deceptions over Vietnam had proved costly to him.

But we should not conclude that every President schemes to keep information from the public; rather it seems to be the case that every President seeks to have himself portrayed in the best possible light with the public. And when this is not the case it simply reminds us that no matter how powerful a President, the power of the Presidency is shared with other institutions in our political system.

Now that the importance of access by the media to the news and its effect on political relationships involving the President, the public, and Congress have

been examined, we must examine the impact of the news
media itself in covering White House actions. The
principal aspect of news media impact is that which
publications have on the public. This impact can also
be analyzed in terms of how such publications affect
public officials, especially the President. Some
Presidents such as Truman and Kennedy have reacted
nonchalantly to press disclosures which put their
Administrations in a bad light; other Presidents, such
as Nixon and to some extent Johnson, have reacted in a
retaliatory fashion, seeking to even old scores with
the press. It would be mistaken to say that Presidents should never take the press to task, since the
news media in their competitive desire to meet deadlines sometimes distort the truth, and there may even
be cases where media people desire to publish information damaging to a particular administration. But
that is a long way from accepting the Nixon Administration's apparent basic premise that the press "is
the enemy".[10] A kind of adversary relationship exists,
in that the White House is always seeking the most
favorable image to be projected to the public and the
journalists are always seeking to pry beneath that
favorable image in an effort to determine whether the
reality matches the image. This inevitably puts the
media and the President at cross purposes some of the
time. But the relationship is not naturally one of
enmity; it is rather a bargaining situation in which
each party has something of use to the other. The
Administration's power can be used to give the
press something it wants, normally disclosures of
major events in the news; the media's power on the
other hand lies in their peculiar ability to
project to the public a favorable or unfavorable
image of those in power. But it is just as
inherent in this relationship that Presidents
and the news media seek patterns of cooperation
as that they should seek patterns of discord and non-

_____

[10]A Nixon aide put the anti-media viewpoint this
way: "Walter Lippman once wrote: 'The power to determine each day what shall seem important and shall be
neglected is a power unlike any that has been exercised
since the Pope lost his hold on the secular mind.'
That power is best reflected in the double standard of
headlining stories against the media's philosophic
opponents and omitting stories that could have brought
a negative response toward the media's own philosophic
allies."--Bruce Herschenson, _The Gods of Antenna_ (New
Rochelle, N.Y.: Arlington House, 1976), p. 95.

co-operation.

Perhaps some examples from recent administrations would suffice. I will cite an example where favorable publicity was generated by the Administration, and to match it with an example where unfavorable publicity accrued to the Administration. During the Kennedy era, 1961-63, the news media in general gave the Administration favorable publicity even though there were occasions when by simply reporting the truth, they made the President and his aides look like something less than supermen. In one notable example of favorable coverage, stories of the Kennedy inaugural put great stress on the idea of a new generation of leadership replacing an older one, and quoted statements in the Inaugural, such as "Ask not what your country can do for you; ask what you can do for your country" were featured. The new Administration captured the imagination of the news media in large measure and the media coverage was positive. Perhaps this was the traditional honeymoon; but again basically favorable coverage can be found in the press when Kennedy faced the Cuban missile crisis and made the controversial 1962 decision to impose a naval quarantine on Cuba until the missiles were withdrawn. Or again, when the controversy between Kennedy and the steel industry arose over a projected price increase by U.S. Steel, the Administration got basically positive coverage despite the fact that it used rather strong tactics against the business community. The generally favorable tone of coverage was reflected as well in the results of public opinion polls indicating a popularity rating for the President ranging in the 60 and 70 percent level for much of his Administration. Kennedy's popularity rating was 62 percent at the time of his death. It was chiefly in the realm of controversy over Vietnam, which was just growing at the time of Kennedy's death, and the unfavorable reportage about the Bay of Pigs fiasco in April 1961, that the Kennedy Administration drew a bad press.

As for the Johnson Administration and its relations with the news media, one must discuss two different time segments, since the country's preoccupation was different in each one. This affected the media coverage and ultimately its impact on public attitudes toward Lyndon Johnson's Presidency. The first period can be referred to as the Great Society era, extending from Johnson's sudden accession to the Presidency on November 22, 1963, until sometime in 1966, when attention had focused away from domestic reform onto the

war in Vietnam. The time of November 1966 could be
arbitrarily selected, since it was in the off-year
elections of 1966 that Republican gains indicated a
waning popularity for Johnson and his administration.

During the Great Society segment of the Johnson
era, two observations can be made about the image of
President Johnson projected in the news media. One is
that the image was never as strongly a positive one as
that portrayed of President Kennedy in his time.
Secondly, despite this, President Johnson was generally portrayed as a benign reformer with a great deal
of political skill which he devoted to the achievement
of his program of domestic reform legislation known as
the Great Society. He was given much credit for
legislative achievement, even though many influential
columnists and commentators were critical of his
leadership style and some compared him unfavorably
with Kennedy in that he was seen as provincial rather
than cosmopolitan, Texas-oriented and earthy rather
than New England-oriented and suavely sophisticated.
Other contrasts of this kind were made. Except in a
minority of conservative publications where his
reform programs would never have been popular, Johnson
and his programs were widely praised. He also was
given much credit for his part in shaping the Civil
Rights Act of 1964 and the Voting Rights Act of 1965.

The trend which became dominant in the second
segment of the Johnson era (1966-1969), the period
when Vietnam was the overriding concern of both the
Administration and the news media, was a mounting
criticism of the Administration for its handling of
foreign policy, especially in Vietnam. This was
accompanied by a growing disillusionment, contributed
to by his opposition, about the Johnson approach to
social reform. Welfare programs and other programs
such as the War on Poverty which had been praised in
the early Johnson years came under increasing criticism as costly and of dubious value when the early
promises made for these programs seemed to fall short
of fulfillment. Urban rioting and growing criticism
of the Johnson programs were contributing factors to
the President's decline, as well as the fact that Vietnam inevitably drained off funds which might have gone
into domestic programs and budget cutbacks began to
cripple what had begun as promising new federal programs. But Johnson's continuing pattern of proclaim-
ing the success of American efforts in Vietnam when it
was becoming increasingly apparent that American
efforts in Vietnam were less than successful eventually

undermined much of the President's credibility. The
Vietnam failure dimmed the luster of the President's
early domestic successes to the point that when he
stepped down under the mounting pressure of anti-Viet-
nam politicians and the public, much of his early
achievement in domestic reform had been largely forgotten. The media played a role in this in that they
were projecting a different image of LBJ and his
Administration at the end than they were in the beginning. Perhaps had President Kennedy lived out his
term and gone on to serve a second, he might have
fallen heir to some of this kind of criticism. But
his premature death prevented that and contributed to
a Camelot-like legend, which clouded all our perceptions of the successes and failures of his administration. But Lyndon Johnson was not spared the normal
pattern of success and ensuing failure, or at least
erosion of support, that is frequently found in the
history of two-term Presidents.

When one explores Richard Nixon's relationships
with the news media and the impact of the media on his
administration is examined, it becomes clear that a
very special kind of relationship existed. Often it
appeared that the media brought out the worst in Nixon
with its criticism and Nixon brought out the worst in
the media by his Administration's official harassment.
This perception of the Nixon era Administration-news
media relationship tends to obscure for us the fact
that in the early months of the Nixon period, he
received a relatively good press. The reporters and
correspondents were supportive of his efforts to bring
about a Vietnam withdrawal, and he appeared to have
had a good deal of support from moderate public opinion even though those in the peace movement felt he
was moving far too slowly to extricate the United
States from the Vietnam quagmire. For a time too, it
was the tendency of the press to give Nixon and Kissinger and others in the Administration the benefit of
the doubt. This was not really a standard White House
honeymoon; the previous relations between Nixon and the
news media had been too embittered for that, but it was
at least a kind of respite.

The only problem for the news media was that
the Nixon Administration did not really reply in kind.
It seemed to feel that favorable publicity was its
just due, and any kind of criticism no matter how
minor must be considered as a sign of enmity. It was
this chip-on-the-shoulder attitude toward the news
media that eventually brought great grief to Nixon

and his Administration during the time when his fortunes were in decline. But early in the Nixon period, the press was relatively kind, and at the time of the campaign against McGovern in 1972, the press turned out to be more critical of McGovern--who after all was readily accessible--while treating Nixon kindly, and at the time of the truce in Vietnam in early 1973 he was given much credit, as he also was for foreign affairs achievements during the trip to China for the summit with Mao and Chou in 1972. But with all this, there was a turning away from Nixon just as there had been with Johnson. Was it simply because of disgust at Watergate, or was it a combination of factors that brought this development? Watergate was an important factor, but it certainly was not the whole story of the abysmal news coverage the Nixon administration received in its last two years, and various additional factors must be considered. One is the normal antagonism or at least adversary relationship growing out of the watchdog role of the press. Even without Watergate, the news media in playing this watchdog role would have been on the lookout for other scandals and it would eventually have found some, to the ultimate detriment of the Nixon Administration. Another factor was the long-standing bitterness between Nixon and those liberals in the news media. This feud dated back to the events surrounding Alger Hiss in the 1948-50 period and the Helen Gahagan Douglas campaign against Nixon for the U.S. Senate in 1950 as well as Nixon's record in encouraging the activities of Joseph McCarthy at a time when McCarthyism and Red-hunting were popular exercises in Washington.

Still another factor can be considered institutional and has been referred to as the Imperial Presidency. In Nixon's era it took the form of a high-handed attitude by the President toward public, press and Congress. Nixon was encouraged in his attitude by staff people who should have served him better but did not. Ultimately, as his fortunes went into an irretrievable slump, he was nearly cut off from reality. By the time of the impeachment debate in Congress, he had few strong supporters. So his own political maladroitness contributed to the situation. To some extent, this was true of Johnson and his dogged determination to stick to his Vietnam policy, but there was never the same flavor of vindictiveness in Johnson's attitude toward the news media as there was in Nixon's. All of these factors together, however, made the final part of the Nixon era a case study in how a President should not handle relations with the news media,

Congress and the public.

Where President Ford is concerned, the verdict
is still out. During the time from his accession
August 9, 1974, until the 1976 presidential election,
the news media had been relatively kind to President
Ford. Even during the campaign and up until his
retirement in January 1977 the media were not greatly
unkind to Ford, although they sometimes portrayed him
as clumsy and a bit of a "clown". The President had
not been immune from criticism, especially at the time
of the Nixon pardon, but through the media he was able
to project an image of sincerity and calmness which
was a welcome one after the heated controversy of the
Nixon years. During the presidential campaign, the
news media reported the charges of Reagan, Carter and
other presidential candidates, but it was still not
clear to what extent the charges made by his political
opponents and reported in the media would be damaging
to Ford. However, the public opinion polls showed
President Ford's popularity rather mercurial and it
slipped sharply during the onset of the economic
recession even as it bounded back rather strongly at
the beginning of economic recovery in late 1975 and
early 1976. The coverage of the second debate with
Carter and the economic slump probably contributed to
Ford's narrow defeat by Carter.

It is too early to project what kind of long-
term relationships between the White House and the
news media may develop during the Carter Administration. (Early relationships were reasonably good.) It
does seem sufficient to say, however, that today's
television-oriented reportage of political news does
make image politics a strong ingredient in the public's perception of the man in the White House, and
despite loud criticism of this fact by those in and out
of the journalism profession, it is likely to remain
that way for the foreseeable future. Carter had a good
press up to April 1977 but the Republican opposition
was becoming more outspoken by that time.

The media will provide an important link in a
positive way between President and public in the
future too. The media in and of themselves are basically neutral, and that means that any adroit and
politically astute President, whether he be Ford,
Carter or someone else, can seize on a great potential
for communication of ideas as well as an image in taking advantage of the mass media to promote programs
and political aims.

As Nixon and Johnson learned to their sorrow, the neutrality of the media contains an obverse danger for any President. The media that can buttress presidential popularity and build up a President with the American public over a period of months and years can also generate the forces which help to bring down a President, once the public views him as not acting in its own perceived best interest. That appears to be the one basic conclusion that we can draw: that it is still Presidents themselves who make or break their own political reputations, despite the magnifying impact of the news media. The media's magnifying effect simply means that when a President is successful, the public gets a magnified image of his success, and when he is a failure, it also gets a magnified image of his failure. But the medium remains only a messenger, and it cannot undermine a President unless he gives it something to undermine him with; nor can it build up a President to have a powerful reputation unless he also gives it something to work with on that score, in the form of achievements, popularity which reflects leadership ability, and the like.

Linkage Between President and Other Parts of Political System

The linkage between the President and other parts of the political system through the mass media will be explored in step-by-step fashion in this section of the chapter. The other components in the American federal system in addition to the Presidency consist of the Congress, the President's Cabinet and the bureaucracy--the ongoing federal civil service--in addition to the judiciary. The White House staff as a supporting element of the Presidency must also be analyzed.

The Presidency does not exist in a vacuum but rather in relationship to the Congress and all other elements of the federal system. So it must be stressed that the news media's coverage of the Presidency is not limited to the Presidency alone, but gives impressions to the nation and its public of the relationships and dealings between the President and Congress as well as between the President and other

systemic elements.[11] This discussion then will be
phrased not in terms of the simple relationships
between the Presidency and other elements of the system, but in terms of the public's perception of those
relationships as derived from coverage of daily events
of national government and politics in the nation's
news media.

The media can have a significant impact on the
President's relationship with Congress. This is
because members of Congress judge a President's reputation both on the basis of their personal contacts
with him and his staff, and his leadership of public
opinion. The public's broad perceptions are significantly influenced by the mass media. To an additional
extent, the attitudes of congressmen toward the President are influenced by comments of columnists and commentators from the mass media, as well as by the way
the news is covered on television, on the radio, and
in the newspapers. Thus a significant factor in this
relationship is the public's perception of the President and Congress. Taking it a step further one finds
the degree to which members of the public act on this
perception is influenced by communication of their
views on current political issues to the White House
and to members of Congress. If the public reacts
inertly or in an apathetic way to statements from the
White House or Congress on an issue, or if public
opinion surveys show there is little public interest
or feeling about that issue, this may lead both Congress and the President to feel it is an issue lacking
in political urgency and they may give priority to
other issues. This sometimes happens, for example,
with foreign policy issues about which the public is
relatively unconcerned until some crisis arises.
Then an aroused public opinion may belatedly cause the
Congress and the President to concern themselves with
that issue. But an element of leadership is present
in this relationship. It is more difficult for a
President to exert leadership when the opposition controls Congress, as was the case with Presidents Ford
and Nixon, but fortunately for them and unfortunately
for the Democratic leadership, on some issues the conservative coalition in Congress has had enough
strength to help these conservative Republican Presi-

---

[11]Richard E. Neustadt, _Presidential_ _Power_: With
Reflections _on_ _Nixon_ _and_ _Johnson_ (New York: John Wiley
& Son, 1976).

dents on certain key issues. Even in Carter's
Administration, his moderate stance has brought him
into conflict with conservatives (e.g., the Warnke
nomination) and liberals (e.g., the extent of the public works program).

The President's relationship with his Cabinet
and with the bureaucracy, i.e., the permanent government, is somewhat different from his relationship with
Congress, but it is similar in one respect. That is
that like Congress, the bureaucratic agencies, like
most Cabinet officers, react with some sensitivity to
certain constituencies. Constituency relationships
fall along interest group lines more clearly than with
members of the House and Senate in Congress, who may
represent districts or states with a variety of parochial interests. But if we examine the White House
and its relationship, for example, with the Secretary
of Agriculture and the bureaucracy within the Department of Agriculture, we can see that the secretary and
his bureaucracy have a constituency of client groups
in the nation's farming community that will be particularly sensitive to such issues as the level of
price supports for some farm commodities and the
arrangements for import-export trade of commodities.
Mass media of general circulation may affect these
relationships to the extent that they report agricultural news, but there are a number of periodicals and
daily publications aimed at the farm constituency that
could have a broader and more direct influence on the
President's relation to farmers at least through the
providing of news and recent information, even in
instances where they do not carry editorial comment.

Similar illustrations could be given with other
policy areas, such as Health, Education and Welfare,
for example, but the point has been sufficiently made
to move on to look at some of the other interrelations
within the federal structure involving the White House.

In the President's relationship with the federal
judiciary, two points are basic. The federal judiciary
is independent once appointed, and can act without
reference to the other two branches on the basis of
established law. However, all federal judicial
appointments are made by the President, from Supreme
Court justices to federal district judges, and it is
only natural for Presidents to look into the political
views and background of such men before they are
appointed. They are normally lawyers and the over-
whelming majority of appointments have been made from

30

the incumbent President's own political party. Designated justices are sometimes drawn from the ranks of elected officials with some legal or judicial experience, and sometimes drawn from the ranks of state and lower court judges. One way the media can enter into this appointment process is through published speculation about the President's intentions, for example, in the appointment of a Justice to the Supreme Court or to a lesser court. There may also be speculation in the press about the likelihood of a court ruling a certain way on a controversial case, and the likelihood of a White House reaction to such a ruling. Recent examples of this would be in school busing cases and the 1973 abortion ruling, which was criticized by President Ford (as well as Jimmy Carter). At any rate, the linkage between the judiciary and the White House provided by the press can be seen as readily as that with Congress or the agencies, even though it may in some instances be a more tenuous or indirect kind of linkage than in the other two instances we have cited.

In the relations of the President with his own key White House aides, relationships are only tangentially affected by news stories published or broadcast in the media. But in the "real world" of politics, the media obviously have a good deal of influence in their ability to embarrass Presidential aides with their boss by publishing things that may be displeasing to the President. Of course, the White House press secretary, and the President both have a direct concern with media coverage of the President and his activities, and they discuss media coverage of major events frequently.

In the linkage between the President and other components of the political system, normally there is a degree of competition between the President and his political rivals for media coverage. The President can normally be expected to dominate this competition; for example, when Senator Fulbright was holding his hearings with the Senate Foreign Relations Committee on Vietnam, President Johnson overshadowed the hearings in the news media by planning presidential activities such as trips abroad and various other events susceptible of White House manipulation. Johnson was only partly successful since Fulbright's views won a broader audience and the public became more fully acquainted with the Vietnam issues. Here it was not only media coverage of the hearings that had an influence--indeed, the media coverage was more limited than

31

some network newsmen such as Fred Friendly of CBS
desired--but it was also the correspondents' coverage
from South Vietnam itself which was damaging to the
image of his Vietnam policy which Johnson wished to
project. We have referred to this competition for
coverage in the context of public policy issues, but
its occurrence in the campaign setting will also be
discussed in a later chapter. However, despite much
talk about the Imperial Presidency and the restoration
of power to Congress, any incumbent President who has
the imagination and the boldness to seize a popular
and important issue is likely to capture the public's
attention away from his adversaries in Congress whenever he really wishes to do so. He can do this
through televised press conferences, through television speeches, through TV and newspaper interviews
and in many other formats. But he can nearly always
draw a higher rating on the networks than any one person or group within the Congress, or any other one
political figure for that matter. This is largely
because of the high visibility of his position.

Three case studies will be cited in which the
President had to compete with Congress for the attention of the public. The first, alluded to briefly
above, will be discussed later in more detail. This
was the series of hearings held by the Fulbright committee on the escalation of the war in Vietnam during
1965 and 1966. These hearings were widely covered in
the media, and they began to have an effect during the
period when the President was able to dominate the
public debate on Vietnam. As a result of the Fulbright hearings, much of public opinion eventually
swung against the war and important congressional
voices began to oppose it, including Senators McCarthy,
Robert Kennedy and McGovern, each of whom played a
leading role in opposition to the war at various times.
Many of these public officials may not have reversed
their positions or become so vocally outspoken had not
the media communicated new facts to the public and had
not many influential people in the news media lent
respectability to the opposition to the war. It is
reported that President Johnson felt the tide had
turned against his Vietnam policy when Walter Cronkite
reported on CBS News that despite the military defeat
of the Tet offensive of 1968 in South Vietnam, the
Communists had scored an important psychological victory. These various developments on Vietnam policy
were not all attributable to the series of hearings
conducted by Fulbright, but that certainly had a major
role in the ensuing events.

32

During the Nixon era, another good example of
success of the President's rivals in popularizing an
anti-Administration point of view came during the
Ervin committee investigation of the Watergate scandals. The hearings, conducted during the summer of
1973, brought out many facts and allegations that
later proved damaging to President Nixon, and ultimately helped lead to his downfall. The coverage of
the impeachment hearings held by the House Judiciary
Committee under the chairmanship of Rep. Peter Rodino
in the summer of 1974 contributed further to the under-
mining of public confidence in the President. It
ought to be noted that this was not merely a matter of
the Congress taking the limelight away from the President, as his own actions in the Saturday Night Massacre of October 1973 and the failure to explain the 18½
minute gap in the White House tapes contributed also
to Nixon's ultimate dilemma.

During the Ford era, President Ford to some
extent neutralized the criticism of his pardon of
former President Nixon in the fall of 1974 by appearing voluntarily before the House Judiciary Committee
to make a full explanation; this no doubt blunted some
of the criticism even though it did not end it
entirely.

Another Ford era congressional investigation
which drew some attention away from the White House
might be said to have ended in a draw with both the
White House and Congress conceding some points. This
was the Church Committee investigation made into the
CIA and FBI by the Senate Select Committee on Intelligence. The committee made a critical report, but the
President somewhat blunted the effect of that by having the Rockefeller Commission report made and by himself announcing some internal reforms within the CIA.
In this instance, Ford showed more adroitness than
Nixon had in the preceding case we cited, even though
he may not have received a great deal more favorable
coverage in the news media.

In general, the public forms its own opinions
on presidential-congressional disputes and conflicts
largely through its impressions gained by the news
media, but it does not receive news media reports
uncritically. And the news media themselves appear to
be monitoring their own performance somewhat more
effectively than in the past. Nonetheless, the press
and the media in general perform a vital linkage role
which makes the political system's operation possible

Shambaugh Library

to a considerable degree.

Aspects of Presidency-Media Relationship to Be Explored

It is obvious that successful use of the mass media constitutes a vitally important factor in the achievements of modern Presidents. This is because of the media's all-pervasive nature.

This relationship, however, may be undergoing a profound change since the media may be developing and finding a new role as responsible critic of politicians. Merely relating to the public accounts of events previously allowed "objectivity" to masquerade a partial or deceptive description of governmental affairs. But the media have moved into a new relationship with government officials as they attempt interpretation of officials' activities, and to some extent play the role of a public advocate or critic. Here the term critic is not used in the sense of one always condemning every move, but in the sense of one questioning whether the public's interest is being served. Raising this issue brings the media into an interpretive role. But there is still no consensus about such a role for the media.

Thus we ask of public officials: What are the boundary lines for permissible behavior? What can governmental leaders do that serves the public interest and when have they stepped over these boundaries? The recent Watergate events clearly show where the boundary line of public tolerance was overstepped. But we are still left with the question of when public awareness develops.

For the news media too we must ask: What are the boundary lines for permissible behavior? The news media encountered legal problems not only in the coverage of Watergate (where did "executive privilege" begin and end, for example?) but it also encountered a related problem in coverage of the Pentagon papers case: Where should the line of secrecy vs. disclosure be drawn?

In analyzing these questions about the proper role of each of these major institutions--the Presidency and the mass media--the remaining chapters of this book will deal with six specific concerns.

Chapter Two will analyze reasons for development of the mass media's function of linkage--providing a bridge between governmental officials and the public. It will examine why mass media linkage has become important, how linkage has become important in the governing system, and consequences of mass media linkage already seen. In exploring these consequences case studies will deal with the Roosevelt, Truman, Eisenhower, Kennedy, Johnson, Nixon and Ford eras, the 1976 campaign, and tentative trends in the Carter period. Attention will also be paid to the media connection to the Presidency in the public policy process and the media role in presidential nominations and elections. A summary statement will examine the evolution of linkage and why it is important today.

Chapter Three will be concerned with the basic features of the institutional structure of the Presidency. Case studies will illuminate modern Presidents' roles to explore the man in the office. The Presidency will be analyzed in terms of structure of the office and its evolution from Roosevelt to Carter. The President's relations with the bureaucracy, with Congress, with the courts, and with the public will be explored. A summary will conclude with the outlook for the future in terms of the man and the office.

Chapter Four will explore the basic features of mass media's institutional structure. Types of media examined include newspapers, magazines, radio, and television. Structure of the newspaper, radio and television industries will be analyzed, followed by a discussion of the roles of individuals in the media, and some current theories of mass communication.

Chapter Five will attempt an explanation of actual linkages of the Presidency and the mass media. How the linkage occurs in the operation of the two institutions will be analyzed separately in terms of each one. Definitions of linkage terms will be provided and illustrations will be used to explore how image linkages occur. Image linkages with the system of government and politics and with the interaction of the Presidency with other parts of the system will be explored. The past role of the mass media connection will be analyzed, together with what the recent and current mass media linkage appears to be. The chapter ends with an analysis of the prospect for linkage of the two in the future.

Chapter Six will explore the impact of Presidency-media linkages on the political system as a whole. The following will be analyzed: (1) the impact of linkages on executive-legislative relations; (2) the impact of linkages on executive-bureaucracy relationships will be analyzed; (3) impact of linkages on executive-judicial relationships. All three will be probed in such terms as exploring the phenomenon of "leaks" and what this does to the dynamics of the relationship. Other matters covered will include the impact on the executive-public relationship, the result of the impact on the policy-making and electoral processes, and a summary of the various linkages.

In conclusion Chapter Seven will explore prospects for the future of the Presidency-media relationship. Matters examined will include: (1) possible technological development in broadcasting; (2) possible technological development in the print media; (3) possibilities of institutional reform in the Presidency; (4) interview data from Washington interviews on reform; (5) the likely relationship between technological development and institutional reform; (6) trends for the future of the Presidency in terms of democratic ideals; (7) analysis of how television has helped and hindered the Presidency as a more responsive office, and (8) conclusions about prospects for the future of the Presidency-media relationship.

In the next chapter, I will begin by looking at reasons for the development of the mass media's linkage function.

CHAPTER TWO

REASONS FOR DEVELOPMENT OF THE MASS MEDIA'S

LINKAGE FUNCTION

The situation was ironic. Agnew, after all,
had been a master of the news media; indeed,
the press had been both his servant and his
scapegoat. . . . In every role Agnew was
lavishly publicized. Even his attacks on the
press were dutifully reported by the very
newspapers and television networks he criticized. The press did not seem to know how to
cope with Agnew. He was an irritant, but he
was also good copy. For all his protestations
and invectives, the press had been Agnew's
best friend, had helped make him who he was.
Though what he did was virtually ignored, what
he said got maximum attention. . . .

--Richard M. Cohen and Jules Witcover, in
A Heartbeat Away (pp. 200, 201)

The reporting of the first two weeks of
August was to raze to the ground George
McGovern's reputation for candor and trust;
more than that, it was to make him look like
a fool. The first weeks of August are always
the low passage of the summer news doldrums,
when television's evening news shows scratch
to fill their time and editors wrestle with
making the front page attractive. And in this
news vacuum stood McGovern--he was prey (to
comment on the Eagleton fiasco), and the press
was on the hunt. . . .

--Theodore H. White, in The Making of the
President 1972 (p. 275)

* * * *

Why Mass Media Linkage Has Become Important

In Chapter One I explored the mass media's
function in linking the public with government, and
more specifically in linking the President with the

37

public and other components of government. In this chapter I will seek to explain some of the reasons why this mass media linkage has become so important in both government and politics in the 1970's.

In this section of the chapter, I'll examine some of the reasons for the public's growing dependence on mass media coverage of governmental affairs for an understanding of the personalities, issues and other aspects of government. I'll also consider the reciprocal development of the growth of dependence of government officials and political figures on the mass media for disseminating information to the public. This two-way dependence on the media for the linkage role sometimes puts the media in a vulnerable position, since they must work with imperfect sources but always get the blame for any distortion that results from the process, and may be blamed also for being more powerful than they actually are in reflecting the political reality that they seek to convey to the public.

I'll also look at four periods in the historical development of the mass media's linkage function in American politics and government, consider the growth of the media linkage function in party politics and the electoral system, and conclude by examining 20th Century developments in the coverage of presidential campaign politics.

As for the growth of public dependence on mass media coverage of governmental affairs, one must recall that two major factors are involved in this trend--the rapidly growing population of the nation, now in the range of 220 million, which makes it unlikely that most citizens will witness political events directly at the personal level, and secondly the technological revolution in communications. The latter has made the average citizen rely more today on the electronic pictures of television than on the printed page for his or her information about government and politics; the printed page, however, still plays a significant role in providing depth of information about political and governmental events and figures.

The implications of these two changes are that communications media for the mass public, and especially television, will play a central role in shaping the average citizen's perceptions of the political and governmental processes in his or her daily environment.

If this were the only change brought about by the shifting socio-political and communications environment, it would be significant enough. But this change has been compounded by the fact that political leaders and public officials, like the mass public itself, have also responded to this changing environment. They too have become more dependent on the mass media for conveying information to the public about their views on issues of the day as well as about facts of political and governmental life. This accounts for the preoccupation of many leaders today with the "image" they project through the media to the public. This is because these leaders sense, correctly, that if they do not project that image accurately, or at least in a positive way, the public reaction may be negative, and they may wind up losing office or facing defeat of their cherished programs.

In either case, the situation has made public officials hypercritical of the performance of the mass media in doing its reporting and interpretive job, in part at least because the stakes are higher for those in public life. Thus, in the examples cited at the beginning of this chapter in the Spiro Agnew investigation of wrongdoing during 1973 and in the events related to Thomas Eagleton's withdrawal from the Democratic ticket in 1972, the mass media inevitably played a significant role in hastening the downfall of both men because its linkage role had been magnified by the factors already alluded to. The technological revolution of which television is a part also includes new techniques in public relations and the development of refined techniques of scientific polling. Both these factors simply hasten the whole process of building up the reputation of unknown public leaders in the public's mind and the reverse process of destroying or damaging such a reputation. We can see this process at work in both directions in looking at recent Presidents and in considering the downfall of Agnew and Eagleton, and later of Nixon. It was also true of George McGovern.[1]

---

[1]See the following: Richard M. Cohen and Jules Witcover, A Heartbeat Away (New York: Viking Press, 1974); Theodore H. White, The Making of the President 1972 (New York: Bantam Books, 1973); Jules Witcover, White Knight: The Rise of Spiro Agnew (New York: Random House, 1972); Jules Witcover, The Resurrection of Richard Nixon (New York: Putnam, 1970); William L.

I've just suggested in a functional way why the mass media, always important to political figures, have become a key element in their relationship to the public in recent decades. Perhaps some case studies later in this chapter will illustrate in more detail, but it seems worthwhile to shift for a moment from the functional analysis of this changing and dynamic relationship to the whys and wherefores of the development of this situation by looking briefly at the historical development of the mass media linkage function.

For this analysis, I've arbitrarily chosen four periods in the growth and development of the political system to suggest that part of the explanation for the modern media's magnified influence, and the fact that this influence is perceived to have grown recently, lies in its unfolding through nearly two centuries of our political history.

The first period to be examined briefly is that between 1789 and 1860. This can be described as a time of newspaper dominance of the communications process, also a time when the party-dominated press enjoyed its greatest popularity. Unlike the modern age of ticket-splitters and preoccupation with image-building, the early era of our history involved some bitter disputes over issues, and the newspaper was peculiarly fitted to present viewpoints about issues. When a public controversy was aired in print, the newspaper subscriber could go back and read and reread points made by those arguing on each side. In that more leisurely time, detailed discussion of issues in newspaper editorials and news stories was the counterpart in the media of the lengthy debates in the public forum or the two-hour political stump speech.

Safire, Before the Fall: An Inside View of the Pre-Watergate White House (Garden City, N.Y.: Doubleday, 1975); Theodore H. White, Breach of Faith: The Fall of Richard Nixon (New York: Dell, 1976); Bob Woodward and Carl Bernstein, The Final Days (New York: Simon & Schuster, 1976); Gary Hart, Right From the Start (New York: Quadrangle, 1973); Eleanor McGovern, Uphill (Boston: Houghton, Mifflin Co., 1974); Gordon Weil, The Long Shot (New York: W. W. Norton & Co., 1973).

Although when George Washington became the first President in 1789, the Founding Fathers had hoped to avoid bitter partisanship and the development of a party system, it became obvious soon thereafter that a system first of factions and then of parties would develop. Even before the ratification of the Constitution, the first factional division occurred between Federalists and Anti-Federalists, the former favoring and the latter opposing the Constitution. The latter group insisted that a Bill of Rights, writing protections of individual and state's rights into the Constitution, be added to the document as a precondition for going along with approval. Ultimately, they won much of what they wanted. Then, early in Washington's Administration, the President's hopes for non-partisan unity were dashed when Alexander Hamilton and Thomas Jefferson, the secretaries of the Treasury and of State, clashed openly over foreign policy and economic issues. Hamilton was pro-British and Jefferson was pro-French; Hamilton was pro-business and Jefferson was for the agricultural and urban laboring interests; Hamilton was for a strong central government while Jefferson favored state's rights. These were the issues which brought about division along partisan lines as the Hamiltonian faction became the Federalists and the Jeffersonian faction became Democratic Republicans.

Eventually the Federalist party faded away after the triumph of the Jeffersonians in 1800, but the so-called "era of good feeling" when most of the battles were fought out internally within the dominant party was merely a transition phase to a new party system in which the Jacksonian Democrats were opposed by the National Republicans who later became known as the Whigs. This Democratic-Whig system lasted several decades until it finally was dashed on the rocks of the slavery issue which caused the birth of the Republican party, and by the end of this period the Democratic-Republican party system had come into being.

Along with these developments for the framework of party competition, institutions such as the presidential nominating convention, introduced in the 1830's, were developing. And a key feature of this period was the party leaders' practice of financing newspapers to propagandize their issue positions with the reading public. In the eras of both Thomas Jefferson and Andrew Jackson, the party in power and the opposition (particularly in the Jackson era) funded newspapers which promoted the party line. The idea of the independent daily press had not yet taken firm hold; it was some years before this became the norm and the so-called party-oriented press largely faded from the scene.

The above discussion covered the period from the establishment of the Constitution just after the Revolution to the eve of the Civil War. The next period, from 1860 to 1900, saw some additional significant developments. The rise of the wire services with their implications for standardization of national news coverage was one major development. By this time also, the party system had settled down into competition between Republicans and Democrats, although the Republicans became the dominant party for many decades after the Civil War. The wire services, most prominent of which was the Associated Press, a co-operative venture of daily newspapers, grew in coverage and extent of membership. They could trace their origin to the invention of the telegraph which made it feasible to distribute news dispatches on a nationwide basis, but the Civil War brought them into greater prominence and after the Civil War they played a major role in the dissemination of political news. Metropolitan daily newspapers were becoming a major part of the media in this period as well. Such papers as the New York <u>Tribune</u> and the New York <u>Times</u> were coming to fore by the end of the 19th Century. This period of mass media development was marked by the rise of influential editors, some with important power within their own political parties. Such men as Horace Greeley, James Gordon Bennett, and Henry Watterson were noted for their brilliantly written editorials, and they were widely respected around the entire nation.

The third period corresponds roughly with the first half of the 20th Century, between 1900 and 1950. During this time the influence of local newspaper editors began to be eclipsed by the rising influence and visibility of syndicated columnists whose work was published on a nationwide basis. The newspapers probably reached their peak of influence in this era, not only with much attention paid to their candidate and party endorsements but also with the added clout given them by the influential columns they carried along with the editorials. A new element entered the picture during the 1920's with the advent first of radio stations and a few years later of radio networks. The radio at first supplemented newspaper coverage of political events, but it was a different medium in that it possessed an immediacy that newspapers lacked. As

42

radio grew and developed, the old newspaper "Extra" of earlier years became outmoded. Instead, attention began to focus on radio commentators carried by the networks some of whom also wrote for the newspapers as well. Names like those of H. V. Kaltenborn, Elmer Davis and Edward R. Murrow became known nationally and eventually worldwide as their reporting encompassed not only political events, but also diplomatic and military events connected with World War II.[2]

The rise of modern television really was a post-war development and this marks the modern era, from 1950 to the present. Network television on a nation-wide basis really came into its own during the 1950's and it has gained an increasingly dominant role since then. In the mid-1960's, the audience for network television began to exceed the total readership figures for newspapers, and television began to expand what was originally a kind of skeleton news coverage into a broader based coverage, including more docu-mentaries, half-hour evening newscasts and wider use of commentary.

As this occurred, newspapers also shifted their function somewhat. While retaining the popular columns with their commentary on national and interna-tional politics, they also began to do interpretive and investigative reporting in a depth which the format of television did not normally permit. It may be significant that for all the influence of network television and all the attacks made on it by Agnew, Nixon and the others of their era, it was still two newspaper reporters, Woodward and Bernstein, who broke the original story of the Watergate scandals of the

---

[2]See an account of early radio correspondents in David Holbrook Culbert, News for Everyman: Radio and Foreign Affairs in Thirties America (Westport, Conn.: Greenwood Press, 1976), especially Chapter Three, "H. V. Kaltenborn: The Gentle Art of Self-Publicity," pp. 67-95; Chapter Five, "Elmer Davis: Radio's Hoosier," pp. 125-152, and Chapter Seven, "Edward R. Murrow: The Foreign Correspondent as Broad-caster," pp. 179-200. This book also covers the radio careers of Booke Carter, Raymond Gram Swing and Fulton Lewis, Jr. See also Robert Sobel, The Manipulators: America in the Media Age (Garden City, N.Y.: Anchor Press/Doubleday, 1976) for a broader history of the mass media and a discussion of contemporary trends.

Nixon administration which ultimately prompted the television networks to cover the same story. The new trend toward investigative reporting may have been a factor in this, but it also appears that with wealth and success the temptation was great for the networks to play it safe in their coverage of controversial events, although each network--particularly CBS--has some noteworthy expose coverage to its credit. Television not only lent a celebrity status to politicians but also to its own news people, and when Barbara Walters landed a million-dollar contract with ABC in 1976, it merely reflected the way in which some of the media celebrities were in some ways almost overshadowing the political notables whose activities it was their job to cover.

A final point to be commented on here is the effect of the rise of TV on politics. Initially the impact was probably to shift the emphasis in politics from issues to images and personalities, but perhaps more sophisticated TV viewers are now beginning to demand more substance from their political leaders. That is far from sure, however, even in the aftermath of Watergate.

While Truman and Eisenhower were the first Presidents to serve in the era of television, each man had begun his career in the pre-television era and neither realized the full potential of the new medium. Truman came across much more woodenly on TV than he did in person, and Eisenhower always seemed to be somehow the product of a slick Madison Avenue production effort even though TV did reflect his evident sincerity.

The first two Presidents to use TV to its fullest potential were probably John F. Kennedy and Richard M. Nixon, although each used it in a different way. Kennedy used it to get elected in 1960 partly through the medium of the TV debates against Nixon. Then he proceeded to make the most skillful and imaginative use of the large set-piece news conference which any modern President has probably made. He was also prior to his untimely death developing some new formats like the interview with one or a few network correspondents which successors like Johnson and Nixon used fairly effectively.[3] Lyndon Johnson never did come across well on TV; like Truman, he was better speaking informally in person or even out on the hustings; but Nixon, having learned the importance of TV when he lost to Kennedy after the 1960 debates, resolved to make effective use of the medium in his 1968 race and he did exactly that by use of a controlled-exposure campaign which carefully let the public see just exactly what Nixon wanted it to see of him. He was aided also by the Wallace defection from the Democrats and the disastrous Humphrey campaign, but this should not detract from the fact that Nixon used television most effectively in 1968, and in some ways he used it well in 1972 although the 1972 Republican convention may be recalled by some observers as more a piece of showmanship than of genuine politics.[4]

President Ford, while he performed acceptably well in front of the cameras, did not really use television as effectively as some of his predecessors. In fact some think Mrs. Ford came across on TV better than her husband. But he did project an aura of sincerity even if some saw his image on television as sometimes massive, heavy-handed and even, in the opinion of some, occasionally bumbling. On the other hand some major candidates who ran in the 1976 presidential

---

[3]See Pierre Salinger, With Kennedy (Garden City, N.Y.: Doubleday & Co., 1966), especially some discussions of JFK's innovations with TV on pp. 113-115. Also see Newton N. Minow, John Bartlow Martin and Lee M. Mitchell, Presidential Television (New York: Basic Books, 1973), and Martin Mayer, About Television (New York: Harper & Row, 1972).

[4]See Theodore H. White, The Making of the President 1968 (New York: Pocket Books, 1970), especially pp. 245-247 and the discussion of the "Hillsboro Format" for TV, pp. 165-167. See also Joe McGinniss, The Selling of the President 1968 (New York: Trident Press, 1969) and Dan Nimmo, The Political Persuaders: The Techniques of Modern Election Campaigns (Englewood Cliffs, N.J.: Prentice-Hall, 1970), especially pp. 142, 143, for a further description and account of the Hillsboro format. See also Theodore H. White, The Making of the President 1972 (New York: Bantam Books, 1973), especially pp. 318-326 for an account of the "programmed" GOP convention of 1972 in Miami Beach.

campaign along with Ford made effective use of television. These included former California Governor
Ronald Reagan, whose acting background made him a
natural for TV even though some of his statements,
when analyzed in black and white, raised questions in
the public's mind. Jimmy Carter, the Democratic front-
runner in the 1976 primaries and the eventual winner,
also had a real knack for dealing with television;
some felt that he had a Kennedy-like image in his
media efforts. A new figure who appeared to use TV
well although perhaps more abrasive than Carter was
Governor Jerry Brown of California, making his first
presidential race in 1976. But since 1976 was the
first post-Watergate campaign, some doubted prior to
the completion of the primary season whether having a
good TV image which enabled one to win primaries in
key states would also be helpful in the final election
stage in the fall. The public was apparently seeking
to look beyond the context and issues of the campaign
of 1976 to seek men of character and ability; perhaps
the public realized that the only real test of
character and ability usually lies in the acts of an
elected incumbent, since voting in an election is
always to some extent an act of faith.

     In looking at the growth of the media linkage
function in party politics and the electoral system,
it is clear that the media today have come to have a
major impact on the presidential selection process;
this is particularly true of television. The media's
impact can be seen through the entire selection process, but it should be analyzed in the context of the
technology of new forms which political campaigning
has taken. Television is a communications tool which
has immediacy, but it has had a great impact during
presidential primaries because of a kind of cause-and-
effect cycle which has developed involving candidates
making a strong (or weak) showing in public opinion
surveys, the same candidates winning (or losing) in
presidential primary contests because of their standing in the polls, and ultimately as further surveys
are taken, the shifting of their standing according to
their latest performance in the primaries.

     All this reflects the new technology of polling
and campaign surveys. But television tends to speed
up this process of building up new candidates and
destroying or damaging the reputations of established
candidates, because it furnishes an immediate communications link between voters and candidates for the
Presidency. Thus modern media, as a part of the

complex of modern technology, have made a significant difference in the workings of the selection process. The co-existence of polling and modern survey techniques along with the rapid communication potential of television probably helped to add to the proliferation of primaries until now 31 of the 50 states hold presidential primaries. And in the other 19 states, television extensively covers the selection processes which include precinct caucuses and state and district conventions. In all this the candidate projecting best on television is usually the one who wins the primaries and leads in the public opinion surveys. Thus the mass media dimension of this changing process appears to be a dynamic factor in producing the changes that have occurred in recent years.

Going beyond presidential politics, it ought to be noted that modern mass media, and particularly television, have had a transforming effect on the electoral process in general. Most statements made about presidential primaries apply at the state and local level to other contests as well, but one additional point should be added: the increasing use of television in campaigning has caused considerable increase in the cost of conducting a campaign, and this in turn has had implications for the system--the number of persons able to sustain the cost of a candidacy, the kinds of persons able to function well in the related fund-raising activities for a contest for public office and matters of this kind.

The added cost may have caused an indirect benefit in that the excesses of the Watergate scandals, which were closely involved with arm-twisting fund-raising efforts in the Nixon re-election campaign, brought about the passage of a new law putting significant curbs on campaign fund-raising and spending. Even though parts of the new law, enacted in 1974, were voided by the Supreme Court as unconstitutional, it represents a political landmark in that it marked the beginning of a process of attempting to restore sanity to a system that had become increasingly cumbersome and expensive.

Estimates of expenditures in the Nixon and McGovern campaigns for the Presidency in 1972, for example, had been in the range of $60 million for the former and $46 million for the latter. Even for a U.S. Senate contest in a major industrial state, the cost of a campaign had come to exceed $1 million before the new law was passed. So it doubtless

47

represents a step in the right direction after much unrestrained spending. The new law could have a bad effect, in one sense, however, in that it might hamper development of a new type of campaign consulting operation which certainly appeared more effective than older forms of traditional party organization effort.

Along with considering the considerable changes in the management of campaigns themselves, it is important to examine 20th Century developments in the coverage of presidential campaign politics from the viewpoint of the media's function. In other words, in this part of the analysis I'll focus on the effect these changes have had on the media themselves rather than on the political system.

The media's relationship to the primary system is basically that they have tended to popularize the primary system. But this has not been true consistently ever since the primary system was first established shortly after the turn of the century. The primary system was popular in its early years until after World War I. Then for a time the number of states with primaries actually decreased. They drew greater attention after World War II. But as recently as 1952 when Senator Estes Kefauver defeated President Harry S Truman in the New Hampshire Democratic primary, many people agreed with Mr. Truman when he referred to the primaries as so much "eyewash" and felt that despite Kefauver's primary victories he would never win the nomination because during Kefauver's crime investigation in the Senate he had offended too many of the powers within the big city organizations of the party.

However, in that same year the primaries, extensively covered by the news media--particularly the growing television networks--doubtless contributed much to the success of General Eisenhower. Eisenhower came across much better on TV than did his main opponent, Senator Robert A. Taft, although Senator Taft would have fared well through traditional organization politics and even with the newly added influence of TV made a strong bid for the nomination. In 1952, a nationwide audience for the first time saw both parties' nomination conventions from Chicago on network TV. From that time forward presidential campaign coverage has been different. The exposure through television has focused public attention on the primaries more than before. Through the impact on the polls and surveys which this has had, the effect has been

48

that the media follow events closely from the final part of the pre-presidential year (when candidates are planning their strategies) through the primary season and the convention season, and finally through the fall campaign when the process culminates in the presidential election. Therefore, the more extensive media exposure has made the process more long-drawn-out at least in appearance. Saturation coverage probably has also had the dysfunctional effect of dampening public interest in the process, although in years where important issues such as Vietnam have been debated this has not necessarily been true.

The media's relationship to public opinion surveys has been basically to establish certain polls and surveys as the most credible; some effort has been made to establish which have the greater reputation for accuracy, and poll-takers such as Richard Scammon and Louis Harris have been hired by the networks (NBC and ABC, respectively) to do analysis for them. In addition, other survey analysts who work on contract for the candidates, such as Pat Cadell (who worked for McGovern in 1972 and for Jimmy Carter in 1976) have been frequently interviewed on network news programs. The polls have had considerable impact on the voters' thinking, but this may be at least in part because like the primaries their effect has been magnified by the magic lens of television. One observer has gone so far as to refer to the polls as "the invisible primary" and to indicate that the candidate leading the polls at a point early in the presidential year is the one most likely to achieve his party's nomination and to win the fall election.[5] (George Gallup for example conducts trial heats pitting possible nominees against each other in his surveys.)

The media's relationship to the new technology of politics should be explored as well. The advent of television has made possible campaigns devoted almost entirely to the use of media with a great de-emphasis on personal appearances of the candidate. This was the kind of campaign run by Nixon in 1968, and again to some extent in his re-election campaign in 1972. It is a campaign in which media images are used to reach a wide audience, but the candidate's actual appearances are carefully controlled and contrived to develop an

---

[5] Arthur T. Hadley, The Invisible Primary (Englewood Cliffs, N.J.: Prentice-Hall, 1976).

agreed-upon image. Joe McGinniss described the 1968 Nixon campaign in the book, The Selling of the President 1968, and it appears to fit this pattern but it should be said in fairness to him that other previous campaigns such as that of Eisenhower in 1952 and Kennedy in 1960 made extensive use of media advertising.[6]

The usual pattern was to engage in heavy use of media commercials for the candidate in the large industrial states such as New York and California where reaching each voter by personal contact was very difficult and expensive. One of the running controversies about this wide use of media commercials (in addition to the allegation that a contrived image is somehow "put over" on the voters) is that the dependence of candidates on this kind of campaign limits the field of candidates to those who can afford the very expensive and slick media campaign that has most frequently proved successful in the past. Those who argue against this claim point to successful low-budget campaigns like that of Senator Lawton Chiles of Florida and Governor Dan Walker of Illinois (both engaged in a meet-the-people campaign, walking from one corner of the state to another). But there does seem to be some correlation between campaign finances for media campaigns and the degree of success of candidates, granting that there are more than a few exceptions to this general pattern.

There have been controversies, too, about the proper format for such campaign commercials. Some argue that 30-second commercials ought to be banned because they can only present slogans and an image of the candidate. Others say that five-minute and 30-minute presentations may not hold the interest of the viewers. An additional controversy has arisen over equal time from the networks in presidential campaigns. Section 315 of the Communications Act of 1934 provides that when one candidate for public office is given time for a presentation, all his opponents must be given an equal opportunity to speak. This would open up the air waves to minor and frivolous candidates. The roadblock of Section 315 was circumvented for the Kennedy-Nixon debates in 1960, when it was temporarily waived. But since then the political circumstances have never been right to secure passage of another waiver, although the FCC has made a ruling that press

----

[6]Joe McGinniss, The Selling of the President 1968 (New York: Trident Press, 1969),

conferences are not covered by Section 315 and the Democratic National Committee is challenging this ruling in the courts because it feels it gives an unfair advantage to an incumbent President. In 1976 another debate series was held between Ford and Carter after a favorable FCC ruling, but no new waiver was passed.

Whatever one's views of the controversy over "phony" commercials and the debilitating effects of "image" politics, one study made by the authors of The Ticket-Splitter indicated that there is some dubiousness on the part of the public about campaign commercials, and that each candidate now tries to generate as much news coverage of his campaign as possible.[7] The feeling is that viewers look on news coverage of the campaign as objective but tend to view commercials as subjective and to discount their content. Most campaigners today, of course, seek to use both, and in fact when negative news coverage develops seek to counter it, as Jimmy Carter did fairly successfully when the 1976 controversy about his remarks on "ethnic purity" erupted during the primary season. It turned out that Udall and Jackson basically agreed with Carter's views when the smoke of battle had cleared.[8] It appeared that each candidate was in favor of open housing laws, but that none of them were in favor of rapid changes in the ethnic composition of neighborhoods. Nonetheless statements made on television, because of its magnifying effects, can be damaging to candidates. The best example of this is the widely

---

[7]Lance Tarrance and Walter DeVries, The Ticket-Splitters (Grand Rapids, Mich.: Eerdmans Press, 1972). For a different point of view, see Thomas E. Patterson and Robert D. McClure, The Unseeing Eye (New York: G. P. Putnam's Sons, 1976). These authors suggest that news casts provide little campaign news, and that commercials give more information to those with little knowledge of politics. See their discussion of "opinion persuasion" and "information persuasion", pp. 154, 155.

[8]See Kandy Stroud, How Jimmy Won: The Victory Campaign From Plains to the White House (New York: William Morrow & Co., 1977), especially Chapter 23, "Ethnic Purity," pp. 271-281. See also Jules Witcover, Marathon: The Pursuit of the Presidency, 1972-1976 (New York: Viking Press, 1977), especially pp.302-309.

publicized statement by George McGovern in 1972 that he was "1000 percent behind" Senator Eagleton, his erstwhile runningmate, when the realities of politics eventually forced McGovern to drop Eagleton from the ticket. This was greatly damaging to McGovern's credibility at a time when his campaign had many handicaps anyway.[9]

The direction of modern politics under the influence of the mass media is somewhat hard to determine at this point, but an effort should be made. Some good things have come from the all-pervasive presence of the media; scandals in campaigning are much harder to cover up, as we learned during the Watergate episode. On the other hand, because the public can learn so much so easily about the candidates and the campaign, it is possible to reach a saturation point which may cause a kind of revulsion against the whole process. This is undesirable because a democratic system can only function on a healthy basis if there is widespread popular participation in each step of the process.

The media have probably been more of a force for good than for bad, however, if an objective appraisal is made. They at least make much more information available to the public, and one can readily believe that the public is more sophisticated now and can make better judgments. It may be true that the public was badly deceived by some of the events surrounding Watergate. It is probably also true that in many cases the media have helped the public see the political system as it really is; that may make for fewer uncritically acclaimed heroes, but the kind of political realism it fosters may be beneficial in the long run.

How Linkage Has Become Important in the Governing System

So far discussion of media's linkage function has focused on the importance of linkage to the poli-

---

[9] See Gary Warren Hart, Right from the Start: A Chronicle of the McGovern Campaign (New York: Quadrangle, 1973), pp. 250-254. See also Theodore H. White, The Making of the President 1972 (New York: Bantam, 1973), Chapter Eight, "The Eagleton Affair", pp. 256-289.

tical system and especially presidential campaigns.
It is also important to look at how linkage has come
to play a vital role in the governing system, that is,
the system concerned with policy-making and decision-
making between elections.

Let's begin the discussion of the significance
of the mass media's linkage function by viewing it
from the White House viewpoint, since the central relationship being explored in this book is that between
the Presidency and the mass media. I'll be concerned
in looking from the White House outside, rather than
looking from the outside into the White House--in
other words, I'll be concerned with the viewpoint of
the President and his aides rather than with that of
the public.

The media obviously have, and can have, considerable impact on the policy-making process at the
presidential level. Recent presidents have been
almost preoccupied with their media image. In Richard
Nixon's case he may have become so preoccupied with
this and so involved in hostility toward the media
that he had overlooked the attitudes of the public
beyond. Presidents in their approach to decision-
making presumably want to serve the public interest,
but they are obliged by political necessity to protect
and preserve their own private interest as well. Thus
in their political calculations, they are desirous of
having the best motives put on their actions by the
news media. Every decision must be put in the best
light possible, and the media can make or break a
President's effort to do this because he must depend
on them to some extent in the final analysis. A favorite stratagem of Richard Nixon was to rely on direct
television speeches rather than press conferences, but
he knew he must get his message across.

The best way to clarify the importance of media
coverage to presidential policy-making is to contrast
the effect of favorable coverage with that of unfavorable coverage. Lyndon Johnson during the Tet offensive
got a great deal of unfavorable coverage for his policy
in South Vietnam, where military successes were scored
but at the same time the enemy was achieving psychological successes. Public reaction was negative as
reflected in voting in the New Hampshire presidential
primary early in 1968. The President's reaction was
ultimately to modify his Vietnam policy by starting
in motion a train of events leading to a peace conference in Paris and, at the political level, by announc-

ing that he would not be a candidate for another term. Johnson may have been reacting to public opinion, but few would deny that the image of events portrayed by the media had a considerable effect on the shaping of that public opinion.

So this three-element model must be kept in mind; the media usually do not work directly in affecting presidential decision-making. They have an indirect effect in that when the media affect public opinion either negatively or positively, the President cannot ignore that dimension in his decision-making responsibilities. A more positive example would be the public reaction to President Nixon's November 1969 speech on Vietnam policy and the slow withdrawal of American troops. Peace activists reacted negatively but the mass public reacted positively, and this helped Nixon to decide to continue along the course he had chosen. Later of course, he incorrectly gauged the reaction of public opinion to the events of Watergate and he paid the penalty for this, but at least at this early moment in his Presidency he did effectively employ the mass media to turn public opinion in the direction he desired.

The media also significantly affect executive-legislative relations in the way in which presidential-congressional transactions are reported. Perhaps the most dramatic policy area in which this is true is that of foreign policy, an issue area basically entrusted to the executive branch but one which it is obliged to share control of to some extent with Congress. Such issues as the effort to cut off funds for the war in Vietnam, the approval of American agreements with foreign governments for military bases, and declarations of future policy in undeclared wars have brought the President and Congress into conflict.

The side of the controversy getting the most favorable treatment in the news media has an obvious advantage. In the controversy over the secret bombing of Cambodia, for example, President Nixon doubtless felt that Congress' side was given more favorable treatment. However, if he had operated more openly and made some information about his policy available to the public through the news media, he may have had a better chance to convince the public there was some merit in his actions. This illustrates too that in some instances where the President does not want to take on Congress directly in a confrontation, the media serve as a scapegoat for a frustrated President--and

most Presidents are frustrated in some of their policies during their White House tenure.

The White House view of the presidential selection process and the media's role in it is an interesting one too. When an incumbent President seeks re-
election, he wants all possible favorable coverage.
When he leaves office, he may want to influence the
media coverage in a certain way or not, depending on
whom he favors as his successor. Lyndon Johnson
apparently did not object to letting the media report
that he was displeased with some of Hubert Humphrey's
policy positions, even though he ostensibly supported
Humphrey.

To take another example, Presidents seeking re-
election or election in their own right after succeeding to the office have a special view of the
presidential selection process, since their aim is to
prolong their own tenure. Thus when Dwight Eisenhower ran for a second term in 1956, he was concerned
with portraying his image in the media in a way favorable to his effort to retain the Presidency. He used
television appearances, filmed news conferences and
other devices to help convey that kind of image. So
it can be said that knowledge of the importance of the
media did affect the way in which the strategy for the
Eisenhower campaign was developed that year.

Examples of Presidents seeking re-election with
considerable awareness of the news media's importance
include Richard Nixon, whose re-election effort in
1972 was successful partly because he managed to keep
out of the public eye and let the news media focus on
George McGovern's mistakes in the campaign. When
Nixon did get extensive coverage, it was usually in
controlled situations such as his summit visit to
China and the Moscow summit or at the Republican
National Convention in 1972 at Miami Beach.

Presidents seeking election in their own right
after succeeding to the office view the electoral
process from a peculiar vantage point. It was important to Lyndon Johnson in 1964, for example, to
develop his own media image and not to allow himself
to be overshadowed by the Kennedy legend; this is one
of the more important reasons, apart from their political differences, why he did not select Robert

Kennedy as his running mate in 1964.[10] At this time
Johnson still had a relatively favorable press and
much public sympathy because of his taking office
under difficult circumstances after the Kennedy assassination, so he won in a landslide, probably helped by
his media image.

The other recent example that comes to mind is
that of Gerald Ford. While Ford had some problems
with his media image in his effort to win the Presidency by vote of the people after succeeding to the
office from the post of non-elected Vice President, it
appears that Ford's problems were at least as much
those of political strategy. Early in 1976, when it
appeared that his chief primary foe would be Ronald
Reagan and that if he won the nomination his Democratic opponent would be Jimmy Carter, the chief problem Ford had was his connection with the Washington
establishment, a factor which might have been an asset
in ordinary years when more public trust was present.
But now it was a liability because Ford had spent 25
years or more in Washington, and he was also associated in the public mind with Richard Nixon and the
Watergate scandals. He had not been implicated in the
scandals, but he had pardoned Nixon and there were
from time to time reminders of this relationship, such
as the report made by Nixon to Ford on his China trip--
an embarrassment to the Ford White House--or the
deluge of publicity given to the movie, All the President's Men, or to the book, The Final Days. On the
other hand, both Reagan and Carter had the ability and
the know-how to use the media well so either would
present formidable problems for Ford.

---

[10]Doris Kearns, Lyndon Johnson and the American
Dream (New York: Harper & Row, 1976), Chapter 7, "The
Transition Year", pp. 170-209, especially pp. 199-202
on "the Bobby problem." See also Lyndon B. Johnson,
The Vantage Point: Perspectives on the Presidency,
1963-1969 (New York: Holt, Rinehart and Winston, 1971),
for the former President's account of his relationship
with Robert F. Kennedy, pp. 538-543. See also Theodore
H. White, The Making of the President 1964 (New York:
Signet New American Library, 1965), pp. 310-319. See
also Edwin Guthman, We Band of Brothers (New York:
Harper & Row, 1971), pp. 244-258, for an account of
this relationship from Kennedy's viewpoint.

In summary then, from the White House viewpoint, no President can be disinterested in the presidential election process because he will either be a leading candidate himself or he will be supporting the presidential bid of someone whose election he feels will vindicate his policies. Even when retiring Presidents are ostensibly neutral, it is hard to believe that they are in fact neutral, and they must be aware in all cases that media coverage of the campaign from start to finish has a solid impact on public opinion polls and public reaction in general.

As viewed from the White House, the mass media can have a significant effect on the President's relations with his Cabinet and with the executive branch bureaucracy, although not to the same degree as with the electoral process where much activity is public. News coverage in the media about President-Cabinet member relationships may concern various things: The selection of a Cabinet appointee by the President; conferences held between the President and a Cabinet member to discuss policy differences or the formulation of policy; discussions they may have about other matters, either governmental or political. Most Cabinet members today do not have the same degree of visibility that some of the President's close aides may have. Nonetheless, there are incumbents in certain key positions, such as Secretaries of State and Defense and the Attorney General, who will get more attention from the news media than their Cabinet colleagues. For example, one can feel sure the relationship between President Ford and Secretary of State Henry Kissinger was affected considerably by what was reported in the news media about the two men. Kissinger was a hold-over Cabinet member to begin with, and columnists noted that Ford felt dependent on him for foreign policy advice; later they said that Ford felt more self-confident about foreign policy decision-making, and downgraded Kissinger's role when Kissinger gave up his post as national security advisor to the President. But as to the true relationship between the two men, many of their political and diplomatic dealings were in private and the media could not publish all that was known about it, although they did have access to each of them and could bring out bits and pieces of facts in interviews and news conferences.

In general, the White House probably views Cabinet members with some suspicion because members generally have a constituent group they maintain some links with, and these kinds of relationships may under-

mine in some cases the Cabinet member's allegiance to
the President who appointed him. This is doubtless
one reason why in recent Administrations the importance
of Cabinet officials has been downgraded and that of
staff aides has grown, although President Carter has
sought to change this somewhat. Staff aides, not subject to the confirmation process required for Cabinet
officials, are less subject to the influences of the
various client interest groups that importune Cabinet
members with such ease. The President's chief of
staff, for example (or in Carter's case, any key staff
aide), owes his position and political influence
entirely to the President who appointed him. On the
other hand, a Secretary of Agriculture may have support from agricultural interest groups and other interests that may make it possible for him to have a degree
of independence from the President that a staff aide
would never have. Nonetheless, even before Carter some
movement had occurred toward restoring some of the
prestige and high standing of Cabinet officers simply
because the whole Watergate experience tended to dis-
credit White House staff aides, at least as they have
operated in recent administrations.

The President's relations with the bureaucracy
occasionally come under the news media's purview.
Some examples that come to mind relate to the Justice
Department revolt of young lawyers under the Nixon
Administration who refused to go along with John Mitchell's and President Nixon's policies on the handling
of civil rights litigation. Those who were not fired
resigned.[11] On another occasion, President Kennedy
ordered a shake-up in the State Department and trans-
ferred Chester Bowles from one position to another
because he felt the State Department bureaucracy was
unresponsive to the wishes of the White House.[12] At

---

[11]William Safire, Before the Fall: An Inside
View of the Pre-Watergate White House (New York: Bel-
mont Tower Books, 1975), Part Four, "Lowered Voices,"
Chapter 2, "The Wayward Bus", pp. 232-245.

[12]For an account of Bowles' service in the Ken-
nedy Administration, see Chester Bowles, Promises to
Keep: My Years in Public Life, 1941-1969 (New York:
Harper & Row, 1971), Part III, "Working With Kennedy",
pp. 335-528. Also see Arthur M. Schlesinger, Jr.,
A Thousand Days: John F. Kennedy in the White House
(Boston: Houghton Mifflin Co., 1965), pp. 437-447.

the beginning of the second Nixon term, the President began a practice of putting a "White House man" in each line department to keep an eye on the bureaucrats, because Nixon felt he could not trust a bureaucracy that he felt had become entrenched under Democratic predecessors. Doubtless there are instances of conflict between the White House and the bureaucracy which never get into the public prints, but examples already cited indicate that the news media are very much aware of such conflict and frequently seek it out. The reaction of a President to the bureaucracy may be different in some cases from that of the institutional White House, as different Presidents involve themselves in differing degrees in the interrelationships between the departments and the White House itself. A President like Eisenhower, for example, may have been less aware of such conflicts as they may have been settled by underlings without being brought directly to him, while a President like Kennedy or Roosevelt may have been more aware of the conflicts simply because he normally made himself more involved in the details of administration.

The media also strongly affect the President's relationship with the party structure and the public. I'll discuss each of these relationships separately. The President's relationship with his own party normally changes after he gives up the role of a candidate seeking the office, or even that of nominee of his party, and actually becomes President. As President he will usually seek control of his own party's national committee and seek regularized working relationshipswith his party's congressional leadership in both houses. As a candidate of the out party or a candidate of a faction of his own party with someone else in the White House, the presidential candidate of course does not have that kind of control although he may work toward it in winning the nomination and the election. Insofar as media coverage of this relationship is concerned, the relationship between the President and his own party tends to get little attention from the media when it is harmonious but a great deal of attention when it is conflictful. This partly grows out of the definition of news as defined by the media, in which the conflict situation is normally more newsworthy than the situation where there is no discord and harmonious relationships predominate.

The news media's impact on the President's relationship with the public can be considerable, and it usually is either helpful or harmful. For one thing, the media cannot ignore any President for what he does can be expected to affect the whole nation for good or ill. Presidents successful in handling the media have usually been able to go on to achieve legislative and diplomatic successes and in general to work toward building a good record for their Administrations. But on the other hand, Presidents--even the most popular-- sometimes get negative treatment in the media. They can respond like Nixon did, with bitterness and vin- dictiveness, which is self-defeating because eventually if they pursue this course they will lose the support of the public as well as the media. This is what ultimately happened to Nixon in the Watergate trauma.

On the other hand, they can respond by fines- sing the media attacks. President Kennedy, for example, used to say that he was "reading it more, but enjoying it less" but he responded in a kidding fashion indicating that the media's criticism did not bother him. President Truman, once said that "if you can't stand the heat you should get out of the kit- chen". He may have been less nonchalant than Kennedy, but in general he knew how to cultivate good media relations. Even President Roosevelt, who along with Kennedy and perhaps Eisenhower may have had the best media relations of any 20th Century President, once said petulantly to a reporter at a White House press conference, "You should put on a dunce cap and go sit in the corner." But the key thing in public percep- tion of Presidents through the media is that over the long haul the President should project a strong posi- tive image. If that occurs, he can usually earn the public's support.

The mass media's role can be important too, in how Congress views the White House. While members of Congress do get first hand impressions of the Presi- dent and his close aides, the fact remains that they get much of their information about the Administration and its activities from the news media, including daily newspapers, magazines, radio and television.[13]

---

[13]See the discussion of the President's "pro- fessional reputation" in the Washington community in Richard E. Neustadt, _Presidential Power: With Reflec- tions on Nixon and Johnson_ (New York: John Wiley & Sons, 1976).

One way in which Congress may feel the media's influence in its relationship with the President is that the media may furnish an amplifying factor for the President's policy statements. Thus, for example, the President may send the leadership a letter stating his policy proposal on an important issue like military aid to Turkey or Israel. The letter will be read in both Houses, and the Congressman will receive a copy or hear about it from his committee chairman, the Speaker or majority or minority leader. But if this same letter is covered in the news media and widely commented on, or if that coverage in the news media stirs the public to write many letters to its congressmen about it, the impact on the congressman will be much greater. Thus does this magnifying or amplifying factor seem to work.

The news media are also viewed by members of Congress as an instrument for congressional response to the President. Again using the Turkish aid legislation as an example, President Ford vetoed legislation cutting off funds for aid to Turkey and ultimately a compromise was reached. But before it was reached, the President and his opposition in Congress made an effort to mobilize public support for the position of each. A key weapon in this effort, of course, was to get broad and favorable mass media coverage of the policy positions involved; congressmen turned to newspapers, television and the other mass media for this purpose. The existence of an important Greek-American lobbying group on the issue probably made it easier for congressmen to generate media coverage of their views.

A final element of the mass media impact on the relationship between President and Congress is the degree to which the media promote conflict between Congress and the White House. Even when the President's own party controls Congress--as under Jimmy Carter--a certain degree of conflict exists between the White House and Congress. But the media can promote further conflict by heavily emphasizing controversies which in some instances both the President and Congress would rather play down. The media can do this because they have the freedom to do so, but this does not mean the public will react in the same fashion on every issue. On an issue like Watergate and the impeachment crisis, the public may react very strongly to coverage of such conflict in the media. On the other hand, a controversy may arise between the Congress and the President over an issue like the

61

composition of the Federal Election Commission. This
conflict may be duly reported in the news media, but
it may arouse the public very little, because it basically sees the FEC issue as one concerning professional
politicians and whether they will get federal matching
funds for their presidential campaigns. Again, as in
the Watergate-impeachment example, the media may cause
the public to react strongly as in the instance of the
controversy over Vietnam policy in the late 1960's.

The media's role may also be examined as this
affects the President's relationship with other officials. It may have some parallels with the President-
Cabinet or the President-Congress relationship,
although there will be differences. I'll consider the
mayors of major cities, governors of the larger
states, and Supreme Court justices. As in the previous discussion, one can cite both the importance of
these relationships and the distinction between the
public and private dimension of these relationships.

As far as mayors and governors are concerned, a
good example of how the news media affect their relationship with the President may be seen in the way in
which the New York City fiscal crisis was covered by
the news media in late 1975 and early 1976. The public
awareness of the crisis came after the media quoted
Mayor Abraham Beame and Governor Hugh Carey on the need
for federal aid. Then the President's views that the
city and state should do more for self-help were
quoted, and it appeared that there was a wide gap
between the President on the one hand and the city and
state officials on the other. Eventually, publicity
brought public recognition that it would be a bad thing
to let New York City go into default because this would
be harmful to the national economy. The public began
to voice this opinion and the President, in reacting
to it, eventually agreed to a compromise solution. It
is likely however that had the media not given the
matter extensive coverage, and that had public opinion
not become more sympathetic to the plight of New York
City, nothing at all might have been done, or at least
nothing very effective. One particularly recalls the
New York _Daily_ _News_ headline: "Ford to City: 'Drop
Dead'".

The President's relations with Supreme Court
justices are publicized primarily at the time of the
justices' appointment, because the Court is supposed
to be independent and free of political influence.
But there are exceptions to this general pattern. In

62

the case of President Lyndon Johnson and Associate
Justice Abe Fortas, it was known that Mr. Justice
Fortas sometimes served as an informal adviser to the
President. But when President Johnson sought to ele-
vate Fortas to the Chief Justiceship and appoint a
replacement for him on the Court, this relationship of
"cronyism" was brought up by the opposition who felt
that Richard Nixon, then expected to be elected President, should be given the right to appoint a successor
to Chief Justice Warren. Later a scandal came to
light and Fortas resigned, but the media played a key
role in the blocking of the Fortas nomination.

        In summarizing the discussion of how linkage
has become important in the governing system, it would
be wise to look at the functional relationships
involved and concede that even though the mass media
do not constitute a formal part of the government,
they should be considered an integral part of the
opinion-formation system which impacts on government.

        Media linkage of the Presidency with the other
elements of government and with the public is important today because the media provide a much-needed
channel of communication and dissemination of information in a large continental nation of more than 200
million people. The function performed by the media
could not be performed so well by any other institution, so its function of linkage has arisen partly out
of a need. The concern of any President must be that
that linkage is carried out in a way that is beneficial to him and his Administration's goals. It ought
not to be assumed that the mass media are "out to get"
any President and his official colleagues. The media
perceive their function as merely that of a watchdog
and a gatekeeper to help insure the public that
elected officials such as the President will perform
their duties of office in the manner which the public
has come to expect. The watchdog function of the
media is the function basically of "blowing the
whistle" on any element of government where wrongdoing
is perceived or suspected. The media can "blow the
whistle" on Congress or state government or any other
governmental institution just as readily as it can on
the Presidency, as it has in the Korean lobby investigation. The reason it has watchdogged the Presidency
more in recent years may be because that is where the
chief power is believed to be found. The gatekeeper
function is that function of deciding what information
can be relayed to the public; it is performed by government officials as well as the media and it is an

important function too.

Consequences of Mass Media Linkage Already Realized

In this section of this chapter, I'll focus attention on some of the consequences for the Presidency of mass media linkages already realized during recent administrations. It is sometimes said that the modern White House news conference originated with Theodore Roosevelt and Woodrow Wilson, but for our purposes the analysis will be limited to Presidents who have used the electronic media. Since Harding, Coolidge and Hoover made only limited use of radio during their terms, in effect this means that meaningful analysis of use by Presidents of the electronic mass media should begin with the Administration of Franklin D. Roosevelt.

President Roosevelt showed great skill in the use of the media. He was a master of the radio address, the fireside chat and the informal White House news conference, all three. How he used these various devices will be described in some detail, followed by an analysis of the apparent impact of his use of the media on the public and on Congress.

A good example of the broadcast public address, while not a fireside chat designed solely for broadcast, would be the First Inaugural of FDR, in which he stated on March 4, 1933, that "the only thing we have to fear is fear itself." Roosevelt was speaking of course in the context of the Great Depression at a time when there were 15 million unemployed across the nation and bank failures had created widespread doubts about the soundness of the currency. There was a kind of economic paralysis setting in across the nation, and Roosevelt properly sensed that the way to deal with it was through immediate action, unlike Hoover, whose ideas of rugged individualism and laissez faire dogma had prevented him from taking bold governmental action. The rest of the story is well known, but Roosevelt's First Inaugural was an important milestone on the road to restoring the nation's self-confidence during the Depression crisis. Another example of a public address by Roosevelt broadcast by radio which brought a widespread positive public response was his acceptance speech at Philadelphia at the 1936 Democratic National Convention, in which he spoke of "economic royalists" and the entrenched privileged class which was resisting his social and economic reforms. Still another was his

64

Pearl Harbor address to Congress, delivered on December 8, 1941. Those who remember that period in recent history felt this speech galvanized the nation into a united war effort against the Axis powers. Other examples could be cited, but these should be enough to demonstrate that Roosevelt had oratorical powers that excelled those of his contemporaries, and that he knew how to make best use of them on radio.

Despite his prowess with the use of the broadcast formal address, Roosevelt perhaps will be best remembered for the use of the "fireside chat", an informal radio talk which he made usually two or three times a year to the public. One of these dealt with the economic crisis of the Depression in 1933, and another dealt with his proposed Social Security legislation in 1935. Still another well-known fireside chat was given on the occasion of the announcement of the D-Day invasion in Normandy in June 1944, and there was one following the Pearl Harbor attack. In each instance, the President was able to convey the feeling that a neighbor had dropped in to chat with the typical American family in its living room, and that he was able to speak in the plain language of the average citizen. It was perhaps the fireside chats more than any other device he used which helped Franklin Roosevelt to get such a hold on the American public and to carry its support through war, depression and other serious national crises. It did not diminish the zeal of his opposition, but it did reinforce the loyalty to FDR of the many millions who supported him through the more than 12 years during which he served in the Presidency.

While he had his difficulties during his final term and even to some extent after 1937 when the conservative coalition had strong influence in Congress, Roosevelt was able to make as effective use of the White House press conference as any modern President with the possible exception of Kennedy. A good illustration of this use of the informal news conference in FDR's time, in which a group of perhaps 40 to 50 newsmen stood around the President's desk in the Oval Office and fired away with questions, is the press conference in which he detailed his support for the Social Security legislation of the mid-1930's. Perhaps one reason for the effectiveness of the Roosevelt press conferences was that they were held frequently; until the onset of World War II, he often held them as often as twice a week and he sometimes held them in

Hyde Park and Warm Springs as well as in Washington.14

   Roosevelt's skill in the use of the media was
not limited to his ability to exploit the use of the
media to convey his ideas to the public. He was also
gifted in the ability to keep in close touch with public opinion through regular reading of the newspapers;
this was supplemented by reports he received from Mrs.
Eleanor Roosevelt, who served as his "eyes and ears"
around the nation and even around the world (and who
also wrote a regular column, "My Day"), and reports of
political intelligence he picked up from his many
friends and associates.15 In getting the most positive
results from the news media, Roosevelt also was
shrewdly capable of making the distinction between publishers and editors who frequently opposed his Administration editorially, and the reporters who were frequently favorably inclined toward his policies and
more likely to give him sympathetic coverage in the
news columns. We should not leave this subject without taking note of the pioneering use he made of
radio,16 and his willingness to experiment with new
approaches to the public. In general, Roosevelt was
one of the most skillful Presidents in the positive
use he made of the media. One can only speculate on
how he would have made use of television if it had
been available to him, but given his personal magnetism and exuberant personality, he would doubtless have
projected well on this medium also. Roosevelt had a
zest for politics, and this came through to the public
by way of the media in nearly everything he did.

   14See Elmer E. Cornwell, Jr., Presidential
Leadership of Public Opinion (Bloomington, Ind.: Indi-
ana University Press, 1965). See also Arthur M.
Schlesinger, Jr., The Politics of Upheaval (Boston:
Houghton Mifflin Co., 1960), pp. 633, 634.

   15See Joseph P. Lash, Eleanor and Franklin: The
Story of Their Relationship Based on Eleanor Roosevelt's Private Papers (New York: W. W. Norton & Co.,
1971), especially Chapter 38, "Publicist for the New
Deal--Columnist and Lecturer", pp. 434-451.

   16See David Holbrook Culbert, News For Everyman:
Radio and Foreign Affairs in Thirties America (Westport, Conn.: Greenwood Press, 1976), especially pp.
141-144 regarding Elmer Davis and the Office of War
Information.

Those who talk about "image" politics as a new development in the age of television would do well to consider that "image" politics in the sense of exploitation of electronic media may well be traced back to
FDR and his fireside chats.[17]

The impact of Roosevelt's use of the media on
the public and on Congress can be viewed overall as
being very positive. In his final years in office,
especially during the latter part of World War II, age
had taken its toll and he did not appear to have the
same magnetism he did as a younger man in his first
term. But even then a strong bond existed between the
President and the public because he had been able to
enlist public sympathy and support through effective
use of the news media. With Congress, the story was a
little different because Roosevelt made some tactical
errors in his second term, such as the abortive "purge"
of conservative Congressmen and the effort to "pack"
the Supreme Court which hurt him in the esteem of Congress. But one would definitely have to say that his
overall record in this regard was good. His personal
magnetism affected his supporters in Congress as well
as his effective use of the media, but the media did
help him with Congress in that they provided the
instrument through which he was able to maintain a
strong hold on public opinion during the longest term
any American President has ever served.

In continuing our look at the Presidential linkage with the public through the mass media in recent
times, we shift our focus of analysis to the Truman
Administration. The first thing that needs to be said
here is that the Roosevelt Presidency was a "hard act
to follow". I would frankly state that President Truman was not a media-oriented President in the same way
that FDR was. Truman was perhaps most effective making stump speeches or doing "whistle-stop" campaigning
in which he was able to project an image of sincerity.
As far as his media relations were concerned, he never
did achieve the skill which Roosevelt showed in press
conferences, but he did eventually develop an easy
rapport with the working press and thus to some extent

---

[17]For an account of an early FDR Fireside Chat,
see Elliott Roosevelt and James Brough, A Rendezvous
With Destiny: The Roosevelts of the White House (New
York: Dell Books, 1975), pp. 44, 45.

earned himself good newspaper coverage, which was still of major importance during the Truman era.[18]

Truman had several difficulties in the use of the media. One of these was previously alluded to, his handicap of being compared to FDR. He could basically not do very much about it, as the comparison was inevitable. But in time he did develop a style and approach of his own which helped him to do a better job of reaching the public. Truman's basic openness and frankness made him controversial sometimes, but it posed problems as well as giving him advantages in the use of the media. Early in his term he began to earn the reputation for being outspoken, unlike FDR who sometimes used tactful or at least devious phrases in order to avoid offending people. Truman did not seem to mind offending, because he put a high premium on frankness in his public dealings. But this sometimes led him to make press conference statements which were misinterpreted by the media and the public, such as one press conference in Tennessee in which he referred to American use of atomic weapons and had to reassure Prime Minister Attlee of Great Britain that there had been no change in U.S. policy. Another example was the press conference at which he referred to the charges against Alger Hiss as a "red herring", something which proved to be embarrassing to him when Hiss was convicted of perjury. But Truman did win some respect and admiration for his frankness, and after a few miscues of the kind referred to, he did learn to be more careful without blunting his disarming frankness to too great a degree. Eventually Truman worked

---

[18]For accounts of Truman's relationships with the New York Times, Kansas City Star and St. Louis Post-Dispatch, see the memoir of a one-time Roosevelt press secretary who worked for Truman in the 1948 campaign: Jonathan Daniels, The Man of Independence (Philadelphia: J. B. Lippincott Co., 1950). For a different viewpoint on Truman's press relations, see Margaret Truman, Harry S Truman (New York: William Morrow & Co., 1973), pp. 229, 230. For Truman's own description of his first press conference as President, see Harry S. Truman, Year of Decisions (Vol. I of Memoirs) (Garden City, N.Y.: Doubleday & Co., 1955), pp. 47-49. Truman commented here, "The President's relations with the press are of the utmost importance. . . ."

out his own style, which was earthy rather than patrician as in FDR's case, and he gave the public and the reporters an idea of what kind of behavior to expect in his news conferences. But this took time. The public's reaction to Truman was rather volatile; during the time of the V-E and V-J Day announcements, he was one of the most popular Presidents in 20th Century history, but toward the end of his first term he had lost popularity due to problems of economic dislocation, inflation and price control controversies, and the like. His 1948 whistle stop campaign regained some of that support for him, but when he left office after the 1952 election, his support had declined, partly due to the stalemated war in Korea. It is likely that it was the impact of events more than his media image which affected Truman's popularity, but had he possessed the skill of a Roosevelt in using the media he may have been able to retain more of his popularity than he did. He was respected as a President with some integrity, even though he never did achieve the long-term popularity which Roosevelt did. The reaction of Congress to Truman's use of the media was sometimes negative; this was partly due to Truman's use of the media to put responsibility for policy differences on Congress--much in the manner used in recent times by Gerald Ford. But Truman's background in Congress and the fact that many veteran legislators knew him well probably mitigated this to some extent.

Perhaps one factor which should not be overlooked is the effective use of the media by Truman's opposition and the likelihood that this helped to lead to a change of party control in the executive branch in 1952. The Eisenhower-Nixon campaign in 1952 made effective use of the media, and Senator Joseph McCarthy, Truman's nemesis (although later discredited and censured by the Senate), exploited the media through widespread anti-Communist charges. In sum, it was as much the opposition's effective use of the media as Truman's failure to use the media as effectively as Roosevelt had, which led to the decline in influence he suffered during his second term. In all, however, he did learn a good deal about using the media and did show some improvement. The basic problem was that his early career had been a period in which public speaking rather than radio and TV had been important, and he had to use the techniques which came best to him. Less skillful media usage by Truman was probably not as harmful to him as it would have been to some Presidents in 1948, for example, because he did very skillfully conduct a "whistle stop" campaign that helped turn the election around (aided by the fact that his opponent, Governor Thomas E. Dewey of New York, did not appear to be speaking very much about the issues).

Dwight D. Eisenhower was not the President who most effectively used TV--indeed it could be said that Kennedy, Nixon and Carter among recent Presidents used it more effectively--but Eisenhower nevertheless had a charmismatic personality which projected well on the visual medium. Also, another factor which would lead one to rate Eisenhower ahead of Truman in the use of TV is that Eisenhower did some pioneering work in the use of TV and he also got good advice from news people and technicians in how to use it more effectively. James C. Hagerty, who served as Eisenhower's press secretary, helped Eisenhower to develop new techniques for filmed press conferences shown on TV which doubtless helped the President in communicating with the public; also, Eisenhower was given advice by Robert Montgomery, the actor, in use of TV in a more effective way. The main asset he had was still his personality, however, because no amount of coaching can help a would-be speaker on TV who possesses a wooden manner and dull way of speaking. Eisenhower developed his own style after a time, and he made use of sincerity much as Truman did but he seemed to be more effective in communicating.[19]

The public and congressional reaction to Eisenhower was for the most part positive; he won both his elections by landslide margins, and he got reasonably good support in Congress for six of his eight years in the White House, although he had a Democratic Congress to deal with for much of that time. It was only in his final two years that he had greater difficulty with congressional relations, and this may have been due to factors other than his media usage, for example, his lame-duck status and his declining influence at a time

---

[19]For an account of how Hagerty handled press relations for Eisenhower at the time of the President's heart attack, see Robert J. Donovan, Eisenhower: The Inside Story (New York: Harper & Brothers, 1956), pp. 366-369. For numerous discussions of Eisenhower's media relations and Hagerty's role, see Marquis Childs, Eisenhower: Captive Hero, A Critical Study of the General and the President (New York: Harcourt, Brace & Co., 1958).

when liberal ideas were once again becoming more popular. On balance, despite his sometimes complicated
syntax in press conferences and a tendency toward
blandness in some of his media appearances, Eisenhower
used the media effectively more often than he did not.
His TV exposure may have had some relationship to his
good showing in the polls; to some extent that may be
explained as well by the political context of the
times in which he governed. He appeared to have a
more down-to-earth manner than the erudite Adlai
Stevenson, his opponent in both of his presidential
races, but part of Eisenhower's immense popularity
stemmed from his record as a World War II hero rather
than from unusually effective employment of the media
to communicate his policy positions.

One final note about Eisenhower is that he
began some innovations in dealing with the news media
which were enlarged and expanded on by his successors.
One of these was the use of TV experts for presidential appearances on camera; another was the filmed
news conference already mentioned which eventually led
to the live news conference in Kennedy's time. Eisenhower held fewer news conferences than either of his
immediate predecessors, but he got skilled counsel
from Hagerty and the other press aides who served him.
In all, his media operation was good.

Controversy could be aroused about President
Kennedy's use of the media in shaping his image for the
public, but a fair-minded person would have to say that
like Eisenhower he used the newly developing techniques of television effectively, and further he had a
charismatic personality like Eisenhower which was
enhanced to some degree by Kennedy's youth and vigor.[20]

Elected at 43 as the youngest elected President,
and the object of much media attention during the 1960
campaign because of the controversy over his Catholic

---

[20]See Harold W. Chase and Allen H. Lerman,
eds., Kennedy and the Press: The News Conferences
(New York: Thomas Y. Crowell Co., 1965), an annotated
edition of all JFK's news conferences as President,
with an introduction by Pierre Salinger. Also see
Pierre Salinger, With Kennedy (Garden City, N.Y.:
Doubleday & Co., 1966), which contains detailed
accounts of JFK's relationships with newspapers, TV
networks and correspondents.

religion and the TV debates with Richard Nixon, Kennedy came into office with great potential for using the new media devices available to him. He did make effective use of the media, but the one main problem in assessing the Kennedy Administration in this regard is that the Camelot legend which grew up around him rather rapidly after the assassination in 1963 may make it difficult to recall the living John F. Kennedy.

He did demonstrate skill in the use of all the mass media; he had a background in the news media which his predecessors did not possess, as he had for a time before his congressional service worked for a news agency, the International News Service; he had many friends in the Washington press corps, and he was capable of securing friendly coverage in part because of this. It is true that he had Irish wit and a warm personality, which perhaps hid a great deal of political depth and shrewdness, but in general it may be this media background as well as the experience he had gained in campaigning and service in Congress, both in the House and Senate, which prepared him to seize the opportunity to use the media most effectively once elected. Indeed, there are those who say that JFK might never have been able to win the 1960 election had it not been for the television debates with Nixon. In any event, he had an understanding of the importance of a good media image, and this led him to develop several new techniques for effective use of the media to promote his policies and his own popularity with the public.[21]

These new techniques either pioneered in the White House by JFK or developed to a fuller extent included the full-fledged live televised press conference, informal television interviews usually done with a small group of correspondents, and a series of

---

[21] For an account of one Washington correspondent's relationship with President Kennedy, see Benjamin Bradlee, Conversations With Kennedy (New York: W. W. Norton & Co., 1975). For a more general discussion of Kennedy's media relations, see Hugh Sidey, John F. Kennedy, President (New York: Athenaeum, 1964), especially Chapter Seven, "The Corps," pp. 98-109. During the Kennedy years, Bradlee was a Washington correspondent for Newsweek and Sidey was a Washington correspondent for Time.

exclusive interviews in which Kennedy made skillful use of accessibility to influential correspondents. The press conferences were handled well by JFK because he developed an extensive briefing system which was an outgrowth of the way he handled these during his campaign. The TV interview with a small group was effective because it was an intimate atmosphere which tended to give the President a good forum for explaining his policies and it discouraged overly hostile questions; he was quite likely to come out looking good after these interviews.

The exclusive interviews with print-media reporters did cause some criticism, but this was muted because Kennedy was not too restrictive with this technique. Pierre Salinger was JFK's press secretary and while he did not have the full background of experience enjoyed by Hagerty, he did have a keen sense of humor and knew how to handle the Washington press corps quite well, so he contributed to JFK's successful use of the media. Kennedy also used the set speech on TV quite well, as for example his speech on the Cuban missile crisis in October 1962, but he probably excelled to the greatest degree in his press conferences.

In securing public and congressional support, Kennedy supplemented his direct media appearances and interviews by carefully cultivating important correspondents, publishers and editors by extending White House invitations to them for "backgrounder" sessions. The backgrounder session was one in which the President talked about a wide range of issues on a not-for-attribution basis. By this means he would enhance the understanding of an issue by media people; he used this technique quite well in handling the civil rights issue for example. It may be asked how it was that Kennedy began with a bare majority at the time of his election, and by the time of the assassination how he enjoyed a wide degree of popularity. One reason is of course that he employed the media skillfully, but another is that Kennedy understood that timing is important in politics and he did not push hard for controversial proposals when he felt he had little chance of winning his goals. His sense of timing showed up in his handling of civil rights (exemplified by his support of a strong civil rights bill in a TV speech in June 1963) and in the handling of foreign policy (the test-ban treaty which he finally achieved a few months before his death, after the missile crisis had created the proper climate of acceptance

for it). This sense of timing was related to his
skillful use of the media in that he prepared the
interested parties by working quietly behind the
scenes before putting the prestige of his office
behind more controversial proposals. His administration was sometimes called pragmatic, and it was in
this sense.[22] The major failure of the Kennedy
Administration was probably the Vietnam involvement,
but that was a failure of other administrations as
well and the record there should not detract from the
fact that Kennedy used the media extremely well.

This was alluded to before, but the massive
media coverage of JFK's assassination and the role of
the media in the development of the Camelot legend,
make Kennedy's place in modern White House history
somewhat unique. But the media seem to have a tendency to develop heroes and to then cut them down to
size. This appeared to happen with JFK during the
Nixon era when the conservatives in power wished to
promote a debunking of his legend, and it continued
when various unconfirmed stories about his sex life
were circulated during the Ford years. This may have
been more a result of the mood of those times than an
animus against the memory of JFK, however, and it
appears that an objective appraisal of his record and
his effective use of the media would be that he was a
leader of great potential whose record was cut short
before he could realize it fully.[23]

During the Johnson Administration, President
Lyndon Johnson had some problems similar to those of
Truman, since he inevitably would be compared to Ken-
nedy just as Truman was compared to his predecessor.
But Johnson began his Administration with much good
will from both the public and the media, because he
started it under difficult circumstances following the
Kennedy Assassination.

It soon became apparent, however, that Johnson's style was less well adapted for the modern media
than was that of Kennedy and he began to suffer by
comparison. He never felt completely at ease with the

---

[22]Bruce Miroff, _Pragmatic Illusions_ (New York:
David McKay Co., 1976).

[23]Theodore C. Sorensen, _The Kennedy Legacy_ (New
York: New American Library, 1969).

full-dress live televised press conferences such as
Kennedy held, so he began to experiment with other
formats. Johnson chose various different settings for
meetings with the news media; he would hold walking
news conferences on the White House grounds while walking his dogs; he would hold news conferences in the
East Room, in the State Department auditorium, in the
Executive Office Building, and he would even try out
again the old format of the small informal news conference for White House regulars in the Oval Office
which had been used by FDR. He never completely
settled on one format, but he seemed to communicate
better in the small informal conference setting rather
than the large press conference at which Kennedy excelled. Johnson had some able press secretaries
including George Reedy, Bill Moyers and George Christian, but two factors began to hamper his relations
with the media after the honeymoon period was over.[24]
One was the frequent criticism of his style in the
news media, particularly the Eastern press which was
wont to make comparisons with Kennedy which put Johnson in a bad light. The other was the mounting difficulties Johnson had with the press over his secretiveness about Vietnam policy. The coverage continued to
be favorable until after he had won election in his
own right, but after the Great Society legislation had
been put through in 1965, press comment shifted from
comments about his domestic program and his great
legislative skills to more negative comments about his
foreign policy, his handling of Vietnam, and what came
to be referred to as the "credibility gap".

Johnson did not have an arrogant contempt for
the media the way Nixon did; rather when he had
adverse coverage, he would feel that somehow he had
been misunderstood and he developed a hurt feeling that
somehow those he thought were his friends had betrayed
him. He made more of an effort than Nixon did to meet
the needs of the media, but the combination of his
style and the "credibility gap" factor complicated the
relationship and in the end caused Johnson to get
worse treatment in the media than he sometimes
deserved, certainly worse than he needed to have. As
this trend developed, Johnson more and more began to
rely on the technique of the "quickie" news conference,
called on short notice for White House regulars. This

---

[24]George Reedy, The Twilight of the Presidency
(New York: World Publishing Co., 1970).

prevented specialists in foreign and defense policy covering the State Department and Pentagon beats from coming and asking hard questions. Johnson did make some effort to be friendly with media correspondents, inviting them to his ranch, including them on some social occasions at the White House, and the like, but try as he might, he never achieved the degree of success with the news media that Kennedy did.[25]

Apart from Johnson's difficulties with the media themselves, he got mixed reaction from the public and Congress. The public elected him overwhelmingly in 1964 partly because of good media coverage, but the support Johnson had was thin if broad, and when controversy over Vietnam and related issues such as urban riots and campus disorders began to develop, some of the fair-weather support began to melt away. So it can be said that Johnson began with broad public support but was unable to maintain it all the way through his tenure, largely because of the growing unpopularity of his Vietnam policy. When Johnson finally did change his posture on Vietnam in 1968, he had long since lost his public support and was not a candidate for another term in 1968.

The process of attrition in Johnson's loss of backing in Congress was perhaps a slower process, because he began with the respect and even admiration of many of his former colleagues but again Vietnam worsened these relationships and as public opinion shifted, it became more and more difficult for Johnson to enlist support in Congress for his programs. This became markedly more true after 1966, when Republicans made gains in the off-year elections, and then he began to lose support within his own party as first Eugene McCarthy and then Robert Kennedy joined Wayne Morse, Ernest Gruening and others in the Senate who had spoken out against Johnson's Vietnam policy. Much the same thing occurred on the House side as well. It was Johnson's sad fate to lose much of the good will of media, public and Congress largely because the focus shifted from the domestic arena, in which he achieved many solid accomplishments, to foreign policy in which Vietnam loomed large as his greatest failure. Thus it would be fair to say that Johnson began with a reason-

[25]Doris Kearns, Lyndon Johnson and the American Dream (New York: Harper & Row, 1976), pp. 246-249, 302, 303.

ably good image but that the Vietnam issue nearly destroyed his relationship with the public.[26]

One point is noteworthy here if we keep in mind the way the news media spoke glowingly of Johnson's legislative achievements and the way in which he was later castigated for his Vietnam policy. That point is the tendency of the news media to exaggerate achievements and failures of Presidents. We can see the same thing operating posthumously with Kennedy in the development of the Camelot legend mentioned earlier, and the more recent stories in the news media debunking some of the achievements of the Kennedy era. There seems to be a pattern in which the media build up a new figure to celebrity status with a degree of adulation and positive comment, only to tarnish the image created by the media themselves when that particular President--being only human--fails to live up to the high expectations created in the public by the media. There may be exceptions of course but this does seem to be a common pattern.

Perhaps one of the most fascinating case studies of media relations with Presidents in the modern era is that of Richard Nixon. It was largely the publicity which Nixon received in the Alger Hiss case in the late 1940's as a young congressman which gave him the reputation of being a rising star in the Republican party. Then in the 1952 campaign, after he was nominated for Vice President, the Nixon fund scandal and the "Checkers" speech on television gave him a further lift largely through the instrument of the media. Nixon's travels to South America and the Soviet Union during the latter part of the Eisenhower years were also widely covered in the media, but it was apparently during the 1960 campaign when he was considered to have "lost" the TV debates to Kennedy and especially two years later when he lost his bid for the governorship of California against Edmund (Pat) Brown, that the hostility of Nixon toward the news media began to come more into the open.[27]

He was never popular with the liberal press or liberal commentators, but he had received the support

---

[26]Doris Kearns, op. cit., pp. 286-352.

[27]See Earl Mazo, Richard Nixon: A Political and Personal Portrait (New York: Harper & Brothers, 1959).

of those in the media who were more ideologically sympathetic, but in 1962 after the California gubernatorial race, he held his famous "last press conference"
in which he made his famous statement that "you won't
have Nixon to kick around any more". It was thought
that he was finished politically, but then in the 1968
campaign he actually won a rather sympathetic coverage
from many in the news media because of the comeback
role he played in that campaign.[28] In the early part
of his Administration, he received generally favorable
coverage for his Vietnam policy.

But Nixon continued to nurse a grudge against
the news media, because he felt it was his due to have
only the kind of coverage that would normally be
expected by the leader of a totalitarian state--that
is, totally favorable coverage. This is of course
something no President has ever had, and all Presidents have at times received favorable and at times
unfavorable coverage, but Nixon always acted as if
unfavorable coverage were directed at him personally
rather than merely an effort to objectively present
both sides of the story. Thus his misperception of
the role of journalists in the media tended to
embitter the relationship which he had with the media.

This attitude of Nixon's was exacerbated by
sycophantic staff people who encouraged him to carry
these feelings of hostility toward the news media, and
in the end it so poisoned the relationship that it
ultimately hurt Nixon with the public. This was
partly true because, since Nixon was the most hostile
to the media of any recent Presidents, inevitably he
generated hostility from the media in return, in the
form of negative editorial comments, in the form of
negative comments from television correspondents, and
ultimately in the form of widespread expose reporting
in all the media, including not only the Watergate
scandal but various disclosures about his income tax
short-cuts, about his lavish spending on his estates
at San Clemente and Key Biscayne and the like. While
some of the public did not ever become upset about
Watergate, they did become upset about the implications that Nixon was cheating on his income tax. So
his whole attitude toward the news media was self-

---

[28]See Earl Mazo and Stephen Hess, <u>Nixon:</u> <u>A</u>
<u>Political</u> <u>Portrait</u> (New York: Popular Library, 1967).

defeating in the end, and it was a factor although far from the only factor in his eventual downfall.[29]

Formats used by Nixon included rather infrequent press conferences, for which he was usually well briefed and which he handled reasonably well until Watergate so intensely embittered his relations with the press. Another format he used perhaps more than his precedessors was the public address on TV, because he felt that by using the medium in this way he could go directly to the people without running the risk of having his words distorted by newspaper, radio and television correspondents. He also used direct interviews on TV with one or a small group of newsmen.

Nixon always tended to view the news media as the enemy and never ceased in his efforts to manipulate the media to try to put himself in the best possible light. He sometimes used threats and pressure as when his political associates tried to have the license of a Washington Post TV station in Florida cancelled in favor of applicants who were pro-Administration. Another tactic he used was the establishment of the Office of Telecommunications Policy headed by Clay Whitehead. This was an effort to co-ordinate his media efforts, and it was accompanied by a design for having Vice President Agnew travel about the country attacking the news media in a series of speeches criticizing "instant analysis", "querulous criticism" and the like. The media reacted defensively and the tactic did achieve a modicum of success when CBS announced it was dropping the analysis of presidential speeches which Agnew had criticized (the practice was later restored and was never dropped by ABC and NBC).[30]

As for public and congressional reaction to Nixon's policies, it tended to follow the pattern that occurred with Johnson. It was essentially supportive

---

[29]William Safire, Before the Fall: An Inside View of the Pre-Watergate White House (New York: Belmont Tower Books, 1975).

[30]Jonathan Schell, The Time of Illusion: A Historical and Reflective Account of the Nixon Era (New York: Vintage Books, 1975).

in the first part of Nixon's tenure, but this support eroded after the Watergate scandals came into full public view. On the Vietnam issue, Nixon received basic support from the public and Congress, although he was put under increasing pressure to withdraw from Cambodia and to end the war at an earlier date. But once the truce was achieved in 1973, and the focus of attention moved to the Watergate investigation, Nixon's popularity with both public and Congress began to slide precipitately. Just prior to the resignation, only about one in four voters were supportive of his policies. While Nixon loyalists claimed that constant media criticism was responsible for eroding his popularity, there is a real question of how much Nixon contributed to his own downfall and how much the media helped the process. It was a mixture of both, it would appear.

It is perhaps too early to make definitive statements about the Ford Administration and its relations with the news media or the kind of linkage the media have provided it with the public and with Congress. But a few statements can probably be made; one is that while relationships were far from perfect, they were much better than they were during the Nixon years. When Ford came into office, he knew about the shortcomings of his predecessor and he was conscious that he would have to work at restoring public confidence and that this would entail better relations with the media than Nixon had ever had. Fortunately for Ford, during his years in Congress and in his brief term as Vice President, he had had a good working relationship with the media and that was carried over to some extent after he entered the White House, because he sought to take an open, more above-board approach to the Presidency. Ford engaged in frequent travels, in which he gained exposure to the local media in visits to various regions of the country. This was true of him in the early part of his Presidency, as well as in his 1976 re-election campaign.[31]

---

[31]See Jerald F. ter Horst, Gerald Ford and the Future of the Presidency (New York: Third Press, 1974). Also see Gerald Pomper, The Election of 1976: Reports and Interpretations (New York: David McKay Co., 1977), and Jules Witcover, Marathon: The Pursuit of the Presidency, 1972-1976 (New York: Viking Press, 1977), pp. 44, 45, 588, 589, 600-604.

Thus there was a considerable contrast between Ford's and Nixon's media relations, which put Ford in a good light. He made real efforts to be conciliatory with the press, and to some extent these efforts paid off.

This is not to say that Gerald Ford has not had problems with the news media. The first test of his media relations probably came about a month after his take-over in August 1974. In early September 1974, the pardon of Richard Nixon was announced. Ford's press secretary, Jerald F. ter Horst, had not been notified in advance, and the surprise announcement of the pardon ended Ford's brief honeymoon with the media and the public.[32] Ter Horst resigned in protest, and Ford selected Ron Nessen, an NBC correspondent, as his new press secretary. Nessen has not had the problems with the media that his immediate predecessor, Ron Ziegler, had. But neither was he as successful as Hagerty and Salinger, or perhaps even Moyers, were in dealing with the news media. This was not entirely Nessen's fault because from time to time he simply was not let in on major developments by Ford's inner circle. But at least he has not had to term his statements "inoperative", as Ziegler did on one occasion during the Watergate scandals.

Another problem area for Ford was the coverage of the Ford-Reagan primary campaign of 1976.[33] The White House would normally be expected to get the best of the exchange and to dominate the primary campaign process, as well as the media coverage of it. But to some extent, because Ford reacted defensively to Reagan's charges and went on the defensive in the campaign, media coverage reflected this. This is not to say that Reagan's media coverage was all good, but rather that the White House did not handle that phase of the primary campaign as effectively as it might have. An example of this was the statement made by Ford's campaign manager, Rogers Morton, to the effect that "we aren't going to rearrange the furniture on the deck of the Titanic" made on the night of Ford's loss to Reagan in the Indiana primary.[34] The comment

_____

[32]Clark Mollenhoff, _The Man Who Pardoned Nixon_ (New York: St. Martin's Press, 1976).

[33]Witcover, _op. cit._, pp. 373-432.

[34]_Ibid._, p. 420.

was made to deny an allegation made by an observer that the Indiana primary was a disaster for Ford, but it came out in such a way as to make it appear that Morton was confirming that the primary loss was such a disaster. Ford did have some things going for him in the primary, such as his ability to point to non-involvement in a major war and improvement in the economy, but somehow in the media coverage the Ford campaign--and the President--never communicated these points effectively through the news media.

Public and congressional reaction to Ford was somewhat shifting and volatile. When Ford entered office, he was like Lyndon Johnson at the start of his Administration, the beneficiary of much public sympathy and support because of the trying circumstances under which he was obliged to take over the Presidency. Some of this public support was dissipated by the manner in which he precipitately announced the Nixon pardon, and he created doubts about his judgment about economic policy by shifting from an emphasis on the war against inflation and a request for a tax increase to an emphasis on the effort to do something about recession and a request for a tax cut. The "WIN" button (signifying Whip Inflation Now) suddenly became unfashionable; but Ford did generate some favorable coverage in the news media by calling an "economic summit conference" in 1974.

However, the public and Congress were somewhat put off by the President's running controversy with Congress over a wide range of issues, including his request for funds for South Vietnam at a time when it was obvious the fall of South Vietnam was imminent, his vetoes of major bills for appropriations for domestic programs, the form of the tax cut and many others. The fact that Watergate reaction led to the election of a more liberal Congress in 1974 made things more difficult for Ford, who had hoped for a less damaging outcome in the election.

But all was not a disaster, as Ford could point to the summit meeting at Vladivostok and the Helsinki conference as achievements of his administration, and he could also note that Secretary Henry Kissinger had been able to keep an uneasy peace in the Middle East. But the Angola crisis and Reagan's criticism of Ford's policies on Panama, as well as the controversy over the firing of Defense Secretary Schlesinger, all earned Ford some unfavorable media coverage. So the conclusion would have to be drawn that his standing with the media, the public and Congress was mixed at best, although certainly not so disastrous as Nixon's came to be. Again it may be partly the media, but also partly the White House, that brought about this mixed result.

Thus far, I've been examining case studies of the linkage function involving incumbent Presidents in recent administrations. It may be instructive, as well, to look at how the linkage function of the media operates in the case of presidential candidates running in primary campaigns. I've briefly mentioned some problems and situations which arose for President Ford during the 1976 primary season; let's also turn to some of his principal rivals for the office in the campaign.

The first candidate to be examined will be former Governor Ronald Reagan of California, Ford's only serious opponent for the 1976 GOP nomination. Reagan came to the California governorship with a background as an actor, so he was well equipped by background for the effective use of the media. Reagan's skillfulness in the use of the media was indeed demonstrated during the primary campaign. He had been conducting a more or less traditional campaign of public appearances and had lost New Hampshire, Florida and Illinois to Ford, when he decided to shift tactics and arranged for a nationwide TV address on the issues of the campaign. Following this, he won the North Carolina primary and making more extensive use of the television exposure he had begun at this point in the primary season, he went on to defeat Ford in the Texas, Alabama, Georgia, and Indiana primaries. While many made sport of Reagan as appearing on the late, late show movies and as the star of the old TV production "Death Valley Days", it was apparent that his media skills stood him in good stead.[35]

In Reagan's campaign, he used the media effectively in other ways besides his television appearances during paid time. He recognized that controversy is newsworthy and he began to attack Ford policies in foreign policy, on detente, on the Panama Canal negotiations, and on other matters where he found Ford was vulnerable. He did indeed get more

---

[35]Witcover, op. cit., pp. 388, 389, 398, 399.

news coverage as a result of these attacks on Ford and his policies, and thus seemed to be benefiting again from careful use of the media in his campaign. His use of television in the campaign can be said, therefore, to have had considerable impact. Before he began using it extensively he had lost a series of primaries, all of them fairly close, but he was perceived as not a serious threat to Ford. He shifted his tactics and began heavy use of the media and he was gradually able to turn the campaign around and take a lead over Ford in elected delegates. Although Reagan ultimately lost to Ford, there could be little doubt that Reagan had improved his chances by imaginative and effective use of TV.

As far as the television images of Reagan and Ford were concerned, Reagan appeared to come across with conviction in hard-hitting speeches. They may have seemed glib to some, but he conveyed the image of an exciting, hard-hitting candidate. Ford, on the other hand, continued to project sincerity but also conveyed an image of dullness not associated with Reagan. So on balance it would have to be said that images projected by the two men left the impression that Reagan was using the medium more effectively.

What about the impact of the Reagan campaign on the public and on public officials? The impact on the public could be measured in Reagan's improved performance in the primaries. As for public officials, only a few leading Republicans did finally desert Ford for Reagan, but they definitely took notice of Reagan's improved performance in the primaries.

The other candidate I'll look at closely is one who appeared to have a knack for effective use of the media, but one who used it in a different way than Reagan did. That candidate was former Georgia Governor Jimmy Carter, the front-runner in the early phases of the Democratic primary season of 1976. Carter, unlike Reagan, used the technique of providing ambiguity to the issues rather than that of sharpening the issues. This was probably a proper technique for a Democratic candidate running in 1976, because the broader constituency of the Democratic party needed to be brought together and unified and highly defined issue statements might tend to divide the party. Also, Carter chose to run his campaign by de-emphasizing issues and emphasizing the character of the candidates.[36]

While Carter did run on a campaign platform of opposing the Washington establishment, he also made many statements about the need for leadership which would bring out the best qualities of the American people and was supposed to have made the statement, "I'll never knowingly tell you a lie." Sensing the public mood of disillusionment in the wake of the Watergate scandals, Carter doubtless felt there was a hunger in the people for new leadership in which they could trust. Thus the emphasis on an image campaign, even though he did make statements on the issues-- often in the form of position papers. When pressed to make issue statements, he would do so, but always in the context that the need for a trustworthy leader of good character was just as important as the specifics of various issues. Carter also declined to let himself be labeled as either a liberal or a conservative,[37] although he seemed to be a fiscal conservative but a liberal on human rights issues and clearly more liberal on foreign policy issues than either Ford or Reagan, both of whom talked a hard line. Carter showed an ability to generate news coverage by some of the things he did. Campaigning in Pennsylvania, he was photographed emerging from a coal mine wearing a miner's hat. A day or two later, his opponent, Senator Henry (Scoop) Jackson, was photographed wearing a miner's hat. Winning the Wisconsin primary, Carter held up for photographers a newspaper headline saying, "Udall Defeats Carter."[38]

Carter's TV style was cool and he had a great deal of poise and he appeared to be an effective media campaigner when contrasted with his primary campaign opponents, or even with Ford. For example, Congressman Morris (Mo) Udall had an earnest manner and had popularity with a narrow constituency of liberals and even had a useful sense of humor when campaigning. But on television, his personal warmth did not seem to come across in the same way Carter's did. Also Sena-

---

[36]Witcover, op. cit., pp. 51-52, 196-197, 232-233, 245-247, 534-535.

[37]Ibid., pp. 128, 207, 225, 528.

[38]Ibid., p. 286.

tor Jackson seemed wooden and dull in his speaking style, and even when he tried to make a conscious effort to improve it, he did not seem to have the natural sense of ease before the cameras that Carter did.

It should be said that Carter did not win his primaries solely because he knew how to use the media effectively. He began his campaign early, right after McGovern's defeat in 1972 (at least as to planning), he organized effectively on a national basis, and he developed with his closest advisers a strategy that appeared to have effectively sized up the mood of the nation's voters at the beginning of 1976.[39]

As far as the reaction to the TV campaign is concerned, it can be said that Carter appeared to score more effectively with the voting public as attested to in his showing in the primaries and in the polls. He did meet some resistance among party leaders, accustomed to liberals who talked specifically on the issues in the style of Hubert Humphrey, but they did soften their opposition and even in some cases enlisted in his campaign after his string of primary successes. Union leaders too were impressed by the public response and began to swing into line, as Carter received the endorsement of UAW President Leonard Woodcock before the Michigan primary, and was received by George Meany, the head of the national AFL-CIO, who never wanted to have much to do with George McGovern in 1972. Public officials also seemed to be impressed with Carter's early showing, and after he won the Ohio primary, he won endorsements from Mayor Richard Daley, Governor George Wallace and Senator Edward Kennedy. One thing was sure, however, Carter did know how to use the media effectively and made his mark on the system.

Media Connection to the Presidency in the Public Policy Process

I'll now shift the focus of analysis from the politics of presidential campaigns to the way in which the Presidency functions with the aid of the media in the public policy process.

---

[39]Witcover, op. cit., pp. 245-247, 534, 535.

First it is important to consider ways in which the media help the President to project a positive image in the decision-making aspects of his office.

An incumbent President like Gerald Ford has ready access to the public through television, newspapers and the radio. He has the potential to exert tremendous influence on public opinion simply because of his incumbency. But as we have seen in looking at the record of Ford and past Presidents, this great potential has not always been realized. Still when a President is articulate, when he has a good sense of timing, when he knows what his aims are in terms of the policy process, White House statements clearly appear to have a magnifying effect. The President can command attention which is never on the same scale for governors, congressmen and senators, and he can command it because the institution of the Presidency is perceived by the public to be a powerful one and it can have great clout when properly employed by the incumbent.

The effective use of the White House by the incumbent involves the ability to enlist public support in part through effective use of the media, the ability to mobilize support in Congress through deft handling of relations with individual congressmen, especially the leadership, and finally the effective handling of relationships within the President's own party to ensure the kind of support he needs. When all of these things are efficiently done, the President can usually muster successful leadership efforts. But as the past record has shown, some Presidents have been effective in one area only to perform less well in another. Franklin D. Roosevelt could most of the time mobilize support in all three of these ways. Kennedy was good at mobilizing public support through effective use of the media, but he had difficulty in congressional relations partly because he had to deal with the dominant conservative coalition in Congress. Johnson on the other hand was a master at congressional relationships, but lacked some of the skills with national politics and public opinion which Kennedy had. Nixon handled some of these things well for awhile, but in the end succeeded in turning media, public and Congress all against him as a result of his deceit. Thus the record of recent Presidents shows that it is the exception rather than the rule for any incumbent to realize the full leadership potential of the office.

In the President's use of the media to perform his tasks, some measure of credibility is lent to his words by the prestige of the office; this probably remains true despite the damage done to that prestige by Nixon. But the Nixon experience does raise the question: To what extent has the office been permanently damaged (if it has) by the Watergate experience, and to what extent will future Presidents repair the damage done by Nixon? It may be said that modern conditions cause some distrust of the Presidency on the part of the public and Congress, simply because of the great power wielded by recent Presidents in foreign policy matters alone. When the public perceives that the act of a President alone can involve the nation in unwanted wars, or when it feels that Presidents operate in secrecy, such distrust is bred. It may require a whole series of Administrations operating with candor and in the open before the pre-Nixon kind of trust accorded the Presidency can be restored; but it must be assumed it is possible, or the implication would be that the nation must give up on the viability of its institutions simply because of the experience with one or two Presidents or Administrations. So the answer to the question is simply an open-ended one: the experience of the next decade or two will tell us what is possible.

Before leaving this topic, I would emphasize that television can be an effective tool for public image-building when properly used by Presidents. It ought to be clarified, too, that Presidents do not normally concern themselves about image-building simply because they like to be popular with the public and their colleagues. They are concerned with a good image in large measure because they want to translate that popularity into success for their programs and a record of achievement. And each President knows that inevitably there is a limited amount of that popularity that can be so translated, because most Presidents suffer a decline in popularity after some point in their Administration in which the necessity of public policy formation has obliged them to do things which make enemies.

Thus far I've looked at ways in which the media can be a positive help to a President seeking to generate positive leadership and to make constructive achievements. But there is another side to this coin too. Since the media are by nature essentially neutral (as simply a tool or an instrument for what politicians seek to do), it follows that the media can in

numerous ways hinder a President by projecting a negative image in the decision-making aspects of the
office. Presidents can be made to seem indecisive by
the media, or they can be made to seem decisive and
effective. When Nixon changed his policy on price
controls and China policy, he did a complete policy
reversal and could have been made to appear indecisive,
but instead the media projected these acts in a positive way as effective action to deal with inflation and
effective action to handle foreign policy. But when
George McGovern reversed his position in the campaign,
as on the Eagleton nomination or on the $1,000 welfare
reform plan, the media made him appear to be indecisive.[40] So much depends on how the President's image
is conveyed to the public, and on the public's perception may well depend the success or failure of his
policies. This is a vital point to remember in the
linkage function of the media between Presidents and
the public, because the important thing is not that
the media portray a President in a good or bad light,
but what perception of him the public forms (in good
measure on the basis of what is contained in the media,
but in part on the basis of pre-existing attitudes in
the public).

Looking at specifics of how the media can
hinder the President from effective performance in
policy-making, in some cases damage can be done by
"leaks" which prematurely disclose developing policy.
Lyndon Johnson and Richard Nixon had an obsession with
preventing such leaks, but even their predecessors
were annoyed by them and on occasion Kennedy, Eisenhower and earlier Presidents tried to prevent them.
The danger in leaks is that they may cause the President to lose influence in the policy-formation process
because of the securing of information by a wider
group of officials who then can have an impact on the
process. It may be less a matter of secrecy than of the
timing of disclosure in order to have the maximum
political benefit to the President.

Damage can also be done to a President by
ineffective use of TV and the other news media. The
television camera is a cold, hard thing when a President is seeking to engage in policy pronouncements
without proper preparation, for example. Also the

---

[40]Theodore H. White, The Making of the President 1972 (New York: Bantam Books, 1973).

question naturally arises: When does the President
define and when does his opposition define what is
effective and ineffective? Again each must possess
skills in the use of the media to turn it to their
advantage. No one can be guaranteed these skills; the
effective politician must learn how to command them,
through experience or through seeking advice from the
soundest advisers.

Damage can also be done to a President when the
White House, intentionally or not, contributes to a
climate of media and public hostility to the President.
This happened with both Johnson and Nixon and for
basically the same reason--a feeling on the part of
media people and the public that important facts were
being withheld from them. Unfortunately, more often
than not in the case of the important issue of Vietnam
this was true--certainly in many cases.

Considering all of these factors, there are
ways in which damage can be limited by the President.
He can seek sympathetic outlets in the media which
will tell his side of the story; when he feels certain
facts must be kept secret, he can convey this to the
public through the media, or he can convey it to other
key decision-makers in private conferences. He can
also realize that secrecy is sometimes damaging and
try to limit it to issues and matters where he feels
it is absolutely essential. But much depends on the
climate of opinion and trust in his leadership that a
President has developed during his campaign for office
and in the early days of his incumbency.

Media Role in Presidential Nominating and Election Process

It has become a truism that the mass media play
an important if not central role in the presidential
nominating and election process. In order to analyze
this statement, it is useful to examine it in terms
of the basic components of that process.

Effect of friendly media coverage can be considerable for a candidate in the stage of preliminary
strategy planning. By being open and accessible to the
news media at this stage of the campaign process,
candidates may be able to win sympathetic media coverage at an early stage before the campaign is really
underway. The degree to which this is possible may of
course be limited by the extent of public attention

being paid to candidates and the incipient campaign. Also, public opinion survey results and the way in which they are handled in the media can either help or hinder a candidacy. If a candidate can secure 6 per cent support in the early stages of a campaign, this may be par for the course if he is a "new face" in the campaign, someone who has never run for President before. But the media can convey one impression by simply publishing polling results showing that a long established figure has 40 per cent support and the new man has 6 per cent support. On the other hand, a different idea is conveyed in the media coverage if the media point out that pre-campaign polls usually inflate the standing of those whose names are already familiar to the public. Thus an error of omission, unintentional though it may be, may create problems for a new candidate.

The effect of media coverage of presidential primaries in both parties is considerable. In 1972, public expectations encouraged by the media were partly responsible for front-runner Edmund Muskie dropping out of the campaign at an earlier stage than had been expected. The entry of Hubert Humphrey into the race, pre-empting some of Muskie's funding sources was doubtless a factor too, but the factor mentioned above plus coverage of Muskie's "tears-in-the-snow" incident in the New Hampshire primary doubtless crippled his campaign. Conversely in the primary season, George McGovern benefited from a kind of "Cinderella syndrome" in the media which commented widely on how his support had grown from a low level early in the primary season. In the Republican primary season in 1972, no one could really mount an effective challenge to Richard Nixon because he had a solid hold on foreign policy, the most significant issue, through his summit visit to China and later to the Soviet Union, and the progress apparently being made toward a negotiated end to the war in Vietnam. Looking at the 1976 primary season, Jimmy Carter on the Democratic side benefited from some of the same "underdog" factors that helped McGovern in 1972. This was also true of former Governor Ronald Reagan on the Republican side. Suffice it to say that at the primary stage, media coverage has important modifying effects on the public's attitude toward candidates, in part at least because the public may still be unfamiliar with some candidates and want to know more, thus relying on the media.

If media coverage is vital to the presidential candidates in the primaries, it is also important to them during the season of convention politics and the fall campaigns. During the 1972 Democratic convention, for example, George McGovern benefited from broad attention paid to the controversy over the California delegation at the convention, but this same controversy may have been damaging to him in the fall campaign as the public's perception of the whole matter changed in part due to the changes which occurred in media coverage. McGovern generally got favorable coverage during the primaries and convention, but after the Eagleton episode the coverage turned bad and in part this interacted with unfavorable public opinion polls projecting a Nixon landslide. It cannot be denied that the perception of McGovern as a weak candidate during the final phase of the campaign contrasted with its more positive perception of him during the primaries, and this was at least in part because media coverage was more unfavorable, even though in part it may have been due to the political context of that year and to McGovern's own tactical and strategic mistakes in the campaign. Another factor doubtless was that the public was bored with hearing about Watergate, and only after Nixon was safely re-elected did many people realize that McGovern's charges were not simply campaign talk.[41] In convention and fall campaign coverage in 1976, the media again played a major role, although not necessarily a decisive one, despite the debates. We operate on the assumption that most voters start out with predispositions built up over a long time, and it is easier to prove that the media have a modifying than a controlling effect on public attitudes.

Looking generally at primary, convention, and campaign politics, positive factors are present in media coverage in each of these. The media are necessary for a build-up for unknown candidates and for retention of a positive image by incumbents. They often do perform such functions for candidates.

There are also present negative factors of coverage in each of the three stages of the campaign. Negative factors may involve media attention paid to

---

[41]White, Chapter 11, "The Watergate Affair", op. cit., pp. 360-400.

opposing candidates' charges, lack of attention to or
enthusiasm about a particular candidate, or in unusual
cases a candidate may even be the object of expose
stories about wrongdoing that have come to light
through the media. In each case, of course, the candidate tries to present himself to the public in the best
possible light and the media seek to discover what is
controversial. Each is presumably seeking to serve
the public interest, but from a very different viewpoint and the politicians and the media in the nature
of things may often come into conflict although this
is certainly not a foreordained outcome.

The linkage of Presidents with the public has
occurred differently in different channels of communication. Each can be examined separately since each
medium is different. In newspapers, the function of
the print medium has changed from one of being the
sole or principal source of news to being that medium
which conveys explanations and in-depth analysis which
people can study and reread. In this way, the public
does gain greater understanding about public officials
and should be better able to pass judgment on their
official acts at election time. Radio always did and
still does serve as a medium which provides immediacy
of communication; it can convey bulletins, it is a
medium which is sometimes accessible when others are
not, but today it clearly plays a secondary role to
television which has become the dominant medium.
Television has started from small beginnings but today
is the vital link between Presidents and public; it
has been used in many different ways for news coverage
and by politicians in an effort to win broad public
support, but it has a major impact because of its
large audience and its visual effects.

The importance of each of the media cannot be
denied in the current political environment. From the
standpoint of politicians, the different media can be
examined separately.

Newspapers perform the function of giving a
more detailed and in some cases elaborate presentation
of the news. Magazines such as news-weeklies may provide a broader perspective of the news as well. Each
performs a unique function, and there are pitfalls to
be avoided by would-be successful politicians. For
example, in newspapers headlines can be slanted or
news stories distorted, either intentionally or unintentionally. Monitoring the press and seeking the

93

advice of a knowledgeable press aide will help a politician to avoid making poor use of newspapers. This is as true for Presidents as it is for lesser politicians.

Radio today becomes a secondary medium to the other two leading ones, because it cannot provide the detail possible in newspapers or the visual impact possible in television. It can be best used by politicians with good speaking ability who may not be able to provide the strongest TV image. Some pitfalls to be avoided by politicians in radio are those growing out of the nature of the medium; every pain should be taken to avoid using short catch-phrases which can be misinterpreted, phrases such as "ethnic purity", "1000 per cent", or "pitiful, helpless giant".

Television as the dominant medium today performs the function of helping the public shape its images of the candidates and the issues they are identified with. It has a solid visual impact and is relied on as a main news source by at least a plurality of the public. In using it, politicians should be on guard against some of the difficulties mentioned in connection with radio, but they should also take care to see how the images projected by television affect the public--if a candidate wants to project an image of respectability, he does not do something on camera that would go counter to that, for example.

In general, it is fairly certain that the future impact of the mass media will be considerable on both public policy-making processes and the electoral process. However, it ought to be emphasized that the mass media impact represents only one of a number of variables which are factors in the formation of public opinion about policy and about candidates. The great attention paid to the media's important role in recent years should not be allowed to obscure the importance of purely political factors or that of the historical context in which political decision-making occurs, as well as other factors which affect political outcomes, such as socio-economic attributes of voters and public officials, or psychological factors which pre-exist prior to the impact of the media. In short, the media clearly have a strong impact but they do not have the sole impact on the public or its leaders and it would be overly simplistic to imply that they do.

CHAPTER THREE

BASICS OF THE INSTITUTIONAL STRUCTURE

OF THE PRESIDENCY

> . . . I have come to tell you in Georgia
> that there is absolutely no reason to trade
> in your Ford in 1976.
>
> > --President Gerald R. Ford, speaking in
> > Atlanta, April 23, 1976 (Weekly Compila-
> > tion of Presidential Documents: 1976,
> > p. 692)

> In my campaign for the Presidency, I
> pledged to end this war in a way that would
> increase our chances to win true and lasting
> peace in Vietnam, in the Pacific, and in the
> world. I am determined to keep that pledge.
> If I fail to do so, I expect the American
> people to hold me accountable for that failure.
>
> > --President Richard M. Nixon, White House
> > Address, May 14, 1969 (Nixon: The First
> > Year of His Presidency, p. 106-A)

* * * *

While this book's theme is the relationship of
the Presidency to the mass media and through the mass
media to the public and other governmental institutions, I want to devote one chapter to examining the
Presidency as an institution. Therefore, I'll be concerned here with the basic features of the institutional structure of the Presidency; I'll also seek to
define the distinction between the man and the office--
the incumbent President and the ongoing institutional
Presidency.

To further an understanding of the institution
of the Presidency, I propose to examine the man in the
office by looking at presidential roles in recent
Administrations. This will be followed by an analysis
of the office's structure and its recent evolution
since Franklin D. Roosevelt's time. Then in turn I'll
examine the President's relations with the bureaucracy,

with Congress, with the Courts, and finally with the public. This will be followed by a summary statement about the Presidency as an institution as the nation enters its third century.

The Man in the Office: Presidents Since FDR and How They Fit Presidential Roles

Although this chapter is concerned more broadly with the Presidency as an institution and its evolution and development (as well as the way it functions in modern government), one cannot examine the Presidency without first looking at the President, the incumbent who is the centerpiece of the office. This is so because the whole institution of the modern Presidency is built around the person of the President; in this sense it is a very personalized institution.[1]

One way to examine the President in the office is to list the roles the people normally expect Presidents to perform in their leadership function. One can then examine recent Presidents to determine how they have fulfilled these varying roles. The comparison can give us a better idea of what Presidents themselves contribute to the ongoing institution of the Presidency. The Presidency as an institution has been in existence since 1789, and no single incumbent has served more than slightly over 12 years; furthermore, under the 22nd Amendment no future President can serve more than 10 years. This means that though individual Presidents can have considerable impact on the institution, it is the combined effect of all which has made the Presidency what it is today. The major Presidents, who have usually served in times of significant national crises, have left their imprint more strongly than the others, so it is not the length of tenure that is as decisive as the nature of events with which they have had to cope.[2] With this in mind, let's begin to examine the various roles the people have come to expect Presidents to fulfill, especially during and since the time of Franklin D. Roosevelt,

---

[1]See Dorothy Buckton James, The Contemporary Presidency, Second Edition (Indianapolis: Pegasus Division, Bobbs-Merrill Co., 1974), especially pp. 307-311.

[2]See Louis W. Koenig, The Chief Executive, Third Edition (New York: Harcourt, Brace, Jovanovich, 1975).

which many scholars identify as the true beginning of
the modern Presidency.

Some roles in which Presidents function can be
traced to Constitutional requirements of the office,
and other roles of Presidents can be traced to the
development of informal practices and customs. An
example of the first type of role is that of the
President as chief executive. In Article II of the
Constitution, the language provides that the President
"shall take care that the laws be faithfully executed",
and it is from this Constitutional provision that the
chief executive role is derived. This will be discussed in more detail below. An example of the second
type of role is the President's role as leader of his
party. In no place in the Constitution is this particular role provided for; yet as soon as the party
system developed in this country, the custom evolved
that an incumbent President would be looked to as the
leader of his party. This is for the obvious reason
that the President has the central role in carrying out
the party's platform and its programs.

The chief executive function should be differentiated from the role of chief administrator, since
the two are similar but different. When the President
functions in his role as chief executive, he is concerned with executing policies written into law by the
Congress as well as developing and carrying out policies on his own initiative under the President's own
powers. The latter type of situation is most likely
to be true where foreign policy decision-making is concerned, since the President has the principal responsibility for foreign policy. Basic policy-making and
policy execution are involved in the chief executive
role of the President, and it is a familiar role to the
American public since all of the thirty-eight men who
have served as President in thirty-nine administrations
have functioned in this capacity since the Washington
Administration through the Carter Administration, and
Carter's successors will be expected to continue to
perform this role.

The President's role as chief administrator,
unlike his role as chief executive, involves oversee-
ing the details of administration. Thus in a sense it
involves a second step in the same process. The President functions as chief executive in developing foreign policy in the Far East, for example. But when he
instructs an American ambassador to Japan or the Secretary of State on carrying out details of that policy,

he functions in his role as chief administrator. As chief administrator, the President is also responsible for managing and supervising the operation of various executive branch line departments and other agencies that are entrusted to his authority. This may involve appointment of subordinate officials, from the Cabinet level on down. It may also involve requiring them to make reports of their activities and other steps to follow up with administrative detail once basic policy outlines are determined. It may be difficult to say where the President's role as chief executive leaves off and where his role as chief administrator begins, but the basic distinction should be clear.

The President also fulfills a role as foreign policy chief. Just as in the case of his role as chief executive, this role grows out of the Constitution's requirements of the President's duties and its provisions setting forth his powers.

Article II, Section 2 of the Constitution states of the President's foreign policy powers:

> He shall have power, by and with the advice and consent of the Senate, to make treaties, provided two-thirds of the Senators present concur; and he shall nominate, and, by and with the advice and consent of the Senate, shall appoint ambassadors, other public ministers and consuls, judges of the Supreme Court, and all other officers of the United States, whose appointments are not herein otherwise provided for, and which shall be established by law. . . .[3]

From the Constitutional treaty-making power and the authority to appoint ambassadors, Presidents have derived the power to conduct diplomacy and engage in foreign policy decision-making. The everyday conduct of diplomacy and foreign policy is normally left to the Secretary of State, but recent Presidents have tended to become rather heavily involved in foreign policy, especially in the 20th Century since the emergence of the United States as a major world power. The wording of the Constitution makes it apparent that while the Senate shares the foreign policy powers through its

---

[3]See Rocco J. Tresolini, <u>American Constitutional Law</u>, Second Edition (New York: Macmillan, 1965), Chapter Seven, "Powers of the President," pp. 178-208.

power to ratify treaties and confirm the nomination of
Secretaries of State, ambassadors and other foreign
policy officials, the principal foreign policy power
is vested in the President and the executive branch.

In recent years, foreign policy has been closely
related to defense policy and the President has normally administered what has come to be referred to as
his national security policies through the Secretary
of State and State Department and the Secretary of
Defense and the Defense Department. However, an
increasing amount of co-ordinating machinery for
national security policy has come within the White
House itself, especially since establishment of the
National Security Council and the growth of responsibilities of the President's national security advisor,
himself an official of the NSC. This trend accelerated under the Nixon Administration, in the latter
part of which Henry Kissinger served both as national
security advisor and Secretary of State. But even
prior to the Nixon Administration, McGeorge Bundy,
national security advisor under both Presidents Kennedy and Johnson, wielded probably as much influence
as Secretary of State Dean Rusk.

The foreign policy power has been one traditionally entrusted to the President. It is this role
along with the President's commander-in-chief role,
which has led to expansion of the President's powers
in international affairs to the point where recent
Administrations have been referred to as manifesta-
tions of the "Imperial Presidency".[4] Although the
growth of the President's foreign policy powers has
recently been checked by Congress and the public to
some extent (for example with the passage of the War
Powers Act of 1973), it is far from certain that this
growth will not continue in the future. This is
partly because foreign policy matters are of such
character that often an emergency decision is
required, and it is a much easier matter for the
President acting alone to respond to a crisis than to
refer it to the 535 members of Congress acting through
the collective decision-making process involved in any
legislative body. Thus it would be overstating the
matter to say that Presidents have sought to aggrand-
ize their power by pressing it further in foreign

---

[4]Arthur M. Schlesinger, Jr., The Imperial
Presidency (Boston: Houghton Mifflin, 1973).

policy; other factors have been at work, but clearly such Presidents as Franklin Roosevelt, Truman, Kennedy, and Johnson were enlarging presidential authority in this area, even before the ill-fated Nixon Presidency.

As has been indicated, another component of national security policy is defense policy, which involves the President's role as commander-in-chief of the armed services. This role, like his foreign policy role, is essentially based on Article II powers. The Constitution provides in Article II, Section 2, clause 1 that: "The President shall be Commander-in-Chief of the Army and Navy of the United States, and of the militia of the several states when called into the actual service of the United States . . ." Thus while the Constitution does give the Congress power to declare war and to appropriate funds for defense, it is clear that the President has the power to conduct wars and deploy troops on behalf of the United States.

It is sometimes believed that American involvement in undeclared wars is a recent development typified by American involvement in the Vietnam conflict or the Korean hostilities. But in point of fact examples of undeclared wars involving the use of troops by American Presidents can be found in our early history. The undeclared war engaged in under President Jefferson against the Barbary pirates in 1803 was one early example, but there are other examples which can be cited which involved use of American troops without congressional assent in both early and modern times. These included the sending of American Marines to Vera Cruz by President Wilson during the Mexican Revolution in 1914, the dispatch of troops by President Johnson to the Dominican Republic in 1965, the movement of troops by President Eisenhower to Lebanon in the 1950's, and in a recent instance the orders for American troops to move into Cambodia during the spring of 1970, issued by President Nixon. President Ford used American Marines to deal with the Mayaguez incident in 1975 off the coast of Cambodia, and he only complied with the technical language of the War Powers Act in notifying Congress of his decision.

Thus not only is there a long precedent for the use of Presidential power in undeclared wars, but also the practice will be very difficult for Congress to control. This is because this is a policy area in which the President usually has the first information and therefore the initiative. The war power or commander-in-chief power which the President employs when functioning in this role has been a principal means through which the expansion of Presidential power has occurred. Along with the war power has developed the President's emergency power of the type used in the Civil War by Lincoln, in World War I by Wilson, and in World War II by Franklin Roosevelt. In fact, some emergency actions of recent Presidents were taken under legislation enacted to give President Lincoln emergency power in 1863 during the Civil War. The illustrations given here should amply demonstrate the importance of the President's commander-in-chief role. This and his foreign policy role are the chief supports for the so-called Imperial Presidency, as it has come to be known.

The President's role as crisis leader is derived from his emergency powers, but when one refers to the President as crisis leader this role need not be limited to foreign policy issues. For example, when President Franklin Roosevelt dealt with the Great Depression in 1933 he was functioning in the role of a crisis leader, even though it was a domestic crisis he dealt with.[5] In a speech to Congress, Roosevelt referred to it as "an emergency as serious as war itself", and it was so viewed by the nation which gladly accepted his leadership as a welcome relief from the policies of his predecessor, who had done very little about the economic crisis. President Carter more recently referred to the energy crisis as "the moral equivalent of war". In the context of wartime situations, or conflicts such as Vietnam or Korea, the President's emergency powers provide an underpinning for his role as crisis leader. But the President's crisis leader role stems partly from a President's ability to mobilize public support behind his Administration in a time of great stress. Successful crisis leaders in the past have included such men as Jackson, Lincoln, the two Roosevelts, and in more recent times Truman and Kennedy.[6] In each case,

---

[5]See Rexford G. Tugwell, The Democratic Roosevelt (Garden City, N.Y.: Doubleday & Co., 1957), and James MacGregor Burns, Roosevelt: The Lion and the Fox (New York: Harcourt, Brace & Co., 1956).

[6]See Louis W. Koenig, The Chief Executive, Third Edition (New York: Harcourt, Brace, Jovanovich, 1975), pp. 369-380, for a detailed account of the Cuban missile crisis. See also Robert F. Kennedy, Thirteen Days (New York: Harper & Row, 1969).

the President in office had a strong sense of purpose
in a time of emergency, and he acted with self-confidence in developing policy and mobilizing public
leadership. Crisis leadership has failed to develop
on some occasions such as when President Buchanan
failed to act to prevent the Civil War, or when Nixon
failed to deal effectively with the corruption of
Watergate. But it is clear that the President's role
as a crisis leader is a very important one in today's
complicated world.

The President's role as legislative chief is
really one which has developed with the modern Presidency. During the 19th Century, it was felt that
Presidents except in serious emergencies could afford
the luxury of reacting to initiatives of Congress and
executing laws passed by Congress. This was essentially a "Whig view" of the Presidency, a conservative
view following a "strict construction" of the Constitution.

But in the 20th Century, most Presidents have
moved away from this concept to exert a positive
impact on the legislative process in Congress. From
the early examples of Theodore Roosevelt (who was
interested in trust-busting and conservation or
environmental legislation) and Woodrow Wilson (who
used an activist leadership approach to secure the
enactment of a program of domestic reform legislation),
the pattern has been well established that modern
Presidents will establish the legislative agenda, and
Congress will in large measure conduct its business in
reaction to White House initiatives. This does not
mean that Congress has surrendered its initiative
entirely, or even that it may not recapture more of it
in the future, but it does signify that modern Presidents have come to perform a true leadership role in
the shaping of legislation, as compared with their
predecessors.[7]

In some degree, at least, this has occurred
because of public dissatisfaction with the way in
which Congress performed its legislative role, and

---

[7]See Koenig, op. cit., Chapter Seven, "Legisla-
tive Leader," pp. 150-180. Also see Nelson W. Polsby,
Congress and the Presidency, Third Edition (Englewood
Cliffs, N.J.: Prentice-Hall, 1976), especially Chapter
Seven, "Conflict and Cooperation," pp. 176-198.

also as a reaction to public demands that the President furnish leadership when the Congress would not. It remains to be seen what the future of executive-legislative relations will be in this area. But it seems a good bet that for the foreseeable future, the President will continue to play a dominant role if not perhaps the kind of overbearing role some recent Presidents have played toward Congress.

The President's legislative role is derived in part from the Constitution, which states in Article II, Section 3: "He shall from time to time give to the Congress information of the state of the union, and recommend to their consideration such measures as he shall judge necessary and expedient; he may, on extraordinary occasions, convene both houses, or either of them, and in case of disagreement between them with respect to the time of adjournment, he may adjourn them to such time as he shall think proper . . ."

The President's role as leader of his party is a role not referred to anywhere in the Constitution. Rather it is a role which has grown out of custom and practice. The party out of power gives a leadership role to its titular head, who is usually the most recent Presidential nominee, but this individual unlike the President cannot support his leadership authority with the power of the Presidency.

Still an incumbent President, even one preparing to retire and unpopular with a broad segment of the public, can wield a good deal of power. This was demonstrated in 1952 when President Truman was able to bring about the nomination of Adlai Stevenson, the Governor of Illinois, by the Democratic Party, despite considerable support for Senator Estes Kefauver. Again it was demonstrated in 1968 when President Johnson, who was stepping down, was able to bring about the nomination of Vice President Hubert Humphrey despite much support in the party for Senator Eugene McCarthy.

The President's party leadership role also involves him in shaping party policy, as in the platform writing process at the convention, and in campaigning for other candidates of his own party. When an incumbent President declines to campaign for other candidates of his own party, as President Nixon did in 1972, this is widely resented. This resentment played a part in Nixon's ultimate downfall following disclosure of the Watergate scandal, and most of Nixon's supporters in his own party deserted him when it became clear he had probably acted illegally and deceived the public.[8]

Another informal role of the President is one which has always been important, but which has become tremendously important since the suffrage was broadened to most of the American public and since the communications revolution of recent decades made television an important factor in American politics. This role is that of leader of public opinion, and it is important for a President in two ways. He must mobilize the support of public opinion to achieve adoption of his legislative program and success for his foreign policy. In addition, a President who desires to seek re-election must mobilize favorable public opinion in support of his effort to win a new term of office. Since the relationship between the Presidency and public opinion is widely discussed elsewhere in this book, it will not be elaborated on in detail here, except to note that it is in this role that the mass media become vital to any President. If he can make successful use of the media, he will be successful in his public opinion leadership role. If he cannot do this, he will almost certainly be unsuccessful.[9]

In discussing the last two of these roles of the President, I would emphasize that this is by no means an exhaustive list but merely a list of the Presidential roles which appear to be the most important ones. These last two roles may differ for different Presidents, because the role as leader for social justice and reform is usually an obligatory role for

---

[8]See Koenig, op. cit., Chapter Six, "Party Chief," pp. 115-149. Also see James MacGregor Burns, Roosevelt: The Soldier of Freedom, 1940-1945 (New York: Harcourt, Brace, Jovanovich, 1970), Chapter Seventeen, "The Grand Referendum", pp. 497-531.

[9]See Koenig, op. cit., Chapter Five, "Publics", pp. 92-114. Also see Elmer E. Cornwell Jr., Presidential Leadership of Public Opinion (Bloomington, Ind.: Indiana University Press, 1965), especially Chapter Seven, "The Modern Press Conference: 1933-1952", pp. 142-175, and Chapter Eight, "The Modern Press Conference, 1953-1964", pp. 176-207.

Presidents who consider themselves as liberals. On
the other hand, the role of preserver of order and
tradition is usually an obligatory role for Presidents
who consider themselves as conservatives. However,
these two roles are not mutually exclusive, as Presidents as conservative as Richard Nixon have attempted
to present themselves as advocates of reform and
Presidents as liberal (on domestic issues) as Lyndon
Johnson have sought to represent themselves to the
public as preservers of law and order. Each role
should be discussed briefly in turn.

The role of leader for social justice and
reform has not been attempted by all Presidents, but
the most liberal ones have usually taken such a stance.
If the liberal Presidents are considered, each one can
usually be identified with some such cause. Jefferson,
for example, can be identified with the struggle for
freedom and independence of thought in his opposition
to the Alien and Sedition Acts and his support for
freedom of speech and the press. Jackson can be
identified with the interests of the poor in his support for reducing the power of the Bank of the United
States. Lincoln can be identified with the cause of
emancipation and the end of slavery during the Civil
War. Woodrow Wilson and Franklin D. Roosevelt can be
identified with social reform legislation enhancing
the rights of labor and the protection of women and
children, as well as the opening up of economic opportunity to the deprived through government programs.
This type of legislation was also supported by Truman,
Kennedy and Johnson and in each case a particular area
of reform was stressed--for example, Truman backed
civil rights reform, Kennedy depressed areas legislation, and Johnson the war on poverty. So it can be
argued that this role of champion of the oppressed or
leader for social justice and reform has been taken
proudly by most liberal Presidents.[10]

On the other hand, the preservation of order
and tradition has been of greater importance to conservative Presidents. The law and order emphasis of

---

[10]See Koenig, op. cit., Chapter Twelve, "Social
Justice", pp. 293-325. Also see Carl M. Brauer, John
F. Kennedy and the Second Reconstruction (New York:
Columbia University Press, 1977), which deals with the
Kennedy Administration's civil rights record.

Ford and Nixon can be noted, along with the appeal
made by Eisenhower to the traditions of patriotism and
nationalism. And to Coolidge, Harding and Hoover, as
well as to Taft, the tradition of the capitalist system was one they felt was of great importance. So in
the case of each of the conservative Presidents cited,
they felt it was important to fulfill the public's
expectations of them in this role as preserver of
order and tradition.[11]

One could cite additional roles normally taken
by Presidents in the performance of their duties of
office, but at this point it may be more interesting
and instructive to look briefly at recent Presidents
and examine how they saw themselves as filling their
Presidential roles.

Franklin D. Roosevelt enjoyed to the hilt the
role of chief executive, and he came to the office
with a natural gift of executive ability. His background had been a period of service as a New York
State senator, assistant secretary of the Navy under
Woodrow Wilson,[12] a vice presidential candidate for
his party with James M. Cox in 1920, and finally two
terms as governor of New York. In his experience as
governor, he had functioned as chief executive of a
major industrial state, and he relished the policy-
making and decision-making aspects of the executive
role.[13]

---

[11]See Dwight D. Eisenhower, The White House
Years, 1953-1961, 2 vols. (Garden City, N.Y.: Doubleday, 1963-1965).

[12]Frank Freidel, Franklin D. Roosevelt: The
Apprenticeship (Boston: Little, Brown & Co., 1952),
Chapter Seven, "Progressive State Senator", pp. 117-
133; Chapter Thirteen, "A Navy to Cope With Any Situation", pp. 220-235, and Chapter Nineteen,"War Administrator", pp. 318-336. See also Joseph P. Lash,
Eleanor and Franklin (New York: W. W. Norton & Co.,
1971), Chapter Sixteen, "The Wife of a Public Official",
pp. 167-182, and Chapter Seventeen,"The Roosevelts Go
to Washington", pp. 183-192.

[13]Lash, op. cit., Chapter Thirty-two, "Return to
Albany", pp. 321-336. See also Frances Perkins, The
Roosevelt I Knew (New York: Viking Press, 1946), espe-
cially Part Two, "The State", pp. 41-108.

There has been much controversy about Roosevelt's performance as chief administrator. Two
schools of thought have developed: according to one,
Roosevelt was a sloppy administrator, careless of
detail, and not terribly efficient in this role;
according to the other, Roosevelt knew exactly what he
was doing in setting up overlapping lines of authority
for his underlings, and this system assured that he
would have ultimate control over the decisions that
really mattered. Those who defended FDR's system of
dividing up responsibilities among his subordinates
said that he was more concerned with the effective
exercise of Presidential power than he was with neat
administration, and that he felt his system served
that purpose. Scholars in recent years have come to
accept the view that Roosevelt functioned admirably
as an administrator in that he usually knew what he
needed to know, and wielded his power accordingly.[14]
Still the minority view has prevailed that Roosevelt
was a less efficient administrator than some of his
successors, for example Eisenhower, who used the Army
staff system of hierarchical authority. One's opinion of how well Roosevelt performed in this role
depends on one's ideal concept of presidential   ·
behavior.

As foreign policy chief and commander-in-chief,
Roosevelt functioned in difficult times and was faced
with important decisions in the period leading up to
World War II and nearly to the end of the war, since
his death occurred just a few months before the end of
the war. Roosevelt usually had definite foreign
policy aims and carried them out to the best of his
abilities, but he was unable to mobilize public opinion very rapidly when he felt that the democracies of
Western Europe were threatened by Hitler's expansion-
ist policies, and he got a very negative reaction when
he proposed a "quarantine of the aggressors" in a 1937
foreign policy speech in Chicago. As a wartime commander-in-chief, Roosevelt functioned quite successfully during World War II insofar as his goals of winning the war against the Axis powers were concerned.
He let his Chief of Staff, General George Marshall,
play a major part in strategic decisions, and turned

---

[14]Perkins, op. cit., Part Three, "The Nation",
pp. 111-396. See also Lash, op. cit., Part Four, "The
White House Years ", pp. 381-723.

other important matters over to able aides such as
Harry Hopkins and Averell Harriman. There was some
criticism of Roosevelt for not taking into account
long-term foreign policy aims in the conduct of the
war; for example, the Yalta agreements were widely
criticized. On the other hand, Roosevelt acted as the
leader of a nation which was relatively new to its
role as a major world power and he knew that after
World War I, a strong isolationist position had been
the dominant foreign policy view in the United States.
Therefore, he may have felt somewhat hampered in any
effort to develop long-term foreign policy, remember-
ing the fate of Woodrow Wilson's effort to promote the
League of Nations, which proved unsuccessful as far as
American participation was concerned.[15]

Franklin D. Roosevelt's performance in his role
as crisis leader must be considered superb insofar as
comparisons with other 20th Century Presidents are
concerned. Roosevelt gave new confidence to the
nation in the depths of the Depression and he furnished resolute leadership to the American people during the crises preceding and during World War II. One
skill which Roosevelt possessed in abundance which
helped him a great deal in his crisis leadership role
was his ability to inspire public confidence through
his oratory, particularly the use of the "fireside
chat", which he developed into a very effective form
of communication in the age of radio broadcasting. He
had many other political skills which helped him
greatly in this role, but it was his outstanding performance in this role which has led many observers of
the Presidency to consider him as perhaps the outstanding incumbent in the office during the 20th
Century.

As legislative chief, Roosevelt earned above
average marks in this role, although he began to lose

---

[15]See Burns, op. cit., especially Part One,
"The Miscalculated War", pp. 33-167; Part Three,
"Strategy", pp. 305-417; Part Five, "The Last Hundred
Days", pp. 557-612. See also Robert E. Sherwood,
Roosevelt and Hopkins: An Intimate History (New York:
Harper & Brothers, 1948). Also see Jim Bishop, FDR's
Last Year: April 1944-April 1945 (New York: William
Morrow & Co., 1974). Also see Elliott Roosevelt and
James Brough, A Rendezvous With Destiny: The Roose-
velts of the White House (New York: Dell, 1975).

influence with Congress after the unsuccessful effort
to "pack" the Supreme Court in 1937. His most successful period was during the First 100 Days of the New
Deal when the outlines of a major domestic reform
program were enacted. Roosevelt also had a respectable record in wartime legislation, but the war brought
to an end most of the major policy initiatives associated with the New Deal. In general, Roosevelt was successful in dealing with Congress but he had his problems as most Presidents have had.

In his role as party leader, Roosevelt won a
unique position as he was the only Democratic President ever to win the nomination of his party for four
successive times and also to win the Presidency four
successive times. Unless the 22nd Amendment restric-
tion on the Presidency, limiting incumbents to no more
than 10 years in office, is repealed in the future,
this record of Roosevelt's is unlikely to ever be
exceeded. It demonstrates how effectively Roosevelt
functioned as leader of his own party.

As public opinion leader, Roosevelt performed
brilliantly most of the time, although there were .
times when he fell short in this area. His greatest
success as a leader of public opinion lay in his effective use of the radio "fireside chat" and his ability
to use press conferences as a significant means of
communicating his ideas and his programs to the American public.[16] The exceptions to his outstanding performance in this area came on such occasions as his
abortive "purge" of conservative Democrats in the 1938
congressional primaries and the proposal for "packing"
the Supreme Court in 1937. On both occasions, Roosevelt misgauged public reaction and overestimated his
own influence, but these were exceptions to the general
rule. In the Depression crisis, during World War II,
and in the case of selling his legislative proposals to
the public--as with the Social Security bill--Roosevelt
performed admirably in his role as leader of public
opinion. He probably ranks as the most effective
modern President in this regard. This is doubtless one
reason for his great success and one reason why some

---

[16]See Elmer E. Cornwell, Jr., *Presidential
Leadership of Public Opinion* (Bloomington, Ind.:
Indiana University Press, 1965), especially Chapter
Six, "Leadership: Franklin Roosevelt", pp. 115-141.

experts on the Presidency feel he was the outstanding
President of the 20th Century to date.

Roosevelt was active as a leader for social
justice and reform, as can be seen in many facets of
his social reform legislation. But interestingly
enough he also saw himself as a preserver of order and
tradition in such areas as his contribution to the
conservation movement through the Civilian Conservation Corps and such projects as the Tennessee Valley
Authority. Ironically, the latter project was viewed
by his contemporaries as radical and socialistic, but
it appears to have been one of his more outstanding
and enduring achievements.

Harry S. Truman functioned in the chief executive role as a President who had no great difficulty
in making decisions. He took each matter as it came
to him, studied it carefully, then made his decision,
and the decision once made was not worried over after-
ward. This was true in many instances, including the
decision to use the atomic bomb against Japan, the
decision to conclude the war with Japan while leaving
the Emperor's position intact, the decision to go
ahead with the Truman Doctrine and the Marshall Plan,
the decision to intervene in Korea, and the firing of
General Douglas MacArthur. These were a few of the
major decisions he made, some of them very controversial, but he never worried about them once made. So
it can be said that Truman functioned as chief executive in an effective fashion.

In the role of chief administrator, Truman
earned high marks from many specialists in administration. He tended to prefer to have Cabinet departments
rather than special agencies handle problems, and he
tended to prefer to have Cabinet officers to handle
major matters rather than ad hoc advisors. Thus the
State Department and Secretary of State Dean Acheson
functioned with a greater degree of authority under
Truman than they would probably have had under Roosevelt, who tended to employ special emissaries like
Harry Hopkins and Averell Harriman to conduct diplomacy, sometimes to the embarrassment of Secretary of
State Cordell Hull. It probably would be going too
far to say that either method is preferable; it would
be correct to say that Truman approached administration in a more orthodox fashion than did FDR.

As foreign policy chief, Truman relied a bit
more on his Secretaries of State than was the case

with Roosevelt, but after his first year he came to
exert more initiative in this field on his own.   He
appointed outstanding men to serve as Secretary of
State, including General George Marshall and Dean
Acheson, who had been an Undersecretary under Marshall
and previously held a high position in the Treasury
Department under Roosevelt.   Truman also had a good
grasp of the basic foreign policy issues, and he did
not permit intrusion onto his authority on the part of
lesser officials.   He dismissed Henry Wallace as Secretary of Commerce when Wallace made statements critical of Truman's foreign policy, and he also dismissed
General of the Army Douglas MacArthur from his command
in the Far East when MacArthur defied Truman's foreign
policy directive by writing a letter expressing his
criticism of Korean policy to Minority Leader Joseph
Martin, the Republican spokesman in the House of
Representatives.

As commander-in-chief of the armed forces, Truman also acted with equal firmness.   His argument with
MacArthur was as much over foreign as over military
policy, but one of the reasons he gave for the dis-
missal was that MacArthur had been insubordinate to
his civilian chief, and General Marshall advised Truman that he would have dismissed MacArthur much
earlier.   MacArthur had a triumphal return home and a
congressional investigation of the matter was conducted, but MacArthur's presidential hopes were dashed
when General Eisenhower was nominated instead by the
Republican party in 1952.   Truman will be remembered
for major military decisions such as the decision to
aid Greece and Turkey, known as the Truman Doctrine,
the Berlin airlift, and the decision to intervene in
Korea under auspices of the United Nations in 1950.
This had both diplomatic and military aspects, but was
decided on in compliance with provisions of the United
Nations Charter.

As crisis leader, Truman functioned ably and
firmly although inevitably there will be controversy
over some of his decisions.   He was widely criticized
for his decision to enter Korea, after the war turned
into a stalemate, but at the time of the decision it
was generally popular.   He also kept his head in refusing to dismiss MacArthur at the time of the Communist
Chinese invasion of Korea, even though he might have
been justified in doing so.   He did not want to put
down MacArthur at a time when the general's fortunes
were at a low ebb.   Instead, he decided on the dis-
missal after the Inchon landings had occurred and

MacArthur had regained some of his reputation. He also withheld action until it was clear that MacArthur meant to defy clearly stated presidential directives.

In domestic policy, Truman sometimes acted a bit forcefully for the taste of some, as in the 1946 railroad strike when he asked for emergency legislation giving him the power to draft railroad workers, or in the 1952 steel strike when he ordered seizure of the steel mills and later saw his order countermanded by the Supreme Court on constitutional grounds. But Truman's domestic decisions reflected his genuine interpretation of the problems he dealt with. He did not abandon his principles when he was under heavy pressure, as for example in 1948 when many in his party were pressuring him not to run for another term or in 1952 when many less courageous Democrats were suggesting that he fire Dean Acheson, who had become a liability. To his credit, Truman acted firmly and courageously in these matters and thus can be described as an effective crisis leader for the most part. His integrity clearly was reflected in most of his decisions, and even his political enemies respected him for that.

As legislative chief, Truman had a mixed record. In the area of foreign policy legislation, such as the Marshall Plan and Truman Doctrine as well as ratification of the United Nations Charter, Truman had a rather good record with Congresses controlled by both parties. But in the area of domestic legislation, Truman proposed a great deal more reform legislation than ever made it through the Congress. In this he resembled Kennedy who proposed a great deal to an unenthusiastic Congress, and the strength of the conservative coalition in Congress made it unlikely that much of his program, especially new proposals, would win approval. Thus Truman and Kennedy could be considered in a different context than Roosevelt and Johnson, who had great legislative success but had it with liberal and sympathetic Congresses.

Truman's record as party leader was probably average. He did not have the popularity with Democrats that FDR had, but he was a party loyalist and he followed the party line perhaps more religiously than some Presidents would have. He did help Democratic candidates for lesser offices by campaigning for them, although some said his 1948 victory was won because they helped him to win a term on his own rather than because he helped them to win--in other words, a

"reverse coattail" effect. Truman was basically
orthodox in his approach to his party leadership role
and did what was expected of him as a party leader.

As a leader of public opinion, Truman had a
mixed record. He lacked the effectiveness in speaking
which Roosevelt possessed, but he did manage to communicate his ideas fairly effectively in his press
conferences and he did communicate effectively in his
"whistle-stop" campaign of 1948. In general, however,
because of the fact that he was tagged with the record
of Korea, communism and corruption by his political
enemies in the last two years of his Administration,
Truman must be judged at best only partly successful
in this role. He certainly did not perform as well as
Roosevelt in this role, but then relatively few Presidents have. He might be considered average in this
regard.

As a leader for social justice and reform, Truman clearly fit this role in his fight for civil
rights for minorities, particularly for black people,
and he was generally on the liberal side of most such
controversies. Truman did not particularly fit the
role of preserver of order and tradition, unless one
considers protecting the Constitutional prerogatives
of the President as maintaining such a role. He did
protect Presidential prerogatives against encroach-
ments of a sometimes hostile Congress, as for example
in the controversy over his veto of the Taft-Hartley Act.
The bill became law because Congress overrode his veto,
but Truman did not supinely give in to the wishes of
Congress when there was a major policy disagreement
between the executive and legislative branches. In
this sense Truman was a preserver of tradition, but in
most senses his liberal legislative program and
inclinations toward reform would indicate he better
fulfilled the role of a leader for social justice and
reform.[17]

---

[17]See the following: Margaret Truman, *Harry S
Truman* (New York: William Morrow & Co., 1973); Jona-
than Daniels, *The Man of Independence* (Philadelphia:
J. B. Lippincott Co., 1950); *Memoirs by Harry S.
Truman* (2 vols.) (Garden City, N.Y.: Doubleday & Co.,
1955-1956); Alfred Steinberg, *The Man From Missouri:
The Life and Times of Harry S. Truman* (New York: G. P.
Putnam's Sons, 1962).

General Dwight D. Eisenhower came to the Presidency from a life-long career in the military service, which extended from his days at West Point through his service as commander of NATO (with the exception of a brief period as president of Columbia University). Thus he can be considered in a different light than Roosevelt and Truman, whose principal preparation for the Presidency had been in the public service, mostly in elective office. In this regard, Eisenhower can also be contrasted with his four immediate successors, Kennedy, Johnson, Nixon and Ford, all of whom spent most of their public careers in Congress or the Vice Presidency prior to becoming President. President Carter, though never in Congress, held state elective offices before becoming President.

As chief executive, Eisenhower was clearly able to function forcefully and effectively when he felt it was necessary, but he was much more likely to defer to the wishes of Congress or the bureaucracy than some of his immediate predecessors or successors. He did not make a great number of policy decisions, but when they came to him he made them on the basis of his best judgment. Some of the major decisions he was faced with making on the executive level were the decision to conclude the Korean truce in 1953, the decision to defuse McCarthy's attack on the Army in 1954, the decision to side with the Soviet Union against Britain and France in the Suez crisis of 1956, and the decision to attempt summit diplomacy in Geneva in 1955, at Camp David in 1959, and in Paris in 1960. Eisenhower was a President who had a mixed record in this area of executive decision-making, largely because he shied away from making unpopular decisions. Thus he sometimes had to deal with domestic crises like the Little Rock civil rights crisis of 1957, because a problem had been neglected. Or he had to deal with foreign policy crises like the Sputnik crisis of 1957, when the Russians showed great strides with their space program, because of earlier acts of omission. This was his greatest weakness, although in some cases his willingness to wait situations out could have been a strength. The latter may have been true in the case of the Hungarian uprising of 1956, when precipitate intervention by the United States might have been disastrous for world peace, or when he declined to intervene in Indochina in 1954. On the other hand, Eisenhower sometimes came up with dramatic initiatives for peace, as when he proposed the Atoms-for-Peace program at Geneva in 1955. So his record can be described as mixed in this regard.

In his role as chief administrator, Eisenhower liked orthodox pyramidal decision-making patterns and he liked tidy administration with well-prepared paperwork, a preference which carried over into the Nixon Administration later on. Eisenhower was a good administrator in the technical sense, but because of his essential apolitical or non-political stance (probably growing out of his Army background), he sometimes missed the political dimensions of policy problems and he later suffered for this shortcoming. His basic idea of good administration was that only the difficult decisions were to come to the President. As he told Kennedy in a pre-inaugural conference in 1961, the easy decisions are made further down the line and ordinarily never reach the President.

As commander-in-chief, Eisenhower perhaps functioned best in handling defense policy. For one thing, his Army background kept him from advocating overly extravagant expenditures for defense, particularly on new gimmicks and weaponry which a less experienced President might have favored. Eisenhower's best record may have been in this role, although at the time of his second Administration, there was much talk about a "missile gap" and the Gaither Report which was suppressed in 1958 suggested that more effort and expenditure should have been devoted to the defense and space programs. Eisenhower was better able than many Presidents with a non-military background to pare money away from the defense budget without worrying that such cuts would be harmful.

As a crisis leader, Eisenhower was usually coolheaded and calm. He did not panic easily, and he never advocated precipitate action as his disposition was conservative in nature. However, he may sometimes have had the shortcoming of not recognizing a crisis situation soon enough to take timely action. This was perhaps his main fault in this area. He had a mixed record in this role, if one examines such matters as the McCarthy affair, the Sputnik and Little Rock crises, or other events of his Presidency. It could be argued that he did function effectively as in such situations as the 1954 decision whether to intervene in Indochina after the fall of Dienbienphu. However, on this matter, Eisenhower was getting a great deal of pressure from Congressional leaders not to accede to the efforts of Nixon and Dulles to involve the United States militarily in Vietnam. Unfortunately, his successors were less fortunate, but he should be given credit for this decision which was essentially a

115

negative one.

As legislative chief, Eisenhower had a mediocre record, but he served at a time when the public did not seem to be demanding new policy initiatives for the most part. So he could rest content with the passage of the mildly worded Civil Rights Act of 1957 or the Interstate highway legislation approved in the mid-1950's. Indeed in his relationship with Congress, especially in the last two years, it could be argued that Eisenhower had a kind of negative success reflecting a degree of public support in his successful effort to veto many Democratic appropriations bills which he felt were excessive. This was true of depressed areas legislation as well as appropriations for education, health and welfare programs as well as other socially-oriented legislation.

Unlike Nixon and Ford, however, he did not compensate for this by advocating higher defense expenditures. Instead, he opted for keeping budget figures low across the board, and the strategic situation at the time made it possible for him to do this. However, the increasing difficulty he had with the Democratic Congress elected in 1958 indicated that in the long run, his vetoes would probably not prevail; this was the case in such areas as depressed areas legislation and aid to education under his two Democratic successors. In general, Eisenhower had a kind of negative success with Congress. He was able to keep it from adopting legislation he did not really want; in nearly all cases he made his vetoes stick, although the Democrats later were able to use them effectively as campaign issues when the public began to shift its views.

As a party leader, Eisenhower must be considered, if not a failure, a President who missed many golden opportunities to help his party build up a continuing constituency in the South, in the suburbs, and elsewhere in the nation. He was not much interested in party affairs and tended to leave them to Vice President Nixon, the national chairmen, and others who thought in those terms. In this role, Eisenhower sacrificed the interests of his own party to the extent that he wished to appear non-partisan or bipartisan to further his own purposes. This was clearly one of his weakest areas of performance.

As leader of public opinion, Eisenhower had a mixed record, in part because there were few issues--

116

those mostly in the foreign policy area or regarding his fiscal orthodoxy about the budget--on which he would stake his popularity. He would rather in most cases remain highly popular than spend his popularity to promote an issue he wished to be identified with. This was not true in all cases, but it appeared to be true most of the time. An example of it was in the controversy over Senator Joseph McCarthy; in this case, Eisenhower was finally forced by events to deal with the situation, but by the time he did so he was not risking much of his popularity in opposing McCarthy, who was becoming discredited by the time of his censure following the Army-McCarthy hearings.

As a leader for social justice and reform, Eisenhower paid lip service to such ideas as equality and civil rights but he never really gave much effort in this area. He felt that government could achieve very little in this issue area, and consequently he did not do very much about it himself. Other examples could be given as well; Eisenhower never felt strongly about social reform legislation and he never pushed it; he tended to share the status quo orientation of his friends from the business and industrial community.

As a preserver of order and tradition, Eisenhower was a traditionally conservative President and devoted much of his attention to the maintenance of conservative values, honoring the flag, motherhood and the nation. But he did so sincerely and could not be accused--as Nixon for example might have been--of doing so for reasons of expediency. He was sincerely a conservative and this was reflected in nearly all of his policy stances, especially domestic ones, with very few exceptions.[18]

In the chief executive role, President Kennedy was a forceful leader; he did not shy away from the policy-making responsibilities of his office. Some difficult crises he had to deal with included the Cuban missile crisis of 1962, the Berlin crisis of

---

[18]See Sherman Adams, First-Hand Report; The Story of the Eisenhower Administration (New York: Harper & Brothers, 1961); Robert J. Donovan, Eisenhower: The Inside Story (New York: Harper & Brothers, 1956); Marquis Childs, Eisenhower: Captive Hero: A Critical Study of the General and the President (New York: Harcourt, Brace & Co., 1958).

1961, the Bay of Pigs debacle of 1961, the domestic controversy over steel prices in 1962, and the civil rights controversies of 1962 and 1963. In each case, he stated his position clearly and without equivocation and did not hesitate to accept the responsibility for his decisions. On the evidence, Kennedy was a decisive and thoughtful decision-maker. The carefulness with which he arrived at decisions in his executive capacity was demonstrated by the Cuban missile crisis, in which he opted for the naval quarantine rather than a surgical air strike or some lesser action such as a diplomatic protest. The decision proved to be a wise one because it eliminated the danger of missiles in Cuba while at the same time avoiding war with the Soviet Union. This crisis is the only known one since World War II in which the nation actually faced the danger of a thermonuclear war, although the Eisenhower Administration did threaten the use of nuclear weapons against China during the Korean War in 1953.

As chief administrator, Kennedy used methods somewhat similar to those of Franklin Roosevelt but he was a somewhat more tidy administrator. He resembled Roosevelt in that federal officials at all levels never knew when he might intervene personally in matters with which they were concerned. Kennedy made wide use of the device of the task force, which prepared options for decision-making at his request in a number of policy development areas. Kennedy was inclined to put less emphasis on the Cabinet and more emphasis on the White House staff, in part because of his frustrations with delays in the federal bureaucracy, but he was somewhat less inclined than FDR to set up overlapping lines of jurisdiction for his subordinates.

As foreign policy chief, Kennedy did a creditable job although he must share with Truman, Eisenhower, Johnson and Nixon some of the blame for the American involvement in Vietnam. But in other areas of foreign policy, Kennedy had an outstanding record. For example, he successfully negotiated the test ban treaty with the Soviet Union in 1963. He prevented a Communist takeover in West Berlin in 1961 and ended the Cuban missile crisis of October 1962 on terms acceptable to the United States which avoided involvement in an all-out war with the Soviet Union. He also took a great interest in the developing nations and tried to improve American relations with nations which had taken a neutral stance in the Cold War, such as Yugoslavia and India. This was a contrast with the previous policies of the Eisenhower Administration.

In addition to the commitment of military forces
to Vietnam, which led to the later escalation under
Johnson, Kennedy also made a foreign policy error in
allowing American participation in the Bay of Pigs
invasion, which was a failure largely because it was
based on faulty intelligence estimates. Indeed, the
role of the Central Intelligence Agency in this activity was disastrous and has led some to suggest that the
CIA was involved in the Kennedy assassination, although
there has never been direct proof of this allegation.
In general though, Kennedy, who was the son of an
Ambassador and had traveled widely overseas before he
became President, had a good grasp of diplomacy and
conducted it in an effective manner. He may have done
a better job in the foreign policy leadership role
than did Johnson and Nixon, although some of Nixon's
achievements were widely acclaimed at the time. Kennedy laid the groundwork for further achievements such
as the nuclear non-proliferation treaty and the SALT
agreements which were achieved under Johnson, Nixon
and Ford. He must be given above average marks for
his record in foreign policy, relatively brief though
it was.

As commander-in-chief, Kennedy made some important decisions related to defense policy. As a candidate for the Presidency, he had criticized what was
thought to be the missile gap in the development of
American missiles as compared to those of the Soviet
Union. But when Secretary of Defense McNamara got
access to the intelligence reports, it was determined
that the missile gap was largely fictional and the
United States was staying ahead of the Soviet Union in
this area.

However, one policy which Kennedy did initiate
was the policy of ending the Administration's heavy
reliance on nuclear weapons and developing a stronger
capability in conventional weapons, a policy proposed
and promoted by General Maxwell D. Taylor, chairman of
the Joint Chiefs of Staff during the Kennedy Administration. Taylor's approach did perhaps help to mount
a credible deterrent during the Berlin crisis and the
Cuban missile crisis, when American conventional
forces became an element in the strategic considerations of both the United States and the Soviet Union.

The concept of limited war which was related to
the idea of the conventional deterrent, however, had
some unfortunate results in that this probably encouraged American involvement in Vietnam. Kennedy should

not be given too much of the blame for this involvement, however, since his aide, Kenneth O'Donnell,
reported that Kennedy was making plans for withdrawal
of American military forces from Vietnam just prior to
his death. According to O'Donnell's account, Kennedy
planned to withdraw the remaining forces in 1965. But
of course, this never occurred because when Johnson
became President he escalated the war. It can be said
that Kennedy functioned effectively in his role as
commander-in-chief during his White House years.

As crisis leader, Kennedy was undoubtedly effective as he had a great ability to rally public support.
One example of a domestic crisis in which he proved
his effectiveness as a crisis leader was the continuing crisis in civil rights. When Kennedy was elected
in 1960, the Congress had passed the Civil Rights Act
of 1960, but there was considerable action going on in
the developing civil rights movement. In 1961 the
Freedom Riders began their assault on the segregated
transportation system in the South by riding Greyhound
busses through the Carolinas, Georgia, Alabama and
Mississippi. In addition to this, the sit-in movement
had begun among young black college students in North
Carolina and was spreading throughout the South as
blacks began demanding equal treatment in restaurants
and other businesses offering public accommodations.

Also, desegregation had been proceeding in the
field of education; at the University of Mississippi
it had been necessary for President Kennedy to order
federal troops onto the campus of Ole Miss at Oxford
before Governor Ross Barnett would bow to the regis-
tration of James Meredith as the university's first
black student. During the Ole Miss crisis in October
1962 bloodshed had erupted along with rioting, and the
following summer an additional attempt to desegregate
the University of Alabama developed and Governor George
Wallace made his famous "stand in the schoolhouse door"
only to be ordered by federal marshals to step aside;
the federal marshals were later backed up by the
federalized Alabama National Guard.

President Kennedy at this point, and following
rioting in Birmingham over a black boycott of white
businesses, went on television to appeal for racial
justice, equality and calmness in the crisis. Kennedy
called on the Congress to make a commitment that it
had not made in this century, and he announced that he
was sending to Congress the most sweeping civil rights
legislation since the Reconstruction a century before.

Although he annoyed black leaders by waiting until the situation became very tense before putting the weight of his office behind the civil rights movement, Kennedy had been able to enlist the support of moderates in both North and South for his position. He could do this because television coverage of the Birmingham riots and other events had disturbed the average American's sense of fairness and justice as nothing else had done in recent years. So his sense of timing was good, and his leadership in a crisis situation was effective. The same kind of observation could be made about the major foreign policy crisis which occurred during Kennedy's brief term, the Cuban missile crisis of 1962. Once again, Kennedy proved adept in his timing, keeping the news from the public until he was certain that the crisis situation did indeed exist, and then his decision was made only after several days of careful deliberation. Both of these instances indicate that as a crisis leader, Kennedy was an above average President.

As legislative chief, Kennedy had a record which was merely average, but there were extenuating circumstances. For one thing, like President Truman, he had to deal with a Congress which was dominated by the conservative coalition of Southern Democrats and Republicans. He also was just beginning to develop public support for much of his program when he was killed in Dallas, so that the civil rights legislation, the tax cut legislation, and other major policy initiatives being prepared by the Kennedy Administration, including the war on poverty in large measure, actually were enacted under Lyndon Johnson. Thus Kennedy's successor got much of the credit, partly deserved of course, for matters which Kennedy had set in motion. Our judgment then of Kennedy's record as legislative chief must be that like Harry Truman he had only limited success, but that it was not entirely his own fault. He probably achieved as much as it was possible for him to achieve, with the adoption of his foreign trade legislation and the test ban treaty and depressed areas legislation. Had he lived, he might have accomplished more.

As party leader, Kennedy was perhaps more effective than his successors, as he was willing to help other candidates in his own party in their election contests. But Kennedy did engage in one practice which has been typical of recent Presidents and has not contributed to the development of party strength. That practice was to develop a personal organization loyal

121

to the President rather than an organization loyal to the party. Of course Kennedy had to do this to win the nomination, and then to some extent his personal organization took over the party machinery, but he did have this shortcoming. To some extent, it is more a shortcoming of the party system and the way party politics is practiced in the present era than it is a reflection on Kennedy. By the time JFK served as President, the old era of strong party loyalties was past and it would do no good to pretend that he could have, or would have wanted to restore it as it was in the time of McKinley and Bryan. So Kennedy filled this party leader role satisfactorily but not in an outstanding fashion.

As leader of public opinion, Kennedy excelled more than in any of his other roles. He had a friendly press for the most part, and the way in which he handled his relations with the news media could set a pattern for modern Presidents. That has been discussed in a previous chapter, but essentially Kennedy's genius was in his ability to project a warmth and a degree of inspiration which has been absent in most recent Presidents. It is true that Kennedy would probably have been chagrined by the Camelot myth, because he had a wry ability to poke fun at himself, but he certainly would not have been dismayed at the many evidences that he had a considerable hold on the loyalties of the American public at the time of his death. In this role, Kennedy probably matched, if he did not exceed, the performance of FDR.

As a leader for social justice and reform, Kennedy did a good deal to fulfill the role, although there were those who had serious doubts about his commitment to reform at the time of his inauguration. This may have been because of his cool, non-committal leadership style. But when the real decisions came to be made, Kennedy usually opted for reform and social justice as when he announced his support for extensive civil rights legislation and for other social legislation. Kennedy did not achieve passage of aid to education during his term, but that was another reform which he gave his full support to, as well as the Medicare legislation which, like federal aid to education, was another achievement of the Johnson Presidency. So Kennedy must be viewed as fulfilling this role in the tradition of liberal Presidents.

As a preserver of order and tradition, Kennedy was unique among progressive or liberal Presidents in

122

that he seemed to value tradition without being shackled by it. In his book, Profiles in Courage, written when he was a Senator, Kennedy indicated his sense of history and his respect for the great traditions of the Senate. But when he became President, this did not prevent him from moving to seek a way around such Senate traditions as that of the filibuster against civil rights legislation. Kennedy only partly fits this role, and only in the way we have suggested. He was conservative in the sense that he valued the traditional American values, but he was not conservative in a policy sense. That description better fits Hoover, Nixon and Ford, all of them basically fiscal conservatives.[19]

Lyndon Johnson is a very interesting case study among recent Presidents because for the brief period of the Great Society, he so nearly dominated Washington and national politics. Then as the Vietnam war became the dominant issue, he quickly lost this domination. A look at Johnson's performance in the various White House roles may be instructive.

As chief executive, Lyndon Johnson performed with mixed results in the policy-making area. His domestic policies at least potentially could have been very fruitful in the time of the Great Society; he achieved great breakthroughs in the areas of civil rights legislation, aid to education, Medicare, and

---

[19]See Theodore C. Sorensen, Kennedy (New York: Harper & Row, 1965); Arthur M. Schlesinger Jr., A Thousand Days: John F. Kennedy in the White House (Boston: Houghton Mifflin Co., 1965); Richard E. Neustadt, Presidential Power (New York: New American Library, 1964) which contains an early appraisal of the Kennedy era; John F. Kennedy, Kennedy and the Press: The News Conferences, edited and annotated by Harold W. Chase and Allen H. Lerman (New York: Thomas Y. Crowell Co., 1965); Elie Abel, The Missile Crisis (Philadelphia: J. B. Lippincott Co., 1966); Roger Hilsman, To Move A Nation: The Politics of Foreign Policy in the Administration of John F. Kennedy (New York: Doubleday, 1967); Robert F. Kennedy, Thirteen Days (New York: W. W. Norton & Co., 1969); Tom Wicker, JFK and LBJ: The Influence of Personality in Politics (New York: William Morrow & Co., 1968).

other domestic reform legislation. The record is studded with Johnson successes in domestic policy, especially in the 89th Congress which took office following his landslide victory over Senator Barry Goldwater in 1964. In foreign policy, the disaster of the war in Vietnam overshadowed other modest successes such as the nuclear non-proliferation treaty, a limited step forward in the arms control area, and the Administration contribution to the settlement of the Six-Day War in the Middle East in 1967. The Administration record was quite a mixture of successes and defeats when one looks at the Johnson years. Certainly, the Johnson Administration did not realize its full potential, and this was largely because of the corrosive effect of Vietnam on domestic policy. Even the urban riots of the 1960's which Johnson had to deal with could be traced in part to the situation in Vietnam.

As chief administrator, Johnson had a great record as an innovator but a rather poor record for administrative efficiency. He attempted to start too many new programs at once, and he employed too little follow-through with the ones he did start to be considered an effective administrator. It is true that the war in Vietnam made this difficult, but Johnson was (like many Democratic Presidents) more interested in innovation than in the details of mundane but sound administration. In this area, he would not be termed a failure but could be described as a sloppy administrator.

As foreign policy chief, it was to Johnson's credit that he avoided American involvement in a general war with the Soviet Union or China. Beyond that, his foreign policy in Vietnam must be considered a disastrous one and his foreign policy elsewhere in the world must be considered only a limited success. He had to deal with an often intransigent government in the Soviet Union and he had to cope with questions like Panama and the Dominican Republic without easy answers. But clearly, foreign policy was not Johnson's long suit, despite the inordinate amount of time he devoted to it in his administration between 1963 and 1969.

As commander-in-chief, Johnson unfortunately must be judged by observers of the Presidency largely on his record in Vietnam; that was basically a policy which was a failure. However, he took his responsibilities seriously and worked in foreign and defense policy to seek to further the advancement of arms control and easing of tensions with the Communist bloc (even though because of Vietnam, the Czechoslovakian invasion and other events this did not prove very feasible during his Administration). Perhaps Johnson's greatest error as commander-in-chief (this applies to his foreign policy record as well) was to make the faulty assumption that American military and diplomatic power could be the primary influence on the outcome of the struggle in Vietnam. That was simply a major error of judgment, and there is no way to minimize it. So again Johnson's record was marred by the war. This is all the more reason why we should give him credit for the relatively minor things he did achieve in other areas, such as keeping American technology abreast of military needs and his contribution to developing the space program.

As crisis leader, Lyndon Johnson handled most domestic crises with a sure hand, including the Selma crisis in 1965 when the Voting Rights Act was passed following the violence in Alabama, and the urban riots, when Johnson delayed sending in federal troops until he was assured it was necessary to end the violence. But in the foreign policy area, on many occasions Johnson showed a tendency to overreact, as if he had to prove the machismo of both himself and the nation. This occurred when he sent troops into the Dominican Republic in 1965, and also when he asked for passage of the Gulf of Tonkin Resolution by the Congress in August 1964. This does not mean that he always overreacted, because Johnson handled the troubles with Panama in a sensitive and sensible way--with negotiation--when difficulty erupted there in 1964 (certainly in a different way than one might expect from Ronald Reagan in the recent dispute). But by and large that was one weakness of Johnson's crisis leadership. His record would have to be described as mixed.

As legislative chief, Johnson's record was outstanding. He probably was responsible for the passage of more domestic reform legislation than any other President in this century, with the possible exceptions of Wilson and Franklin Roosevelt. It should not take anything away from his great legislative achievements to say that the way was prepared for them by Kennedy, because Johnson's whole career in the Congress prepared him magnificently for this role which he undertook as President. If there was one role he excelled in, as Kennedy did in the public opinion leadership role, for Johnson it was the role of legislative chief. His skill at congressional maneuvering could be seen in many pieces of legislation, but no more so perhaps than in his role in the adoption of the Civil Rights Act of 1964, when he enlisted the help of Senator Everett Dirksen.

As party leader, Lyndon Johnson shared with Kennedy and Nixon the tendency to put his own personal organization and his own personal needs as President ahead of those of the party. Under Johnson, much emphasis was given to the President's Club as a fund-raising device. The more emphasis Johnson placed on building up his own personal organization, the more the party organization was allowed to fall into disarray, and the Democratic party suffered for this in Hubert Humphrey's campaign in 1968. In general, Johnson had a weak record as party leader, even though he did help the party in compiling a substantial legislative record in domestic policy. Certainly he did not help it with his Vietnam policy which divided the party down the middle.

As public opinion leader, Johnson lacked the skills which JFK possessed. Johnson never had the same grasp of the levers of public opinion. The secretiveness with which he operated soon created the credibility gap of his Administration, which left the press and public disbelieving about many of his statements. Johnson did make a good beginning after the Kennedy assassination, and he did have the sympathy of public and the mass media for a time but within a year of his accession he had in large measure lost this support and sympathy.

Certainly even during his election campaign in 1964 he was beginning to lose his credibility with the news media, because of the way in which he handled the selection of his vice presidential running mate, Hubert Humphrey, and also the way in which he handled the controversy over the Mississippi Freedom Democratic party, which he tried to compromise. By this time, the compromise worked out by Johnson and Humphrey appeared rather pallid, and did not impress Johnson's black constituency very much. He did however get good black support in the 1964 election, in part because Barry Goldwater voted against the Civil Rights Act of 1964. Johnson was essentially unsuccessful in his role as public opinion leader, with some early exceptions.

As leader for social justice and reform, Lyndon Johnson can take credit for major achievements and, like the other liberal Presidents we have mentioned, he fulfilled this role superbly. Among the steps toward social justice and reform for which he was responsible were at least three major legislative enactments, the Civil Rights Act of 1964 (plus the Voting Rights Act of 1965), the Education Act of 1965, and the Medicare Act of 1965. There were many other legislative achievements made by LBJ (such as the War on Poverty), but these alone assured him of a place in history as a major leader for social justice and domestic reform.

As preserver of order and tradition, LBJ was not much concerned with tradition. He was however concerned with preserving order during the urban riots which occurred in Harlem in 1964, in Watts in 1965, in Cleveland in 1966, in Detroit and Newark in 1967, and in Washington and Chicago in 1968. He did restore order, and he was responsible for proposing and securing the passage of the Safe Streets Act of 1968. This began efforts in this area which were later continued by Nixon in sponsoring the Law Enforcement Assistance Administration.[20]

In examining Richard Nixon's record, one must remember his unique role as the only President who ever resigned under fire, and the likelihood of his impeachment had he attempted to remain in office in 1974 after the deceptions of Watergate and the cover-

---

[20]See Doris Kearns, Lyndon Johnson and the American Dream (New York: Harper & Row, 1976); Lyndon B. Johnson, The Vantage Point: Perspectives of the Presidency 1963-1969 (New York: Holt, Rinehart, Winston, 1971); Alfred Steinberg, Sam Johnson's Boy: A Close-up of the President From Texas (New York: Macmillan Co., 1968); Jack Valenti, A Very Human President (New York: Pocket Books, 1977); Theodore H. White, The Making of the President 1964 (New York: New American Library Signet Books, 1965); Eric F. Goldman, The Tragedy of Lyndon Johnson (New York: Dell, 1969); Lyndon B. Johnson, The Choices We Face (New York: Bantam, 1969); Michael Davie, LBJ: A Foreign Observer's Viewpoint (New York: Ballantine Books, 1967); Lyndon B. Johnson, A Time For Action (New York: Pocket Books, 1964).

up had been exposed. The exposure came as the result of Washington Post exposes, the disclosures made by James McCord (formerly of the CIA) at the urging of Judge John Sirica, and the investigation conducted by the Senate Watergate Committee led by Senator Sam Ervin of North Carolina. Following all of these developments and the firing of Special Prosecutor Archibald Cox in October 1973 in the "Saturday Night Massacre", the public outcry against Nixon and his refusal to turn over the Watergate tapes led eventually to the impeachment proceedings conducted by the House Judiciary Committee under the leadership of Chairman Peter Rodino. This committee after conducting extensive hearings. approved a bill of impeachment with three articles against Nixon in the summer of 1974. He was accused of obstruction of justice and abuse of power among other charges, but the impeachment never came to trial in the Senate because just as the House was preparing to debate the articles of impeachment, Nixon decided on August 8, 1974 to resign the next day. Then a month later, President Ford precipitately decided to pardon former President Nixon, which resulted in suppression of much of the remainder of the Watergate evidence.

As chief executive, Nixon was very power-oriented but he did not always have a clear purpose for the exercise of his power. Many of his actions were negative; he vetoed appropriations bills for health, education and welfare and other domestic programs, he impounded funds legally appropriated by Congress for programs he opposed such as the Office of Economic Opportunity, and did other essentially negative things. He did act with some effectiveness in foreign policy, in the initiative to improve relations with China and to some extent the Soviet Union, but he was relatively unsuccessful in the domestic policy area in taking new initiatives. Despite the much touted Family Assistance Plan, Nixon never gave it solid support in Congress and it died in the Senate after twice being passed by the House. This ended any meaningful chance for much-needed welfare reform during the Nixon years. Most of the rest of his energies were devoted to the settlement of the Vietnam war and other foreign policy matters, although prior to the time when Watergate broke wide open, he had begun some potentially useful administrative reforms which never came to anything. He was quite overbearing his relations with Congress and the public, and his rating as an effective President dropped more sharply than that of any of his predecessors. At the time of the Vietnam truce in early 1973, his rating as President was near 70 per cent in public approval; at the time of his resignation about a year and a half later, his approval rating was around 24 per cent. So although he concentrated more power in the White House than perhaps any President in history, especially during the second term, his period as an executive with near-dictatorial powers was very short-lived because the Congress and more importantly the public literally revolted against this state of affairs.

As chief administrator, Nixon must be given better marks than as chief executive. Like most conservative Republican Presidents, he was interested in improving the style and character of public administration, and he had proposed a system of four super-cabinet positions. The secretaries of four departments, under this system, would have also been White House aides, and he felt this would give the President firmer control of policy. He never really got to try out this functional system, first proposed in 1971, however, because just as he began to implement it, he was forced to ask for the resignations of Haldeman and Ehrlichman, his principal aides. During most of the remainder of his term, he was consumed with Watergate matters or foreign policy crises. So one can conclude that his record was mixed, but that he probably had good intentions to improve the quality of administration. It will be interesting to see how President Jimmy Carter handles some of these problems, since he too has some novel ideas about improving the soundness of administration. That will be discussed in a later section of this chapter.

As foreign policy chief, Nixon performed as well as most modern Presidents, since it is extremely difficult to turn in a good record in this area and he had to devote much of his efforts to ending the war in Vietnam rather than taking new policy initiatives. The outstanding achievement of his Presidency will probably turn out to be a reopening of diplomatic dialogue with the People's Republic of China, which the United States had never recognized and fought against in the Korean war between 1950 and 1953. This step was made possible through the secret negotiations of Secretary of State Henry Kissinger, who had been an advisor to Governor Nelson Rockefeller of New York at the time he was appointed by Nixon in 1969. Kissinger also had been a professor of international relations at Harvard University, and his tenure ended with the end of

Ford's term in 1977. Nixon also made a treaty for the SALT agreement for arms control with the Soviet Union. Nixon went ahead with plans for the anti-ballistic missile in 1969 and 1970, but this was halted after the SALT agreement in Moscow in 1972. He signed space cooperation and trade agreements, including the pact for sale of American wheat to the Soviet Union, when detente was in its heyday in 1972. Today, however, some of those agreements appear less attractive to the American public than they did in 1972 when Nixon concluded them.

Nixon tried to improve U.S. relations with Western Europe, but may have damaged them by imposing trade restrictions in 1971 and may also have damaged U.S.-Japanese relations by not keeping Japan informed about his negotiations with China. He should be given credit, along with Kissinger and William Rogers, Kissinger's predecessor as Secretary of State, for several truce agreements in the Middle East. When Nixon came into office, the Six-Day War in 1967 had not been over long and during his tenure the Yom Kippur war of 1973 occurred. Nixon had good relationships with Prime Minister Golda Meir and her successor, Yitzhak Rabin, but Kissinger's efforts to negotiate separate truces with Egypt and Syria were only partly successful. At least Kissinger and Nixon managed to buy more time for U.S. policy in the Middle East.

As commander-in-chief, Nixon's chief concerns were with the conduct of the war in Vietnam from 1969 through 1973. He began a slow, measured withdrawal of American troops from Vietnam and put the South Vietnamese on their own for the defense of their country. He concluded a truce which left North Vietnamese and Vietcong troops in position and probably made inevitable the fall of the South in 1975, so in a sense it was a kind of "fig leaf" for American retreat and defeat. But Nixon may have handled that as well as he could have, except that he prolonged the war much longer than many people, including Senator George McGovern, his 1972 opponent for the Presidency, felt was necessary.

Nixon also conducted a secret war in Cambodia, carrying out bombing raids without informing Congress for some two years, and he brought about a major domestic flare-up including the Kent State incident when he ordered troops into Cambodia in the spring of 1970. He also allowed the CIA to conduct a secret war for a time in Laos; clearly there were some probable constitutional violations of his power in some of these acts, especially the deception of Congress about the Cambodian bombing. Ultimately Congress voted a cut-off of funds for the more questionable operations. Nixon's record as commander-in-chief is essentially a rather dreary one, although he should not be blamed for the initial American involvement in Vietnam because that occurred under his four predecessors.

As crisis leader, Nixon was found wanting during the Watergate situation. He fared somewhat better with his leadership on Vietnam, but overall, his handling of crises would have to be rated as poor. He allowed a postal strike for example to occur in the spring of 1970 before stepping in to do something to remedy the situation which caused it. Also his record on dealing with civil rights was rather abysmal, and he helped to bring on a crisis of sorts in other domestic areas by his refusal to spend legally appropriated funds voted by Congress. Nixon was clearly deficient as a crisis leader.

As legislative chief, Nixon had a fair record in foreign policy matters (he obtained ratification of the SALT treaty, a major step in arms control), but he was continually at war with Congress over domestic policy and was constantly attempting to undermine policy initiatives of Congress by vetoing bills for new initiatives in domestic policy, as well as appropriations bills for social reform programs and environmental control. A major dispute erupted between Nixon and the Democratic majority in Congress when he vetoed a bill appropriating funds for water pollution control. The bill was passed over his veto in an override, and then Nixon impounded the funds and refused to spend them. He was taken into court by Senator Kennedy, and he was also challenged by several governors on the issue of his impoundment of funds for construction of Interstate highways and for state education programs from the federal aid appropriations. In almost all of these cases, Nixon lost. His record as legislative chief has to be judged a failure by most standards, even given that his opposition was in control of Congress.

As party leader, Nixon's record was also abysmal. Although he started out helping other members of his own party and taking a few token steps toward broadening the Republican constituency, in his re-election campaign he selfishly concentrated on his own re-election, declining to even campaign for all but a

few other Republicans. Nixon even set up his own campaign organization completely outside the GOP structure, the Committee to Re-Elect the President (known
as CREEP) and it was for this reason that major Republican figures like Ford were not involved in the
unsavory Watergate scandals which involved not only
the payment of hush money for blackmail but also the
collection of illegal contributions from corporate
treasuries to Nixon's re-election campaign.

As leader of public opinion, Nixon was rather
successful on Vietnam policy and some domestic social
issues such as law and order in his first term, but in
his second term he almost completely lost the confidence of the American public. He was capable of communicating directly with the public on television
rather effectively during his first term, but he never
was able to achieve a "good press" in the fashion of
some of his predecessors, apparently because he
appeared to hate the news media and to engage in a
campaign of vilification and persecution against it,
as exemplified by his actions in the case of the Pentagon Papers in 1971. In general, Nixon has to be considered a failure in this role.

As a leader for social justice and reform,
Nixon talked a great deal about reform, and even proposed a major departure in the area of welfare reform
with his Family Assistance Plan, but it must be
assumed that this was mostly talk. When the FAP came
up for passage in the Senate and committee hearings
were going on in relation to it, Nixon did not lift a
finger to help it. It has to be noted here that key
Democrats like Senator Russell Long were also opposed
to it, but a bit of White House support could have
possibly brought about its passage. Nixon did achieve
one significant reform in the decentralization and
modernization of governmental programs in the inter-
governmental relations area. This came with the
acceptance of his General Revenue Sharing plan by Congress in 1971. This five-year plan represented a
major advance in the administration of federal aid
programs, and Nixon should be given credit for this.
Like most conservative Republican Presidents, however,
Nixon did not worry a great deal about making achievements in this policy area and he was not disturbed too
greatly when some of the proposed reforms failed to
make it through Congress.

As preserver of order and tradition, Nixon paid
lip service to the traditional functions of conserva-

tive Republican Presidents and talked a lot about the
conservative values of the Republican party. But in
fact through his behavior as President he departed
from these values in many ways, particularly in his
high-handed behavior toward Congress and in his con-
doning and possible participation in the Watergate
scandal. So he really did not fulfill the role of a
preserver of tradition in any serious way. He also
talked a great deal about law and order, and his
appointee, Attorney General John Mitchell, worked on
his ideas in this area, establishing major programs
for the Law Enforcement Assistance Administration,
cracking down on demonstrators, and engaging in wiretapping of White House aides suspected of making
"leaks" to the suspect press, especially the New York
Times and the Washington Post. But it was later found
that there was a good deal of corruption and mismanage-
ment in the LEAA, and John Mitchell himself was convicted for his part in the Watergate cover-up, so again
Nixon did not really measure up very well in his role
as preserver of order. Nixon in the end did not really
measure up very well as preserver of his own Administration, as he had to resign under pressure in 1974.
In all, his record showed many shortcomings.[21]

In the role of chief executive, Gerald Ford
gradually developed a self-confidence in policy-making
which he did not exhibit in as sure-footed a way in
the early months of his presidency. He was in the
pattern of conservative, status quo Presidents, and to
some he appeared as a caretaker President, at least

------

[21]Richard M. Nixon, Six Crises (New York:
Pocket Books Giant Cardinal Edition, 1962); Earl Mazo
and Stephen Hess, Nixon: A Political Portrait (New
York: Popular Library, 1968); Garry Wills, Nixon
Agonistes: The Crisis of the Self-Made Man (New York:
New American Library Signet Books, 1971); Theodore H.
White, The Making of the President 1968 (New York:
Pocket Books, 1970); Theodore H. White, The Making of
the President 1972 (New York: Bantam, 1973); Bruce
Mazlish, In Search of Nixon: A Psychohistorical
Inquiry (Baltimore, Md.: Penguin Books, 1973); Theodore
H. White, Breach of Faith: The Fall of Richard Nixon
(New York: Dell, 1975); William Safire, Before the
Fall: An Inside View of the Pre-Watergate White House
(New York: Belmont Tower Books, 1975).

until he announced in 1975 that he was running for a term in his own right. Ford made an effort to strip away some of the trappings of the Imperial Presidency, and he also made more of an effort to make himself open to the people and to at least make a show of working with Congress, but as his term in office neared a close in 1977, it seemed that Ford--while much less imperious than his immediate predecessors--was still not shrinking from defying the Congress when he felt he was justified. His leadership style was much less pretentious than that of Nixon and perhaps that of Johnson and Kennedy, and he made much more of an effort than Nixon to maintain his contacts with the public. He may have been obliged to do this because of his peculiar status as the nation's first President who was not elected by the people, but the fact remains that he did so. Although Ford appeared to fill the minimum requirements of the chief executive role, he was challenged by the candidacy of former Governor Ronald Reagan of California on many of the key decisions and policies he followed. Reagan for example challenged Ford on the basic foreign policy of detente with the Soviet Union and also on the negotiations with Panama over the Panama Canal, to mention but two examples.

As chief administrator, Ford tried to run the government more efficiently and in a less costly manner, but his Democratic opposition charged he was making cuts in domestic spending only to divert the funds to the defense program. Like most of his conservative Republican predecessors, Ford sought to keep budgets down. But in his first two years large deficits were run by the federal government, in part because of the recession of 1974 and 1975. Ford's critics charged that his traditional laissez-faire policies caused the economy to produce at only a fraction of its full potential and that this reduced the government's tax revenues, but he of course argued that recovery had to be dependent on the private sector more than the public sector and he threatened a veto of the Humphrey-Hawkins bill, a New Deal proposal which would have made the federal government the employer of last resort. As chief administrator, Ford paid lip service to the conservative Republican ideal of reducing the size of the federal government, but in practice he like Nixon did not do a great deal of reducing. He simply diverted funds from domestic reform programs and welfare and food stamp type spending to the defense budget instead. Ford did show some concern with the fact that the regulatory agencies no longer seemed to be

134

doing the job they were created to do, and he proposed
various reforms to streamline administration and reduce the functions of the regulatory agencies. Some
of these proposed reforms won Democratic support,
especially his proposals to reduce regulation of small
business, but his opposition was suspicious of other
proposals which they felt would lift the restraints of
regulation from big business and might be harmful to
consumer interests, which had come to have more powerful representation through lobbying groups. Ford was
making an effort at the end of his term to fulfill the
chief administrator role more adequately.

As foreign policy chief, Ford came into office
with a limited background in this area and was known
as a hard-liner toward the Communist bloc. However,
his chairmanship of the Defense Appropriations Subcommittee in the House during his Congressional tenure
made him knowledgeable about defense policy and the
defense budget. In general, Ford relied for his first
year at least on the advice of Secretary of State
Henry Kissinger, but during the 1976 primary campaign
season when Kissinger came under attack from Ronald
Reagan, Ford's challenger for the nomination, Ford did
not rush to come to Kissinger's defense. Ford did
actively involve himself in shaping foreign policy,
however, and his trips to Japan and to the Vladivostok
summit in late 1974, as well as his trip to Helsinki
for the Helsinki Conference in 1975 and his visit to
Peking in late 1975 indicated a growing interest in
foreign policy. He seemed to become less dependent on
Kissinger's advice and to function more on his own in
this area as he developed more self-confidence in his
own judgment. Voters who supported Ford in the primaries felt, for example, that he showed sounder judgment on the issue of Panama and the canal than did
Reagan, who made some very belligerent statements.
Ford pointed out that following the policy Reagan
advocated could involve the United States in a Vietnam
type war in Central America at a time when the American public did not want involvement in such avoidable
hostilities. As for detente with the Soviet Union,
Ford dropped the term detente which had been given a
bad name with some Republicans by Reagan, but he
talked about a policy of "peace through strength"
which on closer analysis did not sound very different
from detente. Like most recent Presidents, including
those like Ford who may have felt more at home with
domestic policy matters, Ford seemed increasingly
drawn into involvement in foreign policy issues. He
may have found, like his predecessors, that in this

area the President has greater freedom and therefore found it more attractive. In general, Ford fulfilled his foreign policy chief role in an adequate way in that he was preserving the peace, but his policies came under increasing attack from both the political right and left during the 1976 election campaign.

As commander-in-chief, Ford was obliged to preside over the liquidation of the unpopular Vietnam commitment. He tried to get funds from Congress to provide military aid to the doomed government of South Vietnam, but Congress--probably wisely--refused to go along. So Ford was stuck in a sense with the policy of his discredited predecessor. Ford also acted with some vigor in sending Marines in to retake the SS Mayaguez in the spring of 1975 when this American merchant ship was seized by Cambodian Communists. In the process, the crew of 25 or so men was saved but about 20 Marines were lost in the skirmish. To Ford, it was a symbolic test of American power, and his move was popular. Another major move made by Ford early in his second year in office was his decision to remove Secretary of Defense James Schlesinger, a hard-liner, at the Pentagon and to replace him with his chief of staff at the White House, Donald Rumsfeld, a former Congressman and ambassador to NATO. Some thought this meant that Ford was planning to take a more conciliatory line toward the Soviet Union, but when the Communists moved into Angola and the Soviet position hardened, Ford accepted Rumsfeld's recommendations and recommended an increase in the Defense Department budget to $110 billion. Congress went along with this for the most part, even though controversy over the B-1 bomber and the cruise missile, two expensive new weapons systems, continued, despite this basic decision. The B-1 bomber had a price tag of $500 million for each plane, and in May of 1976 the Senate voted to defer a final decision on operationalizing the B-1 bomber until the election of a new President. Thus Carter as Ford's successor would not be stuck with an unwanted weapons system. Carter later cancelled the B-1 but decided to proceed with the cruise missile. Ford clearly took his responsibilities as commander-in-chief seriously and this was one of his main areas of interest as President.

As crisis leader, Ford had relatively few crises to deal with in his 2½-year tenure, but he did have a few. The Mayaguez crisis was one which he dealt with, and another was the final collapse of South Vietnam. In each case, he indicated that he

136

would follow a hard-line policy. This was also true in Angola, but unlike Nixon or previous Presidents who had fairly substantial backing in Congress, Ford was unable to win support in Congress for American action in Angola or South Vietnam and this weakened his stance as a crisis leader. Ford also created a crisis of his own making with his unannounced and precipitate pardon of Richard Nixon. He thought this was the way to end the Watergate controversy but his action apparently only embittered the controversy.

As legislative chief, Ford was handicapped by working with a Congress controlled by the opposition. While that alone might not have been an insuperable obstacle, the difficulty was compounded by the fact that the Democrats scored substantial gains in Congress in the Watergate elections of 1974, and Ford's base of support in Congress was thus narrowed as more liberal Democrats were elected. Ford thus had to veto many Democratic appropriations bills in order to follow his conservative philosophy, and this hampered his efforts to provide leadership for Congress. The situation in 1976 was such that the stalemate was likely to be resolved either by the defeat of Ford or by the defeat of his liberal Democratic opponents. With Carter's election in November 1976 this stalemate appeared to have been ended. Somewhat like Kennedy and Truman, Ford had to deal with an extremely difficult situation in Congress, so the fact that he had little accomplishment to show for his efforts was not entirely his own fault. He was largely suffering the results of Richard Nixon's misdeeds and the political effects of the Watergate scandal.

As party leader, Ford was certainly much more liked and respected by most Republicans than was Nixon. He traveled to many places to give his support to Republican candidates, and it was this fact that brought about his nomination in 1976 despite a strong challenge from Ronald Reagan. Ford was a party regular in a sense that Richard Nixon never was. He was one of the first to condemn the excesses of the Committee to Re-elect the President, and he pledged after taking over the Presidency that his own presidential campaign would be run by giving party regulars a greater voice in the management of the campaign, indicating that he would avoid one blunder made by Nixon. In his role as party leader, Ford must be said to have performed admirably, and perhaps to have a better record than some of his predecessors.

In his role as leader of public opinion, Ford
may not have excelled to the degree that Kennedy and
Roosevelt did, but he did succeed in restoring some
measure of confidence in the Presidency after the public had felt itself much abused by the shenanigans of
the Nixon Administration. Ford tried to project an
image of sincerity and openness, and he was succeeding
remarkably well until he pardoned Richard Nixon, an
action which was a public relations disaster for him.
His standing in the Gallup poll on presidential performance dropped off sharply, although later he regained some of the lost ground. Ford was quite accessible as President, holding press conferences with
more frequency than Nixon and also giving interviews
and holding press conferences with local media around
the country to an unprecedented degree during his
travels associated with the campaign for the Presidency. In general, Ford functioned reasonably well in
his role as leader of public opinion. Though the
leader of a minority party, he was able to maintain a
good deal of good will for himself with the American
public and it was largely because of his own humility
and down-to-earth qualities, something almost totally
lacking in Nixon.

Ford could point to few achievements as a
leader for social justice and reform, although he was
interested in reform in the area of reducing the
bureaucracy and eliminating red tape in government
regulation of business. But as far as social justice
and people-oriented programs are concerned, Ford
showed little sympathy with these and had a record of
many vetoes of appropriations for social reform programs. So his record is spotty on this score, and he
probably feels it is not necessary for a conservative
President to be a leader for social justice. In that
he would not be alone, as some of his predecessors
also felt the same way.

As preserver of order and tradition, Ford was
more interested in this role of the Presidency than
some of his predecessors. He was a conspicuous participant in various Bicentennial observances around the
nation, and obviously valued national traditions.
After a period when the custom was dropped by Richard
Nixon, he resumed the practice of attending church
services regularly each Sunday and was frequently in
the congregation at St. John's Episcopal Church in
Washington. Ford was also interested in attending and
participating in traditional patriotic observances at

such places as Arlington National Cemetery; he went on
one occasion to Independence, Missouri, to unveil a
statue of President Harry Truman, one of his heroes by
his own account. Ford was interested in following
tradition and preserving it. In the preservation of
order, he favored a hard-line policy in law enforcement and indicated he favored the restoration of
capital punishment and was opposed to abortion, among
the many controversial issues on which he has announced
a stand. In this role, Ford felt comfortable and has
stuck with the tradition of his conservative predecessors.[22]

We will conclude this part of the chapter with
a brief discussion of how Jimmy Carter is handling the
presidential roles and how another popular candidate,
Ronald Reagan, might have been expected to handle the
presidential roles. This discussion will of necessity
be brief, but it is important to include it, since the
public should learn to think in terms of how it sees
candidates fitting into the presidential roles and
should learn to give more serious thought to the choice
of a President, since the public obviously failed
rather badly in its part in the selection process in
1972. We will look at Carter first.

As chief executive, Carter has taken the policy-
making responsibilities of the President quite seriously. In a speech to the Washington Press Club during
the 1976 primary season, he indicated his view of the
executive-legislative relationship. He said that Congress should be a partner in the policy-making process,
but he felt that the President should exercise vigorous, aggressive leadership. This indicates that while
Carter might be a somewhat more moderate President
than recent Democratic liberal Presidents like Truman,
Kennedy and Johnson, he would be progressive and
aggressive in his leadership style much as they were.

---

[22]Allan P. Sindler, Unchosen Presidents: The
Vice President and Other Frustrations of Presidential
Succession (Berkeley, Calif.: University of California
Press Quantum Books, 1976); Bud Vestal, Jerry Ford Up
Close: An Investigative Biography (New York: Berkeley
Medallion Books, 1974); Jerald F. terHorst, Gerald
Ford and the Future of the Presidency (New York: The
Third Press, 1974).

As for the role as chief administrator, Carter has shown a lot of interest in that and has developed some rather detailed plans for streamlining the structure of the federal bureaucracy. He maintained during the campaign that he could take the more than 1,000 federal departments and agencies and through appropriate consolidations and dropping of unneeded agencies reduce this number to about 200; he said he did this successfully in state government as governor of Georgia. There are many who are doubtful that he could do this successfully, but as President he has already begun working on executive reorganization.

As foreign policy chief, Carter has been somewhat dependent on the advice of appointees such as Zbigniew Brzezinski, national security advisor, and Secretary of State Cyrus Vance--but like Ford, he did assume full command of foreign policy as soon as he felt confident of his own judgment and competent to do so. Prior to the Democratic National Convention of 1976, Carter had already been asked by spokesmen for several foreign embassies to talk with their ambassadors so they could learn more about his views, but he said he felt this would be inappropriate until he had won the nomination. He proved to have a somewhat more flexible policy than Ford, but he appeared to agree with Henry Jackson and others that simply having a policy of detente is not enough, that we must ensure that the Soviet Union will cooperate with such an approach. Although Carter came under a great deal of pressure from constituencies within the Democratic party to take a more pro-Israeli stance in the Middle East, he did announce he favored a homeland for Palestinian refugees. He explored the possibility of moving toward normal diplomatic relations with the People's Republic of China and also with Cuba, although the intervention of Cuban troops in Angola and elsewhere in Africa has perhaps delayed that step for a time. In general, Carter has followed an activist foreign policy but is not an advocate of peace at any price. His emphasis on human rights has been popular but controversial. He appears to feel that some reductions in defense spending are possible through increased efficiency, but he has not advocated cuts in defense spending of the magnitude favored by George McGovern in 1972. He would also be likely, as a former naval officer, to give more attention to a restoration of a naval build-up than in the air arm of the U.S. armed forces. In 1977 he finally chose to put American defense funds into the cruise missile rather than the B-1 bomber, and cancelled the latter project. It is unlikely that he would follow a belligerent policy toward Panama and the Latin American neighbors of Panama who are concerned about statements by Governor Reagan about the Panama Canal. Indeed Carter by mid-summer of 1977 had completed the negotiation of a new canal treaty with Panama, the object of controversy.

As crisis leader, Carter would probably be coolheaded in the manner of John F. Kennedy rather than acting hastily and precipitately as Johnson and Nixon sometimes did. He appears to have the detachment and maturity which would stand him in good stead in times of crisis; certainly he has shown these qualities in his own campaign for the Presidency, and it is a fairly safe assumption that he could be expected to show them as President. He had not faced a major foreign policy crisis in his first six months, but could have to deal with such crises in Korea or the Middle East.

As legislative chief, Carter was expected to have excellent working relationships with the Southern Democrats in Congress, even though he lacks a background in Congress himself. His congressional relations got off to a shaky start but were improving after six months. He probably could be an effective leader in promoting legislation in Congress, although those who observed his record as governor in dealing with the Georgia legislature have mixed opinions as to how effective Carter would be with Congress. He appears to have a good deal of charm and persuasive ability, which are important in this kind of relationship, so it is likely he could be more successful than Nixon or Ford were, primarily because he would not have to deal with an opposition Congress.

As party leader, Carter can be expected to have some problems as he ran for the Presidency as a candidate opposing the Washington Establishment. But that was true of John F. Kennedy too, and he seemed to manage the party leadership role rather well. The same should be true of Carter too, as unlike Richard Nixon, he does not appear to carry grudges.

As leader of public opinion, Carter has proved to be imaginative and effective; he demonstrated these qualities in his handling of the news media during his campaign for the Presidency. As President he used news conferences, fireside chats and a telephone call-in effectively.

As a leader for social justice and reform, Carter was expected to fight for progressive programs in order to maintain his leadership in the Democratic party which has always been oriented in that direction. He was criticized by Democratic liberals for his slowness in this direction, however. His reforms began with his effort to reform the federal bureaucracy, a much needed reform, but it was a good expectation that there would be plenty of others. So he would probably fill this role rather well.

As for acting as preserver of order and tradition, that may be of less concern to him than to conservative Republican Presidents, but he may keep a modicum of tradition since he is viewed as a moderate person who would probably not seek to bring about overnight transformation of American political institutions. Carter has already put much emphasis on a balanced budget by 1981. It should be remembered that all of these statements about Carter's Presidency are based on early impressions he has given the public during the campaign and as President.[23]

It seems quite plausible that as President, Ronald Reagan would pretty much have taken up where Richard Nixon left off as the two men have many things in common besides their basic conservatism. As chief executive, Reagan's record as governor of California indicated he would have given his top policy priority to retrenchment and reduction of government spending and government services; he would also have been quite

_____

[23]Jimmy Carter, Why Not the Best? (New York: Bantam, 1976); Howard Norton and Bob Slosser, The Miracle of Jimmy Carter (Plainfield, N.J.: Logos International, 1976); David Kacharsky, The Man From Plains: The Mind and Spirit of Jimmy Carter (New York: Harper & Row, 1976); Martin Schram, Running for President: A Journal of the Carter Campaign (New York: Pocket Books, 1976); Jules Witcover, Marathon: The Pursuit of the Presidency, 1972-1976 (New York: Viking Press, 1977); Gerald Pomper et al., The Election of 1976: Reports and Interpretations (New York: David McKay Co., 1977), especially Chapter Six, "The Outlook for the Carter Administration" by Ross K. Baker, pp. 115-146; Kandy Stroud, How Jimmy Won: The Victory Campaign From Plains to the White House (New York: William Morrow & Co., 1977).

outspoken in support of his policy positions and would have taken decisive actions. He might well have been the most conservative President in this century, even more conservative in the context of his times than Richard Nixon or Herbert Hoover.

As chief administrator, Reagan would probably have been concerned with the details of retrenchment and budget cutbacks. Richard Nixon talked about economy and cutbacks in government, but he did not always follow through in his actions; Reagan probably would have. So he would probably have pared back the federal establishment, unlike Carter who may reshuffle it in an effort to achieve greater efficiency. Reagan would also have been likely to be most concerned with administrative panaceas and streamlining of administration and he would have been very hard-hearted toward federal bureaucrats, since he apparently actually believes his anti-government line. This is in sharp contrast to Ford, who was in government long enough to know what can and cannot be done. Reagan might have brought about a major revolt within the bureaucracy; it is difficult to predict how he would have handled this, but he would probably have moved in conservative and even reactionary directions. As foreign policy chief, he would have been a hard-liner judging by his statements on Panama, and he could be expected to follow a tough policy toward the Communist bloc. This could have involved the United States in a war either as a supplier of arms or as an active participant; he might have gotten the United States involved in a guerrilla war in Panama if he really meant what he said about the Panama Canal.

In defense policy, as commander-in-chief, Reagan during the campaign led the public to believe he would be a hard-liner. In point of fact, events might make him less so. In a book about Reagan's record as governor of California, Here's the Rest of Him, a critic found that Reagan proved less conservative than expected. It could have proved to be the same way with his hard-line foreign policy pronouncements.

As a crisis leader, Reagan would probably have been a tough talker but whether he would match his words with actions is problematical. His record as governor indicated that he was a flexible politician, but he took a tough line in condemning student radicals, Angela Davis and other left-wingers, and he perhaps would have matched his actions to his words at least part of the time. Much of the public might have sus-

143

pected his sincerity, since the chief thing that most of the public identifies him with is his actor's image.

As a legislative chief, Reagan would be faced with having to compromise with the opposition or having to lose on some key policy issues. If he had followed the pattern set by Ford, he would have vetoed a great deal of legislation but would have wound up making some compromises. The extent to which this would have been true may always remain uncertain.

As party leader, Reagan would have functioned more like Kennedy or Nixon than like Ford since he is not a life-long Republican, and makes his appeal to Independents and Democrats as well as Republicans. He would not have been a strict party-liner in comparison to Ford, but he would have tried to accommodate the wishes of conservative Republicans since they would have been his "core" constituency.

As leader of public opinion, Reagan would have used his histrionic ability to mobilize public support, making frequent use of television addresses or press conferences to project his views and image. He would probably have been fairly effective in mobilizing conservative opinion, at least as effective as Nixon was.

As leader for social justice and reform, he would probably have talked a good deal about reform especially in the area of putting a limit on taxes and federal spending, but he doubtless would not have made major proposals in the area of social justice, as this was not one of his main concerns. He might have proposed some things such as welfare reform (as did Nixon) and might have tightened up on federal spending in some areas, but that hardly makes him fit the role of leader for social justice.

As preserver of order and tradition, Reagan could have been expected to pay lip service to conservative values but actually might not have gone very far in this direction. Rather he could have been expected to follow the example of Richard Nixon and follow an opportunistic path. In all, he would have fulfilled some roles and seriously neglected others, but no President has ever managed to fulfill all these roles satisfactorily.

Conjectures might be made about other candidates. Congressman Morris Udall might have been an active leader for social justice and reform, for example, or Governor Jerry Brown might have been a fairly effective leader of public opinion. But we will probably not learn how most of these men would have functioned as President because only a few of them are ever likely to be elected.

The Institution of the Presidency

The discussion up to this point has been about the man in the office rather than the office itself. Now I'd like to consider the office of the Presidency, and examine this office as an ongoing institution in American politics. The Presidency has been in existence continually since 1789, and it was conceived as an institution of American government in Philadelphia between May and September of 1787 during the Constitutional Convention debates. But it has been observed that the Presidency represents an elective kingship, and that it combines the powers of a British monarch with those of a British prime minister. The Presidency today has enormous powers, but it did not always have powers of the magnitude it possesses today and especially those it possessed during the heyday of the Imperial Presidency. Let's begin to look at the structure of the office.

One can best describe the structure of the Presidency, what the office includes as an institution, by looking first at the President and working one's way out to the outer edges of the White House establishment. The pattern can be represented by this diagram:

The "core" of the White House establishment, the nerve center of the Executive Branch, consists of the President and his immediate staff. The President normally is served by personal aides. In the Kennedy Administration, these men were known as Special

145

Assistants to the President. In the Nixon Administration, they were known as Counsel to the President or Special Counsel to the President. But whatever the title, they shared the attribute that they were the President's personal staff, not subject to Senate confirmation and subject to serve at the pleasure of the President.[24]

Governors and big-city mayors have similar staff people, and they usually perform functions in which they act in effect as an extension of the executive himself, dealing with details of administration and policy-making he normally does not have the time or inclination to involve himself with. The White House chief of staff (when there is one) may be the co-ordinator of this group, as Donald Rumsfeld and his successor Richard Cheney were. Or the President may have one or two top assistants, as Nixon did with H. R. Haldeman as chief of staff and John Ehrlichman as domestic chief. Or he may operate as Kennedy did with an informal chief of staff such as Ted Sorensen working as first among equals. Hamilton Jordan has performed a similar role for President Carter. Or the President may operate as Eisenhower did with a hierarchical system with one man, Sherman Adams, serving as the Assistant to the President, in the sense that everyone but a select few must clear all presidential business through that key aide.

In effect, then, each President has operated differently but each has had his personal staffs serving him and each has had someone performing the function of a co-ordinator or chief of staff. Whether the chief of staff worked informally like Ted Sorensen or Hamilton Jordan (without that title) or formally like Haldeman or Adams, he performed this co-ordinating function for the President.

Besides the presidential assistants authorized following the Brownlow Commission Report in 1937, who may have served in these various capacities, the President also relies considerably on his press aide. The men who have served as press secretary to the President

_____

[24] Louis W. Koenig, The Chief Executive, Third Edition (New York: Harcourt, Brace, Jovanovich, 1975), see especially Chapter Eight, "Administrative Chief"; pp. 181-212.

have for the most part been capable men, such as
Stephen T. Early for FDR, Charles Ross for Truman,
James C. Hagerty for Eisenhower (generally considered
one of the best), Pierre Salinger for Kennedy, Bill
Moyers, George Reedy and George Christian for LBJ,
Ronald Ziegler for Nixon, Jerald ter Horst and Ron
Nessen for Ford, and Jody Powell for Carter. Under
the Nixon Administration, a Director of Communications
functioned over the press secretary; Herbert Kline and
later other men served in that position but that was
more of a policy position and less of an operational
one on a day-to-day basis.

Nixon also introduced the position of Director
of the Office of Telecommunications Policy (Clay T.
Whitehead). This post was downgraded by Ford; Nixon
who had an obsession with the news media wanted to
have someone monitor the performance of the media,
especially television networks. (Nixon, unlike LBJ,
did not have three finely-tuned color TV sets in the
Oval Office, but he shared LBJ's preoccupation with
the media, and indeed even Kennedy who was less ob-
sessed with such things paid a great deal of attention
to media coverage.) Without listing the names of all
recent aides, this discussion should give a good idea
of what is meant by the President and his immediate
staff, the "inner circle" of the diagram.

If one conceives the White House institutional
structure as consisting of three layers, the second
one would be the White House mini-bureaucracy, consisting of two component parts. The mini-bureaucracy
is the co-ordinating machinery under supervision of
the President and his closest aides which makes sure
that policy recommendations from the various departments (State, Defense and all the rest), get properly
co-ordinated and thoroughly considered before staff
work is given to presidential aides and ultimately to
the President. It is a check on the departmental
bureaucracy in that it is intended to take from the
departmental bureaucrats the negative power to stall
or delay decisions. Sometimes it works this way and
sometimes not; it is sometimes a layer of insulation
which is harmful to the President, as in Watergate.
But sometimes it serves a useful function.

The mini-bureaucracy can be subdivided for convenience sake into two sub-units, the Domestic Council
which was established under Nixon and continued under
Ford (under Carter a domestic advisory panel), and
this is concerned as the name indicates with the

shaping of domestic policy and related matters. The second sub-unit is the National Security Council, which is concerned with the co-ordination of foreign and defense policy. These can both be described in greater detail, but the basic idea is that the function in each case is to provide a co-ordinating unit for policy before final policy recommendations reach the President. Thus NSC and its staff can co-ordinate matters coming up from the Defense and State Departments and sometimes the Treasury, if foreign economic policy is involved, and all can be weighed from the White House perspective. The Domestic Council, first headed by John Ehrlichman, served as the same type of co-ordinating unit for domestic policy recommendations coming from HEW, Interior, Labor, Commerce, Transportation and other departments primarily concerned with domestic policy.

The arrangement is in theory sound, but in practice there are sometimes some difficulties in providing the necessary co-ordination. For example, in some cases the NSC staff's recommendations may cause the Secretary of Defense or the Secretary of State to appeal to the President or his chief of staff for a review of their recommendations. Or the Domestic Council may have made a recommendation, only to have it appealed to the President or his chief of staff by someone like the Secretary of HEW or the Secretary of Commerce. In each case, the co-ordinating machinery usually co-ordinates but not always successfully. And in some cases, such as the review of the Pentagon budget for Fiscal Year 1977, when the case is carried to the President, he may amend the original recommendations or modify them, since he after all has the final policy-making authority.

The outer ring of the White House establishment is the Executive Office of the President, which incorporates not only the previously discussed arms of the Presidency, but also such bodies as the Office of Management and Budget (formerly Bureau of the Budget) and the Council of Economic Advisers. The OMB is required to make independent recommendations to the President on each year's federal budget, based on its analysis of income and expenditures and apart from the policy-oriented recommendations of the departments, NSC staff and domestic policy staff.

The OMB may be overruled, but it has a very important function in that it is supposed to give the President an accurate estimate of what the federal

government can "afford" in a given fiscal year. The
Council of Economic Advisers, established in the Full
Employment Act of 1946, is required to advise the
President on what steps he must take to see that the
domestic economy is properly managed. It is concerned
with recommendations on taxation policy as well as on
the general posture of the federal government toward
national economic policy, as for example in the use of
monetary and fiscal policy and the establishment of
interest rates paid by the federal government on its
bonds and other indebtedness (although the Federal
Reserve Board has power over that).

The Executive Office of the President also includes other statutory bodies such as the Space Council and various other agencies, such as the recently
established White House Office on Science Policy,
which are placed by enactment of Congress or by executive order of the President in the White House structure. These could be detailed at much greater length,
but the examples already mentioned should suffice.[25]

The evolution of the Presidency from Franklin
D. Roosevelt's time will be briefly discussed, because
most of this administrative super-structure has grown
up since FDR's second term. I'll first examine the
evolution of the Presidency as an institution from
FDR's time to Eisenhower's, and then I'll examine the
evolution of the Presidency from Kennedy's time to
Ford's, as these are two distinctly different eras in
the evolution of the office. Finally I'll endeavor
to draw some general conclusions about the institution
of the Presidency from the period from 1933 to the
present.

Until President Franklin Roosevelt's first term,
most Presidents had functioned with a very small personal staff and President Herbert Hoover had only a
handful of secretaries. As long as Hoover's philosophy
of laissez-faire rugged individualism prevailed in the

---

[25]For a detailed discussion, see Louis C. Gaw-
throp, Bureaucratic Behavior in the Executive Branch:
An Analysis of Organizational Change (New York: The
Free Press, 1969), Chapter Three, "Controlling Con-
flict--The Federal Executive Structure," pp. 47-81.
See also Louis C. Gawthrop, Administrative Politics
and Social Change (New York: St. Martin's Press, 1971),
Chapter Two, "The Administrative Structure," pp. 18-40.

White House, a larger staff than this was probably not necessary. But under the pressures first of the Great Depression and later of World War II, this began to change rather rapidly under FDR. During the "First Hundred Days" of the New Deal and the remainder of FDR's first Administration, between 1933 and 1937, there was a growth of White House personnel, but this came about largely through the practice of temporarily "borrowing" staff aides from various executive departments. The Depression crisis, and FDR's response to it, however, soon made it clear that some permanent reorganization of the White House structure was needed, and in 1937 a report was made by a presidentially-appointed group known as the Brownlow Commission, headed by Louis Brownlow, former city manager of Knoxville, Tennessee, and an official of the Tennessee Valley Authority on loan for the purpose of making this report. The Brownlow Commission stated that "the President needs help" and recommended that Congress immediately authorize six assistants to the President. The report suggested that these aides should be men "with a passion for anonymity" (it is indicative of the male chauvinism of the day that it was understood that the President's key aides would be men) and it was expected that this kind of help should bring the President through the economic crises of the 1930's and any future crises.

During World War II, the staff was spread thin and the practice of "borrowing" from agencies and departments was resumed, but eventually the Administration won the approval of Congress for an enlargement of the White House staff. By this time, bright aides such as Tommy (the Cork) Corcoran, Rexford G. Tugwell, John R. Steelman and Clark Clifford, had received considerable notice and the aides were somewhat less anonymous but still nowhere near the celebrities they became in the era of Sorensen and Bundy and Haldeman.[26]

The White House staff grew under President Truman. Truman was unlike President Roosevelt in that he did not try to keep all major decisions among himself and the key White House staff; he tried to have some of the key recommendations for presidential decisions come from Cabinet officers such as Secretary of State

_____

[26]See Patrick Anderson, The President's Men (Garden City, N.Y.: Doubleday & Co., 1968), Chapter Two, "The Roosevelt Staff," pp. 7-85, especially pp. 8-10.

Dean Acheson and Secretary of the Treasury John W. Snyder. Nonetheless, the growing volume of White House business in post-World War II America brought about an increase in the size of the White House staff under Truman.[27] This increase was continued under President Eisenhower, because Eisenhower brought about the bureaucratization of what had been a relatively free-wheeling and loosely operating staff under FDR and Truman. Eisenhower formalized many things and set up a hierarchical structure; this meant further growth of the staff although major matters were always brought to the President's attention through "the" Assistant to the President, former Governor Sherman Adams. The Eisenhower staff system meant more red tape, more bureaucratic structure, and it had draw-backs because of this. But it also meant more thorough preparation and more detailed paperwork, and in this case it had some strengths as well as weaknesses. It worked well for Eisenhower, but it probably would not have worked so well for his Democratic predecessors and successors. At any rate, this brought about continued growth of the White House staff as well as its increase in hierarchical form. This trend did, however, end with the end of the Eisenhower Administration.[28]

With the advent of President John F. Kennedy, who liked informal administrative processes, and worked with a spokes-of-the-wheel approach according to some administrative experts, the White House took a look at the administrative machinery. Kennedy decided that the highly pyramidal structure set up under Eisenhower, which was highly formalized and depended a great deal on paperwork and detail, was too bureaucratized for his taste. He dismantled some of the committees and co-ordinating machinery which Eisenhower had established, and he involved himself in decision-making at a point much farther down the line than Eisenhower ever did.

The story is told of one minor State Department

---

[27]Anderson, op. cit., Chapter Three, "The Truman Staff", pp. 87-132, especially p. 91, for a discussion of President Truman's belief in a strong Cabinet.

[28]Anderson, op. cit., Chapter Four, "The Eisenhower Staff", pp. 133-193. See also Adams, op. cit.

desk officer receiving a call from President Kennedy, answering the phone, and hearing the voice at the other end, "This is President Kennedy." The desk officer, thinking a colleague was playing a prank, was startled and hung up in disbelief. The phone rang again, and indeed it was the President, who this time asked for a report on a minor event in an obscure Middle Eastern country. Thus did Kennedy attempt to keep the bureaucracy on its toes. But his system had its pitfalls, as he discovered at the time of the Bay of Pigs fiasco in 1961, when more thoroughly prepared staff work might have helped to prevent the disaster. Kennedy then restored some of the co-ordinating machinery and ordered a reorganization of the Central Intelligence Agency, but he continued to follow his preference for a more informal modus operandi as much as possible. This could be seen in his handling of the Cuban missile crisis in October 1962. At this time, Kennedy established an Executive Committee of the National Security Council, which came to be referred to as EXCOMM, and he put Robert Kennedy in charge of it, absenting himself from its discussions on several occasions so the discussion would be more free and open. It was this committee which ultimately came up with the recommendation that the naval quarantine be imposed around Cuba, rather than a surgical air strike as originally proposed. The system worked quite well, but Kennedy never convened the entire NSC for the whole series of deliberations. The ad hoc decision-making pattern continued to be followed during the remainder of the Kennedy Administration.[29]

This approach to administration represented the beginning of a new phase in the evolution of the Presidency from Kennedy to Ford, because it was accompanied by the establishment of an inner mini-bureaucracy in the White House by Kennedy in an effort to speed up decision-making. Kennedy, who was frustrated by the slow response of the State Department (using regular bureaucratic procedures) in the drafting of a diplomatic note during the 1961 Berlin crisis, decided

---

[29]Anderson, op. cit., Chapter Five, "The Kennedy Staff," pp. 195-298. See also Kenneth P. O'Donnell and David F. Powers with Joe McCarthy, "Johnny, We Hardly Knew Ye": Memories of John F. Kennedy (Boston: Little, Brown & Co., 1972), especially Chapter Ten, "The White House," pp. 250-283.

that a counterpart structure within the White House
for national security policy, co-ordinating the State
and Defense Departments, was needed. Eventually this
resulted in the establishment of the office of the
President's national security affairs advisor first
headed by McGeorge Bundy, and later under Johnson by
Bundy and Walt W. Rostow, then under Nixon by Henry
Kissinger, under Ford by General Brent Scowcroft, and
under Carter by Zbigniew Brzezinski. But the important thing is that a potential rival to the Secretary
of State was established within the White House.
Bundy and his successors may have been performing the
same kind of function for JFK and his successors as
Harry Hopkins and Averell Harriman performed for FDR
during World War II, but the important point is that
now the position that was informal under FDR was
formalized and given power under Kennedy and his successors. Thus a new layer of bureaucratic structure
had developed within the White House.[30]

Under President Lyndon Johnson, this trend
begun under Kennedy was accelerated under the pressures of decision-making for the war in Vietnam. The
mini-bureaucracy grew in part because of Vietnam and
in part because of the mushrooming domestic programs
of the Great Society, even some of the latter proved
to be short-lived. It is suggested by Joseph Califano, a former Johnson aide and author of The Presidential Nation, who is now HEW secretary, that LBJ
thrived on this kind of hyperthyroid activity.[31] But
it was perhaps ill-suited to Johnson's successor,
Richard Nixon.

Although the trend began even under Roosevelt
and was visible under Kennedy and Johnson, the Imperial Presidency truly reached its modern peak under
Richard Nixon, who seemed to have a regal conception
of the office. Nixon further aided and abetted the
mushrooming growth of the White House staff, and under
his leadership it exceeded 1,000 in number. Nixon

---

[30]See Koenig, op. cit., pp. 196-200 on "Kennedy's Personal Management".

[31]See Califano, The Presidential Nation (New
York: W. W. Norton & Co., 1975), and Anderson, op.cit.,
Chapter Six, "The Johnson Staff", pp. 299-388. Also
see Koenig, op. cit., pp. 200-202 on "Johnson's Consensus Method".

viewed all this as simply a necessary extension of the President's person, and saw it as essential that he have an estate at San Clemente, an estate at Key Biscayne, two Washington offices in the White House and the Executive Office Building, and a retreat at Camp David, Maryland. This does not count another informal retreat in the Bahama Islands provided by presidential friend Robert Abplanalp, the aerosol-spray-can king. At any rate, by the time of Nixon's resignation in August 1974, the trend had clearly gotten out of hand.[32]

Under President Gerald Ford and his chief of staff, Donald Rumsfeld, the former congressman and NATO ambassador, some reforms and adjustments were made including a reduction of the size of the White House staff, transfer of some staff persons back to the executive departments, and a reorganization which made the Ford chief of staff, Mr. Rumsfeld and later Mr. Cheney, a sort of first among equals.[33]

After his election, Jimmy Carter began to reform the White House staff. Ronald Reagan, if elected, would have probably also done this because both men have made it a point to talk about streamlining government to make it more responsive to the people. Reagan also talked about reducing the size of government, and it is hardly credible that he would have entered the White House without reducing the size of the President's White House staff. What other candidates such as Udall and others would do is less clear from their campaign statements.

Some general conclusions can be stated about the growth and development of the Presidency as an institution, and its evolution during the period from 1933 to 1977 (i.e., from FDR to the beginning of Carter's term).

One of the main trends during this period of forty-plus years was the rise and fall of the Imperial Presidency. The rise of the "Imperial Presidency," foreshadowed in the 20th Century under Theodore Roose-

_____

[32]See Koenig, op. cit., pp. 202-208 on "Nixonian Centralism ".

[33]See Koenig, op. cit., pp. 208-210 on "Ford: Centralism Diminished ".

velt and Woodrow Wilson (who said the President should
be "as big a man as he can"), really got underway in
earnest under Franklin Roosevelt, who was jealous of
presidential prerogatives in his effort to cope with
the depression and the war. It did not develop too
much more under Truman and Eisenhower, except that
both men had to deal with the Cold War, and Truman in
setting up a loyalty program for federal employees and
Eisenhower in extending it paved the way for abuses
under the administrations of later Presidents. Both
men wielded a great deal of power overseas, but both
were essentially rooted in the democratic culture and
neither could have been expected to have imperial aims
for themselves. This was also true of John F. Kennedy,
although he developed a kind of imperial style for the
Presidency which may have led to later abuses by his
successors. The pattern for Presidents from FDR
through JFK was that they probably had no imperialistic
designs for themselves but that they unintentionally
expanded the powers of the office so that it could be
abused by their successors.

Lyndon Johnson and Richard Nixon had the most
powers to abuse and in connection with Vietnam policy
and the collection of scandals known as Watergate,
both men abused their powers. Enough has been said
about those matters that it should not be necessary to
elaborate on how they contributed to the Imperial
Presidency. The decline of the Imperial Presidency
may have been foreshadowed by the "abdication" of Lyndon Johnson in 1968, but it was clearly at hand when
Richard Nixon resigned under fire in 1974 just before
a scheduled impeachment vote in the House of Representatives.[34] Under Gerald Ford, a beginning was
being made in scaling down the Imperial Presidency
to a more normal size, but even Ford had temptations.
The manner in which he pardoned Richard Nixon in 1974
indicated that even Ford could act in an imperial
fashion at times, even though he seemed more in the
pattern of earlier Presidents who merely considered
themselves as first citizens of the nation rather than
emperors. Time would tell about the future developments, but the outlook for post-Ford administrations
was that the public would demand a further scaling
down of the Imperial Presidency. Jimmy Carter seemed

---

[34]Arthur M. Schlesinger, Jr., The Imperial
Presidency (Boston: Houghton Mifflin, 1973).

to heed this mandate, and perhaps Gerald Ford would
have if he had been re-elected. What Ronald Reagan
would have done was hard to predict, because ironically
he believed in a smaller government but not necessarily
less power for the President.

President's Relations With the Bureaucracy

In his relationships with the federal bureaucracy, the President acts as head of the Executive
Branch. But it is an Executive Branch whose components, the departments and agencies, frequently have
constituencies of their own which tend to bring
Cabinet officers and the departments which they head
into conflict with the Presidents under whom they
serve. This is a natural state of affairs, but it may
be considered in the light of the traditional role of
the line departments and the Cabinet members.

The Secretary of State is a kind of exception
since he has a set of overseas clients who have
limited influence on American politics, but in most of
the domestic departments there is a ready-made
clientele or constituency that has a direct interest
in what a Cabinet secretary does. Thus the agricultural constituency is interested in what the Secretary
of Agriculture does, the Western interests are concerned with what the Secretary of the Interior does,
the business interests care what the Secretary of Commerce does, and the labor interests notice what the
Secretary of Labor does. There are limits to this,
but the President wants his Cabinet appointees to
follow what is best for his interests, and those interests sometimes come into conflict with the client
groups the Secretaries and their departments serve.

When these conflicts become too great, a Secretary sometimes resigns, as did Secretary of Commerce
Charles Sawyer when President Truman seized the steel
mills in 1952, or when Secretary of the Interior Harold
Ickes resigned when he and Truman had a dispute over
the appointment of an oil man, Edwin Pauley of California, a Truman friend, to a key post during the Truman Administration in 1946. These conflicts can sometimes be contained and sometimes not, but they are
part of the traditional relationship between line Departments and the Cabinet on the one hand, and the
President on the other. This relationship is unlikely
to change, and it is one reason Presidents have seldom
wanted to give most of the Cabinet members a key role

156

in the Administration. Secretaries of State and in recent years Secretaries of Defense have sometimes played key roles, but most Cabinet members in recent years have had less influence with the President than his key staff aides. Most Presidents have wanted to keep it that way, because they have not fully trusted some of their Cabinet members.[35] This is particularly true when they have their own political base. Jimmy Carter, however, has sought to upgrade the Cabinet's status.

One factor which has contributed to clashes between line Departments and agencies and Cabinet members on the one hand, and the President on the other, has been the growth of a counter-bureaucracy within the White House. This has occurred since Roosevelt's time, but especially since Kennedy's time. It has been detailed above in the description of the evolution of the White House mini-bureaucracy. The firing of Secretary of the Interior Wally Hickel is a good example of this; he offended staff aides of President Nixon in 1970 when he released to the press a letter criticizing the President's failure to listen to the views of young people. The "German mafia" in the Nixon White House, Haldeman and Ehrlichman, sent Fred Malek to the Interior Department after Hickel had been notified by Nixon and John Mitchell of his firing, and Malek ordered six of Hickel's key aides to vacate their offices by the end of the day.

Another example was the freezing out of George Romney and Melvin Laird. Romney had been Governor of Michigan and Laird had been a Wisconsin Congressman and a leader of the Republicans in the House. Romney was Secretary of Housing and Urban Development and Laird was Secretary of Defense, but both men were resented by the Nixon staff because they had independent political bases, so they persuaded Nixon to replace both in his second term with men who were not so independent. Nixon appointed Dr. James Schlesinger as Secretary of Defense and he appointed James Lynn, nationally unknown, as Secretary of HUD. Thus the

---

[35]See Richard F. Fenno, Jr., The President's Cabinet (Cambridge, Mass.: Harvard University Press, 1959).

White House staff won another battle with the Cabinet.36

Some revisions in the counter-bureaucracy were made under Nixon and Ford. Nixon wanted to concentrate power even further and he would have made some Cabinet members a part of a super-Cabinet, whose members would also have been White House staff aides and thus beyond the reach of Congress.37 This plan fell through. Ford, however, did try to decentralize some of the power in the mini-bureaucracy and also to cut down its size. Carter has tried to continue this trend.

It may be instructive to examine some of the revisions made in the bureaucracy under recent Presidents, let's say since Johnson's time. Johnson added a number of new agencies to the bureaucracy and these were in charge of Great Society programs, for the most part. Typical of these was the Office of Economic Opportunity, liquidated by Nixon but in Johnson's day in charge of poverty programs. It was typical of the kind of bureaucratic infighting which occurred during the Johnson Administration that many of the Community Action Programs set up by Great Society legislation ran afoul not of federal bureaucrats, but of mayors of major cities and bureaucrats in city governments. This was rather typical of the Johnson era, and its approach to the problems of the time. Another example which could be cited is the Model Cities Program, which encountered similar difficulties.38

When Nixon became President, he began liquidating a number of the Johnson programs such as OEO and Model Cities, but he also introduced a few changes of his own. One of these was the considerable expansion of the White House staff, and another was the expansion of the Law Enforcement Assistance Administration, one of Nixon's pet projects. He also was interested in tidying up some administrative loose ends, and even

---

[36] See Safire, op. cit., Part Two, "It Sure Beats Losing ", pp. 97-117, especially Chapter Three, "No End Runs ", pp. 112-117.

[37] See Gawthrop, Administrative Politics and Social Change (New York: St. Martin's Press, 1971), pp. 34-37.

[38] See Califano, op.cit.

though it was never enacted into law, one effort to do this was the Family Assistance Plan for welfare reform. Nixon also promoted with partial success the idea of revenue sharing, which was passed in its general but not special form under Nixon. Another of his innovations, and a much needed one by all accounts, was the establishment of the Domestic Council within the White House as a kind of co-ordinating instrument for domestic policy similar to the National Security Council for foreign and defense policy. In another sensible move, which led to unnecessary controversy because of the way it was handled, Nixon replaced the old Bureau of the Budget with the Office of Management and Budget. The aim of this OMB structure was to do some longer-range management planning as well as the annual preparation of the executive budget. But the effort of the administration to install the controversial Roy Ash as OMB director and also to begin the policy of heavy impoundment of congressionally appropriated funds at the same time caused the OMB to become clouded with unnecessary controversy. The OMB did stay, however, and may be one of the contributions made by Nixon to a more efficient federal structure.

The Nixon Administration also proposed a reform known to some as the "super-Cabinet". This proposal was for a reorganization of the Executive Branch along functional lines, with four major departments in addition to State, Defense, and Treasury. This proposal was first made in 1971 and proposed reorganizing the remaining seven federal departments into four departments, a Department of Natural Resources (embracing Interior, Agriculture and related departments), a Department of Human Resources (including HEW, for example), a Department of Economic Development (including Commerce, for example, and finally a Department of Community Development (including HUD and Transportation, for example). This proposal made a great deal of sense in functional terms, but it ignored the likelihood that unless a similar functional reform of the congressional committee structure was undertaken, the prospects for its success were quite remote. Finally in 1973, after it became clear that Congress would not approve the super-Cabinet proposal, Nixon implemented it by appointing four of the Cabinet Secretaries as staff aides in charge of each of these policy areas as a first step toward consolidating existing departments into the super-Cabinet departments. But Watergate intervened and after the resignation of John Ehrlichman, who was working on this proposal, it was never brought to a conclusion. So this reform was left for a future administration, but it did appear to have some potential.[39]

Under the Ford Administration, there was not a great deal of experimentation with administrative reforms, but President Ford did favor reducing the size of the bureaucracy and he did order a reduction in the size of the White House staff after he took over the White House. President Ford also slowed down efforts begun by the Nixon Administration to dismantle social reform programs. He continued the OMB but did not propose major shifts in the administrative structure. Rather his emphasis was on reducing the size of the bureaucracy and streamlining existing departments and agencies.[40]

Under the Carter Presidency some administrative reorganization was assured by congressional legislation. Jimmy Carter spoke all during his campaign and after becoming President about reducing the number of federal agencies and modernizing the bureaucratic structure.[41]

Ronald Reagan would have probably cut the size of the bureaucracy even more sharply than Ford had already done; that was the thrust of his campaign statements in this area. Other candidates, such as Representative Morris Udall, spoke more of developing additional programs but making the bureaucracy more responsive while keeping it at the existing level. Actually, a cut in the size of the bureaucracy in a growing nation would mean a net reduction in not only its size but possibly its effectiveness since fewer bureaucrats would be serving more citizens. But according to the Reagan approach, the government was an alien force to be resisted by any means at hand.

The Carter and Reagan campaigns seemed to reflect the popular feeling that government bureaucracy's

---

[39]See Safire, op. cit., and also Richard Nathan, The Administrative Presidency: Nixon and the Plot That Failed (New York: John Wiley & Son, 1975).

[40]See Koenig, op. cit., pp. 208-210.

[41]See Kandy Stroud, How Jimmy Won: The Victory Campaign From Plains to the White House (New York: William Morrow & Co., 1977), "Why Jimmy Won ",pp. 419-434.

growth had gone far enough and that it was time to prune back and consider the possibility of having more problems solved by the private rather than the public sector. If this turned out to be the dominant trend, it would mean a reversal of a 40-year trend begun by Franklin D. Roosevelt.

President's Relations With Congress

The President's relations with Congress, another important aspect of the institutional context of the Presidency, generally follow the lines of the traditional separation of powers. Although this pattern was established in the provisions of the Constitution in 1789, the relationship among the three branches of the federal government has shifted many times and the executive-legislative relationship has also shifted many times.

In the early years, the legislative branch held the dominant position and although Washington and Jefferson could be considered "strong" Presidents, it was not until the administration of Andrew Jackson that a President actually threatened to impose his will on Congress, and Jackson was rebuffed on several occasions and was even "censured" by Congress. The Congress remained dominant until the Civil War, and then during that emergency, Abraham Lincoln again expanded the boundaries of presidential power, but this was a temporary phenomenon, and during most of the remainder of the 19th Century the congressional ascendancy was noteworthy.

Congress almost was successful in bringing about the impeachment of Andrew Johnson in 1868, and some experts believe this might have led to a parliamentary system in the United States.[42] However, Johnson stayed on though weakened, and it was really in the 20th Century that the trend toward executive dominance of Congress began to develop. Theodore Roosevelt and Woodrow Wilson contributed to this trend, but it remained for Franklin D. Roosevelt to push it into its recent

---

[42]See Gene Smith, High Crimes and Misdemeanors: The Impeachment and Trial of Andrew Johnson (New York: William Morrow & Co., 1977).

pattern. Roosevelt's aggrandizement was built on by his successors, but it was really the Johnson action in Vietnam and Nixon's secret actions in the Watergate scandal which brought the executive branch into its recent dominant position in relation to Congress. Now Congress is showing signs of reasserting itself, and it seems likely the pendulum will swing the other way, although not all the way back to the pre-Civil War period.

Although the separation of powers relationship has been discussed in broad and general terms, it may be useful to look a bit more closely (though briefly) at periods of congressional and presidential dominance in American history, and to consider the growth of the concept of the Imperial Presidency and its relationship to World War II, the Cold War, Vietnam and Watergate. I'll also consider the reassertion of congressional powers, how far it can be expected to go, and what some of the presidential responses have been.

Insofar as periods of congressional dominance in history are concerned, the first one which might be examined briefly is that which followed the Jefferson Administration and preceded the Jackson Administration (1809-1829), or a period of about 20 years when Congress was quite powerful, as attested by the fact that during part of this period presidential nominations were largely made through the mechanism of the congressional caucus. Another example of legislative dominance in the relationship with the executive is the manner in which the Congress forced President James Madison to acquiesce in the entry into the War of 1812 against Great Britain. A faction of "war hawks" in Congress had pressed for hostilities, but two years later the British invaded the United States and laid waste part of Washington, including the White House. The period in question also embraced the "Era of Good Feeling", a period of party realignment. The most significant presidential action during this period was probably the Monroe Doctrine of 1823, an action not disapproved by Congress but in fact encouraged by it. This doctrine held that the United States would not stand idly by while outside European powers intervened in the Western Hemisphere. Congress maintained the upper hand during the administration of President John Quincy Adams as well, but it met a real challenge in the Jackson Administration, which included a great deal of controversy.

A second period of congressional dominance followed the Jackson Administration and preceded the Lincoln Administration (1837-1861). During this period, President Van Buren let the leadership which Jackson had asserted fall back into the hands of Congress, and his successor, President William Henry Harrison, was not in office long enough to challenge Congress in 1841 even had he wanted to, which he did not. President Tyler, who succeeded Harrison and served until 1845, attempted to defy Congress but lacked the power to do so and even most of his Cabinet resigned because of policy differences. Nor did President Polk exert excessively strong leadership, although because he had sufficient congressional support he was successful in involving the United States in the Mexican War which made possible the extension of slavery, but also helped to catalyze the forces which led to the Civil War. After Polk, a succession of weak Presidents, Taylor, Fillmore, Pierce and Buchanan, brought the Presidency to one of its low points in history. Pierce was known as a "doughface" or a Northern man of Southern principles, as was Buchanan. The latter resolutely refused to take action at a time when timely action might still have prevented the Civil War. His inaction had the same relationship to Lincoln's crisis actions after March 4, 1861, that Herbert Hoover's inaction had to FDR's crisis actions after March 4, 1933. Of course, the accession of Lincoln temporarily ended this period of congressional ascendancy, but during this time the leading members of Congress, such as Daniel Webster and Henry Clay, easily dominated the Presidents of the era as the slavery issue continued to mount in intensity.

The third period of congressional ascendancy may be said to cover the late 19th Century, and really extends from Andrew Johnson's accession to the Presidency in 1865 to the takeover of the White House by Theodore Roosevelt in 1901 after McKinley's assassination. During this third era, congressional dominance rose to perhaps its highest point in all of American history when the Radical Republicans dominated both houses of Congress, forced a harsh Reconstruction policy on the South and impeached and nearly brought about the conviction of President Andrew Johnson in 1868 for refusing to obey an unconstitutional law, the Tenure of Office Act. The real struggle between Congress and the President lay in the realm of policy,

and on that score Congress won the fight.[43] But Johnson escaped without being convicted, a fate which was
also true of Richard Nixon in 1974 but for different
reasons.

After Andrew Johnson a succession of weak
Presidents gave in to congressional dominance. These
included Ulysses Grant, Rutherford B. Hayes (elected
through a deal with the South, thereby establishing
the modern conservative coalition which has often
dominated Congress), James A. Garfield, Chester A.
Arthur, Grover Cleveland (who served two terms), Benjamin Harrison, and William McKinley. Of these men,
Garfield served less than a year before his assassination and only Grover Cleveland made a concerted use of
the veto power against Congress. Others were Whig-
oriented Presidents who felt that congressional dominance was natural. It was during this period that a
young scholar named Woodrow Wilson, then a graduate
student in political science at Johns Hopkins University, wrote his famous treatise known as Congressional Government, his doctoral dissertation. According to Wilson, the real power lay in the chairmen of
the congressional committees; he saw little potential
for leadership in the Presidency, although he later
changed his mind about this. This book was published
in 1885.[44] After the Roosevelts and Wilson served in
the Presidency, the Congress never had the old aura of
dominance about it, although some Presidents such as
Taft, Harding, Coolidge and Hoover slipped part way
back into the 19th Century pattern. But most 20th Century chief executives, from the Roosevelts through
Nixon, were in the tradition of the strong Presidents.

For the sake of simplifying the discussion of
periods of presidential dominance in American history,
one should speak of Presidents Andrew Jackson, Abraham
Lincoln, Woodrow Wilson, Theodore and Franklin Roosevelt and a group who might be referred to as the "Cold
War Presidents" (beginning with Truman and continuing
through Nixon).

---

[43]Woodrow Wilson, Congressional Government (New
York: Meridian, 1956). Also see Woodrow Wilson, Con-
stitutional Government in the United States (New York:
Columbia University Press, 1908).

[44]Wilson, op. cit.

President Andrew Jackson showed the hallmark of
a strong President when he took strong stands against
the Bank of the United States and the moneyed interests with several important vetoes, and also when he
insisted on the endorsement of federal rights in South
Carolina during the Nullification Crisis of 1832.
Jackson was remembered for his famous toast, "Our
Federal Union, it must be preserved!" The Nullification controversy, which was over the issue of states'
rights and secession, foreshadowed the Civil War, but
Jackson's firm action prevented a break at that time.
Jackson was also an active party leader, as was Jefferson before him, and he popularized the idea of the
President as a "tribune of the people". Jackson in a
sense was the first popularly elected President, since
his predecessors had been elected prior to the broadening of the suffrage. He was the spokesman for the
frontier interests of the nation and made an effort to
furnish aggressive, vigorous leadership.

President Abraham Lincoln was thrust by events
into the role of a strong leader. When Fort Sumter
was attacked in April 1861, Congress was not in session, and Lincoln found it necessary to act rapidly
and with decisiveness in the face of the challenge of
secession and the establishment of the Confederacy.
He did this by calling on the Governors to issue troop
levies and by authorizing the expenditure of federal
funds with the expectation that Congress would approve
the expenditures retroactively, which he did. But he
acted positively and with firmness, and this was true
of Lincoln's leadership all during the Civil War.[45]

Wilson and the two Roosevelts can be considered
as a group of Presidents in the sense that they came
out of the Progressive Era, which was reform oriented.
TR and Wilson were products of the Progressive Era,
and Wilson and FDR were the two wartime Presidents
who extended the boundaries of presidential power
further than it had been extended before under the
pressures of wartime emergencies. Theodore Roosevelt
extended the legislative initiative of the President
and made an unprecedented use of the news conference
to promote the White House point of view. He also

---

[45]Stephen B. Oates, With Malice Toward None:
The Life of Abraham Lincoln (New York: Harper & Row,
1977), pp. 217-280.

165

used the presidential power to promote reform legisla-
tion--up to a point.

Wilson continued the extension of the President's legislative powers, modeling his leadership
after that of the British Prime Minister and making
use in his first term of the "binding caucus" device
in Congress, seldom used in American politics. He
also used the war powers of the President to broaden
the President's emergency powers during World War I,
for example authorizing the takeover of shipyards by
the President when labor disputes interfered with the
production of war goods.[46]

President Franklin D. Roosevelt had to face the
most severe economic crisis in the nation's history,
the Great Depression, and he also had to face the most
extensive war in the nation's history, World War II.
Roosevelt, while respecting the traditions of American
politics, did extend presidential powers further in
the war powers area and in the area of government
intervention in the economy. In both of these actions,
he had the almost solid support of a majority of the
American public and in most of his actions he had
strong support in Congress although this wavered somewhat after 1937. On most wartime issues Congress gave
him solid support.[47]

The Cold War Presidents, from Truman through
Nixon, had to deal with a series of crises, which included the Berlin Airlift, the Korean War and truce,
the Suez crisis, the Hungarian revolt of 1956, the
Berlin crises of 1958 and 1961, the Bay of Pigs invasion of 1961, the Cuban missile crisis of 1962, the
Dominican crisis of 1965, the hostilities in Vietnam
(which went through a whole series of crises), and the
Middle East crises of 1967, 1970 and 1973. This discussion has referred to foreign policy crises, but
many domestic crises, in particular those related to
recessions, civil rights and the crisis of law and
order occurred during these years. These domestic
crises, as well as the foreign policy crises, helped

---

[46]John Morton Blum, Woodrow Wilson and the Politics of Morality (Boston: Houghton Mifflin Co., 1956).

[47]James MacGregor Burns, Roosevelt: The Lion
and the Fox (New York: Harcourt, Brace & Co., 1956).

to bring about the expansion of presidential power through the Nixon years. But by the time of Nixon's resignation August 9, 1974, the use of presidential power had earned a bad name, and it appeared that this period of presidential dominance was perhaps running out. At least Congress was reasserting its traditional powers, many of which had been allowed to atrophy and slip into the hands of the executive branch.

This turn of events was related to the growth of the concept of the Imperial Presidency, a matter tied to the growth of American imperialism and an increasingly unpopular war in Indochina but not entirely related to this sequence of events. The Imperial Presidency can be seen in retrospect from the vantage point of the late 1970's to have had its origins at least in World War II, and the trend was heightened by the Cold War as well as by American involvement in Vietnam. It was perhaps brought to its culmination by the Watergate scandals, which represented a festering of the corruption brought about by the earlier problems in relation to the Imperial Presidency. Public revulsion to the excesses of the Nixon Administration, which included wiretapping and spying and sabotage of the opposition political party, has led to a reassertion of congressional powers. The main question in the 1970's is: How far will this reassertion of congressional powers go? Will Congress, like the President, overreach itself, or will it merely seek a balance with the executive branch? It is too early to say at this point, but the signs are clear in the Budget and Impoundment Control Act of 1974, which mandates a new congressional budgeting procedure; in the internal reform of Congress, which modified the seniority system in 1975, and in the investigations of the Central Intelligence Agency and the Federal Bureau of Investigation by the Church Committee of the Senate in 1975 and 1976, that Congress has not yet ended the trend toward greater assertion of its traditional powers.

A companion question which may also be asked will have to be judged on the basis of the actions of Presidents Gerald Ford and Jimmy Carter and their successors. This question is: How will Presidents respond to reassertion of congressional authority? On the basis of Ford's record, they will respond vigorously but not always effectively. Ford vetoed some 60 congressionally-passed bills, but some of the most important have been passed over his veto. This kind of conflict did not continue between Carter and the

Democratic Congress, but their relationship was still far from smooth. It seems safe to say that Presidents will not give up their power without a fight and in the foreign policy area at least, they may be able to keep a great deal of it. In domestic policy, of course, it is harder for Presidents to resist congressional authority, as the overriding by Congress of Ford's vetoes on measures such as education appropriations seems to bear out. Nonetheless, the veto is still a powerful weapon, even in the hands of a less aggressive President such as Ford. Time alone will answer these questions, but the outlook is for an increase in congressional power and some reduction of presidential power, but not a tremendous loss of presidential power.

In the context of the federal government structure, another important aspect of the Presidency is the President's relationship with the judiciary system, particularly the Supreme Court.

The President's relationship with the judiciary can be defined in several ways. One factor of importance to this relationship is the fact that the President is intimately involved in the appointment process for all federal judges. The President appoints federal judges, who normally serve for life during good behavior. Although the power to make these appointments, subject only to Senate confirmation, is in the hands of the President, in practice the President seeks the recommendations from the state which is affected. For example, if former President Ford wished to make a judicial appointment for one of the federal court districts in Michigan--i.e., a federal district judge--he would normally have sought the recommendations of Senator Robert Griffin, the state's Republican U.S. Senator, and perhaps those of members of the Republican House delegation from Michigan.

Or to take another example, when President Lyndon Johnson made such an appointment from Michigan, he would have consulted the late Senator Philip Hart and the Democratic congressmen from the state. President Carter would have consulted Senator Donald Riegel. When the President's party does not hold a Senate seat, the congressional delegation from that party is usually consulted and if there are no members of either house from the President's party, he may consult with the Governor or some state officials who have standing within the party. At any rate, despite the effort to appoint professional judges of a high caliber for the federal bench, these appointments are essentially patronage appointments. The members of the state bar may be consulted, however, to assure that appointees are technically competent in the law.

The President also has power to appoint justices of the Supreme Court, and this process is somewhat more complicated than the appointment of judges to federal district courts and the circuit courts of appeals, the federal intermediate courts. For one thing, while the congressional delegation from the appointee's home state may be consulted, a President normally takes into account policy considerations in the appointment of a Supreme Court justice, since he recognizes that a nominee, if confirmed, may be sitting on the court for 20 years or more and he may have a considerable impact on the shaping of constitutional law. The President may wish to appoint a member of his own party with legal or judicial experience (all appointees have been lawyers, but not all have been judges prior to nomination), but he will also wish to appoint a person who has views harmonious with those of the President if possible (in a philosophical sense, as to liberalism and conservatism).[48]

Another important consideration is that the President will wish to nominate someone the Senate can be expected to confirm. This was true of John Paul Stevens of Chicago, President Ford's only appointee as a justice, and it was true of Chief Justice Burger, and Associate Justices Powell, Blackmun and Rehnquist, the other Nixon appointees. It was not true of Judge Clement Haynsworth, one of Nixon's choices for the Supreme Court who was rejected because of a conflict of interest. Nor was it true of G. Harrold Carswell, another lower court judge nominated by Nixon, whose nomination was opposed by the deans of many law schools because of the high rate at which his decisions had been overturned by higher courts. Carswell was not considered a judicial craftsman, and Haynsworth's integrity was questioned. On the other hand, the other Nixon appointees were found acceptable and were confirmed by the Senate. The Senate also declined to

---

[48]See Clinton Rossiter, The Supreme Court and the Commander-in-Chief (Ithaca, N.Y.: Cornell University Press, 1951). Also see Danielski, A Supreme Court Justice Is Appointed (New York: Random House, 1964).

confirm Abe Fortas, a Johnson choice, as Chief Justice, and Republicans felt this appointment should be left for Nixon to make after Earl Warren resigned as Chief Justice.

I mentioned briefly the concern of Presidents with the policy aspects of Supreme Court appointments, but no President can be sure how his nominees will vote on the Court, once confirmed. For example, President Theodore Roosevelt expected that Justice Oliver Wendell Holmes, a Roosevelt choice for the Court, would support the Administration's position in the Northern Securities case. Instead, Justice Holmes voted against the Administration position. Eisenhower did not expect Earl Warren to rule as chief justice in the way he did in the Brown school desegregation case, but Warren did so rule.[49] Nor did President Nixon expect that the Court including four of his appointees would rule unanimously against him (8-0) on the issue of whether he should turn over his tapes to the courts in the Watergate case.[50] The life tenure of justices makes it difficult to predict specific decisions, but Presidents have had somewhat better luck in appointing justices whose philosophy was congenial with their own. For example, President Kennedy appointed Secretary of Labor Arthur Goldberg to the Court knowing that he would be sensitive to liberal views, and President Johnson appointed Thurgood Marshall to the Court, knowing that he would be likely to take liberal views, especially on civil rights cases. So there is some policy impact, though it cannot be guaranteed in specific cases.

Some recent examples of the kinds of policy areas where Presidents have been concerned with the Supreme Court's impact on policy have included such issues as school desegregation (we mentioned Eisenhower and the Brown case of 1954), bussing issues (which have been of particular concern to Presidents Nixon and Ford, both of whom have sought the support of opponents of bussing), foreign policy issues

---

[49]See Richard Kluger, Simple Justice (2 Volumes) (New York: Alfred A. Knopf, 1975), pp. 950-952 (Volume II).

[50]See Frank Mankiewicz, U.S. v. Richard M. Nixon: The Final Crisis (New York: Quadrangle, 1975).

(Johnson was concerned that the Court not declare the
Vietnam war unconstitutional, but of course it did
not), and issues such as abortion (the court rules
that abortion was legal under some circumstances ran
contrary to the convictions of President Nixon and
later this ruling was opposed by President Ford.)
These are merely examples of policy areas important to
Presidents in which the Court has handed down opinions,
and which thus involve it in policy-making. Thus it
is incorrect to say, as some in the legal profession
do, that the Supreme Court does not make policy, but
merely applies the Constitution to the law in "slot
machine" fashion. In many controversial areas, where
the President and Congress have sidestepped tough decisions, these decisions get made by default in the
courts. This is essentially what has happened with
various civil rights issues, including school desegregation and bussing and including the recent rulings on
fair employment practices and discriminatory zoning
practices in housing.

        The main reason why the Court sometimes steps
into areas such as these, policy areas not touched by
either the President and Congress (usually by their
own desires), is that the Court is insulated from the
elective process by the independence of its members,
and therefore it is in a better position to make unpopular decisions. This may seem undemocratic, but in
a more profound sense it is a great protection for
civil liberties and civil rights, and indeed for the
more meaningful guarantees of freedom without which
democracy would not be very meaningful for its citizens.

        A final aspect of the analysis of the Presidency
in the context of American political institutions is
the President's relations with the public. While this
has been touched on in earlier chapters in the sense
of the media's impact on that relationship, a brief
discussion is needed here to round out the discussion
of the Presidency in context. The public's perception
of Presidents in modern times depends a great deal on
the issues of the Presidents projected by the mass
media, in contrast to the public's perception of Presidents in earlier historical times, when a smaller population may have had more frequent opportunities to observe Presidents at first hand. Today, the mass media
are very important in this regard and inevitably help
to shape the mass public's perception of the President.
This occurs through all the familiar ways such as
presidential addresses, presidential press conferences

171

and the like, through the newspapers, radio and television appearances by the President. It is not necessary to elaborate on this point, discussed in detail
in an earlier chapter, except to emphasize that the
President is very much caught up in the "image" politics syndrome, and there appears to be no way to prevent this.

One of the interesting things about the impact
of the mass media on a President's popularity with the
public today is that the media have a way of making a
President either a public hero or a public scapegoat.
To use recent examples, for the most part favorable
newspaper coverage gave President Franklin D. Roosevelt a highly favorable image with the public. He was
depicted as a gay crusader against the Depression and
during World War II he was frequently depicted as
Commander-in-Chief of one of the most awesome military
aggregations in the history of man. The public could
hardly avoid making a hero of the President with this
kind of adulation, although he had his opponents as
every President has.

Another example of this kind of favorable image-
building was President John F. Kennedy. Although recent controversies may have tarnished the image somewhat, while Kennedy was living and especially for a
period of a year or two after the assassination, JFK
was certainly a hero to the vast majority of the American public. Again there were detractors, but the hero
image was largely the result of overwhelmingly favorable treatment by the news media, in Kennedy's case
especially television which carried his press conferences and gave him a highly favorable image.

In the case of Lyndon B. Johnson and Richard
Nixon, the mass media gave both men a build-up during
their early days as President and when they were candidates, but eventually the media's attitude changed and
both men received a great deal of criticism, not only
from the media but also from political activists and
the public at large. Whether public opinion followed
the media or the media followed public opinion is a
question of interpretation, but the fact is that both
turned against both Johnson and Nixon and in effect
made scapegoats out of them both. Johnson, who had
been praised as the man who could work miracles in
Congress and the father of the War on Poverty, soon
became the man who got us deeply involved in Indochina
and rather soon the media were covering the activities
of youthful anti-war demonstrators who were chanting

172

such slogans as "Hey! Hey! LBJ! How many kids did you kill today?" According to Doris Kearns, Johnson's biographer and author of Lyndon Johnson and the American Dream, this hurt Johnson deeply. He is supposed to have said that he helped develop programs for education and then the students turned against him over Vietnam.[51]

Richard Nixon did not fare much better, although during the 1968 presidential campaign the media presented him as a man making a comeback and erasing his loser's image, and by limiting his exposure in press conferences and public forums which he did not himself control, Nixon managed to project a contrived image as an attractive alternative--to some people at least--to a Democratic party which had nominated Hubert Humphrey and which tore itself up on the streets of Chicago and in the convention hall at the Stockyards over the issue of Vietnam. For the first year or two of his administration, Nixon as President got a reasonably good media treatment--for Nixon--as he was able to get public opinion (the "great silent majority") to follow his policies on Vietnam. But this began to change during 1971, after the Kent State killings in May 1970 and the invasion of Cambodia and after the release of the Pentagon Papers in the spring of 1971.

Nixon also was developing a bad image because of the recession and the inflation which accompanied it, and he was getting increasingly hostile comments from some of the leading daily newspapers, such as the New York Times and the Washington Post. He had usually had their editorial opposition but until this point they had given him fairly thorough, if sometimes not flattering, coverage. And most of all, Nixon had scored with the public through his direct television addresses. Now he was running into rough weather with the television networks, and newscasters like Walter Cronkite and John Chancellor were not treating him with kid gloves. The networks had been responsible for such broadcasts as the CBS News program, "The Selling of the Pentagon". Although the coverage was very positive during Nixon's 1972 trips to Moscow and Peking, the CBS coverage of Watergate and the Russian wheat deal of 1972 had not been especially favorable to Nixon. Nor had some of the networks' coverage of

---

[51]Kearns, op. cit., pp. 327-334.

the campaign.

But Nixon came through the election fairly well, because again he ran a low-key campaign and kept out of sight as much as possible with the result that the network coverage, and that of the principal dailies, concentrated on George McGovern and his mistakes--the 1000 per cent remark about Senator Eagleton, the $1,000 welfare reform "demogrant" plan that was never satisfactorily explained, and various conflicts within the McGovern campaign organization. Thus while Nixon was not getting the most favorable coverage, he was faring much better than McGovern. The Eagleton fiasco and the unfavorable coverage of it in all the media, including the networks, doubtless played a part in Nixon's turning a landslide over McGovern into a rout in November 1972. But after the election and especially after the Vietnam truce in January 1973, the positive coverage of Nixon hit its peak and from then on it was Watergate which got most of the attention and Nixon's image went into a permanent decline.

It ought to be emphasized that while the media played a major part in Nixon's decline from the time of the Haldeman-Ehrlichman resignations early in 1973, through the investigations of the Ervin Committee and the Rodino Committee in 1973 and 1974 respectively, the President himself contributed a great deal to this decline because of his secretiveness and because certain actions of his, such as his refusal to turn over the Watergate tapes to Judge Sirica and the special prosecutor and his firing of Special Prosecutor Archibald Cox in the Saturday Night Massacre, fed public suspicions.

So in this case the media merely mirrored a growing corruption that was already present. The disclosure that Vice President Agnew had been taking kickbacks from contractors and his resignation in October 1973 along with a plea of <u>nolo</u> <u>contendere</u> to federal charges in Baltimore did not enhance Nixon's image by that time. It was Nixon who had declined to remove Agnew from the ticket, because he didn't want to break up a "winning combination". How soon the winning combination was to become a losing combination! Nixon ultimately of course appointed Gerald Ford as Vice President, and finally resigned under fire in August 1974, only to be pardoned by Ford a month after his resignation. The full details of Nixon's involvement in the Watergate scandal have never been brought out in court, because of the Ford pardon. But it

clearly illustrates how Nixon had become a scapegoat
for both the public and the mass media.52

All this raises one key question which is difficult to answer: How can the American public develop
the ability to appraise its Presidents realistically?
And can it do so? It is doubtful that this can be
done very well, but the public at least could make an
attempt to find out more about candidates for the
Presidency while they are running and make an attempt
to vote on them more intelligently. It might also
consider that not participating in presidential elections does not help keep bad men out of office, but
probably helps to bring about such a result. In order
to do this, the public needs the help of the news media
and their editors, reporters and correspondents. Full
information may not prevent the public from electing
another President like Nixon who would be a participant in obstruction of justice and abuse of power, but
it might help. And it is certainly worth trying.
Otherwise the public would be forced to admit that it
is impossible to elect a President who has integrity,
and it is doubtful that the nation has sunk to such a
low estate in only 200 years. Certainly many Americans have more faith in their country and in themselves
than to accept this cynical viewpoint.

Summary of the Presidency as an Institution

In this chapter we have tried to look at the
Presidency as an institution by examining the man in
the office and the office itself, and we have tried to
discern why the interaction between the man and the
office as well as the interaction of both with the
public and with other institutions of government follows the pattern it takes.

The impact of the man on the office has been
considerable from Washington's time to Carter's but it
has varied among different administrations. The
President's influence has been at a low ebb during
administrations like those of Buchanan and Harding,

52See Elizabeth Drew, Washington Journal: The
Events of 1973-1974 (New York: Vintage Books, 1976).
Also see Jonathan Schell, The Time of Illusion: An
Historical and Reflective Account of the Nixon Era
(New York: Vintage Books, 1976).

but it has been at a peak during administrations like those of Lincoln and FDR. So a great deal does depend on the caliber of the incumbent and he can have a strong even if not permanent impact on the office.

The office also has a great impact on the man in that it conditions his thinking about his performance in office and his place in history. All Presidents have been interested in both of these things, especially the latter. Also the office has been passed along to each incumbent with developing traditions and customs which have conditioned them to function in a certain way as President. This can be expected to continue into the indefinite future.

In view of recent problems with the Presidency, the outlook for the future is uncertain in terms of the man and the office. Much will depend on the public's ability to discerningly choose capable and strong incumbents for the Presidency in the years immediately ahead and much will depend on these Presidents' ability to serve with distinction and integrity. If the public and the Presidents both live up to the potential of the office, it can once again be restored to a place of dignity and respect among the American people. If either the public or its Presidents fail to do so, they may jeopardize an institution which over the years has contributed a great deal to the development and growth of American democracy. We can only hope that the Presidency will be restored in the decades ahead to a place of high honor and trust and that the shame of Watergate and the bitterness of Vietnam will eventually be forgotten as the crimes and the mistakes of the past decade slowly fade into history.

CHAPTER FOUR

BASICS OF THE INSTITUTIONAL STRUCTURE

OF THE MASS MEDIA

. . . "I know of no photographer or newsman
who covered that (1960) campaign, start to
finish", Laura Bergquist of Look magazine later
said, "who didn't come away thinking he knew
John F. Kennedy--they were no longer the press
corps, but his friends. In turn, the President
knew them and all their idiosyncracies." . . .
(R)epresentatives of the New York Times, the
Washington Post, the Chicago Daily News, Newsweek, Time, and other large-circulation and
important periodicals generally found it far
easier to see Kennedy than someone representing a small town magazine or newspaper. . . .

> --Lewis J. Paper, "The Presidential Images
> of John F. Kennedy" in The Promise and
> the Performance: The Leadership of John
> F. Kennedy (New York: Crown Publishers,
> Inc., 1975), p. 322

. . . Fred Graham, a CBS television reporter, called the White House Press Office
for comment on a story scheduled for that
evening's news. Graham had information that
in two of the tapes the President had made dis-
paraging remarks about Jews and had called
Judge Sirica a "wop". When he was asked by
Ziegler, Buzhardt insisted to the press secretary that he had heard no such thing on the
tapes. Ziegler tried but couldn't talk Graham
out of the story, so he moved to kill it. He
told two of his secretaries to get hold of CBS
correspondent Dan Rather. Failing that, they
were to reach Walter Cronkite or the CBS Washington Bureau chief or the producer of the CBS
Evening News, or the president of CBS, Arthur
Taylor. None could be reached. Ziegler blamed
the secretaries and started shouting at them
when the story went on the air. "Ron, we can

only place the calls", responded Anne Grier.
"If you think you can do any better, then be
my guest."

> --Bob Woodward and Carl Bernstein, in The
> Final Days (New York: Simon & Schuster,
> 1976), p. 170

* * * *

Institutional Structure of American Mass Media

Having examined the basic characteristics of
the institutional structure of the Presidency, I'll
analyze now the basic characteristics of the institutional structure of the American mass media. We will
begin this analysis by determining the distinction
between the various media in terms of their roles and
their functions in the political communications process.[1]

First, I'll focus on newspapers, which together
with magazines constitute the major print media today.
I'll stress contemporary newspapers, which have
slightly different characteristics than newspapers
looked at in a historical perspective. The most important daily newspapers are the metropolitan dailies.
These consist of newspapers in two categories, metropolitan dailies with national circulation like the New
York Times and metropolitan dailies circulated primarily in their immediate area, such as the Houston
Chronicle. Out of a dozen nationally known metropolitan dailies, three or four are key newspapers, widely
quoted by wire services and television networks. Here
I'm concerned with the basic characteristics of these
newspapers: readership, editorial policies, influence,
and how they cover the White House news.

The readership of the metropolitan dailies
normally is concentrated in a radius of several hundred miles from their publication site. But in cases
like that of the New York Times, the newspaper is read
nationwide even though circulation is concentrated in
the New York metropolitan area. Usually the readership varies with the nature of the newspaper. The New

---

[1]Warren Breed, "Social Control in the Newsroom:
A Functional Analysis", Social Forces, May 1955, pp.
326-335.

York _Times_, a newspaper of record which prints "All the News That's Fit to Print", has a wide readership among intellectuals and community leaders. It is also influential in government and journalistic circles as it is a bellwether of the national press. By comparison, the New York _Daily News_, a tabloid which competes with the _Times_ as a morning daily, has a wide readership among middle class, blue collar and ethnic citizens of the New York metropolitan area.[2]

As for editorial policies, the New York _Times_ has a progressive, liberal policy on domestic and foreign policy issues; it's considered a spokesman for Liberal Establishment viewpoints, to the extent that they exist. Again contrasting the _Times_ with the _Daily News_, the latter takes a more conservative editorial viewpoint. The _Times_ is independent, but since Kennedy's time has frequently endorsed Democratic presidential candidates. It endorsed Kennedy in 1960, Johnson in 1964, Humphrey in 1968, McGovern in 1972, and Carter in 1976. It did, however, endorse Eisenhower in 1952 and 1956 although it had many favorable things to say about Stevenson. The _News_, on the other hand, endorsed Republican candidates (Nixon in 1968 and 1972, also in 1960 against Kennedy). On issues, too, the _Times_ has usually taken a liberal stand and the _News_ a conservative one, although this has not been automatic.

The _Times_ definitely is one of the most influential newspapers in the nation, largely because both governmental and journalistic elites look to it for information and viewpoints on current issues. It has frequently published the first story on major exposes, such as Seymour Hersh's news break on the Mylai incident in South Vietnam, and the first disclosure by Neil Sheehan on the Pentagon Papers in 1971. It did, however, lose out to the Washington _Post_ in the reporting of the early phases of the Watergate scandal by Woodward and Bernstein. Newspapers like the _Times_ and

---

[2]See Gay Talese, _The Kingdom and the Power_ (New York: Bantam Books, 1970) for a study of the influence of key _Times_ executives. For a conservative study of perceived bias in the _Times_, see Herman H. Dinsmore, _All the News That Fits_ (New Rochelle, N.Y.: Arlington House, 1969).

<u>Post</u> still tend more frequently to "break" major stor-
ies than their television network competitors. It is
partly because of this that the newspapers retain much
influence, although they may be declining somewhat in
recent years.

In covering news about the White House, <u>Times</u>
reporters and editors strive for objectivity, but sometimes show a liberal bent. Editors and reporters for
the Washington <u>Star</u>, a more conservative daily, tend
to interpret the news conservatively. Despite much
criticism, newspaper reporting has remained reasonably
objective in the sense that every effort is made to
give all sides of a controversy. One side may come
out better in the headlines or in the lead of the
story, but an effort is made to provide balance. When
President Ford and Ronald Reagan were slugging it out
in the primaries for the 1976 Republican presidential
nomination, it could be predicted that the slightly
more moderate Ford would get better treatment from the
<u>Times</u> than from the Washington <u>Star</u>; the more con-
servative Reagan would normally expect better coverage
from the <u>Star</u> than the <u>Times</u>. This is not true in all
cases, however, so I refer to a trend or tendency
rather than a general rule. But there is a wide opportunity for the coverage of conservative political
figures in friendly media and for the expression of
conservative viewpoints in editorials and columns, contrary to the impression given by former Vice President
Agnew in his 1973 attacks on the news media. For
example, after the 1972 election, a lengthy interview
with President Nixon was prominently displayed in the
Washington <u>Star</u>; it and other papers made friendly
comments about the Administration, as did such conservative columnists as William Buckley and James Kil-
patrick. So it should not be suggested that the
liberal media are "out to get" conservative politicians, or vice versa. It may be true that they treat
their friends in a more friendly way, but that is true
regardless of ideology and it probably comes much
closer to bringing a balance overall than critics of
the media would lead one to believe or expect.[3]

Characteristics of daily newspapers in small

---

[3]Robert Cirino, <u>Power to Persuade</u>: <u>Mass Media
and the News</u> (Toronto: Bantam Pathfinder Editions,
1974).

cities are quite different from those of metropolitan dailies just discussed. For one thing, small city dailies usually circulate in a limited area and little attention is paid to them outside their own circulation zone. So their readership is more limited, and they are much less likely to gain the attention of national elites in government and journalism than metropolitan dailies.

As for editorial policies, some small city dailies have no overt editorial policies because they never publish editorials. Others do but their editorial policies are most likely to be conservative and they are likely to engage in "Afghanistanism", or commenting on faraway topics while ignoring burning issues at home to avoid offending anyone, especially big advertisers. Lest one be too unfair in this assessment, I note that an occasional small city daily has developed a good record of crusading news coverage, and it has sometimes editorialized for community betterment on many issues--improvement of schools and parks, honesty in city government and the like. Nonetheless, comparing small city dailies to metropolitan dailies is like comparing the bush leagues to the major leagues in baseball.

Geographically, small city dailies have limited influence, but sometimes they can be quite influential (or their editors can) with local elites. They may choose to use their influence broadly, or they may choose not to, but usually there is a potential for influence on community political and social matters, if the papers choose to use it. Most of the time they so choose, it is for community betterment, but sometimes the influence is used to undergird the status quo. Some would consider this a perversion of journalistic influence.

Except for the occasional invitation for a publisher to visit the White House for an off-the-record conversation with the President (often done in election years) or a rare presidential visit to the small city (again usually during a campaign), the small city daily editor has little reason to do more than use the wire service stories and wirephoto pictures of the President and his White House activities.

Characteristics of weekly newspapers are perhaps more different from those of metropolitan dailies than from those of small city dailies. Weekly newspapers,

like small city dailies, usually circulate in a small
area and normally receive little attention from the
national elites or the national news media. There may
be a rare exception such as when a small weekly newspaper has its office destroyed by an arsonist in
retaliation for news stories or editorials are not
well received, but in most instances these weeklies go
largely ignored by the great world outside. They are
also more likely to publish small personal items from
country correspondents, and they are in a sense a
throwback to a more leisurely era in American journalism, a remnant of the kind of publications that were
often found in Benjamin Franklin's day in the colonies.

Weeklies often have no overt editorial policies.
They may publish "canned" editorials. Sometimes they
use locally written editorials, backing a community
betterment project, or perhaps a tribute to a de-
ceased community leader.[4]

Like small city dailies, weeklies usually have
limited geographical influence, but there may be an
occasional exception for a certain type of newspaper.
For example, Harry Golden for years published a small
weekly called the Carolina Israelite, and this was
widely quoted nationally. Another example of a well
known weekly newspaper was William Allen White's
Emporia Gazette, published in Emporia, Kansas, and
noted for various things including a widely reprinted
editorial, "What's the Matter With Kansas?"

Small weeklies' coverage of White House events
is almost non-existent. If the President visits the
area in which the weekly is published, this is almost
sure to get coverage, but the newspaper's focus is so
locally oriented that normally the White House coverage is nil.

As for the role of these three types of newspapers in the communications system within the
national political system, one may make a brief analysis of each of the three types.

---

[4]The reference to "canned" editorials should be
explained. These may be furnished by a syndicate
which prepares such material. These are also used
occasionally by daily newspapers as well, but if weeklies publish editorials it is quite likely that they
will be this type.

The metropolitan dailies play a key role in the communications system because they often originate the coverage of important national stories. In particular, they may be responsible for "first break" on important White House-related stories such as Watergate, the Pentagon Papers or even a relatively minor story, such as the arrest of Walter Jenkins, a Johnson White House aide, on homosexual charges. Thus metropolitan dailies are pace-setters for the national journalistic community. Frequently, but not always, they give sufficient exposure to key stories that the television networks are unable to ignore them. When this happens a situation may occur such as the Washington *Post* coverage of Watergate or the Segretti dirty-tricks squad, when CBS and the other networks were obliged to carry stories dealing with this matter. Dan Rather noted after the Watergate scandals had subsided that the television networks did not have a particularly good record at being first on such stories.[5] Occasionally, as with the disclosure of profiteering on the Soviet wheat deal in 1972, CBS would give detailed coverage, but in many cases networks ignored important stories until the metropolitan dailies gave them extensive coverage. Breaking major stories is probably the key role of metropolitan dailies in the national communications system, although their editorial comments and coverage of their chief correspondents sets the pace for other journalists.

Small city dailies' role is primarily to extend the coverage given by metropolitan dailies into deeper coverage of regional or local political affairs. They are much less likely to use White House-related stories unless there is a prominent local angle involved.

Much the same can be said of weekly newspapers and their role in the communications system as I've just said about small city dailies. The weeklies may be more provincial and parochial in their coverage, but there may be occasional exceptions to this tendency. The function of the weeklies is mainly to provide home-town coverage to events normally largely ignored by

---

[5]See Dan Rather and Mickey Hershowitz, *The Camera Never Blinks: Adventures of a TV Journalist* (New York: William Morrow & Co., 1977).

big city dailies and even small city dailies in the same geographical area. Thus, they continue to flourish because they fill a gap in the existing structure of the news media.

Political News in Metropolitan Dailies

Some observations can be made about political news in metropolitan dailies. The _Times_ is read daily at the White House and it is also read daily by members of the Washington press corps, who help set the agenda of national discussion of issues, along with the President and other public officials. I've mentioned major stories first broken by the _Times_. In addition to the Pentagon Papers case and Mylai massacre story, the _Times_ has often been in the forefront of expository and investigative journalism. The Sunday _Times_ also carries a widely read Magazine in which nationally prominent politicians and authors (primarily its own journalists) write about important issues of the day; the Sunday _Times_ also has an influential Book Review section. _Times_ editorials, while perhaps less influential than in earlier times, are still widely quoted; when for example the _Times_ urged the impeachment or resignation of Richard Nixon in 1974, this was a watershed in the whole Watergate affair. The _Times_ has a number of well-known correspondents and columnists, such as James (Scotty) Reston, Tom Wicker, Russell Baker, Seymour Hersh and William Safire. Many of these men are well-known authors in their own right. Some like Harrison Salisbury, a retired _Times_ man, developed their reputation as _Times_ correspondents overseas (Salisbury was in Moscow for a number of years). The _Times_ would have to be No. 1 on anyone's list of the most influential American metropolitan dailies.[6]

Close behind the _Times_ on most persons' lists of influential metropolitan dailies is the Washington _Post_, a newspaper with a reputation for aggressive investigative reporting even before the Watergate scandals thrust it solidly into the national limelight through the reporting of Woodward and Bernstein. The

---

[6]See Ruth Adler, _A Day in the Life of the New York Times_ (Philadelphia: Lippincott, 1971).

<u>Post</u> has been involved in many other expose stories,
besides Watergate. These include the spring 1976 disclosures about the Wayne Hays sex scandal, the 1974
stories about Wilbur Mills, chairperson of the House
Ways and Means Committee, and the 1977 Korean lobby
scandal expose. In effect these stories marked the
beginning of the end of important careers. This was
true too of former OMB director Bert Lance.

A popular feature of the Washington <u>Post</u> is its
Style section, which carries behind-the-scenes articles
written by such well-known journalists as Maxine Che-
shire and Sally Quinn. The <u>Post</u> is reported to be one
metropolitan daily whose women's features are as
widely read by men as by women; this is because so
much of Washington's official business appears to be
affected by what transpires on the Georgetown cocktail
party circuit. The <u>Post</u> also has its Magazine section,
formerly <u>Potomac</u>, which carries articles giving background on national newsmakers. In addition its Outlook section carries articles by nationally known
politicians and authors on current issues. The two
key people (in addition to the writers themselves) on
the <u>Post</u>, are executive editor Ben Bradlee, a former
intimate of President Kennedy and a major character in
the movie, <u>All</u> <u>the</u> <u>President's</u> <u>Men</u> (an adaptation of
the "Woodstein" book), and Katharine Graham, the pub-
lisher of the <u>Post</u> and a remarkable woman in her own
right. It was Kay Graham and Ben Bradlee as well as
the Woodstein combination who played a considerable
role in the Watergate exposures by sticking to their
guns when everyone else was discounting the story.
They have largely made the <u>Post</u> what it is today--one
of the leading newspapers in the country.

The <u>Christian</u> <u>Science</u> <u>Monitor</u> is strong on background coverage of the news, although it does not go
in so heavily for investigative reporting as the <u>Times</u>
and the <u>Post</u>. It is more conservative than either in
editorial policy, but is independent. It excels in
foreign correspondence and it has carried many outstanding background stories and series by such gifted
journalists as Godfrey Sperling and Richard Strout
(who also writes a column of comment known as "the TRB
column" in the <u>New</u> <u>Republic</u>). The <u>Monitor</u> published
regional editions, an innovation which has added to
its stature as a national publication. It also has
developed a number of serious and important series of
background stories on major issues. It is sober in
its approach and deemphasizes headlines and superfi-

cial events in order to emphasize the backgrounding of news in depth, which it does well.

The Chicago Tribune was long considered the voice of Heartland Republican conservatism. It was the political organ of the late Colonel Robert McCormick; it was known not only for its political conservatism but also for some eccentric causes espoused by Colonel McCormick, including "simplified spelling". During the 1940 Presidential election, the Tribune regularly carried a front page box which referred to the Roosevelt-Willkie contest by saying "Only 10 Days Left to Save the Republic", and each day the number was reduced as the election grew closer. Since Colonel McCormick's death, the Tribune has become more moderate, but it still represents a voice in conservatism in the Midwest and is a nationally known paper. When in the summer of 1974, the Tribune called for Nixon's resignation, it became obvious that the President was losing much of his conservative support. The Tribune has been noted for its staff of Washington and foreign correspondents and along with the New York Daily News, has maintained a syndicate which distributes the columns and stories of these correspondents.

The Boston Globe, once not so greatly respected, has become in recent years a widely noted voice of Eastern Establishment liberalism. It was one of the newspapers which was involved in recent investigative reporting disclosures, such as gambling scandals in Massachusetts, the coverage of Watergate spying activities related to the Chappaquiddick incident, and "leaked" stories such as the Pentagon Papers disclosures. The Globe supported George McGovern in the 1972 presidential election, and it is interesting that Massachusetts and the District of Columbia were the only parts of the nation whose electoral votes he won. The Globe is today considered as perhaps near the quality of the New York Times and the Washington Post in terms of its investigative reporting and liberal editorial policies. It was bitterly attacked by Spiro Agnew, Patrick Buchanan and other media critics who resent newspapers with anti-Nixon and anti-Big Business views.

The Atlanta Constitution, for many years edited by Ralph McGill and now edited by Hal Gulliver, and its sister newspaper, the Atlanta Journal, are widely respected as regional leaders in journalism in the Southeast. The Constitution and the Journal have both

186

had enlightened editorial policies and have generally supported what are considered in Dixie as liberal causes. The Atlanta metropolitan area is one of the more progressive areas in the modern South; this fact is mirrored in the editorial policies of both news-papers. The Atlanta dailies are part of the Cox Enter-prises.

The Miami *Herald* is known for its crusading in-vestigative reporting; it is also widely known not only in Florida but also in the Deep South. It has one of the best metropolitan coverage staffs of any of the nation's largest dailies and is capable of giving top-notch coverage to any major event. During recent political conventions in Miami Beach in 1968 and 1972, it gave outstanding coverage to the convention activi-ties. Still a Knight newspaper, it must be considered one of the nation's leading dailies today.

The Cleveland *Plain Dealer* dominates the news-paper field in Ohio, although the Cleveland *Press* has also been important in this major city. The *Plain Dealer* has followed an aggressive policy in its news coverage and quite often comes out with first-break stories which have led to major disclosures. It fol-lows a somewhat more conservative editorial line than other newspapers discussed in this chapter, with the exception of the Chicago *Tribune.* It follows an inde-pendent editorial policy somewhat like its neighbor in Ohio, the Toledo *Blade*. In 1972, the *Blade* endorsed McGovern for President but did it in such a lukewarm fashion that the endorsement was almost meaningless. It supported Carter in the 1976 election. The *Plain Dealer* supported Nixon in 1972 as did the Cincinnati *Enquirer*. Both backed Ford in 1976. The *Enquirer* has been known as a conservative newspaper, but like the Chicago *Tribune*, its conservatism is probably not so rock-ribbed today as in the past. The *Enquirer* has done a good deal of excellent local reporting, includ-ing exposes about local politicians involved in wrong-doing. Its main competitor, the *Times-Star*, has been the journalistic outlet of the Taft interests in Cin-cinnati and it is also basically conservative. The slogan, "Solid Cincinnati Reads the *Enquirer*", was used for many years.

A leading voice of liberalism in the Border South is the Louisville *Courier-Journal*. While the *Courier-Journal* has limited political influence in Ken-tucky and southern Indiana, its circulation area, insofar as local voters are concerned, it is known for its crusading investigative reporting. About 1969 one of its reporters, named Branzburg, figured in a well-known contempt case for refusing to disclose the source of a marijuana story; in the 1930's, the arrest of another Courier-Journal reporter in connection with a similar contempt episode brought about the enactment of legislation by the Kentucky General Assembly, known as the Armentrout Law (a "shield law"). The courts found that the Armentrout law did not protect Branzburg, however, because a criminal prosecution was involved. The Courier-Journal has a long tradition in Democratic politics, as its various editors and publishers have included such noted persons as "Marse Henry" Watterson, a supporter of Grover Cleveland and Woodrow Wilson; Judge Robert Worth Bingham, appointed by Franklin Roosevelt as Ambassador to the Court of St. James prior to Joseph P. Kennedy, and Barry Bingham Sr., a Stevenson-oriented liberal. Barry Bingham Jr. is currently the editor.

Another Border South newspaper with a long liberal tradition is the St. Louis Post-Dispatch, which has a long history of fighting against corruption and secrecy. It helped to disclose scandals in the Administration of Governor Dwight Green of Illinois which led to indictment and conviction of many in his administration and also some newspaper editors who were accepting "kickbacks" to publish stories favorable to the Green Administration. It also disclosed the scandal about Secretary of State Paul Powell of Illinois, who died with several shoeboxes full of cash in his hotel room which were never satisfactorily explained to the authorities. The Post-Dispatch also contributed to breaking a story (Jack Anderson published it) about the disclosures about Senator Thomas Eagleton's health in 1972. This led ultimately to his withdrawal from the Democratic ticket because of controversy about his history of problems with mental health. The Post-Dispatch has been for many years a leading newspaper in the nation, noted for the distinguished crime reporting of Theodore Link, for the distinguished cartoons of Fitzpatrick, and for the tradition of Joseph Pulitzer, the founder of the Post-Dispatch, as well as for the columns of Marquis Childs and other well-known contributors.

The Kansas City Star is another well-known regional newspaper with a national reputation. It was a spokesman for a conservative viewpoint and for many

188

years was known among journalists for its conservative
front-page makeup. The Star long ago commenced using
pictures on its front page and introduced other innovations, but it remains a leading voice in the Midwest. It may be somewhat less famous for crusading
than the Post-Dispatch, its neighbor in St. Louis, but
it was known for its crusades to expose the Pendergast
machine during the early and middle years of the 20th
Century. In fact, it was the Star's reporting which
led in part to the conviction of old Boss Tom Pendergast.

Another set of newspapers well-known in the Midwest consists of the Minneapolis Star-Journal and Tribune, both of which have followed the traditions of
progressivism in Minnesota, where the Democratic-
Farmer-Labor Party was founded by Hubert H. Humphrey
and his allies back in the 1940's. The Star-Journal
and Tribune had close ties with the old Look magazine,
now defunct, and the Cowles Publications had a well-
known syndicate. Some of those who used to write for
it included Joseph and Stewart Alsop, and Clark Mollenhoff, who for a time worked in the Nixon White
House but ended up asking one of the more embarrassing
questions at the Disney World press conference in 1973
when Nixon stated, "I am not a crook."

Also of considerable importance in the nation
is the Des Moines Register and Tribune, with its own
syndicate and a reputation for Farm Belt reporting.

The Denver Post, perhaps best noted today for
the political cartoons of Oliphant, was long known for
outstanding investigative reporting and the unearthing
of information about scandals. This widely read newspaper in the Rocky Mountain West has a proud history
in American politics; in 1952 it was one of the leading daily newspapers which gave impetus to the Eisenhower movement in the Republican party. It was a
voice for reform in the Republican party and urged
cleaning up governmental corruption early in the 20th
Century. It has maintained its reputation.

The Los Angeles Times, owned by the Chandler
family (one of the nation's best known publishing
families, along with the Grahams and Sulzbergers, the
Tafts and the Binghams), was for many years a very
conservative newspaper, but today it is known as being
considerably more liberal, and like the Chicago
Tribune it has shown noticeable improvement in the

189

caliber of its coverage. It is today joined with the
Washington <u>Post</u> in the Times-Post Syndicate, which distributes many widely read columns in the United States
and around the world.

Other Newspapers and Magazines

Besides these metropolitan dailies, a few
papers have come into prominence which must be classified under a new category--that of the suburban newspaper. Only one of these will be mentioned here, but
it is well-known in the New York City metropolitan
area. That is the Long Island suburban daily, <u>Newsday</u>,
for a time enriched by the talents of Bill Moyers who
served as its publisher for several years after leaving the LBJ White House in the 1960's. <u>Newsday</u> has
passed on to other hands and Moyers is now with CBS
after serving as a commentator for PBS, but the paper
remains one which has a reputation for aggressive investigative reporting. It was reported on good
authority that after stories published in <u>Newsday</u>
about Bebe Rebozo, former President Richard Nixon's
close friend, the reporters involved had their tax returns investigated and <u>Newsday</u>'s request to send a reporter to China with Nixon during the 1972 summit trip
was turned down.[7] The suburban newspaper with a growing circulation is a fairly common phenomenon today
and <u>Newsday</u> is doubtless one of the best known, if not
the best known of this type.

Small city dailies are not so widely known as
the major dailies mentioned above, or even as widely
known as <u>Newsday</u>, but even though it is hard to mention well known examples, it is possible to describe
the nature of small city dailies. They usually depend
mostly or entirely on either the Associated Press or
United Press International wire services for their
national and international news. But they also tend
to emphasize local news coverage, as something the
larger metropolitan newspapers do not cover in as
great depth. Thus, the enactment of an ordinance on
zoning by a small city council may get a top news
play, while the Wayne Hays sex scandal, or even the
primary campaign travels of Ford, Reagan and Carter,

---

[7]See William Safire, <u>Before the Fall</u> (New York:
Belmont Tower Books, 1975).

or Carter's Panama Canal Treaty signing, may get less news play.

The small town weekly may be a disappearing breed of newspaper, but no one has told the many editors who spend much time covering the local news. Small town weeklies are more likely to carry country correspondence and personals columns about local residents; their coverage is strongly localized. They usually tend to ignore largely the news of the world outside in order to give solid coverage of the local community. They can do this because most subscribers also read a metropolitan daily and doubtless frequently watch the network television news and perhaps local news on the nearest TV station. The small town weekly of this type may be typified by William Allen White's Emporia _Gazette_, published in Kansas, which in his time was nationally famous for two editorials he wrote. One was about the death of his daughter, Mary, the object of a 1977 TV biography, and the other was "What's the Matter with Kansas?"

Metropolitan dailies now serve a more interpretive function along with depth news coverage and more detailed news analysis. Their function has changed with the advent of television. With the role of interpretation has come the rise of investigative journalism, and this remains controversial.

The function of the small city dailies is essentially to supplement news coverage of television networks and local stations and metropolitan newspapers by giving the readers more local news. Some may use them as a substitute for metropolitan newspapers, but probably relatively few do. Local news is their lifeblood.

Weekly newspapers' function in the communications system is, like that of the small city dailies, to supplement other news sources by bringing readers things they haven't learned about in any other way. In another sense, in small towns where most of the news travels by word of mouth, the newspaper may serve the function of legitimizing or making official news that has been heard already by the grapevine. In addition they make available classified and display advertising and often sponsor community betterment projects such as spelling bees. The weekly newspaper is definitely one of the facilitators of community pride and cohesiveness.

I turn now to a second type of print media, like newspapers in the periodical category, but with characteristics of their own--the magazines. I'm especially interested in two kinds of magazines, the news magazines and the special audience magazines.

The news magazines contain much material that is found in metropolitan dailies and sometimes much that is in their Sunday Magazine sections, but the news weeklies make an attempt to put the news in perspective by relating the week's most important events and giving some indication of their significance in a historical or other context. They do this in different ways. U.S. News and World Report frequently carries, for example, the text of speeches made by Presidents, presidential candidates, foreign leaders and other key newsmakers. On the other hand, other news magazines may put more emphasis on interpreting the words of these news figures than on simply presenting the actual words themselves. Time, for example, is known for its colorful, punchy style and has sometimes coined new words (for instance, "cinemactor"). Characteristics of news magazines essentially are the featuring of news and efforts to put it into perspective for the readers.

Special audience magazines like Woman's Day, Sports Illustrated, and politically oriented magazines like the New Republic, the Nation, the Progressive, Human Events, and the National Review, have a limited but lively audience. Some sprang up after the old Saturday Evening Post, Life and Look succumbed after the loss of advertising to television. Both Life and Look featured photojournalism. Their general interest approach may also have hastened their demise.

The roles of news magazines in the communications system may be considered as fairly specialized. The role is affected by the fact that, with the exception of some magazines such as People, these magazines are usually read by a leadership elite, the well-informed people across the nation who read beyond the daily newspaper and seek more information than that provided by Cronkhite, Chancellor, and Reasoner and Walters on the national television newscasts. They turn to Time, Newsweek and U.S. News for this information and further, for the kind of interpretation and analysis of the news they are seeking, and except for brief comments by men like Howard K. Smith, David Brinkley and Eric Sevareid, seldom see on TV. Thus the function is that of an extension of the metropolitan daily newspaper, but an extension in a different fashion than the small city daily or the small town weekly newspaper. The audience is relatively high-income and well educated.

It may be instructive to examine examples of news magazines, and four have been chosen for that purpose. The four to be examined are Time, Newsweek, U.S. News and World Report, and New Times. All four practice "group journalism", with much collaboration on stories.

Time is the oldest of the news magazines and therefore the originator of the format. It was founded in 1923 by Henry R. Luce and Britt Haddon, and continues to be published today in a style similar to the breezy one used at the time of its origin. It departmentalizes news of the past week, under such headings as "National Affairs", "International", "Cinema" and "Milestones". A typical article might state something like the following: "Charismatic Jimmy Carter put a hammerlock on the Democratic presidential nomination with an endorsement from Senator Hubert Humphrey--who flirted briefly with the stop-Carter movement but then gave up his flirtation."

Time was indeliby stamped with the attitudes of Henry Luce and it remains today the kingpin of a publishing empire which also includes Fortune, Sports Illustrated, and People. For many years, it also published Life, the first picture news magazine. It also produced for the motion picture screen "The March of Time", discontinued when television made it largely superfluous. The whole idea of Time reflected the flamboyance of the 1920's scene in journalism. Paperback publications such as Time Capsules, each dealing with a specific year such as 1945 (condensations from the original Time articles), and such other ventures as Time-Life Books, Time-Life films and Time-Life records are also outgrowths of the original Luce enterprises.[8]

Newsweek was established during the 1930's,

_____

[8]For more on Luce, see W. A. Swanberg, Luce and His Empire (New York: Dell Publishing Co., 1972).

about a decade after the birth of _Time_. It originally
took the approach to the news that it would strive for
balance and objectivity rather than color as _Time_ did,
but that approach has long since been outdated. Today
Newsweek has a wide readership and is seen by some as
a magazine of the Liberal Establishment, perhaps because of its ownership by the Washington Post Co.,
headed by Katharine Graham. (Ms. Graham, Chairman of
the Board of the Washington Post Co., says the two
publications have separate editorial policies.)

During the 1960's, a Washington correspondent
for _Newsweek_, Benjamin Bradlee, was a close friend of
President John F. Kennedy. He has recently written a
memoir of his experiences with Kennedy as one of the
intimates of that era.[9] In it Bradlee, now the executive editor of The Washington _Post_ and one of the key
figures in Woodward and Bernstein's _All the President's Men_, quotes Kennedy as saying that the only
trouble with Richard Nixon was that "he has no class".
This may give some idea of the inclinations of Bradlee
and, by extrapolation, of _Newsweek_. _Newsweek_ has been
in the forefront of magazine journalism for the past
decade; its correspondents in Vietnam filed some outstanding reportage. It followed the events of Vietnam
and Watergate closely, and it carries the writings of
well-known columnists of all shadings of editorial
opinion. Among those who have written columns for
Newsweek are the late Walter Lippman, the late Joseph
Alsop, the late Raymond Moley, Bill Moyers, Shana
Alexander, Milton Friedman, and numerous other well-
known commentators on the national scene. _Newsweek_
currently carries a column called "My Turn", open to a
different author each week, in a format similar to the
CBS "Spectrum" series on the CBS Morning News. One
"My Turn" column was written in 1976 after publication
of _The Final Days_, Woodward and Bernstein's account of
the last days of the Nixon Administration. The column
was written by Julie Nixon Eisenhower in defense of
her mother, Pat Nixon, loyally denying that her mother
had a drinking problem and that some of the allegations in the Woodstein book were true. _Newsweek_ also
periodically commissions public opinion surveys, and
its surveys are respected and equally as well-known as
the CBS-New York _Times_ surveys. One well-known survey

---

[9]Benjamin Bradlee, _Conversations With Kennedy_
(New York: W. W. Norton & Co., 1975).

commissioned by Newsweek was a survey of black-white opinions on civil rights, open housing and other racial issues. This survey was done by Louis Harris and Associates, which along with George Gallup, Pat Cadell, Burns Roper and others is one of the leading polling organizations in the nation today.

Newsweek attempts prediction of coming events in a column called "Periscope". Sometimes it makes accurate predictions, but sometimes predicts the obvious. This however is a feature of long-standing. It also compartmentalizes news coverage, so that a cover story about Ronald Reagan or Jimmy Carter would normally be found under the heading of National Affairs. Like Time, Newsweek has gone into the publishing business, distributing books on famous places (the Tower of London) and condensed versions of best sellers. It remains influential and has a large readership, so that it competes on almost even terms with Time.

Third in the group of newsmagazines to be examined is the most conservative of the lot, U.S. News and World Report. The original U.S. News was established by the well-known columnist, David Lawrence, in the 1930's, and developed a wide readership among businessmen and moderate conservatives. Later, after World War II, it established a companion magazine, World Report, which was eventually combined with U.S. News. The two magazines respectively covered national affairs and foreign affairs, and as now published U.S. News and World Report carries predictions about trends in national politics and business, as well as foreign policy developments. U.S. News and World Report also is widely respected for its coverage of news events in the form of documents, such as presidential speeches, party platforms, and international leaders' speeches. It is apt to carry a conservative editorial or two. Prior to his death, it carried the conservative commentary of Mr. Lawrence. It sets a high standard of journalism, although unlike Time and Newsweek, it avoids expose-type investigative reporting and tends to stick with objective balanced reporting.

The newest magazine in the group of four singled out for analysis is New Times, only a few years old, but with a growing readership among American youth. It is written for somewhat the same audience as Rolling Stone, but it appeals to a somewhat wider readership. New Times each issue (it is published bi-weekly)

195

carries a summary of news events and people in the
news, together with columns by authors such as Larry
King, Robert Sam Anson, and Robert Scheer. Some of
these wrote for _Ramparts_ magazine in the 1960's and
take a radical or ultra-liberal viewpoint. Anson is
particularly talented and has already written a
biography of Senator George McGovern and a book on the
Kennedy assassination cover-up, called "_They've Killed
the President!_"[10]

The general approach taken by _New Times_ is that
of a feature newsmagazine, which concentrates on human
interest and political features rather than on the
day-to-day events in the news. To some extent perhaps,
most newsmagazines do this to a degree but _New Times_
does it consciously. Among matters to which it has
given wide coverage are the Wilbur Mills scandal, the
Kennedy assassination investigation, and the Patty
Hearst case. A 1976 issue included an article by
Andrew Kopkind on "Eurocommunism on the March" about
the Italian elections, a piece by Maureen Orth entitled "Memoirs of a CIA Psychologist", an essay by
Bob Holland, "The Double Life of Jack Coleman" about
white-collar workers secretly desiring to do blue-
collar work, and an article by Chris Welles, "Warning:
Cosmetics May Be Hazardous to Your Health", dealing
with cosmetics recalled from the shelves by the Food
and Drug Administration. This issue also contained a
final tribute to Martha Mitchell, written by Mark Goodman. The editing is lively, the quality of the writing
is usually good, and the magazine appears to have
carved out a niche for itself among the young skeptics
who tend to reject establishment values. This magazine goes about as far as one can go and remain in the
news magazine category; if it contained entirely
columns and essays of opinion it would have to be considered a special audience magazine.

Special audience magazines are important in the
communications system, especially journals of opinion.
Such magazines obviously appeal to a limited segment
of the population; in a sense they are the counterpart

---

[10] Robert Sam Anson, _McGovern_ (New York: Holt,
Rinehart & Winston, 1972). See also Robert Sam Anson,
"_They've Killed the President!_": _The Search for the
Murderers of John F. Kennedy_ (New York: Bantam Books,
1975).

of the Public Broadcasting System in the magazine
field. Some of the special audience magazines like
Sports Illustrated and Field and Stream or the various
automotive magazines will not be discussed here, other
than to take note of them, but they have a wide readership, as do women's magazines and magazines like TV
Guide and the movie fan magazines. I'll concentrate
on journals of opinion since their political content
is the highest.

Although a number of such journals could be
examined including The Nation, the Progressive, and
Human Events, I'll limit this analysis to the New Republic and the National Review, since these are more
or less prototype publications for the liberal and
conservative viewpoints in the United States today.

The New Republic traces its history back to the
World War I era and its first editor was Walter Lippman, one of the great journalists of 20th Century
America, who wrote admiring essays about Woodrow Wilson and the New Freedom. It has carried over the years
the writings of such distinguished authors as Edmund
Wilson, the literary critic; Michael Harrington, author
of The Other America, and James MacGregor Burns,
biographer of John and Edward Kennedy and a past president of the American Political Science Association.
Recent issues of the New Republic have reflected
liberal opinion about Jimmy Carter; the magazine first
appeared to support Representative Morris Udall for
President in 1976, but by mid-summer of 1976 was carrying articles speaking favorably about Carter and seeing
him as favoring some liberal viewpoints. The magazine
was once edited by Henry A. Wallace, a former U.S.
vice president and cabinet officer and the 1948 nominee
for President of the Progressive Party. The present
principal owner, a Harvard professor named Martin
Peretz, was friendly to the Independent campaign of
Eugene McCarthy for President. Through the years, the
New Republic has been a bellwether of Establishment
Liberalism of the Wilson-FDR-Truman-Kennedy-Johnson
type, and it can be expected to give its general support to at least the more innovative reforms of President Jimmy Carter. Like many Democratic liberals, it
has tended to be a bit skeptical of him.

The National Review is a relative upstart compared to the New Republic; NR only recently celebrated
its 20th anniversary. It is published by William Buckley, conservative columnist and brother of a former

U.S. Senator. Buckley was originally well-known for his book, God and Man at Yale; he is a prolific author. Buckley writes cleverly and the entire magazine is dominated by his touch, but it does serve faithfully as a spokesman for the conservative viewpoint. During 1976, it spoke most favorably about Ronald Reagan as a presidential candidate and it was a supporter of Richard Nixon almost to the bitter end in 1974.

The National Review has performed a signal service for American conservatives in that it has developed a coterie of conservative authors and given them an outlet for their sometimes distinguished writing. These include Brent Bozell, Grayson Kirk and perhaps the most gifted of the group, Garry Wills. These are only a few of those whose work is regularly published in the National Review. When the Buckley brothers called for Nixon's resignation, it was clear that the jig was up. The National Review editorializes about nearly everything; on one occasion William Buckley's tongue-in-cheek letters to himself were taken seriously by a liberal critic of Buckley who wrote him a letter taking exception to an entirely fictitious letter. Buckley apologized but in such a way as to score more points than before. The editorializing function is the chief way these magazines of the character of the New Republic and the National Review can be distinguished from the news magazines already discussed. Time has only carried one editorial in its history; some 50 years after its founding it carried an editorial calling for the resignation or impeachment of Richard Nixon. Newsweek, like U.S. News and World Report, carries only signed columns (something Time has not usually done). New Times also carries signed columns, but except in comments on letters to the editor, does not editorialize directly. The line may be a fine one between these magazines and the journals of opinion, but it is there.

Functions of news magazines in the communications system are fairly easily distinguished. Their main aim is to report the news for a one-week or two-week period and to put it in perspective for the reader. They do this both by carrying summaries of the news (in Newsweek they now carry the authors' bylines) and by carrying signed columns with opinions of the authors. They have gone further into investigative reporting, as illustrated by a recent Time magazine story making allegations about former Speaker Carl Albert's involvement in parties on Capitol Hill.

Time and Newsweek both did some investigative reporting on the scandal involving Elizabeth Ray, a stenographer who "couldn't type" and "couldn't answer the phone", and the once-powerful former Representative Wayne Hays of Ohio, who in his heyday served as chairman of the Congressional Democratic Campaign Committee and the House Committee on Administration. As chairman of these committees, he controlled important perquisites for Democratic congressmen and all congressmen, respectively. But Time and Newsweek, or even New Times, could not claim credit for breaking the Elizabeth Ray-Wayne Hays story. They were beaten to it by the Washington Post, and Ms. Ray did not allow the Post to have the story until her publisher had notified her her book was about ready to be published to cash in on the scandal. Once the story was broken, however, both magazines rushed in pell mell. Newsweek carried a bosomy picture of Ms. Ray which would have only appeared in Playboy a few short years earlier, when such pictures were not considered fit for a family magazine. Time and Newsweek and New Times should not feel bad, however, about losing out to the Post on the breaking of the Capitol Hill sex scandal story. The CBS network lost out to the Post on the Watergate scandal, and so did the New York Times, although the Times later did some distinguished reporting after the original story had appeared in the Post.

Functions of the special audience magazines in the communications system are fairly readily described. They provide a particular kind of news, information or commentary to persons interested in a particular field of human endeavor. Sports Illustrated provides this for sports fans, TV Guide for those who follow television, and the journals of opinion provide it for those who keep careful watch on the American political system and the world in which it operates.

Four additional periodicals of a more academic nature should be mentioned. Atlas gives a summary of the world press. Current History deals with current events in a more scholarly way. Foreign Affairs takes an Establishment viewpoint toward foreign policy, and Foreign Policy takes a more critical viewpoint toward foreign policy and tends to have younger authors.

Structure of Radio Broadcasting Industry

Turning now to the electronic media, one must

look at radio broadcasting.[11] I'll consider in turn
the characteristics of clear channel radio stations,
which are the major ones, and smaller radio stations
which usually serve a small geographic area. I'll
also examine the roles of each in the communications
system, and then discuss some examples of typical
clear channel stations. Next I'll look at functions
of both clear channel stations and smaller stations in
the communications system, and then turn to characteristics of radio networks, both historically and in
today's broadcasting scene. The roles of radio networks in the communications system will be examined,
with specific networks examined individually. The
discussion will conclude with analysis of the radio
networks' functions in the communications system.

Clear channel radio stations usually have a
wide coverage area and a powerful transmitter, normally 50,000 watts. They make an effort to provide regional news coverage and other services, and they are
usually key contributors to the news coverage of the
networks, although the networks have autonomous staffs
of their own. Clear channel stations are given an exclusive frequency because of their historical importance and the large number of listeners they serve.
They have been known for numerous community services;
for example, during the 1937 Ohio River flood, WLW in
Cincinnati and WHAS in Louisville gave round-the-
clock service to broadcast appeals for help to rescue
persons stranded in the flood. The clear channel stations did a great deal during World War II to assist
in the war effort, including advertising for war bonds
and the like. They usually involve themselves in various community service projects as well, at either the
state or local level, and sometimes in an entire region. In one sense they are the backbone of the radio
broadcasting system in the United States.

Characteristics of smaller radio stations are
not vastly different from those of the clear channel
stations. The main difference is that they operate in
a more restricted geographical area and they do not
have exclusive use of their frequencies. They may
operate in a 20-mile radius and it is not uncommon for

---

[11]See David Holbrook Culbert, News for Everyman:
Radio and Foreign Affairs in Thirties America (Westport, Conn.: Greenwood Press, 1976).

their transmitter power to be about 5,000 watts, just a tenth of that of the clear channel stations. They provide local news coverage and they also engage in community service projects just as the clear channel stations do. They usually provide a kind of formula broadcasting, with news and music, and sometimes they may use air time to promote community service projects such as collecting funds for building a swimming pool for the youth of the community. They fill out the system and supplement the large clear channel stations, much as small town weeklies and small city dailies supplement the large metropolitan daily newspapers.

Roles of clear channel stations in the communications system are relatively simple. These stations provide a basic newsgathering staff to assist the networks; they also have the role of providing services for a regional audience, as will be illustrated shortly in looking at specific stations.

Roles of smaller stations in the communications system are also simple. They provide some local news which the big stations do not carry; they provide an advertising medium for local merchants to supplement local newspapers, and they provide community services for the area in which their listeners reside. In general, they supplement the services of the clear channel stations which are the mainstay of the big national radio networks. Most of the smaller stations are independent, but they may subscribe to the AP Radio wire, or the UPI Radio service, which along with local news provides the news coverage they present.

It is possible to illustrate the work of the clear channel stations by looking at some examples. The first of these I'll examine is WGN in Chicago. This station is owned by the Chicago _Tribune_, which called itself for many years "The World's Greatest Newspaper". It is from this slogan that the call letters of the station are derived. WGN competes with WBBM, WMAQ and several other leading stations for the Chicago radio audience. It has popularized the phrase "Chicagoland" to signify its metropolitan area, and it has normally had a network affiliation. WGN long was affiliated with the Mutual Broadcasting System, one of the major networks. It has a first-class news staff of its own, and it has locally written newscasts spoken by local announcers. It also takes a "feed" of national news from the network, and this includes some direct coverage from cities around the world. But

over the years, WGN has been active in community and
regional affairs and has carried out the public service mandate of the Federal Communications Commission
reasonably well.

In Cincinnati, the clear channel station is
WLW, which is affiliated with the National Broadcasting Company. It carries the Cincinnati Reds' baseball
games and it carries NBC News reports, supplemented by
its own local reporting. It has had some well-known
announcers, and for many years its evening newscast
was voiced by Peter Grant, a well-known personality in
Cincinnati media circles. WLW has been regionally active and has provided a force for leadership in Cincinnati.

A competitor station is WCKY, the station owned
by the Taft Broadcasting Company. It too has
attempted to meet the FCC's public service requirements. On WLW, various personalities have become well-
known. One was Ruth Lyons, who appeared for years.
Rosemary Clooney, the pop singer, got her start on
WLW before becoming nationally known, just as Dinah
Shore began on WSM in Nashville before becoming nationally known.

WJR in Detroit has broadcast clear channel
programming for many years. This station prepares its
own newscasts, and a difference of opinion over this
practice caused it to shift its affiliation from CBS
to NBC at the beginning of 1976. It normally airs
fifteen-minute newscasts in the morning, at noon, and
in the evening, and during the remainder of the day
picks up hourly news "feeds" from NBC in addition to
its own locally originated news. The remainder of its
time is filled with music, such as disc jockey programming with announcers like J. P. McCarthy and classical
programming including a daily weekday program with
Karl Haas, a musician specializing in music apprecia-
tion type programs. In addition it carries specialized
features such as weather news, farm news and business
news. Its format is designed for general audiences,
compared with other area stations such as CKLW in
Windsor, Ontario, which appeals to the "youth" audience with rock-n-roll music, and punchy headline-type
news format.

Still another Detroit station, WCAR, for sometime carried programming designed principally for "all
news" 24-hour news coverage with constant bulletin

type coverage of hard news interspersed with occasional feature material, most of it coming from American Information Network, but supplemented by local reports from its own staff. (After AIN was disbanded, the station relied more heavily on AP Radio News and finally went to a music format.)

WOR in New York carries similar type clear-channel programming, and in New York City each of the major networks, as well as PBS, has its own "flagship" station. WCBS features CBS News and some special programming such as "The CBS Mystery Hour"; WNBC features NBC News and audiotape versions of such popular television news shows as "Meet the Press" and occasional excerpts such as interviews from the morning "Today" Show with Tom Brokaw, Jane Pauley and Floyd Kalber; WABC features ABC News and like ABC television puts heavy emphasis on sports coverage, e.g., the Notre Dame games, World Series and tournament tennis.

Other examples of clear-channel stations include WWL in New Orleans, which as one would naturally expect provides some jazz programming as well as the usually found features; WHO in Des Moines; KDKA in Pittsburgh, known in radio history as the nation's first regularly scheduled radio station which broadcast returns from the Harding-Cox presidential election in 1920, and WHAS in Louisville, which features controversial programming such as call-in talk shows. WHAS, incidentally, a few years ago suffered a severe blow to its advertising accounts when tobacco advertising was banned. The effect would be similar to that if WJR in Detroit were suddenly banned from carrying automobile commercials. Many long-time announcers were laid off and younger, less expensive talent was hired. This station, like the newspapers which are affiliated with it, has a long-time record of public-service oriented programming and activities. Most of the clear-channel stations rate very well in this regard, perhaps because they have the resources to carry on high quality programming.

The functions of clear channel stations in the communications system include the basic one of providing wide-area news coverage and entertainment to a general audience, as well as the more specific ones of serving regional programming needs. To some extent they have a more nearly national audience, especially at night. Phone-in programs often include calls from

New York to California when the program is a well-followed and popular one. In general, the clear channel stations are pace-setters and since they usually are key network affiliates they exert a leadership role in the industry. That is to say that they may determine network offerings by what they accept or reject, and they may set a pattern of programming that is emulated by smaller stations.

Various examples can be given of smaller stations. Those already mentioned include WCAR in Detroit, a former all-news station. The Paterson, New Jersey, all-classical station, is another one with specialized programming. Some Black-owned stations and some religious stations serve a fairly specialized audience as well. Then there are the scores of small-town, locally-oriented stations which bring local news to the public. Some of these do a rather good job considering their more limited resources, although some of them have fallen into a formula pattern of merely news and music. Public Radio affiliates do a good job in the sense of providing more feature-type coverage and educational material.

Functions of smaller stations in the communications system may be more specialized as we have seen in mentioning all-news and all-music stations. They may also serve a small local audience, however, much as a small city daily or weekly newspaper supplements the news coverage of metropolitan dailies. Smaller stations also can provide the kind of entertainment and limited-interest news coverage which clear channel stations feel they cannot provide because of their larger, more regional audiences.

Characteristics of radio stations, considered in historical context as opposed to today's stations, have changed a great deal since broadcasting first became common and then became more regulated in the 1920s. For many of the smaller stations, at least, a turning point came when much of the national audience shifted to television. Even some of the clear channel stations shifted away from the kind of entertainment programming with big name performers to more of a formula approach with 10 to 15 minutes of news followed by 45 to 50 minutes of music each hour, with coverage of special events such as local and area football games, and other sports events included. Weekend programming is still rather heavily sports-oriented on both types of stations. In the old days of radio, its

early pioneering days, it was not uncommon for a
typical clear-channel station to carry the broadcasts
of Lowell Thomas, H. V. Kaltenborn and Elmer Davis on
its newscasts[12] and to carry entertainment shows like
those of Bob Hope, "Fibber" McGee and Jack Benny. In
other words, there was more of a national orientation
and much heavier network programming.

In recent years, since the television tube
emerged as the dominant factor in broadcasting, the
emphasis on network programs has faded although it
hasn't disappeared altogether and stations of this
type have tended to build up and develop local personalities. An example of this is the disc jockey on
WJR, J. P. McCarthy, well-known in the city of Detroit and for a time an active broadcaster on the West
Coast.

But the clear channel stations have retained
network news "feeds" and some network programming.
The NBC "Monitor" weekend feature-news type of programming has been popular (a sort of magazine format).

The smaller stations have always depended somewhat more on local personalities and they are more
prone to depend on wire services for non-local news,
even though they have often aired broadcasts by a
local reporter-newscaster (one and the same person).
Entertainment may be geared to the local audience almost entirely. The technology of tape recording also
has made it possible for small stations to have lively
news coverage of local events with timely interviews
and a few have interesting "talk shows" patterned
after those of their clear-channel counterparts.

Characteristics of Radio Networks

Radio networks, historically and today, have
thus performed somewhat different functions. In the
early days, they were a mainstay in programming; today,
they supplement television and newspaper fare, but
they do still retain their importance. The role of
radio networks today is mainly to provide features and
other material not available to local stations; they
also provide material demanded or requested by affiliates and they fill a need for linking together network

---

[12]See Culbert, op. cit., pp. 205, 206.

stations, one of the original purposes of a network
(to make co-operative programming more feasible).

A key characteristic of radio networks is that
they tend to be adjunct to the dominant television
networks (pickups of televised programs for radio use
indicate the continuing link). This may be largely
historical accident and to a degree it reflects the
same kind of phenomenon represented by newspaper-owned
radio and television stations, the result of a newspaper (e.g.) which wanted to branch out into a different medium to reach more people and thus went into
the broadcasting business. The Federal Communications
Commission has considered this kind of tendency toward
monopoly undesirable, but it has tended to permit it
where a showing of effective public service could be
made and where the opposition applicant for the broadcast license could not indicate it would provide as
good or better programming. But this remains a controversial area in broadcast regulation. Radio networks continue to play an important role in broadcasting but today they are overshadowed by their big
brothers, the television networks.

Specific networks must be identified and
examined briefly since each has a unique history and
each has a somewhat different role from the others today. The American Broadcasting Company, which has
several differentiated services such as Entertainment
Network and News Network, FM-Entertainment Network,
and FM-News Network, is the youngest of the major commercial networks. In the old days, the National Broadcasting Company had a Red Network and a Blue Network;
it was ordered by the FCC to dispose of one; it chose
to dispose of the Blue Network, and that eventually
was transformed into the modern ABC network. The
programming of sports and an emphasis on entertainment
seem to be hallmarks of ABC today. It is a growing
and increasingly strong network, and it has made its
mark in the all-important ratings competition which is
the basis for the advertising rate-cards for networks
and affiliates.

The National Broadcasting Company is the
pioneer network, the first one established. It dates
its origins back into the early 1920s and during 1976
was celebrating its 50th anniversary. It carried such
popular entertainers as Paul Whiteman and the Rhythm
Boys, the late Bing Crosby, Billy Jones and Ernie Hare
(the Interwoven Pair), and Singin' Sam, the Barbasol

206

Man, during the 1920's. It also carried some of the early serials like "Vic and Sade" and "Amos and Andy: The Fresh-Air Taxicab Company" in the early days of radio. Then and later it carried news programs by such men as Lowell Thomas and H. V. Kaltenborn and it also carried sportscasts by such notables as Grantland Rice and Graham McNamee.

The Columbia Broadcasting System was the out-growth of William Paley's early network which con-sisted of a small group of stations put together shortly before the depression. It had its beginning in the 1920's and branched out into a nationwide net-work in the 1930's--the first major competition for NBC. CBS was firmly imprinted with the personalities of Paley and Edward R. Murrow, the World War II London correspondent who later led in developing the CBS News operation. CBS continues to this day to have a premier reputation in news programming, and it has only recently lost its dominance in entertainment programming. But this was a long way in the future when Bill Paley sold out his interest in the family cigar company to help finance the building of CBS.[13] Another key figure in the development of the CBS Radio Network was Frank Stanton, a specialist in audience surveys and one of the first trained social scientists to serve as a network executive. CBS really became a household word during World War II when Murrow made his famous broadcasts from London with the nightly opening: "This . . . is London." Murrow had been in educational broadcasting originally and had the good fortune to be in Europe when the 1938 Munich crisis erupted. He and William L. Shirer and H. V. Kalten-born became nationally known almost overnight thanks to Adolf Hitler and the sudden interest in interna-tional events, especially in Europe. Murrow helped Paley build a whole set of foreign correspondents and such names as Eric Sevareid, Hughes Rudd, Winston Burdett, and many others became well-known as a result of their war reportage. NBC had luminaries too, but it was CBS which dominated the hard news field.

_____

[13]See David Halberstam, "CBS--The Power and the Profits", <u>Atlantic</u> <u>Monthly</u>, January and February 1976. Also see Robert Metz, <u>CBS:</u> <u>Reflections</u> <u>in</u> <u>a</u> <u>Bloodshot</u> <u>Eye</u> (New York: New American Library, 1975) and Sid Mickelson, <u>The</u> <u>Electric</u> <u>Mirror</u> (New York: Dodd, Mead & Co., 1972).

National Public Radio is the non-commercial
public service radio network, and its mission is at
least in part educational with a number of campus
radio stations included. Its programming is heavy
with educational, news and classical music program
materials, but pop music, talk show interviews and
other material is also included. It has had some
imaginative programming, but does not have as much
visibility as its television counterpart, PBS.

Functions of radio networks in the communications system can be briefly described as providing
quick news coverage, background material not available on television, providing music and entertainment,
and furnishing an alternative outlet to newspapers and
television. Its impact nationally is probably less
than newspaper syndicates or television networks, but
it retains some importance to the system.

Television Stations and Networks and Cablevision

Characteristics of over-the-air television
broadcasting stations are several in number. First of
all, stations may broadcast on the very high frequency
(VHF) band, with Channels 2 through 13, or they may
broadcast on the ultra high frequency (UHF) band with
Channels 14 through 83. Stations broadcast primarily
in color and for most the broadcast day runs from
6 a.m. to 12 midnight or perhaps from 6:30 a.m. to
1 a.m. For a few stations the broadcast day may be
shorter, but in considerable measure the major stations depend in large part on network programming for
their schedule.

Characteristics of television networks include
their nationwide nature, their firm financial base,
and their ability to contract for outstanding national
talent. They are not limited by the availability of
local talent in newscasting, entertainment and other
broadcast activities, but they are able to pay as much
as $1 million a year for a newsperson like Barbara
Walters, who in October 1976 began serving as co-
anchor for the ABC Evening News with Harry Reasoner.[14]

---

[14]In late 1977, rumors were flying of a shakeup
at NBC News with Tom Brokaw and Tom Snyder likely to
replace John Chancellor and David Brinkley on the NBC

Jane Pauley, the "Today" co-hostess, is reportedly paid between $75,000 and $100,000, a tidy sum for a 27-year-old performer, only five years away from being a psychology major. The TV networks are also very much geared to the audience rating system; programs which do not earn a top rating are in great danger of being unceremoniously dropped.

Characteristics of cablevision systems are still developing, but the typical cablevision system presents twelve-channel selection and the programming is relayed by cable-wire systems after being received through conventional broadcast receivers at a central location. What began as CATV (community antenna television) gradually broadened into cablevision. Cablevision must now originate its own broadcast on one channel, even though this may be merely radio with pictures on many systems. A new FCC ruling which became effective in January 1977 requires all new cablesystems to provide viewers with a choice of at least 20 channels.

The outlook is for a broadening of the cablevision channel spectrum to approximately 100 channels. This new technology has raised for the first time the possibility of "public access" channels for broadcasting by interest groups, minority programming, and a varied type of programming that was not possible under conventional broadcasting and was difficult with the early cablesystems.[15] It appears to hold a great potential for serving the broader public, but the spread of cablesystems may undermine the role of the networks, or it may at least lead to a long business struggle between the networks, built as they are on conventional telecasting, and the cablesystems, geared to the newer technology of the "wired nation" concept. Ultimately, some middle ground may be found but networks and over-the-air stations are going to expect some kind of copyright compensation for the use of their signals by cable systems.

Nightly News. It was also reported that NBC made an unsuccessful effort to contract with independently syndicated Phil Donahue to replace Brokaw on the "Today" show.

[15]See James G. Strouse, The Mass Media, Public Opinion, and Public Policy Analysis (Columbus, Ohio: Charles E. Merrill Publishing Co., 1975), especially the chapter, "The Wired Nation".

Within the communications system, over-the-air
TV stations serve the role of providing conventional
coverage in news, entertainment and other programming
for the general audience. The television networks
provide a linkage for tying these local and regional
stations together and also a major source of programming. The networks themselves increasingly produce
less and less of their regular programming (outside of
news departments) and more and more depend on Holly-
wood production companies, and other sources for their
programs. Local stations use more syndicated material,
some of it newly produced (that is how "Space, 1999"
began in 1974) and some of it previously produced for
regular network use and later made available to local
stations on a syndicated basis. The cablevision systems' role in the total communications picture is
still developing, but it appears that it will make a
broader variety of channels available in each local
market and that will be its major contribution. In
addition, another variant of cablesystems includes the
experimental pay-TV networks. Through these networks,
it is possible for viewers to see first-run movies,
porno flicks (for motels), or various other kinds of
entertainment or information not yet available on
either the standard TV networks or the regular cablesystems.

Examples of various stations, networks and
cablevision systems can be discussed briefly. It may
suffice to identify WCBS-TV, WABC-TV and WNBC-TV in
New York City, the flagship stations for the three
major commercial TV networks. Each of these stations
carries the bulk of the programming originated by its
parent network. Each network may wholly own up to
five member affiliates in the network.

Examples of television networks can be briefly
identified. The Columbia Broadcasting System competes
with the other two commercial networks, the National
Broadcasting Company, and American Broadcasting Companies, for the conventional TV national audience. The
Public Broadcasting Service, financed by a mixture of
government appropriations, private contributions and
foundation grants, is an outgrowth of the old Educational TV Network (ETV) and is an effort to use partial
public financing in a manner similar to that found successful with the British Broadcasting Corporation in
the United Kingdom. This has provided diversity in
programming, even as the British have moved to a non-
governmental network to supplement BBC.

210

The senior network is the National Broadcasting Company, which was founded as part of the Radio Corporation of America. NBC was headed for many years by General Robert A. Sarnoff, whose experience in communications went back to the pre-radio days of Marconi's wireless telegraphy. NBC, the pioneer radio network, worked closely with RCA in the development of modern television technology. The long suit of NBC in programming was its entertainment programs for many years, in contrast to CBS which during the Murrow era at least put a great deal of emphasis on the CBS News Department. Some of the leading entertainers were NBC stars all through the days of radio and up to the beginning of the age of television, when CBS began to lure some of the stars away. NBC for a time lost ground to CBS, especially after the development of the nationwide television networks (although CBS lost heavily on a color television set that was adjuged to be inferior to the RCA set). Until 1976, CBS led the ratings for both entertainment and news programs but it began to run into difficulty with a strong challenge from the third network, ABC. During 1976-77 ABC led the ratings and began the 1977-78 season in the lead. NBC has had strong programming in certain areas, however. It has been extremely successful since 1952 with the "Today" show, which starred Dave Garroway, Hugh Downs, and more recently Tom Brokaw, Jane Pauley, Gene Shallit, and Floyd Kalber. The "Today" show in late 1977 was having some ratings problems.

The Columbia Broadcasting System has been dominated by William S. Paley, much as NBC was dominated for many years by General Sarnoff. Paley served for some 40 years as CBS board chairman. Another leading figure in the growth and development of CBS was a social science researcher named Dr. Frank Stanton. These two men, plus Edward R. Murrow, for many years CBS' chief news commentator, perhaps contributed the most to the reputation of CBS as a leader in news and entertainment programming. The story of Mr. Paley's business feats in the development of CBS has been written in many places, such as David Halberstam's and Robert Metz's volumes about CBS and in the Eric Barnuow trilogy about the history of broadcasting,[16]

---

[16]See Eric Barnuow, The Image Empire: A History of Broadcasting in the United States from 1953 (New York: Oxford University Press, 1970).

but Dr. Stanton's contribution was considerable in
that he insisted on high quality programming. After
Stanton reached 65, he was obliged to retire, although Paley as of 1976 was still chairman of the
board although he resigned his title as chief executive officer at "Black Rock" (CBS headquarters) and
fired the president, Arthur Taylor, because of a severe drop in CBS' ratings during much of 1976.
In 1977, Paley announced his own retirement from CBS.
Edward R. Murrow became a legendary figure. After
Murrow's departure CBS continued to develop talent,
and some of its former correspondents went to other
networks. For example, John Hart became an NBC correspondent and Harry Reasoner (now paired with Barbara
Walters) became an ABC anchorperson. In the post-
Murrow era at CBS, the leading news people in addition
to Walter Cronkite (anchor of the Evening News) have
included Dan Rather, Mike Wallace, Morley Safer, Roger
Mudd, Lesley Stahl (campaign correspondent), Robert
Threlkeld, Susan Spencer, and others.

The American Broadcasting Companies, the third
commercial television network, gained a great deal of
ground recently on NBC and CBS, and since 1976 has led
the prime time entertainment ratings during the late
spring and in the beginning of the fall season. ABC
entered sports heavily, and it was bolstering its
entertainment programming considerably during the
1975-76 season and the 1976-77 season, developing the
"docu-drama" concept with such teleplays as "Eleanor
and Franklin (Part One)" and "The Missile Crisis",
based on actual historical personages and events. CBS
on the other hand had a dismal flop in the 1975-76 season with the failure of the highly touted "Beacon
Hill", and it continued the 1976-77 season with its
successful "sitcom" lineup, only to find itself third
in the ratings much of the time during the "first season" of 1976-77. CBS was still groping for an answer
to ABC in the entertainment area, but NBC made a partial comeback to second behind ABC with its "Big
Events" programming, emphasizing mini-series. A smash
hit of 1976-77 was ABC's "Roots" mini-series on the
history of a Black family in America.

The Public Broadcasting System, partly financed
with public funds, was the only non-commercial network.
Its programs were sometimes underwritten by grants
from Mobil Oil, Ford Foundation and other sources, but
it did a good deal of innovative programming. One of
its most successful series was the Sunday night drama,

<u>Masterpiece</u> <u>Theater</u> which developed the smash hit,
"Upstairs, Downstairs" and "The Forsyte Saga".

In the news production area, PBS introduced
talk-show programs such as "Firing Line with William
Buckley", a news special with Bill Moyers patterned
after "CBS Reports" and "ABC Close-up", and it introduced in the fall of 1976 a new program, "The MacNeil-
Lehrer Report" which gave a depth coverage look at a
specific news item each evening for a half-hour. The
latter was well received by the critics.

Other PBS programs which were well received in
earlier seasons included "Behind the Lines", a critical look at journalism and its coverage. PBS under-
went a crisis during the Nixon Administration when the
Nixon regime put pressure on the Corporation for Public Broadcasting, the federal funding agent for PBS,
to eliminate some of its most controversial public service programming. Sander Vanocur was one of those cancelled and Bill Moyers and William Buckley for a time
were threatened with cancellation, but both were given
a last minute reprieve when the Administration--pre-
occupied with Watergate and the impeachment threat--
relented. But the Ford Administration took a much
kinder attitude to public broadcasting, and the Carter
Administration has done so also.[17]

The networks could be examined in much greater
detail, but the above discussion should give a general
idea of their current activities. Types of cablevision systems are expected to multiply, but the two
most common in 1976 were the 12-channel system, one in
which cable stations are viewed on Channels 2 through
13, and the pay-TV system, on which special programming is made available to subscribers who pay a premium for first-run movies and the like. The 12-channel
cablesystems have been in operation for some time, and

----

[17]In October 1977, the Carter Administration
requested $1 billion, five-year funding for PBS, but
the program faced some tough questioning in Congress.
For a summary of Nixon era developments, see William
E. Porter, <u>Assault</u> <u>On</u> <u>the</u> <u>Media</u>: <u>The</u> <u>Nixon</u> <u>Years</u>
(Ann Arbor, Mich.: University of Michigan Press, 1976).
Also see Douglass Cater and Michael J. Nyhan, eds.,
<u>The</u> <u>Future</u> <u>of</u> <u>Public</u> <u>Broadcasting</u> (New York: Praeger
Publishers, 1976).

most of the pay-TV systems have been in operation for a briefer time, but these are the two dominant types of cablevision systems currently in operation.

The number of cablesystem channels may eventually be expanded to 50 per system or even 100 as this becomes feasible. This has prompted talk of public-access cablevision with various channels being allocated to various minority groups and others who have only limited access to broadcasting with the present technology. A controversy has been growing as cablevision grows, and the conventional broadcasters complain that their programming is being "siphoned" without reimbursement to them for copyright usage. This will be affected by new legislation currently in the works; in the meantime, the Federal Communications Commission requires cablevision systems to use one of their channels for local broadcasting (even if it is without "pictures" in the sense of a camera-oriented broadcasting operation). This means that each system carries radio-like programming with a color test pattern in many instances. This of course could eventually have further potential for direct cablecasting when the economic feasibility of this becomes greater.

Functions of TV stations in the total communications system can be described as providing to local audiences a programming consisting of news, entertainment and sports, as well as other public service features.

Functions of TV networks in the total communications system include the provision of nationwide programming (as for example in coverage of major news events) and the furnishing of a link between individual affiliate stations. They of course provide programming in the areas of news, entertainment, sports and public service.

Functions of cablevision in the total communications system are focused around the provision of programs which are unavailable to communities which would otherwise be without them. Cablevision began in the 1950's with the community antenna television program, and it has matured today into one of the fastest growing aspects of television.

The Structure of the Television Industry and Its Regulation

Next I'll examine the structure of the television industry and its recent evolution. Broadcast regulation has a major impact on political coverage.

One of the foundations of the television industry's structure is the relationship between the networks--primarily the commercial networks--and their affiliates. Each of the three major networks has five wholly owned affiliates, the limit permitted by the FCC. In addition it has scores of other affiliates who agree to take its programming subject to adjustments in local programming, the "family hour" concept and other factors. This means in effect that each network owns five of its affiliates in the major markets but that the other affiliates are largely independent of the networks--entirely in terms of ownership, and largely in terms of control. The networks are dependent on the affiliates for their audience in large part, and the affiliates are dependent on the networks for their major programming in large part. This is especially true of prime-time programming (approximately 8 p.m. to 11 p.m.).[18]

At this point a distinction should be pointed out, that between network stations (those carrying NBC, CBS or ABC programming) and independent stations. Independent stations normally carry locally originated programming, syndicated programming, or an occasional program purchased from the networks in a situation where there is no network outlet for that program on a regular affiliate station. An example of an independent station would be WKBD-TV (Channel 50) in Detroit, a part of Kaiser Broadcasting. The Westinghouse Group stations are also independent although they occasionally produce programming for all members of the Group. Independent stations frequently operate in a market where there are more than three basic stations and therefore there are not enough network programs to fill the needs of all the stations in the

---

[18]For a discussion of this in depth, see Erwin G. Krasnow and Lawrence D. Longley, The Politics of Broadcast Regulation (New York: St. Martin's Press, 1973). A second edition of this book was scheduled for publication in 1978.

metropolitan market. New York City, for example, has several independent non-network stations. The independent stations furnish a source of variety in programming and in addition to this they furnish a market for the growing "fifth network", the increasing number of syndicated programs. A recent hit of this "network" was "The Testimony of Two Men", aired in 1977. Syndicated programs are sometimes tapes of old network programs ("All in the Family", for example or "What's My Line" or "The Brady Bunch"). But increasingly of late some programs have been provided directly for syndication such as "Dinah!" the Dinah Shore prime-time evening show. Syndication has become as important as local programming in filling the need for non-network-originated programming.

A further distinction should be made between "groups" and networks. The networks (NBC, CBS, ABC) are already clearly defined and may include scores of stations with a nucleus of five network-owned affiliates. But "groups" such as Group W Westinghouse may be groupings of independently owned minor chains which make no attempt at nationwide programming but sometimes provide regional programming.

Development and evolution of the major networks has been discussed previously, but this opportunity will be taken to mention some of the emphases of each one. The Columbia Broadcasting System, like the other networks, grew out of the old radio networks. A major emphasis of CBS, ever since the 1930's, has been its coverage of international and national news. It has not only had such well-known commentators as Eric Sevareid, such anchormen as Walter Cronkite and such correspondents as Dan Rather. But it has also been a major training ground for correspondents who have gone on to staff the other commercial networks and even the Public Broadcasting System. This recently worked in reverse when Bill Moyers, a former press aide to Lyndon Johnson, came from PBS to CBS to become a commentator with Sevareid, who retired in November 1977.

CBS has apparently reached what may be a critical turning point with William Paley's announcement of his retirement. It will need to replenish its executive ranks with imaginative, shrewd leadership if it is to gain back its lead from the other networks. It has not been used to being third in the ratings, so it may be expected to try hard to regain its leadership. This may not occur right away, however.

The National Broadcasting Company, as the
senior network, has certain programs which are king-
pins in its appeal for the ratings. "Today" until
recently dominated early morning ratings, and the
"Tonight" show dominated night-time ratings from
11:30 p.m. onward. To this it added the Tom Snyder
"Tomorrow" show, and another entertainment show popular with the youth audience, "Saturday Night" which
until recently featured Chevy Chase with his satires
on former President Ford. NBC, often third in the
ratings, began a big move to win back part of the
prime time audience. The "Big Event" and some "Best
Sellers" programs have been a successful beginning in
this direction. NBC has kept a respectable audience
for the Chancellor-Brinkley Nightly News. Its NBC
White Papers (news documentaries three hours long)
have had slim ratings but they have made up for low
ratings with the prestige accrued from these programs.
One White Paper for example dealt with Vietnam and the
war, and it was a "revisionist" view of President
Kennedy.

The American Broadcasting Companies, the junior
network, with aggressive leadership in programming
(their programming director left CBS to join ABC) have
been making inroads into the ratings of both CBS and
NBC programs. In sports, they boast the Olympics each
four years and they feature such events as the Super
Bowl; they have also outbid CBS for such long-time CBS
fixtures as the Kentucky Derby. ABC clearly has the
outstanding sports coverage, although it continues to
get strong competition for the programming. It is beginning to take the lead in entertainment, a development which just began in 1976 and is not yet firmly
established, but which could continue with good fortune
in the ratings. (Despite high ratings, critics have
not liked some of the new ABC programs.)

In the news area, ABC is just beginning to move.
Here it hired Barbara Walters away from the "Today"
show and it also began a new morning program (successor
to a failure) known as "Good Morning, America". The
latter program starring David Hartman bolstered by
such personalities as Jack Anderson is taking some
audience away from the "Today" show.

The "ratings war" among the networks is of
prime importance to them because high and low ratings
establish the going "rate card" for advertising rates
charged to sponsors. In terms of political television,

ratings are also important because they may frequently prevent high-grade public service programming from appearing on prime time television on the networks. The competition between the networks for high ratings (linked as it is to the advertising dollar) makes them reluctant to give up prime time to all but the most important public service programming. There are exceptions to this, including the presidential campaign "debates" (more correctly joint news conferences) of 1960 and 1976, the nominating conventions, the election night returns, and the like.

A second facet of the importance of ratings to political television is that they make the networks all more vulnerable to indirect regulation by government agencies such as the Federal Communications Commission (the FCC regulates affiliate stations). Also they are very conscious of meeting their public service obligation as licensees, especially since some TV licenses have been revoked or suspended (a case in Mississippi caused changes at a licensed station because of lack of minority programming). The nature of broadcast regulation and its impact will be the last facet of the structure of the television industry to be discussed.[19]

The nature of broadcast regulation grows out of the nature of broadcasting. Since the establishment of the Federal Radio Commission in 1927 and especially since the establishment of the Federal Communications Commission in 1934, the federal government has closely regulated the broadcasting industry. Indeed, not only has the FCC regulated the industry closely, but Congress has kept a close watch on it as well. So it is important to understand why such close regulation is imposed; this grows out of the concept that television and radio stations derive their profits from the use of airwaves owned by the public; thus regulation is imposed for the "public interest, convenience, and necessity" and the FCC's duty is to impose this regulation. Regulation is largely through the device of licensing and establishment of guidelines, as for example in the area of public service programming, where standards are clearly specified in FCC guidelines for newly licensed stations or for new purchasers of existing station licenses.

----

[19]See Krasnow and Longley, op. cit.

The varied regulatory functions of the FCC have been stated above. The FCC's relationship to affiliate and independent stations, however, is different from its relationship to the networks. The FCC does not license networks, but only individual stations. Thus technically the networks are not directly subject to FCC regulations. But immediately this proves to be a technicality, since network-owned affiliates are subject to FCC regulation of individually licensed stations. Thus the FCC has direct regulatory authority over individual stations, but it has only indirect authority over networks. Further complicating the picture is the fact that because of the First Amendment ban on censorship of the mass media, the FCC has no direct authority to impose censorship.

A legal controversy has been raging over whether the "family hour" imposed by the FCC is a form of censorship. At least one federal judge has ruled that it is and therefore violates the First Amendment, but the issue at this writing had not finally been settled by the U.S. Supreme Court. The Supreme Court frequently refuses to hear appeals from FCC rulings on the ground that Congress has delegated the regulatory authority to the FCC and that it therefore is a political question inappropriate for adjudication by the Supreme Court. The Court can indicate where pornography has exceeded the limits, but it cannot impose prior censorship nor according to its rulings can the FCC do so. The only penalty can be a license suspension or revocation after the violation of FCC guidelines. This applies to lack of public interest programming as well as to violation of pornography guidelines (which incidentally are quite generous; "blue" movies can be legally shown on pay-TV, for example).

The politics of license renewal for radio and television stations deserves a brief discussion here. Each station is granted its license by the Federal Communications Commission to serve "the public interest, convenience, and necessity" under the 1934 Communications Act. To the extent that the licensee serves the public interest, convenience and necessity, renewal of a license is likely to be approved by the FCC. In the early years of broadcasting such renewal was often considered almost routine for both radio and television stations. However, there has been considerable controversy over renewals in recent years. TV station license suspensions and even a radio station license revocation have occurred because of

stations' failures to live up to the broadcast regulations promulgated by the FCC. One case involved a
license suspended for a TV station in Jackson, Mississippi, found to be remiss in granting program access
to minorities. A radio station in Nebraska lost
its license and was forced to sign off the air because
of practices deemed unethical by the FCC. The Red
Lion, Pennsylvania, religious radio station was also
obliged to face suspension of its license because it
would not permit other views about religion to be
aired on its facilities.[20] The major point underlying
all these FCC punitive actions has been that the stations are not merely the property of the owner, but
rather are acting with a franchise from the FCC (in
the form of a license) to use the publicly owned air-
ways for broadcasting in the public interest, convenience, and necessity.

License renewal may also be used as a political
tool when an effort is made to control the FCC in a
partisan fashion. Thus the Nixon Administration secured the assistance of friendly broadcast interests
in Florida to challenge the television license of
WJAX-TV in Jacksonville because it was owned by the
Washington Post Corporation which had been publishing
news stories and editorials highly critical of the
Nixon Administration. Ben Bradlee, executive editor
of the Post and a former Newsweek correspondent and
friend of President Kennedy's, and Katharine Graham,
publisher of the Post, were both considered to be on
President Nixon's infamous "enemies list", as disclosed by John Dean of the White House staff. The
Nixon Administration effort to revoke the license of
WJAX-TV ultimately failed, but it represented a kind
of harassment of the station's ownership simply on the
basis of a political disagreement with the Administration. This is but one example of the politics of
license renewal. More likely is the case where someone with political clout is helpful to a station in
securing the approval of a renewal or is helpful in
securing FCC approval for sale of a license to a new
ownership. An investigation of such a case in Miami
occurred in 1955, and it resulted in the resignation

---

[20]Fred W. Friendly, The Good Guys, the Bad Guys
and the First Amendment (New York: Random House,
1975).

of an Eisenhower appointee, Richard Mack, from the FCC.[21]

Political news coverage on television is always a kind of "hot potato" in that the FCC has no power to censor news coverage because of the First Amendment freedom of speech of broadcasters, but it is at the same time holding broadcasters responsible for fairness and equity in their news coverage. Regulation has brought about a number of rules, nearly all of them difficult for the FCC to enforce partly because it has no power of direct censorship.

Two rules which have been most troublesome for the FCC and radio and television stations in the effort to enforce these rules are: (1) that embodied in the Section 315 provision for "equal time" for all candidates and parties, a rule written into the enabling legislation of the FCC which the FCC has been obliged to interpret, and (2) the "Fairness Doctrine", another rule promulgated by the FCC but one difficult for it to interpret also.[22]

The "equal time" provision requires that all presidential candidates, for example, must be given equal time on the networks and stations if any one or two of them are given time. This has had the effect of preventing any station or network from giving them such time. This is because stations fear that free equal time will be demanded by the Prohibitionist, Vegetarian, Socialist Workers and other minor parties. Thus the station would lose valuable advertising revenues from commercial sponsors. This Section 315 provision requiring "equal time" for all candidates regardless of following or popularity was suspended only once, in 1960 when Congress suspended it for the duration of the presidential campaign, so that the Kennedy-Nixon presidential debates could be staged by the networks. But after the last debate the suspen-

---

[21]See Victor G. Rosenblum, "How to Get into TV: The Federal Communications Commission and Miami's Channel 10", Chapter 4 in Alan F. Westin, ed., The Uses of Power: Seven Cases in American Politics (New York: Harcourt, Brace & World, 1962), pp. 173-228, especially pp. 216-219.

[22]See Friendly, op. cit.

sion of Section 315 ended and it has been in force ever since.

In 1976, a loophole was found in the law, and the FCC under Chairman Wiley ruled that news coverage of a "debate" series sponsored by the League of Women Voters did not fall under the "equal time" provision of Section 315. Thus the networks could cover this event as a news event just as they cover White House news conferences without the minor party opposition being given time to reply. This matter was being pursued by the Democratic National Committee in a lawsuit against the Columbia Broadcasting System and the Federal Communications Commission, but the DNC agreed not to press the suit when the Ford-Carter debates were scheduled, and Carter was given the opportunity to debate with President Ford.

The option of suspending Section 315 was again open to Congress, but on this occasion it was decided not to take that route but to let the League of Women Voters rather than the networks sponsor the joint appearances or "debates".

Many feel a suspension would have been preferable, so the debates could have been held in studios. The first debate was plagued with an equipment breakdown when it was held in the Walnut Street Theater in Philadelphia. The 28-minute delay caused by the breakdown of ABC's microphone equipment might have been avoided or shortened if the debate had occurred in a studio. Also a censorship problem arose; the networks did not want to carry the debates without being able to focus their cameras on the audience but the League as debate sponsor would not permit this. The networks resisted but eventually decided to cover the event anyway because of the overriding public interest involved; but many television people felt the debates were not well staged and they would have preferred to have consultation with experts.

The general public was not invited, and only a small audience attended each of the three 90-minute debates, which were held in Philadelphia, San Francisco, and Williamsburg, Virginia. A fourth debate was held between Senators Mondale and Dole, the vice presidential nominees, in Houston. But the debates were held, and while boring to some and criticized by many, did at least juxtapose the candidates so that each man's followers had to watch the other in action in order to see their own man.

As for the "Fairness Doctrine", this has caused a great deal of grief and difficulty of interpretation both for broadcasters and the FCC. The basic intent of the "Fairness Doctrine" is that all sides of controversial issues will be presented to the public. Difficulties have arisen because it is difficult to enforce the "Fairness Doctrine" without interfering with the freedom of broadcasters and those who use their facilities.

Examples of controversy over the Fairness Doctrine might be given in at least two cases to illustrate the problems. In the fall of 1975, CBS broadcast a one-hour program entitled, "The Guns of Autumn", which showed abuses of hunting licenses by hunters and which brought anguished cries of criticism from the American Rifle Association as well as sportsmen's groups. They complained that the presentation was one-sided. CBS did carry a follow-up program, "Echoes of the Guns of Autumn", in which it made an effort to carry rebuttals of the original program by the NRA, hunters and conservationists, but they argued that this did not meet the test of the "Fairness Doctrine" because the original program was slanted against hunters and the second program was merely "balanced" between the two points of view. NRA felt it should have had an entire hour to reply.

Another example is found in the CBS program, "The Selling of the Pentagon", which was critical of Pentagon public relations gestures as misrepresenting facts to the public about the defense establishment. Military spokesmen were given a chance to appear on the program but their remarks were edited and this prompted criticism by Defense Secretary Melvin Laird, Vice President Spiro Agnew and others. It even brought about a congressional investigation in which the Staggers Subcommittee in the House attempted unsuccessfully to subpoena Frank Stanton, the president of CBS at the time, and film "outtakes" from filmed material (outtakes are portions not used in broadcast). CBS refused to honor the subpoena for the outtakes and Stanton refused to appear under duress, and ultimately Congress backed down and CBS and Stanton were not cited for contempt. But again the problems of the Fairness Doctrine were illustrated. In 1976, Daniel Schorr, formerly of CBS, was subpoenaed, and did appear but he refused to testify in connection with a "leaked" CIA hearing document which he turned over to the <u>Village Voice</u> in Manhattan. Schorr resigned from CBS but he was never forced to reveal the source of his information; he argued that this would have had a "chilling effect" on any news correspondent seeking to gather the news and also that it would unfairly force him to act as a prosecutor in violation of his own professional ethics.[23] For every Daniel Schorr, there are scores more of unsung, unknown reporters who face similar problems.

The broadcasting industry feels the Fairness Doctrine should simply be eliminated and that instead the FCC and the courts should be allowed to hear complaints when it is felt that all viewpoints are not given access to the media. This view may ultimately prevail because of all the complications that have arisen from difficulties in enforcing the Fairness Doctrine. It should be remembered that this is a separate question from the "equal time" or Section 315 controversy. One relates to candidates and parties and the other relates to issues.

Political advertising on television also presents problems, some related to equal time and the Fairness Doctrine and some unrelated. One issue which apparently has been settled is that no station or network is required by present FCC rules or the 1934 Communications Act to sell time to a political advertiser (candidate, party, or issue sponsoring group) if it does not wish to do so. The courts apparently reason that if the power to sell or not to sell TV time is abused by broadcasters, public pressure will result in a remedy, and they see the freedom of broadcasters at issue. In a recent lawsuit the United States Supreme Court refused to accept the request of the Democratic National Committee that the Columbia Broadcasting System be required to sell time to the DNC to answer a speech by President Nixon on a controversial national issue. Since this ruling, however, the FCC has ruled that while presidential news conferences at the White House are news and therefore not subject to the equal time restrictions of Section 315, the networks and affiliates have no obligation to carry all

---

[23]For the former correspondent's view of the controversy, see Daniel Schorr, <u>Clearing the Air</u> (Boston: Houghton Mifflin Co., 1977).

White House news conferences or presidential speeches. On one occasion in 1976, one of the networks, ABC, declined to carry a Ford news conference at the White House under this ruling, even though CBS and NBC chose to carry it. The present situation is also that a presidential request for air time to carry a White House-originated presidential speech is not automatically honored. President Nixon made many such speeches, but President Ford did not get the time automatically as did Presidents Nixon and Johnson before him.

As for political advertising itself, especially campaign commercials, some general guidelines have developed in practice. It is increasingly the view that the thirty-second "spot" should be replaced by longer commercials so that sloganeering will be kept to a minimum. Some thirty-second spots were used in 1976 by both the Ford and Carter campaigns, but more one-minute spots were used and for the first time in recent years, a number of "five-minute trailers" were used, which followed regular programming which had a format of 25 minutes instead of 30 minutes, with the trailer at the end. This may represent a new trend, and it was favorably received by television critics and political observers. Political advertising is also controversial as to the ethics of the message. The "daisy petal" commercial of 1964 for the Democrats (implying Goldwater was a nuclear bomb "hothead") was taken off the air after Republicans complained, but complaints were ignored about the "flip-flop" commercial used by the Democrats for Nixon in 1972 to undermine the credibility of the George McGovern campaign. Sometimes a questionable commercial may be withdrawn before being used, as was the case in 1964 with a Goldwater commercial which implied that President Johnson approved of pornography and smut because of a report made by a presidential commission on pornography. Goldwater felt the commercial was unethical and in bad taste; he ordered it withdrawn before it could be used.

The outlook for the future in the coverage of politics is somewhat clouded, because political coverage is affected very strongly by such legal guidelines as the First Amendment, the Section 315 equal time provision (which it has been ruled does not apply to White House news conferences and presidential debates but may apply to other events, subject to the discretion of the FCC), and the Fairness Doctrine. The

prospect is that some of these guidelines will be
clarified, and the interpretation of the First Amendment freedoms of broadcasters will be fairly liberal;
it may however be balanced somewhat by court rulings
recognizing the First Amendment rights of candidates
and their parties. These issues were raised by former
Senator Eugene McCarthy in connection with the Carter-
Ford "debates" in 1976, but the courts ruled that Mc-
Carthy did not have a case and that the FCC ruling
settled the matter.

The Structure of the Radio Industry as Adjunct to TV
and Its Source

        The radio industry, which fostered the tele-
vision industry but now is largely an adjunct to TV,
should not be overlooked. The structure of this industry is similar to that of the TV industry, but
should be examined separately.

        Insofar as radio stations are concerned, the
relationship between networks and their affiliates is
similar to that between television stations and TV
networks. The affiliates of the major networks carry
their news and sports programming, and such prime-time
programming as they offer, such as "CBS Mystery
Theater". The affiliates operate very much as their
counterparts in television do, and the same is true of
the radio networks. The cost of advertising on radio
is today considerably less. The prime-time programming is less comprehensive on radio with local affiliates originating more of their own programming than is
the case with television. But the pattern of the relationship carried over from the days when radio was
more significant than television has not been drasti-
cally altered.

        Independent radio stations are numerous, and
somewhat different from independent television stations, they tend to target a particular audience and
they tend to specialize in programming. Thus all-news
stations such as WCBS in New York and WBBM in Chicago
provide round-the-clock news programming. NBC once
furnished programming for its own affiliate stations
through its News and Information Service, which was
discontinued in 1977. But many of the all-news stations are independent of network affiliation. Other
independent stations, in various parts of the nation
and elsewhere, such as CKLW, Windsor, Ontario,

specialize in rock music. Still others specialize in
"good music" or classical musical programming. Still
others place a heavy emphasis on sports presentations.
They have a clear place in the industry and they have
a loyal audience. Clear-channel stations once were
important in the radio industry, and most of them serve
a large regional audience. But since the coming of
FM their importance has waned. Some examples are WCBS,
New York; WLW, Cincinnati; WJR, Detroit; WHAS, Louisville; WSM, Nashville; WSB, Atlanta, and KSL, Salt
Lake City. Normally, they have a 50,000-watt transmitter and a network affiliation.

     To a considerable extent, the rise and decline
of radio networks can be correlated with the rise of
television networks, since as television increased in
overall importance, radio tended to diminish cor-
respondingly. Today, radio is coming back while TV
continues to rise in importance. The major networks
in the early days of radio were the National Broadcasting Company and the Columbia Broadcasting System.
Later the Mutual Broadcasting System joined the others,
and NBC eventually was split into the Blue Network and
the Red Network. The latter remained as the current
NBC network, and the Blue network was the forerunner
of ABC. The networks in their heyday provided news
programming, sports programming, and youth serial
programs. Networks also provided coverage of major
news events such as political conventions, and they
developed the first co-ordinated nationwide attempt
at news coverage outside the wire services. In addition they provided an audience for such late-night
programs as those afforded by the "big bands" such as
Glenn Miller and his Orchestra. All this did not come
to an end until the beginning of nationwide network
television in the early 1950's. By then it was clear
that the heyday of radio as a medium was past, and
that television's star had begun to rise.

     Today, the same radio networks exist as before:
NBC, CBS, Mutual, ABC, and in addition there is National Public Radio, a public service, partly publicly
financed radio network which concentrates on public
service programming. It is the radio counterpart of
PBS, mentioned earlier in the description of the institutional structure of television. National Public
Radio carries such programming as congressional hearings and classical music.

     In large measure today, radio serves as a

supplement to television. It reaches specialized audiences, old persons in retirement homes, young persons at the beach, drivers commuting in their cars, various other segments of the population which for one reason or another do not have access to television. It remains a medium which calls on listeners for more use of the imagination, and it is a medium which has instantaneousness as one of its main characteristics. TV aan be instantaneous also but it has more problems than radio with program structuring. Thus radio provides a bulletin service, and television comes along a bit later with pictorial coverage and newspapers a bit later yet with the printed page, both written and pictorial. Radio supplements television in serving those beyond the reach of the TV screen; it provides types of programming which are not feasible on television. Some prefer its news coverage because its format permits all-news stations, something not done by TV, and because its format and economics permit more news and fewer commercial minutes per newscast.

The evolution of the radio industry is partly a story of technological progress and partly a story of geographical spread of a new phenomenon. From the beginnings of wireless early in the 20th Century, radio grew until in 1920 the first broadcasts were put on the air--broadcasts of presidential election returns in the Harding-Cox election.[24] The first regular station, KDKA, went on the air that same year, and by 1926, the first major network, NBC, was in business. The radio set and fixed frequency broadcasting made modern ratio broadcasting possible. By 1927, when the Federal Radio Act, was passed by Congress, the federal government began assigning frequencies for broadcasting. By 1934, the mandate of federal legislation was broadened and the Congress established the Federal Communications Commission, which today licenses both radio and television stations and monitors citizens band radio licensing, as well as other forms of communication. The FCC was given the basic regulatory responsibility in order to control the growth and development of the mushrooming broadcast industry, and it oversaw the introduction of FM (static-free) radio, the first television stations, the television networks,

---

[24]See Eric Barnouw, The Golden Web: A History of Broadcasting in the United States, 1933 to 1953 (New York: Oxford University Press, 1968).

and today the development of a nationwide system of cable television. It had a great deal to do with the evolution of the radio industry.

The way in which the radio industry spawned the television industry resembles in many ways the manner in which the newspaper industry spawned the radio industry. The first owners of many radio station licenses were newspapers, and likewise the first holders of many television station licenses were newspaper-radio combinations. The FCC is currently trying to diversify ownership, but it has historically not required radio stations and newspapers to divest themselves of television stations which grew out of their communications operations. This will be done more in the future, however, as the result of a 1977 FCC ruling. The television industry grew more or less naturally out of the radio industry as radio simply began to add pictures and radio stations branched out into television. The background and technology, as to experience of operators of stations, was similar enough that many radio broadcasters found themselves in on the ground floor of the emerging television industry.

There remains a considerable future potential for radio and its use in American politics, especially in local campaigns. It will probably always remain an adjunct to television, which overshadows it, but it has a definite place because of its ability to reach specialized audiences and because of the portability of radio (it can be used in cars and carried anywhere, for example). It may be used in different ways as network television loses some of its importance to cablevision, but it will be a factor in the broadcasting industry for many years, as it now seems to be developing.

Campaign commercials on radio continue to have an importance in local campaigns, and to some extent in statewide and national campaigns. Indeed, many consider radio the best medium for advertising. Radio is peculiarly adapted to the device of repetition of slogans and repetition of arguments on behalf of candidates, issues, and parties. It will doubtless continue to be used in this fashion. As limits on campaign spending remain stringent, radio will probably be of increasing importance in relation to television and newspaper advertising as it is a relatively inexpensive manner in which to reach a large number of people effectively. The 30-second and one-minute spot will probably remain the major type of campaign commercial on radio, although half-hour or hour-long broadcasts may occasionally be used (along with five-minute commercials).

Campaign coverage on radio will probably continue to be relegated to a secondary place behind campaign coverage on television, because television carries a visual impact which radio does not possess. But as I noted earlier in referring to all-news formats on radio, there are certain characteristics of radio as a medium, which make it a desirable forum for candidates to appear on in order to further their campaigns. Campaign coverage on radio will continue to be an important adjunct to campaign coverage on television and in the print media, but it cannot be expected to supplant coverage on any of the other major media.

Coverage of public policy on radio has considerable potential, not only on commercial all-news stations with a 24-hour news format, but also through National Public Radio. Such major events as the Watergate hearings of the Ervin Committee of 1973, the Judiciary Committee impeachment hearings of 1974, and the political conventions of 1976 are particularly well suited for this kind of coverage, and it will probably be expanded. Congress is studying TV coverage of House debates with government cameras.

Structure of the Newspaper Industry and Its Changing Role in the Age of Television

The structure of the newspaper industry has changed considerably since the days when newspapers were the dominant medium and newspaper endorsements of candidates in political campaigns were widely noticed and much discussed. The newspaper industry today shares billing with radio and television; newspapers are no longer the sole source, or even the principal source, of the public's information about politics. Still the newspaper--and especially the prestige paper such as the New York Times or the Washington Post--remains a chief source of important analysis and information about the campaign from the so-called "attentive public" of regular newspaper readers who often are the "community influentials" who influence public opinion in any community. Thus newspapers remain important today, but they are important for different reasons than in the pre-television era.

Since the function and structure of the newspaper industry have both been examined earlier, this portion of the chapter will analyze some developments which have accompanied television's rise and the change in the newspaper's role from a reporter of events to a source of analysis and depth coverage. One of the more important of these relationships is that between individual newspapers and the syndicates which provide them with columns, special news coverage and features. Syndicates may be exemplified by the North American Newspaper Alliance and Newspaper Enterprise Association. Some serve small dailies and even weeklies. Syndicates may be such nationwide organizations as United Features Syndicate, the _Times_-_Post_ News Service (Los Angeles _Times_ and Washington _Post_), the New York _Times_ News Service, and Chicago _Tribune_ News Service, as well as regional syndicates which serve limited numbers of newspapers. The rise of the syndicated columnists, an important development related to newspaper syndicates, has caused the diminishing in importance of the newspaper editorial and the editorial endorsement of candidates by individual newspapers. A candidate about whom a columnist like James (Scotty) Reston or Clayton Fritchey says favorable things may not need many newspaper endorsements. A majority of the daily newspaper endorsements in 1976 went to Gerald Ford, but he still lost the election to Jimmy Carter, perhaps in part because some of the columnists (certainly by no means all) were saying complimentary things--or less derogatory things--about Carter. Syndicates are important for the influence of the columnists and also for the part they are playing in the homogenization of American daily newspapers (and weekly newspapers, for that matter).

The newspapers also have a key relationship with the co-operative newsgathering agencies. Originally there were three major wire services in the United States: The Associated Press, founded in the 1840s; the United Press, originally affiliated with the Scripps-Howard newspaper chain and dating back to the turn of the century, and the International News Service, which was established by William Randolph Hearst, again around the turn of the century. About twenty years ago, the UP was merged with INS, and the merged wire service became known as UPI. Since then

the major wire services operating in the United States
have been AP and UPI. There are also foreign news
agencies, such as Reuters (British), Havas (French),
and Tass (Soviet). These furnish news to clients much
as the American wire services do. The AP consists of
member newspapers who furnish news to AP and take news
from it on a co-operative basis. The UPI's newspapers
are customers or clients who buy its service. Both
AP and UPI furnish wirephoto service as well as news
and feature coverage. They also play a major part in
the standardization of news coverage and reporting in
the United States. This causes a trend toward a common style (through use of the AP or UPI style book by
all newspapers using those wire services) and it also
causes a common consensus of what is newsworthy and
what is not. It should be remembered also that most
radio and television stations also use one or both of
the wire services that serve the newspapers, although
they normally subscribe to the radio wire which is
written differently than the AAA wire which is filed
to the newspapers. The wire services also have an
audio service for broadcasters. State and regional
wires also provide more specialized or limited services to member newspapers and clients, particularly
to small city dailies, some weeklies or other newspapers.

        The relationship between newspapers and radio-
TV station ownership is an important one. The newspapers that own radio and TV station licenses are in
some degree similar to the networks that have owned-
and-operated stations. They control the policy of
these stations and for all practical purposes they are
almost like an extension of the corporate identity of
the newspapers that hold the station ownership. Since
newspapers that have such a monopoly or semi-monopoly
position are aware of the possible abuses of it, they
frequently go to great lengths to assure independence
of the broadcasting operation and to provide access
to the media by all groups in the community or region
which they serve. Some newspapers such as the Washington _Post_ have an ombudsman to deal with the public's complaints against the newspaper and others such
as the Louisville _Courier-Journal_ have customer-ser-
vice columns to deal with complaints, corrections and
the like. The _Post_ also has a critic who writes in
criticism of newspapers and even its own coverage. A
higher degree of social responsibility is thus displayed by newspapers today than, in the opinion of
many, the television stations. But they still fall

short of the standards of perfection, of course. Some
newspapers do fall considerably short of ethical and
other expectations, however, and some of these are
part of "chains" which represent multiple ownerships.
There are of course both "good" and "bad" chains in
the sense of the degree of public responsibility they
represent. The only control the public has over "bad"
chains is that it stop buying their newspapers and
read something else; newspapers, unlike radio and
television broadcasting stations, have no regulation
imposed on them by government.

"Chain" ownership can exercise considerable
responsibility. The Knight Newspapers (Detroit Free
Press, Akron Beacon Journal, Miami Herald) have a good
reputation in this regard. The same is true of the
Cox Newspapers (Atlanta Journal and Constitution,
Dayton Daily News and Journal Herald). Other "chains"
have a less responsible reputation, such as the Newhouse newspapers and the Ridder chain, or Rupert Murdoch's American periodicals, and there are others who
have not the means to do an outstanding job but make
an attempt to serve the public interest as best they
can. Some publishers develop the reputation of simply
being out to make money rather than to serve the public interest, but of course the same charge is sometimes made about television networks and station
owners probably with no greater or less reason.

Effect of "chain" ownership on political coverage can be great or less so, depending on how much
freedom is given individual member newspapers in the
"chain". A paper like the Detroit Free Press apparently did not suffer from being part of a "chain",
while one like the Buffalo Evening Standard may have
suffered if local editors were given little or no freedom in determining the nature and extent of news coverage in their own columns.

The role of news coverage in the modern newspaper is a major one, but news coverage is of a different sort today. The newspaper editor in the 1970's
realizes that many of his newspaper's readers will
have seen a television news program or heard a radio
newscast with the same information before they read it
in his newspaper's pages. Therefore, he will try to
provide depth coverage and analysis to put the news in
perspective. This is something which takes detail, a
thing easiest for newspapers to provide because of
format, but hardest for radio and TV to provide. Thus

an increasing emphasis on analysis and background stories in newspapers fits them best in an era of television coverage of major news events.

The role of commentary in the newspaper of today is usually in two forms--editorials or background stories which provide perspective for the news events on the surface, and columns (either locally written or syndicated) providing analysis of current news events. The newspaper's key role today is perhaps to provide a context for understanding the news. This is made possible through good columns, editorials, analysis pieces and the like. The newspaper thus helps the reader to understand the significance of what is going on around him but which TV and radio have neither the time nor inclination to explain, except in such rare instances as the NBC "White Paper" documentaries.

Television has caused newspapers' role to change in that it has taken from the newspaper the town-crier function of being first to relate the news to the public, and it has caused the newspaper and all the print media for that matter to move toward explaining the significance of the news through analyses, columns and the like.

The newest trend in newspaper journalism is perhaps the rise of interpretive and investigative journalism, a logical extension of the trend toward analysis which was already apparent. This was best demonstrated in the work of Bob Woodward and Carl Bernstein in breaking open the Watergate scandal of the Nixon Administration, but they are only two of the more prominent practitioners of this type of journalism. Another example of it would be the article by Seymour Hersh of the New York _Times_ on the My Lai massacre in Vietnam, or the Daniel Schorr revelations about the CIA released through the _Village Voice_. A controversy has arisen periodically about the manner of publishing such expose material and how it should be released, but it is clear that investigative, interpretive reporting is here to stay. The use of "leaked" information is a major part of such reporting, but it ought to be noted that government officials also "leak" favorable information, as did Henry Kissinger, and that they usually get upset about "leaks" only when they may prove damaging to themselves or the administrations which they serve.

One point remains for discussion. That is the
effort to project where the Woodward and Bernstein
trend may lead in the future of newspaper journalism.
It could lead in two different directions. The
journalists believe it could lead to more honest government and better public responsibility on the part
of public servants, because officials who know that
they won't be able to operate in secret will be open
and above-board and more honest with the public. The
officials tend to believe it may lead to greater
sensationalism and some of them were highly critical
of the book by "Woodstein" entitled The Final Days,
as they felt that there was not enough disclosure of
sources by the authors. Be that as it may, the trend
is still a strong one, and it is unlikely that it will
be arrested any time in the near future.

One thing is sure, officials will always be
able to answer allegations about themselves. News
stories and books can be written by reporters like
Woodward and Bernstein, but there will also be auto-
biographies and memoirs by former officials like
President Nixon. The public will be able to judge who
is right when it is given all the facts, and it is
there that the final judgment should rest. Suppression is unhealthy and all should be given their say.
The First Amendment freedoms written into the Constitution indicate that the best remedy for abuse of
freedom is its exercise by everyone, including those
against whom charges are hurled. If Nixon was guilty
of wrongdoing (and the evidence on his tapes indicates
he was), let the public know and make its own judgment.
If the public felt Ford was wrong in pardoning Nixon,
let the public again make its own judgment. It can
only do this with all the facts, including those
brought to the public through the instrumentality of
investigative and interpretive journalism. In this
sense, Woodward and Bernstein did the nation a service
through their reporting of Watergate.

Current Technology of the Mass Media

The functions of the mass media and their relation to political phenomena are affected by technological advances in the media, such as new applications
of television technology. These will be examined
briefly, with emphasis on implications of the newer
technology for political aspects of the mass media.

Television has recently developed satellite technology to the point where satellites make possible live broadcasts between Peking and New York, or between any two points in the world where equipment can be taken. The use of this technology has also made it possible to receive telecast signals from the surface of the moon and outer space, as well as live TV from China as occurred in 1972 when former President Nixon made his visit to the Great Wall outside of Peking and the late Mao Tse Tung played host to the President.

Satellite technology needs to be summarized briefly. The signal is beamed upward to the satellite from the point of origin, and the satellite then relays it in a fashion similar to microwave relay to various relay points around the globe. The quality of the signal is normally excellent, subject to the usual technical limitations. The satellite has been a major step toward achieving what McLuhan referred to as the "global village".[25]

Another new development in television which has recently been refined to the point that it can be used in regular broadcasting is the "minicam" or camera employing miniaturized equipment. This is a major step forward since it makes it possible for cameramen to get to formerly inaccessible locations, but it is only the first step forward since technology is now being developed for the "microcam" or miniature "minicam". The equipment for the "microcam" could be handled by one person, thus giving reporters and correspondents greater maneuverability. The "microcam" is not yet generally in use, but it will doubtless be in use soon, probably before general use of the large mural-screen TV set or reasonably priced videocassette recorders.[26]

Radio has been affected by the impact of the new miniaturized equipment, because very small portables can be manufactured with transistor circuitry, and the smaller the portables the more easily they can

---

[25] Marshall McLuhan and Quentin Fiore, War and Peace in the Global Village (New York: Bantam Books, 1968).

[26] Videocassette recorders are used to tape television programs for replaying later through a standard TV set with a special attachment. It is possible that copyright problems may arise when cheaper videocassette recorders become available.

236

be carried anywhere. Radio's chief remaining advantage over TV is that it can be taken just about anywhere; even a personal portable TV cannot be taken just about anywhere, so radio retains a slightly greater degree of instantaneousness than does TV. Doubtless the newer technology will make radio even more popular, as a subsidiary news medium. Radio no longer makes an attempt to perform all the functions performed by television, but at one time, in the infancy of TV, the two were competitive.

Newspapers have also felt the impact of new technological innovations. Newspaper printing processes were revolutionized when offset printing on a mass scale, suitable for metropolitan daily newspapers, became feasible. Offset printing gives a superior and more readable appearance and in many instances is gradually replacing conventional letterpress. The new coldtype processes have replaced the older technology of linotype hot-type typesetting for newspapers, and these have been joined by the teletypesetter equipment almost routinely used by daily newspapers today. With the teletypesetter, when telegraph or wire copy is received in the newsroom, a punched tape is delivered at the same time as the teletype copy. This tape is then sent to the composing room and a TTS machine "reads" the punched tape before setting the material into type. Still another technological advancement in the print media is the introduction of electronic editing processes. These involve the use of computer terminals for editing and eliminate part of the older process. Still more changes are occurring, such as the use of the varitype which eliminates the need for linotype composition, but it is not necessary to catalog them all in this brief discussion.

What implication does all this new technology in television, radio and the print media have for the news media institution and the relationship of the media to the political environment they cover? One obvious advantage of all the new technology is the increased speed with which the news dissemination function can be performed, as for example, satellite TV compared with film or tape that had to be flown from the Far East to New York. Still another advantage is that the new technology allows correspondents, reporters, writers and editors to concentrate on their basic job of getting the reportage of news events to the public.

Has the new technology meant that the media are doing a better job for the public? In the technical sense, it no doubt has, but in the sense of the quality of news writing, reporting, editing and other functions performed by the news media, it has not necessarily done so. This is because the basic integrity of the media's newsgathering and news interpreting function depends on the integrity, knowledge and analytic and reporting skills of the people in the media themselves. Better trained reporters have more to do with improving this process than the greatest advances in technology. The networks sometimes overlook this when they advertise all the gadgetry of their convention coverage, for example, but neglect to mention the background of their reporters, analysts and correspondents.

The potential for political coverage and advertising growing out of the new technology is great, even if not yet realized to the full. Perhaps there has been more of an effect on campaign techniques in politics, ironically, than there has been on the use of the technology in the reporting of politics. Every candidate wishes to make use of the latest polling, media and other technology and if he or she is running for a major office, he/she makes sure that this is done. The development of "image" politics with a major role for campaign management and media consultants is a development closely related to this modern technology.

The modern technology also has had its impact on public relations techniques in government. For example, the whole operation of the White House press office is quite different today than it was even in the time of Pierre Salinger or James C. Hagerty. Ron Nessen and Jody Powell have had many more techniques at their disposal for disseminating information, news and even propaganda about Presidents Ford and Carter. This applies to the remainder of government as well as the White House, but because of the pre-eminent importance of the Presidency, the trend is most visible in the White House.

Theories of Mass Communication

The relationship between the White House and the news media can be examined in the light of several basic theories of mass communication. Each of these

A WHO'S WHO OF NOTABLES IN MODERN JOURNALISM

WALTER CRONKITE--CBS Evening News anchorman; former UPI reporter and convention anchorperson for CBS since 1956

BARBARA WALTERS--ABC Evening News co-anchor with Harry Reasoner; first woman prime-time anchor and holder of $1 million contract

JOHN CHANCELLOR--NBC Nightly News anchorman; former Moscow correspondent, "Today" host and convention correspondent

HARRY REASONER--ABC Evening News co-anchor with Barbara Walters; originally with CBS News; has whimsical approach to news

DAVID BRINKLEY--NBC Nightly News commentator; formerly part of team with Chet Huntley; attained fame with convention coverage

HOWARD K. SMITH--ABC News commentator; once considered a liberal correspondent, now considered slightly conservative

ERIC SEVAREID--CBS News commentator, recently retired; featured on Evening News; European correspondent in younger days; did "Conversations"

ROGER MUDD--CBS Capitol Hill correspondent; reputed to be in line to serve as "anchor" when Cronkite retires

PROMINENT CORRESPONDENTS:

CBS--Lesley Stahl, Bruce Morton, Hughes Rudd, Dan Rather, Morton Dean, Susan Spencer, Marya McLaughlin, Ed Bradley, Bob Schieffer, Robert Pierpoint, Winston Burdett

NBC--Judy Woodruff, Bob Jameson, Peter Hackes, Floyd Kalber ("Today" announcer), Jane Pauley ("Today" features); Tom Brokaw ("Today" host; former White House correspondent); John Hart, Bill Monroe

ABC--Ann Compton, Sam Donaldson, Bob Clark, Tom Jarrell, Barbara Walters (also does interviewing)

239

will be discussed briefly before we leave the subject
of the structure of the news media as institutions
serving the public.

One of the basic concerns of all theories about
the mass communications media has been the concern
with their influence on public opinion formation.
Some critics think this influence is great while others
think it is overrated; the data seem to bear out
neither view entirely.

It might be stated that the "devil theory" of
the news media--that they deliberately distort the
news to serve their own ends or those of their political allies--was popularized by former Vice President
Spiro T. Agnew in 1969 after Richard Nixon's early
presidential speeches about Vietnam and the "great
silent majority". Agnew charged that the networks
distorted Nixon's words through "instant analysis"
following the President's speech and he claimed that a
"small band of willful men" in New York--the media
capital of the nation--undermined the wishes of the
public by sneering at the elected leaders of the nation, by raising an eyebrow in an appropriate place,
and by otherwise distorting the news in a most harmful
way for the national interest. Agnew usually identified the national interest with that of the Administration of which he was a part. His attacks drew some
rejoinders from Cronkite and others, and there was a
great deal of controversy.[27] CBS even cancelled its
"instant analyses" for a time, and then the controversy over the Pentagon Papers reignited the basic
controversy. After numerous escapades such as the
Pentagon papers, the coverage of the Watergate affair
and its related events, including the impeachment
movement against Nixon, ultimately quieted down Agnew,
he blamed Attorney General Richardson as much as the
news media for his own ouster as Vice President.
Nixon became too busy to worry much about the news
media, but remarks he made to John Dean on the infamous tapes made it clear that he could hardly wait
until after the 1972 election to make his "enemies"
(and the list was a long one) suffer for what he considered to be their misdeeds. This was not to be, as
Nixon resigned in disgrace, but if there had been no
tapes, many people forget that Nixon might have won
his battle with the news media and imposed a dictator-

---

[27]Martin Mayer, About Television (New York:
Harper & Row, 1972), pp. 214-219.

ial regime, or at least a very authoritarian regime. The media helped to save the country from that fate, however, by their own exposes of the scandals of the Nixon Administration. Agnew made his initial speech excoriating the networks in Des Moines, and the response was so favorable in ultra-conservative and other circles that he went to Birmingham to deliver a similar attack against the anti-Administration newspapers. This was a ninety-day sensation, but after Agnew's resignation this criticism faded quickly.

The conspiracy theory of the media is another view which suggests that the media are somehow part of a subversive plot to take over the country in company with the intellectuals, the liberals and the pro-Communist fellow travelers, to prevent the 100 per cent red-blooded Americans from maintaining control. This theory, indeed, is accepted only by right-wing fringe elements but at one time it was very popular.[28]

Various objective studies of media influence have been attempted, and measurements of media exposure have been developed, but no researcher has yet developed an effective measure of the linkage between exposure and political beliefs or attitudes. However, Edith Efron has made a study of bias in the news. Her study of the 1968 presidential campaign showed that Humphrey was given more favorable and more extensive coverage than Nixon or Wallace in the presidential campaign. But her categorization of the news has been criticized, and her findings are far from being generally accepted. That there may have been bias is quite possible, but that it was in the direction in which she found it is debatable.[29] A later study conducted by Edward Jay Epstein indicated that the existence of

---

[28]See John L. Hulteng, The Messenger's Motives: Ethical Problems of the News Media (Englewood Cliffs, N.J.: Prentice-Hall, 1976). Also see William Small, Political Power and the Press (New York: Hastings House, Publishers, Inc., 1972); Marvin Barrett, ed., Moments of Truth? (New York: Thomas Y. Crowell Co., 1975), and Edwin Diamond, The Tin Kazoo: Television, Politics and the News (Cambridge, Mass.: MIT Press, 1975).

[29]Edith Efron, The News Twisters (New York: Manor Books, 1972).

bias in the news media can more credibly be accounted for by the economic limitations on the television broadcasting industry. He notes, for example, that coverage of out-of-the-way places is difficult whereas appearances of candidates in major cities are more likely to get coverage from the networks.[30]

Another theory has been that there is actually very little media influence on public opinion formation. It is argued that countervailing factors tend to override or offset media influence. These factors include such things as socio-economic variables in the background of each individual voter. Voting studies from the University of Michigan Survey Research Center for Political Studies indicate that while in a time of flux and change, the electorate is more likely to take cues from the news media, the basic attitudes growing out of political socialization or education, the social and economic background variables of the individual, group memberships, and the influence of friends are usually more influential than opinions to which the average voter is exposed through the news media.[31] The "nexus" hypothesis of Klapper is one statement of this view. Thus media influence becomes only one small influence on the voter among the many to which he/she is exposed. A good deal of the findings of empirical research tends to support this viewpoint, although no definitive conclusion can be reached at this point. The reasons why some of these other variables override media influence are many and varied. At least one reason is that people tend to read and watch on television primarily those views and opinions they are likely to agree with. Thus, except for the "debates" of the 1976 presidential campaign, a typical Ford supporter may have never watched Carter and a typical Carter supporter may have never watched Ford and each may have paid very little attention to newspaper stories about the opposing candidate. Many

---

[30]Edward Jay Epstein, News From Nowhere: Television and the News (New York: Random House, 1973). See also Ben H. Bagdikian, The Effete Conspiracy and Other Crimes By the Press (New York: Harper & Row, 1972).

[31]Norman H. Nie, Sidney Verba, and John R. Petrocik, The Changing American Voter (Cambridge, Mass.: Harvard University Press, 1976).

other reasons can be given, but one of the most basic of these is that people usually develop their political opinions and attitudes slowly and are very unlikely to change them very rapidly. This can be illustrated by the behavior of "Democrats for Nixon" of 1972 who returned to their basic allegiance in 1976 in order to vote for Jimmy Carter. Political change may no longer be glacial, but it still tends to be gradual.[32]

Sig Mickelson in The Electric Mirror suggests a kind of "mirror" theory, which is basically that television merely holds up a mirror to the society in which it sees itself reflected. (Mickelson is a retired CBS News executive.) There is a great deal to this, although it can be pressed too far. The phenomenon of selective perception is also at work here; that is, we only see on the tube that which we want to see. Two people can see Jimmy Carter smile on television, and one will think it is a nice smile while another can think it is a deceptive smile. Who really knows which one is right?[33]

Another popular theory with media people is that the public tends to blame the messenger, not the message, when the news is bad. Thus the failure of Johnson to end the war in Vietnam, the failure of Nixon to "come clean" about Watergate, were blamed on the media rather than these leaders, even though in each case the President was more to blame than the news media. Thus a kind of transference of hostility took place, and the messenger was blamed for the message.[34]

Another view of the function and role of the mass media may be found in the idea that the media are themselves limited by the context of what they communicate to the public, for example: The facts that are known, the public's perceptions of these facts, the situation in which the facts are related to the public have a great deal to do with the public's reaction to national and international events. Thus the media

---

[32]Joseph Klapper, The Effects of Mass Communication (New York: Free Press of Glencoe, 1960).

[33]Sig Mickelson, op. cit.

[34]Hulteng, op. cit.

serve as a kind of conveyor belt, but they have as little control over the context of events and perhaps less than the politicians themselves do.

Nevertheless, it is generally conceded that the media do have some influence on political behavior and many studies have been conducted to attempt to find out how great that influence is and under which circumstances it is effective.

Factors indicating high influence of media on the public could include a great deal of effective exposure to television speeches, a great deal of effective exposure to news coverage on television, and the like. The only difficulty with this is that it is relatively easy to measure exposure to the media, but it is almost impossible to measure the true effects of exposure.

Factors indicating low influence of the media on the public, to the extent which it can be determined, would be indications of lack of effect of exposure to TV speeches, lack of effect of exposure to newscasts, press conferences and the like. Here again the data can be interpreted many different ways and lack of effect is as difficult to prove as effect. The data we have tend to indicate a limited effect, but this is frequently overshadowed by pre-existing attitudes and other variables, as already stated.

Some general conclusions can be reached about the impact of the mass media on policy making in the White House, and also about the impact of the mass media on political campaigns for the Presidency.

The impact of the mass media (whether television, radio, newspapers or magazines) on policy making in the White House grows out of perceptions of White House policy makers of the effect, or potential effect of news stories, media dissemination of speeches and the like on the public. The impact of the media will be slight if the White House policy makers believe the public is paying little attention; but if the White House policy makers believe the public is paying a great deal of attention, the impact will be considerable. It will be considerable in two ways: (1) the White House policy makers will take into account the effect the media may be having on the public, and (2) the White House policy makers will make an effort to counteract, through their own media utterances, any negative effects such coverage is having on the public.

The above observations can be extended to refer to political campaigns for the Presidency. The same general rule can be made to apply to the campaign situation as to the policy making situation. If the President who is running for re-election believes the media are having damaging effects on his campaign, he will try to counteract it by his own manipulation of the media or the public and try to offset unfavorable publicity with favorable publicity. If the coverage is good from his viewpoint, he will try to see that it continues. If he feels it is having little effect, he will probably ignore the problem and concentrate on his own direct communication with the public as well as his communication with the public through the news media.

CHAPTER FIVE

THE ACTUAL LINKAGES OF PRESIDENCY AND MASS MEDIA

. . . The (Vienna Summit) session broke up at 6:45 p.m. Kharlamov and I were waiting for the two heads of state in the embassy lobby to prepare a joint communique for the press. The principals agreed that we would omit all specifics and describe the first day's conversations merely as "frank, courteous, and wide-ranging". Kharlamov and I went into a side office and I reduced the communique to two typewritten paragraphs. We then left for a joint press briefing at the historic Hofburg Palace.

I can only describe the scene as bedlam. More than 1200 reporters and photographers, representing at least thirty nations, were jammed into the auditorium. Hundreds of television cables were strewn around the floor. Correspondents were struggling to adjust headsets to hear the instantaneous translation in six languages. . . . To preserve at least a semblance of order, we had agreed on White House rules for the briefing. No one could enter or leave the auditorium until it was over.

I read the joint communique, emphasizing the key phrase, "frank, courteous, and wide-ranging". . . . When (Kharmlamov) took over the mike, he said . . ."This was all that was decided to communicate today so that the meeting tomorrow could be as _fruitful_ as today."

"Fruitful" went much further than the statement on which we had agreed. . . . I was to spend much time the next two days spiking a series of Russian "leaks" that Khrushchev was bringing JFK around to his point of view. . . ."

--Pierre Salinger, "The Russians in Vienna", in <u>With</u> <u>Kennedy</u> (Garden City, N.Y.: Doubleday & Co., 1966), pp. 179, 180

"Mr. President, I have something here you
need to see", I went on, feeling the tension
in my throat as I spoke. I tore open the
manila envelope and removed my letter to him.
He reached for it, leaned back in his big
chair and began reading. . . . The President
finished reading, turned the letter face down
on the desk, spun his chair half-around, and
sat looking past me toward the windows along
the Rose Garden.

"Well, Jerry", he began, "I'm sorry you
feel this way." His voice was even and quiet,
his face betraying no sign of emotion or surprise. For three or four minutes, Ford spoke.
I did not interrupt.

"It was not an easy decision for me to
make", he said of his plan to pardon Nixon.
I thought about it a lot and prayed, too.". . .

"Mr. President, I want you to know this was
a hard decision for me, too", I said, my voice
tightening as I spoke. "But I just felt that
I had no choice under the circumstances except
to do this. I wanted to tell you personally.
I stayed up all night thinking about it. I
just couldn't come to any other choice. So
I--"

The telephone buzzer sounded again. I
stood up, extending my hand. "I'm sorry, Mr.
President". Ford rose and we shook hands.
"I'm sorry, too", he replied, then picked up
the telephone. . . .

> --Jerald F. terHorst, "Epilogue", in Gerald
> Ford and the Future of the Presidency
> (New York: The Third Press, 1974), pp.
> 226, 227

* * * *

How the Linkage Occurs in the Operation of the Two
Institutions

Now that I've examined in detail the institution of the Presidency and the institution of the mass
media, I'll analyze the linkages between these two
institutions. I'll consider how the linkage occurs in

247

the White House, and then how the linkage occurs in the news media.

The linkage occurs in the White House through the operation of the White House Press Office. Under Presidents Nixon and Ford this was under control of the White House communications director. Herb Klein held this position in Nixon's first term. Nixon also appointed Clay Whitehead as Director of the Office of Telecommunications Policy.[1] The communications director conducted his duties in an administrative capacity, chiefly, and he was a co-ordinator of news media activities. Klein functioned by supervising the White House Press Office operation, basically under press secretary Ron Ziegler, and he also traveled around the country giving interviews and propagandizing on behalf of the Nixon Administration. His successor under Ford was somewhat less well known, and for a time before Nixon's resignation Ziegler had the responsibility for these duties.[2]

The White House Press Secretary has traditionally been the key person in the White House Press Office and its operations. The White House Press Secretary under President Carter is Jody Powell, whose appointment was foreshadowed when he served as the press secretary for Governor Carter during the 1976 presidential campaign. The Press Secretary's duties are basically the management of the press office, the preparation and conduct of presidential news conferences, and the handling of daily (or at least frequent) press briefings.

---

[1]For a discussion of the Office of Telecommunications Policy (OTP), see Douglass Cater and Michael J. Nyhan, eds., The Future of Public Broadcasting (New York: Praeger Publishers, 1976), pp. 8, 109, 121ff., 252, 313, 330. The OTP played a major role in the controversy over how public broadcasting would be funded. For a profile of Clay T. Whitehead and the operation of OTP under Nixon, see William E. Porter, Assault on the Media: the Nixon Years (Ann Arbor, Mich.: University of Michigan Press, 1976), pp. 73-79, 145, 147.

[2]Ford downgraded the Office of Telecommunications Policy, and in 1977 at this writing the Carter Administration was reported to be considering complete dismantling of the agency.

Jody Powell's immediate predecessor in this position was Ron Nessen, formerly a correspondent for the National Broadcasting Company. Nessen's predecessor was Jerald terHorst, Washington correspondent for the Detroit News, who resigned after a month because of his inability to support the action of President Gerald R. Ford in pardoning former President Richard M. Nixon for his Watergate crimes. Under Nixon, the press secretary for most of his five-year tenure was Ron Ziegler, a former advertising agency man for the J. Walter Thompson agency in Los Angeles and Nixon's campaign press aide. Ziegler had a famous feud with the Washington Post. When his charges against the Post proved to be untrue, he said merely that the White House denials about Watergate were "inoperative", largely destroying his credibility. After that, Ziegler took Klein's old job and Gerald Warren became Nixon's press secretary for the remainder of his term.

Press secretaries have come and gone at the White House. Lyndon Johnson, the 36th President, was served by Bill Moyers, George Reedy and George Christian. John F. Kennedy was served in this capacity by Pierre Salinger for his 1,000-plus-day administration. Prior to Kennedy, James C. Hagerty, by consensus perhaps the standout in the group, served Dwight D. Eisenhower. In the Truman Administration, the post was held by Jonathan Daniels, Charles Ross, and James Short. Daniels was a newspaper editor and publisher and Ross was a correspondent in Washington before his appointment for the St. Louis Post-Dispatch. He was also a former classmate of President Truman. Franklin D. Roosevelt had Stephen T. Early, Louis Howe, and Marvin McIntyre in this capacity. Prior to Early's time, the press spokesman was usually almost anonymous, and it was under FDR that the press secretary became a specifically singled-out position. Aides like James P. Tumulty had served Presidents like Woodrow Wilson prior to that time, but they had often carried out other duties as well as that of press aide.

Jody Powell served President Carter before his 1976 campaign; from 1971 to 1975 Powell served as the Governor's press secretary when President Carter was Governor of Georgia. A native of Americus, Georgia, without journalistic experience, Powell was the Carter press aide in the 1966 campaign, Carter's first for statewide office. Carter hoped to retain Powell during his entire tenure just as Eisenhower and Kennedy had kept Hagerty and Salinger in the same post during their entire tenure. Powell has an unassuming, self-deprecating manner, which caused ABC Anchorperson Barbara Walters to comment that he returned her phone call with an apology for a delay in returning her call. Barbara Walters expressed the hope that he would continue to be so polite in the Southern fashion after four years in the White House. Powell and Hamilton Jordan, of the Carter staff, were two of the closest aides to the President. They worked hard in all of his major campaigns.

The White House Press Office, under Jody Powell's guidance, is responsible for White House news media operations, including contacts with all correspondents stationed at the White House. The office assists Powell in briefing the President for all his White House news conferences. It also makes contacts with networks, newspapers and other media for special events coverage of the President. Furnishing of background information and conduct of briefings, sometimes handled by Powell's staff, are other duties handled by the press office. The responsibilities of this office are similar to its responsibilities in previous administrations. But every administration has its own press relations style and the Carter Administration is no exception. Its press relations in the early months have been reasonably good, but after a honeymoon period, they begin to become more normal.

Preparation and staging of White House news conferences normally involve much work. The President must be carefully and fully briefed about pending legislative and diplomatic matters. His press staff works with him, asking questions likely to be raised in his news conferences. The President may wish to consult experts on his own staff or such other officials as the Secretary of State or Secretary of Defense on foreign policy matters, or the Secretary of the Treasury or Chairman of the Council of Economic Advisors on fiscal or economic policy. Then he may work with the press staff to determine what questions to expect. He may also expect a briefing from his public opinion experts to establish what matters weigh most heavily on the public's mind before holding a news conference.

If the news conference is for pencil-and-pad reporters and photographers from the print media only, it may be held in a different type of location than

one held before television cameras and radio and TV
microphones. The East Room has been the scene of Ford
and Johnson news conferences and some of the Nixon and
Carter news conferences. Nixon did not hold many, and
he sometimes held them outside of Washington as was
Ford's practice also. This means that local reporters
and White House regulars rather than the full Washington press corps attend such a conference. If a full
dress news conference is held, it may be held in the
State Department Auditorium, large enough to accommodate several hundred members of the working press,
cameras, microphones, lighting and all the other
necessary paraphernalia. Presidents have developed
different formats. President Eisenhower let his conferences be filmed for TV and then his news secretary,
James C. Hagerty, edited the film for security and
other reasons. Pierre Salinger often arranged for
President Kennedy to hold full dress TV news conferences at the State Department, but sometimes JFK held
"conversations" with a small group of TV newsmen, as
his successors have also done. President Nixon once
even exposed himself to an interview with such television correspondents as Dan Rather, at that time CBS
White House correspondent. President Carter seems
pretty much at home with television and he has a home-
spun manner with the public which comes across in his
TV appearances. His news conferences are normally relaxed in manner, and there was some tension at the one
dealing with OMB Director Bert Lance's resignation.

Preparation of White House news briefings and
conduct of such briefings are similar to presidential
news conferences, except that the President is not
present. The President's agent is the press secretary,
who normally handles questions, sometimes with the help
of a Cabinet officer whose Department may be involved.
These were held daily under Ron Nessen, and have been
also held frequently under the Jody Powell press
office. These sessions are more likely to handle routine matters, such as the announcement of minor
appointments, rather than major White House policy
statements, usually reserved for the President's White
House news conferences or perhaps a traveling President's news conferences outside Washington. News
briefings are a miniature of presidential news conferences, but much less is at stake and they are normally
not so heavily attended. They may be limited to White
House regulars, although the President sometimes holds
a "quickie" news conference for the regulars (a step
between a briefing and a full dress presidential news
conference).

When the President is on the road, his news
conferences outside Washington give the news media in
each city visited by the President an opportunity for
a close-up look at the President and an occasional exclusive interview. President Ford in his tenure (1974-
77) used this format frequently, and usually with good
effect.

The White House press office seeks out favorable
coverage in various ways. For example, it may arrange
an exclusive interview with the President for a well-
known television or newspaper personality. Or it may
provide for a background briefing session with the
President or one of his chief aides in order to promote, for example, an administration bill pending in
Congress. The press office makes every effort to secure favorable coverage by making the President or his
staff accessible and by encouraging positive facts to
be publicized about the President or his Administration. The President may be interviewed in a small
group setting with a few Washington correspondents on
television, and this format may be considered superior
from the President's viewpoint to a general news conference. The President's press secretary seeks to ensure that all positive viewpoints will be presented.

Sometimes the White House press office faces
the problem of minimizing unfavorable coverage of the
President. When this occurs, as it frequently did
under Presidents Nixon and Johnson, the press office
may keep the President away from the press by cancel-
ling or postponing news conferences, by letting a
spokesman such as the press secretary speak for him,
or in some other fashion. The press office's normal
behavior is to have the press secretary deny derogatory reports while shielding the President from direct
accessibility to the press. In some circumstances, it
may be felt that a direct appearance by the President
is to be preferred, and in those circumstances, he may
decide to hold a special news conference to deal with
the matter. In any event, the President himself makes
the final decision; it is then communicated by the
press secretary through the White House press office.

Let's examine the operation of the White House
press office by recent press secretaries. Perhaps a
good place to begin is with the Eisenhower Administration (1953-61), during which the press secretary for
the entire time was James C. Hagerty. Mr. Hagerty is
generally considered to have been one of the outstand-

ing press secretaries to serve a President in modern times, and perhaps the best. He was skilled in the art of doling out news to the press corps daily. He made it appear that the President was very active and busy, even when the President was recovering from an illness, for example, such as after his heart attack.

Hagerty had a keen sense of humor and partly for this reason, he had a good working relationship with most White House correspondents. He also had a background as a working newspaperman himself, and he had gone from a career including service on the New York *Times* and the old New York *Herald*-*Tribune* as Albany correspondent, to a position with Governor Thomas E. Dewey of New York. After Governor Dewey's term ended, he became press secretary for Eisenhower during the 1952 presidential campaign and stayed with Eisenhower during his entire eight-year presidential tenure until 1961.

At that time, Mr. Hagerty joined the American Broadcasting Companies as a news executive. He was noted during his tenure as White House press secretary for inaugurating a policy of providing edited news clips of White House press conferences for television; he attempted to use a restrained approach to the editing of such appearances by the President. He was always well-informed, and was an unfailing source of background information for the working press at the White House. Hagerty could be considered a model for a modern press secretary; he gave the media as much news as he could (some of the press felt he provided a flood of information), but he also was loyal and painstaking in his work performed for Eisenhower. He was also consulted by Eisenhower as a trusted aide during his eight-year term.[3]

After Eisenhower and Hagerty left the White House, the next team of President and news secretary consisted of John F. Kennedy and Pierre Salinger. Mr. Salinger, who is now in business in France, served President Kennedy as his press secretary during the

---

[3]For about a year and a half of his tenure as press secretary during 1954 and 1955, Hagerty kept a diary of his routine in the press office. It gives a clear picture of his thorough approach to his duties.

entire Kennedy Administration. Somewhat less skilled than Hagerty, he nonetheless had good working relations with the White House correspondents and was good natured. He was sometimes referred to by the President and the White House correspondents as "plucky Pierre". He was willing to go to great lengths to aid correspondents with their work. Kennedy adopted a policy of allowing frequent interviews with individual correspondents, and it was part of Salinger's job to smooth ruffled feathers of those who could not get an "exclusive" interview with JFK when and where they wanted it. By and large, Salinger did a superior job, but he sometimes was not kept fully informed, as he was somewhat less close to President Kennedy, than Hagerty was to President Eisenhower. Nevertheless, he got good marks from the press corps for his work.[4]

Salinger had been a trained journalist and had worked for the old Collier's magazine before going to work for Robert Kennedy. During the 1960 presidential campaign he began to work for John rather than Robert Kennedy. He stayed with him during his entire term, and for a brief period worked for President Lyndon B. Johnson during the Kennedy-Johnson transition until he was replaced by George Reedy of the Johnson staff.

During the 1972 presidential campaign, he served for several months on the staff of Senator George McGovern when McGovern was the Democratic presidential nominee. He was considered as a candidate for co-chairman of the Democratic National Committee but did not get the job because of the unexpected candidacy of Basil Patterson, a black political leader from New York. Salinger did a good job for President Kennedy, in the press corps' opinion.

President Johnson was served by at least three press secretaries following the resignation of Salinger, so it is more difficult to make generalizations about the White House press office in the Johnson Administration. Perhaps the most colorful of these men was George Reedy, who had been on Johnson's staff in the Senate and during his term as Vice President. Reedy was a skillful press aide and in the beginning had good working relationships with the news media.

---

[4]See Pierre Salinger, With Kennedy (Garden City, N.Y.: Doubleday & Co., 1966).

Eventually he was dropped by President Johnson who had
a turnover in the press office as he began to develop
his "credibility gap" during the Vietnam era. After
Reedy left the White House he wrote a book called The
Twilight of the Presidency in which he stated that
based on his personal experience in the White House,
he felt the President is too closely protected from
unpleasant things by his key aides.[5] He was not on
Johnson's list of close friends and associates after
the book appeared and was not invited to the dedica-
tion of the Johnson Library when this occurred in 1971.
However, he rated more highly with the press corps
than with the President he served. Reedy, who is a
great story-teller and was popular with the working
press partly for this reason, eventually went to the
Marquette University School of Journalism in Milwaukee,
and has been serving as its Dean for several years.

Reedy was succeeded at the White House press
office by Bill Moyers, for a long period a trusted
aide to Johnson. But Moyers eventually had his differences with Johnson also and in 1967 he resigned and
became publisher of Newsday, a Long Island daily newspaper.[6] He sold out his interest in this after
several years and later became a television commentator, first for the Public Broadcasting Service and
later for the Columbia Broadcasting System. He was
widely trusted by the working press for the accuracy
of his information. It was believed he differed with
Johnson over the important issue of Vietnam policy at
the time of his resignation. He had also served Johnson as a speech-writer and policy adviser as well as

---

[5]See George Reedy, Twilight of the Presidency
(New York: World Publishing Co., 1970). See also
Reedy, The Presidency in Flux (New York: Columbia University Press, 1971), based on a provocative set of
lectures.

[6]In an oral history interview, George Christian
indicated that Moyers left the White House for Newsday
because of the financial burden of supporting a
brother's family after his death. According to Christian, Moyers' departure strained relations between
Moyers and Johnson. By common consent, Moyers (now
with CBS) is one of the leading television newsmen in
contemporary broadcast journalism. Janet Murrow,
widow of Edward R. Murrow, has praised Moyers' work
highly.

in the press secretary's role. Moyers had been trained
as a clergyman but joined Johnson's Senate staff after
completing his theological training. He has had a successful journalistic career in the newspaper and television profession after leaving the White House.

George Christian also served LBJ as press secretary; he was more self-effacing than either Moyers
or Reedy. This is perhaps the reason he retained the
position until Johnson's retirement. He was less
respected by the White House press corps, although he
was generally deemed to be a competent staff aide. He
was perhaps less close to Johnson than Moyers, and
perhaps less so than Reedy. But he served Johnson in
this position at a time when Johnson distrusted the
press and perhaps this was one reason Christian was
not taken into the President's confidence more than he
was. He was apparently successful at the routine aspects of the job but not quite as highly regarded as
Hagerty or Moyers, perhaps. He came from a background
as press aide to Texas Governor John B. Connally.

When President Nixon came into the White House,
he reorganized the White House press office and had a
communications director as well as a press secretary.
His press secretary was Ronald Ziegler, who served
until the period of the Watergate scandal, when he was
given Herb Klein's old job as communications director
and a temporary replacement was found for the remainder of Nixon's term in the person of Jerry Friedheim, a former Pentagon information officer. Gerald
Warren also served Nixon as an acting press secretary.
Ziegler's background was in the advertising business
and he had worked for the J. Walter Thompson public
relations firm along with chief Nixon aide H. R. Haldeman. Ziegler was kept in the dark about many matters
as press secretary, and the press at that time had
little respect for him.[7]

_____

[7]After leaving Nixon's service, Ziegler was
more candid about his White House years. At a University of Texas symposium in 1976, he said he was
envious of press secretaries whose bosses had news
conferences more frequently than did Nixon. (Hoyt
Purvis, ed., The Presidency and the Press (Austin,
Texas: Lyndon B. Johnson School of Public Affairs,
1976), pp. 18, 19).

When Gerald R. Ford became President in 1974, he selected as his press secretary Jerald R. terHorst, a correspondent for the Detroit _News_, and a friend of long standing. Unfortunately for Ford, terHorst's tenure lasted only one month and then the press secretary resigned because he differed with the President over the pardon of Richard Nixon. During his brief period in the position, however, terHorst was widely respected by the White House press corps. After terHorst's resignation, a correspondent with the National Broadcasting Company, Ron Nessen, was appointed by Ford as his press secretary and he served during the approximately two and a half years of the remainder of Ford's term, ending in January 1977. Nessen was technically skilled, but he lacked the good working relationship with the newsmen which some of his predecessors had enjoyed. He was known for being rather thin-skinned and sensitive and he was also considered as not always well-informed although this may have been more the fault of the President than his own. He did make an effort to improve his relations with the White House press corps, however, and he was more respected than Ziegler, his predecessor under Nixon.[8]

Jody Powell's appointment as press secretary for the new Administration was the first one announced by President-elect Jimmy Carter after the 1976 election. Powell, like Hagerty and to some extent Moyers, was and is a close adviser and consultant of the new President. He appeared to have good working relations with the press during the Carter campaign, but it remained to be seen how well he would keep his reputation during the Carter Administration. The press corps hoped he would make the President accessible and would perform well, but it was too early to tell how it would all work out early in 1977 when this was written. (Powell suffered temporary damage to his reputation during the heated controversy over OMB Director Bert Lance.)

A special word should be said about the Nixon Administration. During this period (1969-74) Herb Klein (except for about the last year) served as communications director. Klein supervised the entire

_____

[8]Nessen indicated that he benefited for a time from the problems of terHorst, his predecessor. (See Purvis, _op_. _cit_., pp. 39, 40).

White House information operation, in theory at least.
But as Haldeman and Ehrlichman (Nixon's chief of staff
and his principal domestic aide), began to control
more and more of the access to the President by Cabinet
members and the news media, Klein's role diminished
noticeably. He finally resigned and took a position
in the communications industry after leaving the White
House. He had been Nixon's press aide when Nixon was
vice president and left a position as editor of the
San Diego Union, in order to rejoin Nixon's staff during the 1968 campaign. From this position he went to
the White House to become communications director.
His principal duties were to co-ordinate the information effort and to serve in a public relations capacity. Increasingly, toward the end of his tenure at
the White House, his title continued to sound impressive but he had little real authority.[9]

Klein's staff worked with him in these tasks
and nominally at least, Ziegler was supposed to report
to Klein.

Another important aspect of the White House
staff operation is the task of the President's speech
writers, and sometimes press aides participate in this
task. Although often special men are hired for this
duty, it is an important one and has a significant impact on the President's relations with the news media.
Under Franklin D. Roosevelt, Judge Samuel Rosenman and
Robert E. Sherwood performed these duties, and Clark
Clifford was a presidential speechwriter under Truman.
Eisenhower employed the talents of various aides, including Emmett Hughes, during his tenure. Kennedy's
principal speech writer was Theodore Sorensen, originally chosen as President Carter's director of the CIA,
but supplanted by Admiral Stansfield Turner. Kennedy
was also served by Richard Goodwin and others in this
capacity. Goodwin and, for a time, Sorensen also
served Johnson in this capacity, although Bill Moyers
was a more frequent speechwriter. Johnson is also reported to have relied on Marvin Watson, a Texas politician, and various others including Reedy for these
chores. He seemed to rely more than his predecessors

---

[9]For Klein's view of the role of the White House
press corps and that of the press outside Washington
in covering the President, see Purvis, op. cit., pp.
26, 27.

on a constantly shifting group of speech writers.

When Richard Nixon became President, he employed several speech writers who reflected the varying ideologies of the Republican party. One of these men was a Democrat who served for a time as counsellor to the President, Daniel P. Moynihan, now a Senator from New York State. Also prominent among Nixon's speech writers were the conservative Patrick Buchanan and the moderate William Safire. Safire, now a columnist for the New York _Times_, is the author of a memoir of the pre-Watergate Nixon years entitled _Before the Fall_.[10] Nixon was reported to feel insecure in the office of the Presidency and for this reason may have leaned more heavily on his speech writers than some of his predecessors. His speeches always carried an emotional tone that was typical of him and he added his own emphases.

President Ford employed several speech writers including Robert Orben, and relied on the ideas of such close aides as his chiefs of staff, Donald Rumsfeld (later Secretary of Defense), and Richard Cheney (a former aide to Melvin Laird). Laird himself was reported to have had a hand in some Ford speeches; he was Nixon's Secretary of Defense and went to the _Reader's Digest_ after leaving the regular staff of the Ford White House. He and Rumsfeld played key roles in the Nixon-Ford transition of 1974.

President Carter's speechwriting team was relatively new at the job as this was written, but no doubt several of his key aides will emerge as important contributors in this regard. Apparently Jody Powell and Hamilton Jordan contribute ideas.

In the Nixon years, an innovation was begun. The President set up an Office of Telecommunications Policy headed by Clay T. Whitehead. The importance of this office was downgraded by President Ford, but under Nixon it was concerned with in effect the task of "news management", and this office was assigned the task of monitoring television coverage of the President and the White House. Whitehead made several statements interpreted as threatening about the com-

---

[10]William Safire, _Before the Fall_ (New York: Belmont Tower-Books, 1975).

mercial television networks during his tenure, and it
was known that Nixon approved of these statements.

This is but one indication of the Nixon Administration's "war" with the media. President Nixon,
even as Vice President, had distrusted the news media.
He also felt that television had cost him the election
of 1960, when he ran against John F. Kennedy for the
Presidency. He especially harbored a deep distrust of
the television networks and their Washington correspondents and anchor men. Thus it should have been
no surprise when Nixon unleashed the Vice President of
that time, Spiro T. Agnew, in an unrestrained and
threatening assault on the news media. Agnew in a
speech in Des Moines attacked the television commentators for their "instant analysis" of a presidential
speech on Vietnam, and a few days later he attacked
the newspapers, especially the New York Times and the
Washington Post, for what he considered their hostility
to the President. The attacks on the television networks seemed to have a pacifying effect, but the
attacks on the print media may have been regretted,
since it was the New York Times which published the
Pentagon Papers in 1971 and it was the Washington Post
which during 1972 and 1973 published disclosure after
disclosure about the Watergate scandals. Never had
any administration had such a long and bitter quarrel
with the news media as Nixon's did.[11]

When the Ford Administration came into power in
1974, it did make some effort to improve relations
with the news media, which had become poor during
Nixon's terms of office. President Ford got positive
publicity during the first month of his term, going to
the door of his Alexandria, Virginia, home in robe and
slippers to pick up the morning paper, toasting his
own English muffins during his first days in the White
House kitchen, and doing similar things to convey the
common touch. He was off to a brief honeymoon with
the Washington press corps, and his appointment of
Jerald ter Horst as press secretary was greeted favorably by ter Horst's colleagues of the Washington
journalistic establishment. This was considerably
damaged, but not irretrievably, however, when Ford

---

[11]For details of this feud, see William E.
Porter, op. cit.

pardoned former President Nixon and terHorst resigned.[12]

TerHorst was replaced by Ron Nessen, who had
been an NBC Washington correspondent. Nessen was well-
liked, but as press secretary he proved to be unable
to handle some of the press aide's duties without
friction with the working press and he did have to
work hard at keeping better relations with the
press.[13] But most of the White House press corps
found him better to deal with than Ziegler, despite
the difficulties which arose.

The Ford Administration did manage to improve
media relations, but it still had room for improvement.
One source of friction between the news media and the
Ford White House, during 1976, was the extensive publicity given to Ronald Reagan, the former California
governor who opposed Ford for the Republican presidential nomination. Later some White House staff
people felt that Jimmy Carter, the President's Democratic opponent, was given more favorable treatment
than the President in the news media, especially after
the two candidates' second television debate, carried
to the nation on all three major networks. But Nessen
did an adequate job.

How the Linkage Occurs in the News Media

Previously I've described and analyzed the
White House staff and its relations with the news
media. Now I'll look at the news media themselves and
their linkage with the White House.

The White House press corps, sometimes described
as the "regulars", should be distinguished from the
larger Washington press corps, which includes a number
of "specialists". The White House regulars have been

---

[12]For terHorst's version of how the pardon and
his own resignation occurred, see Jerald F. terHorst,
Gerald Ford and the Future of the Presidency (New York:
The Third Press, 1974), "Epilogue", pp. 225-240.

[13]For Nessen's view of his White House responsi-
bilities, see Hoyt Purvis, ed., The Presidency and the
Press (Austin, Texas: Lyndon B. Johnson School of
Public Affairs), pp. 45-57.

accused in the past of developing a rather "cozy" relationship with the President and the White House staff and, as a result, of not probing into matters that should be covered through investigative reporting. For example, in the Nixon period it was charged that the White House press corps did very little questioning about Watergate until the newspapers, especially the Washington _Post_, had unearthed numerous facts about the scandal. On the other hand, the regulars, of whom some have been outstanding reporters like Dan Rather and John Osborne, may develop the kind of relationship with the White House staff and the President which permits them to discover information not so readily available to the Washington press corps. The Washington press corps, on the other hand, includes specialists in such matters as national defense, agriculture, and the like, who cover the line departments in the federal government. When these reporters are in attendance at White House news conferences, because of their specialized knowledge, they can ask more probing questions. It troubled many journalists that Presidents Johnson and Nixon seldom invited these specialists to White House news conferences, although President Kennedy frequently did and President Ford sometimes did. Their presence seemed to some to guarantee that the hard questions would be asked of the President and his staff.

Functions of the media at White House news conferences differ according to the medium. The White House press office may wish to employ each of the media in a different way. Television may not be permitted to cover all news conferences, since television coverage normally requires the presence of either a live camera or a film camera or videotaping unit. But in the cases where live TV is permitted, this medium can provide a unique immediacy and a sense of observing the making of the news. Certainly there has never been any question that television cameras would cover major news conferences about significant developments at the White House. The television news conference in a sense makes "actors" out of White House correspondents, whether they work for the print media or the electronic media, since the viewing public can watch them as they question the President or his spokesman. Television basically provides for graphic and immediate coverage; it may be used to emphasize or underline some major news development.

Radio functions somewhat differently since it

is nearly always possible for radio correspondents to broadcast live or at least to audiotape the proceedings at a news conference. The only kind of news conference radio would not be able to cover is that which is restricted to pencil-and-pad reporters for the print media (newspapers and magazines); there are relatively few of these. Radio provides bulletin-type information; its chief function nowadays may be to provide the first news of a breaking story. Later television and newspapers can fill in the details, but often it is first learned about by radio.

Newspaper correspondents have a special responsibility at White House news conferences, since they are expected to provide depth coverage of presidential news. They are also expected to provide some analysis of the meaning of the events they cover. Thus, if the President and the Director of the Office of Management and Budget announce a new executive budget for the forthcoming fiscal year, newspaper correspondents should examine such questions as how the budget differs from the previous fiscal year's budget, what new programs are included, what old programs have been reduced or eliminated, and similar questions. These are matters the print media are uniquely equipped to examine because they can provide more detailed coverage. As television and radio have more and more provided the bulletin-type material and the first news of an event, it has become increasingly the function of newspapers to interpret and analyze the news and put it into perspective. A good White House correspondent can do this.

The function of wire services at White House news conferences is similar to that of the newspapers in that wire services serve many newspaper clients. However, they also provide information to radio and television outlets, so they will probably function in a more general fashion than do individual newspapers' correspondents. Thus the kind of coverage given to White House reaction to the New York City fiscal crisis would be different from the viewpoint of the Associated Press or United Press International, than it would be from the viewpoint of the New York _Times_. The _Times_ correspondent would provide more information about local effects of the lack of federal aid insofar as New Yorkers are concerned, but wire services would provide more general information for their clients around the nation.

The function of magazine correspondents at the White House differs from that of newspaper correspondents primarily in that the magazine writers have less frequent deadlines and they may have a greater opportunity to do investigative reporting and provide analytical writing in their coverage. The deadline factor does not completely limit investigative reporting by newspaper reporters, however, as the performance of Woodward and Bernstein in the coverage of the Watergate story indicates. On the other hand, some excellent pieces have appeared in magazines such as The New Yorker (such as the writings of Elizabeth Drew) which could probably not have been written for a daily newspaper.[14] The depth research which is required makes this kind of writing more appropriate for a magazine.

From the viewpoint of the President and his press secretary and the White House press office, various alternatives to news conferences may sometimes be used. One of these is the interview granted to a single member of the press as an "exclusive". This is most likely to occur with a correspondent from one of the television networks or from a major newspaper like the New York Times or the Washington Post, but it can be employed by the President when he wishes. From the White House viewpoint, care must be taken not to offend other members of the working press when this is done. However, most of those most annoyed by an "exclusive" interview being given to their rivals can be satisfied if they in turn are also given an opportunity for an "exclusive" interview. During the 1976 presidential campaign, President Ford also made appearances with local news reporters in many communities--a variation of this practice.

Still another alternative to the special interview technique is the television interview, done live on one or all of the networks. This may be done on a one-to-one basis with a single correspondent, or it may be done with the President submitting to an interview by two or three, or even four, correspondents. It is usually done in the White House and it never

_____

[14]For an example of this kind of writing, see Elizabeth Drew, An American Journal: The Events of 1976 (New York: Harper and Row, 1977). Much of this book appeared as installments in the New Yorker.

fails to provide a more intimate setting for the interview than the standard format of the White House news
conference with several hundred reporters present. An
example of the TV interview is the farewell conversation with President and Mrs. Ford done by Barbara Walters of ABC on Sunday, January 2, 1977. This had most
of the characteristics of the one-on-one interview mentioned above. Prior to his resignation President Nixon
once submitted to an interview with Dan Rather and on
another occasion was interviewed by three correspondents. Both Presidents Johnson and Kennedy used this
format as well; it was first used in the Kennedy Administration.

In all this discussion, it must have been apparent that all the news media--but especially the print
media--have a considerable interpretive function. The
public has come to expect that newspapers and maga-
zines--and even to some extent radio and television--
will try to put the news of the President in perspective and will try to interpret what is happening.
Some speculation about the future plans of the President frequently enters into this. But some coverage
inevitably deals with analysis of the political significance of this move or that, the diplomatic significance of foreign policy moves, the meaning of various
presidential decisions for the public. One of the
means by which the President and his press secretary
and sometimes Cabinet officers or White House staff
members contribute to this analysis and interpretation
is the backgrounder.

The backgrounder is a session in which the
President or one of his spokesmen meets "off the
record" with the news media, with the understanding
that information given is for background only and that
no one will be quoted for attribution if any material
is used. If none of the material is to be used
directly in a news story but is provided for background only, it is said that the session is on "deep
background". On the other hand, a background session
may have ground rules that some or all of the material
may be used, but without attributing it directly to
anyone in the Administration. Or the information may
be attributed, but only in a general way, such as "a
high Administration source said today". This is a
device useful for both the news media and the Administration, but it sometimes causes misunderstandings.
Material released this way may be used by either the
media or the Administration in a way best suited to

its own ends. Given the number of "leaks" that occur in Washington, however, the backgrounder appears here to stay as a form of communication with the news media.

The investigative function of the news media has come to be almost as important as the interpretive or analytic function, or perhaps as important. One illustration that could be provided is the segment of the Watergate scandals having to do with former President Richard Nixon's federal income taxes. Through investigative reporting, it was brought out that President Nixon had claimed a large tax write-off through the gift of his papers to the National Archives, but after this was decided on the law was changed and he could no longer claim this write-off. It was determined that the tax papers were back-dated in violation of the law, and a prosecution could have been made except that the statute of limitations had run out. Other findings of this investigative reporting disclosed some unusual real estate transactions involving Mr. Nixon, and it was also reported that he had used campaign funds kept by "Bebe" Rebozo to purchase expensive jewelry for Mrs. Nixon. This is given just as an example of the fruits of investigative reporting. No doubt this information damaged Mr. Nixon's standing with the American public.

During the two and a half years of the Ford Administration, some trends in White House media coverage did become apparent. For one thing, the relationship between the President and the news media, which had been quite strained during the latter part of Nixon's term, began to return to normal. The media remained critical, inquisitive and analytical, but the media and the President were no longer hostile to each other. The whole nature of the relationship changed for the better, although moments of friction did occur, such as the period immediately following the pardon of Richard Nixon by Mr. Ford. This was not tipped in advance to the press. When Ford left the White House, things had largely returned to normal.

Mr. Carter's relations with the news media in the campaign had been reasonably good, although when as President-elect he was questioned about the controversial appointment of Griffin Bell of Atlanta as Attorney General, he had a somewhat edgy exchange with the reporters. But Carter and Ford in general have enjoyed much better relations with the news media than Nixon ever did, even at the beginning of his White

266

House tenure. Carter handled his press relations with equanimity during the Bert Lance scandal of 1977, an early major test.

How Image Linkages Occur: Definitions and Illustrative Material

The use of the term "image" requires a definition. An image, as used in connection with the mass media and political figures, represents the impression or picture of political figures conveyed to the public through the mass media. Thus image linkages refer to the process through which the media help the public develop its images of political figures, such as the President and others associated with the White House.

These kinds of image linkages can be examined in three patterns, all with an impact on the public's image of political leaders. The first of these involves the linkages which occur between the White House and the media. The White House image linkages with the media are important since the media's perception of the President and his Administration will have an impact, either positive or negative, on the public through news stories conveyed to the public through the media. These linkages consist of impressions of the President and his Administration formed by correspondents through their dealings with the President, the press secretary, and others in the Administration. It should be noted that each member of the media may react somewhat differently, so that some will develop a positive image and some will develop a negative image. But the linkages are important because of the key role played by the White House correspondents.

The image linkage with the media inevitably affects the second image linkage, that between the White House and the public. While any President will have some direct contact with the public besides that which occurs through the media--in his public appearances, for example--the major contact the public has with the President is through the news media. Thus the image linkage with the public is dependent on news of the President conveyed through the various media--newspapers, radio, television, magazines. It is also somewhat dependent on the way the President makes direct use of the media--such as presidential speeches on television. In any event, the image linkage

between the White House and the public, which helps
the public form its impressions of a President and
those around him, is hardly possible without the intervening presence of the news media. Thus it is
affected by the image linkage between the White House
and the news media.

Another important image linkage is the linkage
between the news media and the public. Through the
reporting of the media, the public forms an impression
of the reliability and credibility of the news media.
If the public trusts the media, the media's impact on
public opinion is likely to be great and in a positive
fashion. If the public distrusts the media, it is
likely to question the images of public officials presented by the media.

This discussion leads us to the next question:
Can Presidents develop a direct linkage or not? As
far as the mass public is concerned, Presidents probably cannot develop a direct linkage. As far as influential leaders other than himself are concerned, he
may be able to. The most direct means most Presidents
use is the television appearance or the personal
appearance; one is media-related and the other is not.
It really becomes a matter of definition as to how
much of a direct linkage the President can develop.
As a practical matter, he can really develop relatively little direct linkage with the public.

If one examines linkages of this type in the
Ford White House, one finds very quickly that the kind
of linkage that occurs may depend as much on the White
House press secretary as on the President himself.
The press secretary either has a good working relationship with the press, or he does not. If he has a
good working relationship, the likelihood is greater
that news coverage in the media will be favorable. If
the relationship is not good, the news coverage in the
media will suffer. So the linkage depends not only on
the image the President himself conveys, but also on
the image conveyed for him by the press secretary and
other subordinates. During the Ford Administration,
the linkage was reasonably good insofar as the President was portrayed to the public as forthright, outspoken and honest. It was weak when Ford was portrayed as a "bumbler". The image of the President was
damaged by the incident of the pardon of Richard Nixon;
this damage was probably done more by the President
than by the news coverage by the media, although that

is a matter of opinion and interpretation. Generally the Ford White House enjoyed average linkages or slightly above average linkages.

In the Nixon White House, the linkages enjoyed with the public were poor at the end of his tenure. But this should not obscure the fact that during his first term and up until after the Watergate scandal gained greater attention after the Vietnam truce, the linkage was fairly good. Nixon at that time enjoyed an image as a peacemaker, a diplomatic success. But his relationship with the news media was always poor, and when he could no longer project an image directly to the public which carried credibility, he could not count on a media image to protect him. Nixon basically caused his own downfall, but the media helped the process along.[15]

In the Johnson White House, the linkages were reasonably good in the beginning. But after the escalation of the war in Vietnam and the development of the so-called "credibility gap", Johnson fast developed a very negative linkage with the majority of the public. The process did not proceed as far and as rapidly as it did with Richard Nixon, but it was essentially similar. Johnson just never did get to the point where his impeachment was seriously discussed, whereas Nixon did.[16]

In the Kennedy White House, the linkages were good throughout the so-called "Thousand Days" of the Kennedy Administration. This was in part at least because President Kennedy worked hard at cultivating good media relations, saw the importance of these, and the media responded for the most part in a positive way.[17]

---

[15]See William E. Porter, Assault on the Media: The Nixon Years (Ann Arbor: University of Michigan Press, 1976).

[16]See Jack Valenti, A Very Human President (New York: Pocket Books, 1977), pp. 206-209, 212-215, 234-237.

[17]For a view of Kennedy's media relations in the perspective of history, see Benjamin Bradlee, Conversations With Kennedy (New York: W. W. Norton & Co., 1975).

Illustrations of Linkages

Various types of linkages can be discussed
through illustrations, to develop the previous discussion. Types of linkages found in government at large
have to do with the general impression of government
gained by the public through the news media and also
through personal experience in dealing with government, such as the postal clerks and income tax agents.
If government has a bad reputation for not being effective and efficient in the delivery of services, in
part this image linkage on the negative side developed
from the average citizen's personal experiences. On
the other hand, the average citizen may read in the
newspaper or hear on television news programs about
abuse of the welfare programs without having any
direct personal knowledge; but that information may
promote a negative image linkage just as much as his
own direct experiences. In fact, if the public had
more direct experiences, it might develop a more positive image of government at large than it does through
the media. This is in part because of the definition
of news as something that happens when things go wrong.

Executive branch linkages have to do with the
impression and images the publid develops of those in
Cabinet positions, those on the fringes of the White
House Establishment, or those working elsewhere in the
executive branch. Again, positive and negative image
linkages depend a great deal on the extent to which
the media portray these people positively or negatively, since the average citizen's direct contact with
them may be either very limited or non-existent.

Linkages directly involving the President have
already been discussed to some degree. But I should
stress that the image which the President has in the
eyes of the public can be affected a great deal by the
manner in which the media portray the President to the
public.

One interesting thing about presidential images
is that the image linkages of Presidents can grow out
of candidates' linkages. Thus if President Carter
projects an image of down-to-earth interest in the
common man, that image may in large part have been
formed by the public, the news media and Mr. Carter
during the period when he was a presidential candidate.
These linkages grow naturally out of the campaign process, and they are its natural result as the media

affect them.

Image Linkages With the System and With Interaction of Presidency With Other Parts of the System

Presidential images have been discussed in some detail. They are usually most positive in the "honeymoon" period of an administration and most negative during its final days. Images of government in general to some extent are associated with images of the President, since as the man in charge, he may have power to cause some improvement in images of government in general. Conversely, if the public perceives a President as doing a bad job, he may damage the image of government in general. It seems obvious that there is a fairly strong connection between the two.

Linkage of presidential images with those of Congress may depend on the relationship at a given time between the President and Congress. If the two are co-operative, it may be that a positive image of the President will be helpful to Congress, and vice versa. On the other hand, if the two are at odds, the image of one may be improved at the expense of the other. Much will depend on the fluctuating situation in executive-legislative relations.

It is important to note how linkage with the public affects White House interaction with Congress. When the Congress has a definite idea that a President and his programs are popular, it will be much more likely to approve programs sponsored by the President. But if Congress views a President as unpopular and a waning political force, it is much less likely to approve his legislative initiatives.

Linkage with the public also affects the White House interaction with the Cabinet and the bureaucracy. While a Cabinet member can be dismissed if he differs with the President (and there are limits on how the President's linkage with the public can affect his relationships with his Cabinet members), the bureaucracy has seen many Presidents come and go. Thus it is more likely that a positive linkage between President and public will have a positive effect on Cabinet members than on members of the federal bureaucracy. Nevertheless, some of the effect of the President's popularity is likely to rub off on the bureaucracy as well. It is just that the bureaucracy has a different perspective than appointive members of the President's Cabinet.

Linkage with the public has at least an indirect effect on the White House interaction with the judiciary. If the courts believe a President is popular and has a strong positive linkage with the public, they may be more likely to give him the benefit of the doubt when they are ruling on his programs and policies and official actions. However, the judges can be expected to put the principles of the law first and this is a constraint they have which does not apply to the other branches of the government.

Linkage with the public also affects White House interaction with the news media, and in much the same way. The President's popularity may be reinforced by favorable coverage in the news media if media people see him as having a positive linkage with the public. On the other hand, if the media see the President as having a negative linkage with the public, they can contribute to the deepening of this negative linkage, as happened in Nixon's case. Thus the media provide a two-edged sword, which can both help and hurt a President, but which he can never completely control. This is a safeguard at times against abuse of power by the President at the expense of the public.

In an overview of the system and how linkage affects it, it would be fair to say that the image linkage of the President with any one part of the system is interlocked with his image linkage with any other part of the system. The relationships and interactions are interdependent, as the examples given above have illustrated.

Role of Mass Media Connection in the Past

Although many have come to think of the vast influence of the mass media on the public as a feature of modern times, the truth is that mass media in some form have always been influential ever since Washington's time. At this point, it may broaden the perspective to look at this relationship in terms of the history of the Presidency.

In Washington's time the relation of the Presidency to the mass media and to the public was more of an arms-length relationship. It was the age of the

272

Virginia Dynasty in the Presidency, and the principal news medium was the newspaper. Pro-Administration articles were to be found in pro-Administration newspapers, and anti-Administration articles were to be found in anti-Administration newspapers. But they seldom made pretense of impartiality, as this was an age in which modern standards of journalistic impartiality were not being practiced. Thus on an issue such as the foreign policy issue of pro-British versus pro-French attitudes, the newspapers favoring Washington and Hamilton took issue with those favoring Jefferson and his pro-French views, and each carried the sentiment of one segment of the public along with them. That was briefly the way in which the President, the media and public related to each other in Washington's day.[18]

By the time of Andrew Jackson (1829-1837), the public had become more politically aware and property restrictions on voting were more and more being dropped, so the media had influence over a wider readership. The newspaper was still the principal medium of communication, but daily newspapers were more commonplace. The party press was much in evidence so that newspapers were either pro- or anti-Administration as a rule. Except for the democratization of the Presidency by Jackson and the broader interest because of a wider voting eligibility, the relationship had not changed a great deal since Washington's era.

When Abraham Lincoln occupied the White House (1861-1865), some of the modern aspects of journalism had begun to develop. The wire services had come into being and the Associated Press was working as a co-operative of member newspapers; also the ideal in the newspaper profession had changed, and an effort was now being made to develop more unbiased reporting than had been the case in the past. The voting public was essentially the same as in Jackson's day, although the vote was soon to be given to minorities, especially to Blacks. But the daily newspaper had a great following

---

[18]See Doris A. Graber, Public Opinion, the President and Foreign Policy: Four Case Studies from the Formative Years (New York: Holt, Rinehart and Winston, 1968). Graber's cases deal with John Adams, Jefferson, Madison and Monroe in the White House.

and the way President Lincoln was portrayed in the newspapers had a great deal to do with his popularity. During the Civil War, critical newspaper comment made his job more difficult, but conversely when the newspapers played up military victories by Grant and other generals selected by Lincoln, this enhanced the President's image. After Lincoln's assassination, the press played a great part in the development of the myth of Lincoln the great war leader, and undoubtedly contributed to his leading place in the history of the Presidency.

Coming into the Twentieth Century, in the time of Theodore Roosevelt and Woodrow Wilson, perhaps the most important development was the formalizing of the press conference. Prior to these Presidents, the relationship of the White House to the news media had been rather hit and miss, but TR established the precedent of holding regular press conferences, and Wilson followed it also. During this time the daily newspaper remained the dominant mode of communication, but the radio was soon to come on the scene (in the 1920's). Newspapers were now trying to achieve a higher standard of objectivity, and Presidents also benefited by this.

Woodrow Wilson, during his tenure, used the press conference on a regular basis during his first term until World War I prevented him from devoting as much time to direct contact with the press. Then after the war ended, he was ill for much of the remainder of his second term so that regular press conferences were not held.[19]

During the period from 1921 to 1933, the relationship between the Presidency on the one hand and the media and the public on the other was somewhat different. Presidents Harding, Coolidge and Hoover did not feel a need for regular press conferences in which the President could be questioned directly, even though Harding had been a newspaper publisher before beginning his political career. Their favorite device was the use of a White House spokesman who would provide answers to questions which had been written by

---

[19]See John Morton Blum, Joe Tumulty and the Wilson Era (Boston: Houghton Mifflin Co., 1951), pp. 48, 51, 61-65, 171-173.

correspondents and submitted in advance for screening. This changed the format of the press conference from one of direct question-and-answer in the White House to that of indirect question-and-answer in writing, which could be called for lack of a better term, the "documentary press conference". This format enabled the White House press aide to screen out any embarrassing questions, and it also prevented the questioning of the President directly as Theodore Roosevelt and Woodrow Wilson had permitted. However, it did establish the general rule that the President himself, in consultation with his press secretary, has the right to determine the format of his relations with the press. Through the Hoover Administration this format continued to be used.

With the beginning of the first term of Franklin D. Roosevelt, the only President ever elected four times by the American people, the press conference as an institution was again transformed into a direct means of communication between President and public through the mass media. President Roosevelt reinstituted the direct question-and-answer conference. Members of the White House press corps met directly with the President in his Oval Office, usually on a weekly basis. Roosevelt was quite skillful at the use of the press conference as a means of communicating with the public. Elmer E. Cornwell, who made a study in the 1960's of the press relations of 20th Century Presidents from Theodore Roosevelt through Lyndon Johnson, found that Roosevelt made extremely skillful use of the news conference as a means of educating the public about new programs. Cornwell illustrated this by pointing out how FDR used press conferences and fireside chats to help promote the legislative innovation of Social Security, which was adopted by the Congress in 1935.[20]

FDR had few equals in his ability to use radio effectively, and he did quite well with the fireside chats, but presidential news conferences at this time were not being broadcast on radio. In fact, the President could not even be quoted directly without his permission; however, the return to the direct question-and-answer format greatly aided the news media, as it

---

[20]Elmer E. Cornwell, Presidential Leadership of Public Opinion (Bloomington: Indiana University Press, 1965).

enabled them to question the President about controversial issues and events.

The President in this period had a reasonably
good relationship with the public; this was in large
part because of his good relations with the news media.
Reporters and correspondents were invited to White
House parties, where an attitude of informality prevailed. Mrs. Roosevelt herself became a newspaper
columnist, regularly contributing a column entitled
"My Day" to one of the major syndicates. The whole
relationship with the news media was a much warmer one
than in Hoover's day. Roosevelt did not normally
grant many single interviews, but he was able to communicate very effectively through the news conference,
even during World War II, when these news conferences
had to be held less frequently.

During the period of the Truman Administration
through the Kennedy Administration, the major change
in relations among the President, the news media and
the public was the advent of television. Its impact
can be clearly seen in the evolution of the White
House news conference, which in Truman's time was attended by newspaper and radio correspondents, but by
Kennedy's time was attended by newspaper, radio and
television news correspondents and was covered live by
television cameras.

The change came about gradually in the period
between 1945 and 1963, but the steps are interesting
to observe. During the Truman Administration, direct
quotations from pencil-and-pad news conferences were
more frequently permitted and it was at this time that
recorded excerpts from the news conferences were permitted for use by radio. Truman's successor, President Dwight D. Eisenhower, was the first chief executive to permit news cameras to film White House news
conferences for use on television, although the White
House reserved the right to determine what portions of
the film would be released for use on television and
live coverage was still not permitted.

By the Administration of John F. Kennedy, the
President and his press secretary had further relaxed
the rules and restrictions, and live coverage of a
number of press conferences was permitted. This meant
that several hundred correspondents usually attended,
and the conferences were moved from the Executive
Office Building, where Eisenhower had usually held
them, to the State Department auditorium. Here Kennedy skillfully answered questions in the full dress

news conferences which became so closely identified with him. Some but not all of his news conferences were televised live, but the President made such effective use of them that most of his successors have held live press conferences for all the media at least occasionally. The frequency has depended to some extent on how well they have been able to employ this medium.

The presidential news conference went into a temporary eclipse under Presidents Lyndon B. Johnson and Richard Nixon. Although they used the televised live news conference occasionally, they did not use it as frequently as Kennedy had done. This was in part because they felt less at ease with it, but it was also in part because their relationship with the public changed. Johnson lost his popularity after he escalated the war in Vietnam, and the public which had been sympathetic with him during his first year or two (after the takeover from the Kennedy Administration and during the Great Society period) began to become dubious and hostile toward him. The press and other news media began to write and speak about LBJ's "credibility gap" brought about because the news correspondents felt the Administration was no longer telling them the whole truth about the war in Vietnam. This problem grew worse with the events of 1968, which included the Chicago convention riots and the McCarthy and Robert Kennedy campaigns for the Presidency.

Toward the end of his term, Johnson was meeting less and less frequently with the news media. When he did he was mostly holding "quickie" news conferences with White House regulars where he would be embarrassed as little as possible. Johnson had had good relations with the public and reasonably good relations with the news media at the beginning of his tenure in 1963. By 1968, shortly before his retirement, his relations with both the public and the news media had soured; the war in Vietnam and controversy over his policies and statements about Vietnam had been largely responsible for this downturn in popularity and rapport with the media. One author, Eric Goldman, who had been on the White House staff for a time, described this development as "the tragedy of Lyndon Johnson" in a book by that title which he wrote.[21]

---

[21] See Eric F. Goldman, The Tragedy of Lyndon Johnson (New York: Dell Books, 1969).

Richard Nixon had a particularly interesting relationship with the news media because he had become a nationally known political figure in the late 1940's because of the publicity given his role in the Alger Hiss case and the subversion investigation by the House Committee on Un-American Activities of which Nixon was then a member. He then accused the press of unfairly blaming him for a scandal during the 1952 campaign, when columnist Peter Edson wrote that Nixon was accused of collecting a slush fund from California oil men. Nixon went on television to defend himself. He won election as vice president but from that time on he showed a good deal of hostility to the news media, especially to the liberal press which had opposed him. He complained of unfavorable news coverage when he ran for President in 1960 against John F. Kennedy, even though he was given reasonably good coverage as vice president as when he had his so-called "kitchen debate" with Nikita Khrushchev in Moscow in 1959.[22]

But the low point of Nixon's early career in his relations with the news media doubtless came at the conclusion of his campaign for governor of California in 1962. At that time, a tired and belligerent Nixon early on the morning after the election which he lost to Pat Brown held a news conference in Los Angeles at which he made the famous statement: "Well, gentlemen, this is my last press conference. You won't have Nixon to kick around anymore." But of course it was not his last press conference, and when Nixon ran for President in 1968 he very carefully controlled the media coverage by limiting his appearances mostly to controlled situations and preparing his own television campaign against Humphrey and Wallace.[23] After Nixon was elected President, there was a brief period of relatively good relations with the news media, but this did not last long because in the fall of 1969, Nixon permitted Vice President Spiro Agnew to attack the television networks and later the metropolitan newspapers as unfair to the Administration. When the Watergate scandal broke in 1973, Nixon held several press conferences which could only be

---

[22]See Richard M. Nixon, Six Crises (New York: Pocket Books, 1962).

[23]See Joe McGinniss, The Selling of the President 1968 (New York: Trident Press, 1969).

described as shouting matches, such as for example the one in which he told a news conference televised live from Disneyworld at Orlando, Florida, "I am not a crook".

Another well-known Nixon news conference was the one televised from Houston, Texas, at a broadcasters meeting in which he and CBS correspondent Dan Rather had a sharp exchange. Nixon had been hostile to Rather for some time for what he considered Rather's unsympathetic and critical coverage, and this incident resulted in some pressure on CBS to transfer Rather away from the White House beat, which eventually did occur but not at that time. When Nixon finally did resign in 1974, the news media made an effort to be fair to him but it was obvious that he was not popular with the correspondents for the most part. Nixon's relations with the public were somewhat better but many believe he won the 1968 election largely by default and won the 1972 election mainly because he stayed out of the limelight and did not campaign very actively against Senator George McGovern, the Democratic nominee for the Presidency. At any rate, Nixon's popularity plummeted quickly soon after the Watergate disclosures which followed the Vietnam truce in early 1973, the peak of his popularity with the public. By the time of the resignation, only 25 per cent of the public, one voter in four, was still willing to support Nixon. So he like Lyndon Johnson before him, fell short of the performance of Kennedy and Eisenhower in preserving and maintaining good relations with both the public and the news media.

What Current Mass Media Linkage Appears to Be

In discussing what the current mass media linkage with the White House appears to be, one must focus on the recently ended Ford Administration, which now appears as an interlude of two and a half years in which the country recovered from the divisiveness of Vietnam and Watergate, and the early period of the Carter Administration.

The Presidency-media-public triangular relationship under the Ford Administration can perhaps best be described in terms of various time segments. These were: the pre-pardon period (August 9-September 8, 1974); the post-pardon, pre-election period (September 1974 until Ford's announcement of his candidacy in

1975); the 1976 primary season (February-June 1976);
the 1976 convention and campaign season (June-November
1976), and the transition period (November 1976-Janu-
ary 1977).

The triangular relationship among President
Ford, the news media and the public was especially
euphoric during Ford's first month in office. This
period for most Presidents is known as the "honeymoon"
interlude, and Ford's honeymoon lasted for about a
month. He won a great deal of sympathy from both the
news media and the public during his first month in
office. Newspapers carried stories about the man who
picked up the newspaper from his doorstep in the morning while wearing his pajamas and bathrobe, and the
man who fixed his own English muffins in his toaster
on his first morning in the White House--a down-to-
earth, sincere President who made a sharp contrast
with Richard Nixon. This image was to last but a
month, however, as this period ended with Ford's announcement of his decision to pardon Richard Nixon.
From that time on, he was subject to the same kind of
criticism that his predecessors were subjected to, except that it was perhaps less bitter than that against
either Nixon or Johnson.

During the period from the pardon of Nixon
until Ford's announcement in late 1975 that he would
run for election to a term in his own right, Ford was
treated more critically by the press. The public
opinion polls showed his popularity declining somewhat,
although during the Mayaguez incident in May 1975, his
popularity went back up for a temporary period. This
was a period when Ford was adjusting to the Presidency,
and the public was adjusting to him in the White House.
Thus his popularity with the public was subject to
fairly wide fluctuations and his relationships with
the news media were still being established. The news
media treated Ford with relative kindness for several
months (after all, he was very different from Richard
Nixon) but after his WIN campaign and proposal for a
tax increase was changed into a program for a tax cut
to fight the recession, some doubts about his management of the office began to surface in the news media
as well as in the Republican party, and of course with
the public. This period of about a year was one in
which Ford had his ups and downs but survived with a
greater measure of popularity than either of his
immediate predecessors.

After Ford's announcement and until the end of
the 1976 primary season, his relationships with the
news media and the public entered a new phase. The
first thing that occurred which disturbed some people
and encouraged others was the announcement that Vice
President Nelson Rockefeller would not seek to run as
Ford's running-mate in 1976. This brought the expected reactions, approval from the conservatives in
the Republican party and among independents and dis-
approval from the moderates in the Republican party
and among independents. But it was in part a reaction
to the possibility which shortly became a reality--
that Ford would have opposition for the Republican
nomination from the former Governor of California,
Ronald Reagan. The Reagan candidacy was announced in
time for the former Governor to enter the primary in
New Hampshire. Reagan was expected to run well in
both New Hampshire and Florida, two of the key early
primaries. Thus Ford's image was so managed that he
would not offend conservative Republicans who might
desert him for Reagan. He won the two primaries
against Reagan, but this did not cause Reagan to drop
out. It merely caused him to change his tactics; he
suspended his campaign for awhile and made a nationwide television address, which helped him to defeat
Ford in the North Carolina primary and then he went on
to win the Indiana and Texas primaries, making him
very much a contender against Ford again.[24] These developments caused Ford to lose some popular support,
and perhaps more importantly they generated some negative coverage in the news media. Reporters and correspondents began to ask what was wrong with the Ford
campaign; Bo Callaway, the Ford campaign director, was
removed because he got involved in a scandal, and the
news media began to carry frequent stories about how
disorganized the Ford campaign was, and how well
planned the Reagan campaign was. But the issue remained in doubt. When Ford won in Ohio and New Jersey
and Reagan did not do quite as well as expected in
California, it became clear that the primary season
would not determine the winner but that uncommitted
delegates and those chosen in caucus and convention

---

[24]For various accounts of these events, see
Jules Witcover, _Marathon_ (New York: Viking Press, 1977);
Elizabeth Drew, _op. cit._, and Malcolm D. MacDougall,
We Almost Made It (New York: Crown Publishers, 1977).

states would hold the swing votes at the Republican convention in Kansas City in August 1976. All through this period the President's image fluctuated according to how well he was running in the primaries, and the news media continued to compare him with Reagan, who was said to have a better television presence. The June primaries ended this phase of the Ford Presidency, and at the end of it his image was somewhat murky with both public and the news media.

In the next phase, the convention and campaign season, Ford again had his ups and downs. He went to the convention with the nomination in doubt and it was not until Tuesday of convention week, when the Ford faction won a test vote on the convention floor at Kansas City by a slim margin of about 100 votes or so that it became clear that Ford had sufficient strength to win the nomination. The fact that he had barely been able to win the nomination in the face of Reagan's strong challenge made his image shaky at best, with both the public and the news media. At this point, Ford challenged Carter to the debates and Carter accepted. After the nomination had been safely won, Ford was faced with the necessity of conciliating Reagan supporters who had opposed him. He was unable to do this completely effectively, even though he chose a running-mate, Senator Robert Dole of Kansas, who had close ties to the Reagan faction. The choice of Dole may have helped to reunify the divided Republican party, but it turned out that it hurt Ford a good deal with independents and conservative Democrats who had been potential Ford voters.

The campaign season began with Ford's opening appearance at Ann Arbor, but the highlight of the campaign for most of the public and the news media was the confrontation between Ford and his Democratic opponent, Governor Jimmy Carter, in the televised debates sponsored by the League of Women Voters. In the first debate, Ford did well but this advantage was somewhat diminished by the fact that an incumbent President is expected to do well in a debate with his challenger. The second of the three debates proved most damaging to Ford; it was in this debate in San Francisco that he misspoke about the status of the satellite nations of Eastern Europe, and this was damaging in a major way because Carter, who was not considered expert in foreign policy, came out appearing as knowledgeable as or more knowledgeable than Ford on foreign and defense policy issues. Thus this was particularly harmful to

Ford's campaign as the Carter _Playboy_ interview and other controversies had cut Carter's margin and Ford had developed momentum in his effort to overtake Carter. But after the second debate this momentum was practically halted. The third debate in Williamsburg, Virginia, was generally considered a draw and did not bring about a major change in images of the two candidates. But after the debates, Carter's Democratic support (which had been soft) began to solidify behind him. Bad reports on the economy in October were also damaging to Ford in the final days of the campaign, which of course was won by Carter. By the end of the campaign, Ford had the image of a game loser but he also had the image of a President who had failed to capture the imagination of the public. To what extent the mass media had affected this image, it is difficult to say. In general the media coverage probably was not helpful to Ford; rather it was a boost to Carter. The media were not particularly biased, but the coverage presented images of the two men that did not meet the public's expectation that the incumbent President would clearly overshadow his challenger. In this sense it was helpful to Carter and damaging to Ford. Ford's popularity with the public was also damaged by its perception--perhaps aided by the media--that Ford was not doing enough about adverse economic conditions in the United States.

In a considerable sense, the importance of Ford's media image and his linkage with the media and the public seemed to diminish after the election in which Carter defeated Ford. Ford appeared more and more to take on the image of a caretaker President rather than a President in his own right, which he would have had if he had won the election. Thus there was one final phase of Ford's relationship with the public and the mass media, the interregnum. Ford went off to Vail and to other places such as Palm Springs, California, and left the limelight to the President-elect, whose relationship with the public and the mass media would soon be the object of everyone's attention.

White House Press Office: Jimmy Carter and Jody Powell

During September 1977, I held a conversation with Barry Jagoda in the White House Press Office regarding media operations of the Carter Administration. I found the information gathered during this conver-

sation enlightening, because of the considerable use
made by President Jimmy Carter of imagery and symbolism in his interaction with the American public.

Mr. Jagoda, a special assistant to the President, indicated that the Carter Administration employs
a quite informal method of briefing the President for
his news conferences. "In the past there has been extensive briefing of Presidents. When we came in, we
discovered that the (line-item) budget in the Nixon
and Ford White House had authorized two staff people
just to prepare briefing books for the President.
This does not take place here. Carter works more informally. Ten minutes before the President is
scheduled to begin a news conference, (Jody) Powell
and others meet with him. Usually Powell, (Zbigniew)
Brzezinski and (Stuart) Eizenstat chat with the President to see if he has any last-minute questions. In
his overnight reading, Carter gets any new developments and relevant information from the staff."

I asked Jagoda what standard White House procedure is used in the Carter Administration for conducting daily press briefings. I wanted to know
whether Powell uses any new or different techniques
that weren't used by Ron Nessen, the Ford press secretary, or any other of Powell's predecessors. "Powell
prepares for these briefings; he usually sees Carter
alone at 10:30 a.m. each day Carter is in the White
House, for about 20 minutes. (Nessen never saw Ford
alone, but always with others.) Having worked here as
a journalist during the Nixon and Ford Administrations,
I feel Powell has a smoother operation and better
access to the President than was true with Nessen or
(Ron) Ziegler (the Nixon press secretary). Powell has
a principal deputy for news, Rex Granum, who has two
assistants (Walt Duka and Bill Drummond). When they
are not meeting with correspondents in briefing sessions, they hold staff meetings and review the broadcasts and the newspapers."

I wanted to know what is involved in the duties
of the President's television adviser or advisers, and
to what extent the style of communication used by the
President and his staff was a concern of the television adviser's portion of the White House Press
Office. Jagoda stated: "I find myself more involved
in policy-making for communications. There has been a
change here. This is something new. TV advisers in
the past tended to worry about lens angles, makeup,

etc. But my feeling is you can't outwit television;
TV presents actuality and I think the President must
project himself just as he is. Carter is very good at
this, just being natural. He instinctively does the
things he should do, such as to look at the camera if
he is not looking at a questioner (the former in a
less question-and-answer kind of format). I handle
liaison with the networks and to some extent am involved in questions of policy-making."

(A parenthetical note here is that President
Nixon established the Office of Telecommunications
Policy (OTP) with Clay T. Whitehead as its director.
President Ford downgraded the office. President Car-
ter in 1977 removed OTP from the White House and
placed it in the Department of Commerce.)

I asked about Jagoda's view of the way in which
President Carter and Jody Powell use television, particularly by use of illustrations then in the news
such as the Panama Canal treaties. He referred to the
Panama Canal treaties in his reply: "We've been
struggling with that question for some months. To
what extent do political leaders use the 'press backgrounder' for the press? The Panama Canal treaty
signing is an example; some things were disclosed on
background that couldn't be made public. Various options with the news media are explored."

(Parenthetically, Jagoda explained that the
White House Press Office knew for some time that
President Carter was planning the treaty-signing
ceremony eventually held at the Pan American Union in
Washington, which was attended by Latin American
chiefs of state and foreign ministers, former President Ford, former Secretary of State Kissinger, and
Lady Bird Johnson. This information could not be disclosed to the news media officially, however, until
all the appropriate senators and congressmen had been
notified about it.

I asked what the public relations staff does
about holding regular meetings to discuss strategy
and tactics for dealing with the media; I also asked
whether the operation of the Carter White House Press
Office was quite informal, as one gets the impression.
Here is the response: "We've never had a formal meeting of the staff. Some smaller meetings do occur,
with just a few people. Another deputy press secretary has a fairly large staff; he has two principal
assistants. Usually there's an informal discussion of

those who need to deal with the problem, and that's the way it works."

I inquired about Jagoda's view of the effectiveness of White House communication with the public. On the assumption that it is good, I asked why he thought it was. "You've got to remember this President is an engineer, with goals and planning. There's been a sense in Carter's first year that his attempts to stay in touch with the public have been effective. He has been continuing on TV what he did around the country during the (1976) campaign."

I asked for an assessment of how effective the White House Press Office's relationship was with the correspondent corps. On the assumption that it was good, I asked if Jagoda could explain why it was. "It's not as good as it should be. This is partly because the Carter people were not as fully 'plugged into' established institutions as has usually been the case in previous Administrations. Jody (Powell) is a partisan; he doesn't bend over to the reporter's point of view as much as a more accommodating press secretary might. Despite some grumbling because of this, Jody has been a more successful press secretary than anyone since (James C.) Hagerty (in the Eisenhower Administration). But sees his role toward the press as somewhat more of an adversary."

I asked what problems arise in the function of communicating White House viewpoints to the public, and to the news media, and I asked for some details. "The public would be well served by direct communication. The news media don't perceive themselves as a conduit for the opinions of politicians. They see themselves as performing a journalistic filtering process. A classic way around this for the politician is the use of the presidential debates (as in 1976 with Ford and Carter)."

Next I wanted to know to what extent Jagoda felt we are really getting away from the concept of the Imperial Presidency, and whether he could suggest examples that tend to prove the President really wants to have a more democratic, first-citizen image with the public. "In the post-Watergate era there is a premium paid for holding government's feet to the fire. I think Carter is sincere in trying to be humble about his position. Just an example. The other day in the White House mess, the President and Vice President\

Mondale came in and ate with the staff people. They talked with them and treated them on a level of equality, no matter how humble or lowly each staff person was. You wouldn't have seen that with Richard Nixon."

I inquired to what extent the Carter TV aide felt the Administration is using television as an effective medium for educating the public on news, as for example, the Panama Canal treaties or the movement toward normalizing diplomatic relations with Cuba or mainland China (People's Republic of China). "If there were an hour television news show, TV could do this. But it's fortunate from the President's point of view that the Fairness Doctrine is in existence. Carter's not using TV that way any more than LBJ did. We have a more sophisticated press now."

I sought Jagoda's personal viewpoint as to the most effective use of television, not merely for the President, but for any major public official in national politics. Here was the reply: "The most effective means of using TV is to have a grasp of questions which are in the public's mind (such as the energy issue). The best way he could use TV is if there were a crisis so the President can easily get a feeling of the public pulse."

I asked what this media aide considered is necessary in the way of training and experience for the President's press secretary, and whether he needs to know a great deal about all the major media. "The President's press secretary needs to have the full confidence of the President. He should be moderately well educated. He should know as much as possible about the internal dynamics (politics) of the media as an institution, or have a staff that does."[25]

---

[25]James C. Hagerty, widely considered as the most successful White House press secretary in modern times, had a long background in newspaper work including experience with the New York _Times_ and _Herald-Tribune_, as an Albany correspondent for New York City newspapers, and as a press secretary to Governor Thomas E. Dewey. Jody Powell, the incumbent press secretary in the Carter Administration, did not have media experience but he holds degrees in political science and has worked for Carter since Carter's first campaign for Governor of Georgia in 1966. For back-

I asked the White House official about what he considers as the best training and background for the President's television adviser, and who he felt had served most effectively in the past in this role. While not mentioning any one standout TV adviser from recent administrations, he commented: "He must understand the decision-making process of broadcasting organizations and have the confidence of the President and key people around him. It depends on his perception of the job. I would say less on the technical side and more on the policy side. It's useful for him to have served the President during the presidential campaign."

I asked whether Jagoda could think of any examples of the kinds of issues that are particularly susceptible of good presidential communication with the public through the use of television. His reply: "There are definitely bad issues, and fake adversary situations. Nixon pre-selected people to ask him tough questions; this came across in a phony way. It is best when the President is most vulnerable. His authenticity and believability comes from this vulnerability, being able to risk answering any question, no matter how potentially embarrassing it might be for him."[26]

Since Jagoda has been a producer in commercial network television, I asked how his view of the President's use of television differed from the vantage point of the White House as compared with the vantage

---

ground, see "Jody Faces Life", Newsweek, September 19, 1977, pp. 119, 120; Kandy Stroud, How Jimmy Won (New York: William Morrow & Co., 1977), Chapter 18, "Jody Powell, Press Secretary", pp. 217-227; Martin Schram, Running for President: A Journal of the Carter Campaign (New York: Pocket Books, 1976); Elizabeth Drew, American Journal: The Events of 1976 (New York: Random House, 1977), and Jules Witcover, Marathon: The Pursuit of the Presidency 1972-1976 (New York: The Viking Press, 1977).

[26]In the author's opinion, Carter probably exhibited this kind of vulnerability in dealing with the Bert Lance controversy; he was probably more effective because he submitted to questioning even though it was obviously difficult for Carter.

point of a network. "Broadcasters and journalists generally see the President as always out selling. The skepticism and cynicism that most reporters bring to their job is apparent. I have no problem with that."[27]

In noting that the President uses the media for both policy purposes and political purposes (i.e., in selling his programs and in promoting his own candidacy for re-election or helping candidates for lesser offices), I asked whether this official saw major differences in the way in which the President uses the media for these purposes, or in the way in which he uses TV specifically for these purposes. "As President, he has to be more responsible for what he says. The major difference is that when he is President, everything he says is news and will be covered as news regardless of content. Access to the media is easier for him when he is President."

I asked whether the White House press aide could think of any examples where it is imperative for the White House Press Office to impose strict secrecy, or where it is necessary for it to impose temporary secrecy, and what problems this engenders with the White House's relationship with the working press. "The examples go from the serious to the benign; when we knew of the plans for the Panama Canal treaties' signing, the news of this was withheld temporarily while the participants were invited and the arrangements were made. The same kind of thing was true of our efforts to assist in the Hanafi Muslim terrorist story." (The White House quietly sought to help law enforcement officials to negotiate for release of the hostages held by the terrorists in three locations in Washington, D.C., in the spring of 1977.) Jagoda implied that the Carter White House does not believe in the imposition of secrecy for secrecy's sake, or because it does not trust the news media.

In our conversation, I noted that some press secretaries have had a reputation for outstanding work and others had a poor reputation with the newsgathering profession. I asked who might be considered the best and the worst in this regard, excluding Powell,

---

[27]The President is usually seen as selling either himself or his programs.

whom most agree is popular and doing a rather effective job. "Probably James Hagerty was the best, and
possibly Stephen Early under FDR. Hagerty like
Powell was much involved in policy and both Presidents
used them in that regard. Reporters want an authori-
tative story so the press secretary must have good
access to the President. Hagerty was brilliant with
logistics, as for example during the time of Eisenhower's heart attack in the way in which he managed
the distribution of the news."[28]

I asked Carter's TV adviser what he thought was
the ideal relationship between the President, on the
one hand, and his press secretary or TV expert, on the
other. I also asked about the press secretary's relationship with the TV expert. "The press secretary
and the President have to have an open relationship.
The President must be open to hearing bad news from
his press secretary. The President ought to have only
six to eight primary staff members he needs to look to
for guidance, one of whom is the press secretary. The
TV adviser shouldn't be in the front rank, but should
be able to see the President when it is necessary and
should have a good working relationship with the press
secretary."

Noting that political scientists have analyzed
the relationship between the President and the press
corps in different ways (for example, analyzing the
press corps as an interest group, or using transaction
analysis to explain the dissemination of White House
news), I asked whether Jagoda saw either of these
theoretical approaches as fitting the relationship.
His comment: "Both do to some extent, but frankly I
think a third approach, that of institutional dynamics
between the media as an institution and the White
House as an institution, explains more than the other
two approaches. It is a matter of institutional understanding, not so much a matter of interest groups or
just transactions. The most important thing in
analyzing this relationship consists of the goals and
needs of each institution (the Presidency and the mass

---

[28]See elsewhere in Chapter Five some excerpts
from the Hagerty Diary regarding the handling of the
press secretary's responsibilities during the Denver
heart attack.

media) and the institutional dynamics that affect their relationship."[29]

I asked Mr. Jagoda about his view of Richard Neustadt's observation that the media convey to congressmen and other important Washington figures an impression of the President's reputation, and whether he thinks the media or key politicians' personal dealings with the President are more important in this regard. "In terms of professional politicians' impressions of the President, a broadbrush impression comes from the media. But they fill in the details with a small brush from the personal context. For example, Speaker Thomas P. (Tip) O'Neill has met with the President numerous times for lunch. The initial impression he formed from the media about Carter has doubtless become more complex and sophisticated and more insightful as the result of these frequent personal contacts, so I would see both as important. Another example is that of Sam Donaldson of ABC News, who has been covering President Carter for a long time. He knows much more about the President now because of the opportunity to interact with him personally as a part of his coverage duties."[30]

---

[29]See Dan Nimmo, Newsgathering in Washington (New York: Atherton Press, 1963) for interest group analysis of the Washington correspondent corps' interaction with federal bureaucrats. Also see Michael Baruch Grossman and Francis E. Rourke, "The Media and the Presidency", in Political Science Quarterly, Vol. 91, No. 3, Fall 1976, pp. 455-470, as well as Robert J. Sickels, Presidential Transactions (Englewood Cliffs, N.J.: Prentice-Hall, 1974), and Leon V. Sigal, Reporters and Officials: The Organization and Politics of Newsmaking (Lexington, Mass.: D. C. Heath & Co., 1973). The nearest approach to the institutional-interaction analysis suggested by the White House official may be found in Edward Jay Epstein, News From Nowhere (New York: Vintage Books, 1974). Epstein discusses the economics of the broadcasting industry and how this affects its news operations.

[30]See Richard Neustadt, Presidential Power: The Politics of Leadership With Reflections on Johnson and Nixon (New York: John Wiley & Sons, 1976), especially Chapter 4, "Professional Reputation", pp. 126-153, with Neustadt's discussion of the "Washington community".

Elmer E. Cornwell Jr. suggests that President Franklin D. Roosevelt did a superb job of selling Social Security to the public as a new program through radio and newspaper coverage of his various official acts. I asked whether Jagoda could suggest some parallel in the Carter Administration, as for example with energy policy, the Panama Canal treaties, or some other foreign policy initiatives. While not mentioning any specific issue, although several might fit this description when the history of the Carter Administration is written, the White House TV aide commented generally: "The President is not afraid of the technology which makes it possible for his opinions to be widely amplified. Carter's effectiveness has been demonstrated in his news conferences, fireside chats, TV addresses and other formats for using the media to communicate with the American public." (Two examples not mentioned by the press aide but which illustrate his point are the Carter "phone-in" for radio in which he was assisted by Walter Cronkite, and the President's surprise tour of a South Bronx slum during an October 1977 visit to New York City. The "inaugural walk" down Pennsylvania Avenue was another example of Carter's effective creation of a media event.)[31]

The White House official, reminded of James David Barber's view that the leadership style of a President indicates the character of the incumbent and that we should all try to make character judgments about presidential candidates, and that the Carter campaign was based on the successful effort to project Carter's image as that of a leader of strong character, was asked whether he thought this would be true in the future as well. His response: "Barber was right and Barber was influential with President Carter. I think it will be true in the future."

In concluding the conversation, Jagoda was asked whether he had any other observations he would like to add on the basis of his experience in television or working at the White House. He had this

[31] Elmer E. Cornwell Jr., _Presidential Leadership of Public Opinion_ (Bloomington, Ind.: Indiana University Press, 1965), see especially Chapter Six, "Leadership: Franklin Roosevelt", pp. 115-141 for Cornwell's study of FDR's role in popularizing the Social Security program.)

final thought: "I am worried about proponents of a particular policy having difficulty in stepping back and seeing the opposing viewpoint. A good example of this is the Panama Canal treaties. This is why the press is so important; it allows all sides of an issue to be aired, and should be carefully followed by the policy-makers."[32]

The Carter White House has had a quite open policy in press relations and the President himself is accessible to correspondents, as he holds a news conference at least every other week when in Washington. He did this even during the Bert Lance controversy and may be expected to hold to this schedule since he has been urged to do so by Jody Powell. Both Carter and Powell suffered temporary losses in prestige because of the handling of the Lance affair, but it is doubtful that this caused permanent damage to relations with the press. Like Kennedy, Carter has had rather good relations with the news media in general, but has had a more difficult time with Capitol Hill, particularly with the U.S. Senate, where he lacks the kind of close working relationship with the leadership that he has with Speaker O'Neill in the House. Carter has a flair for public relations and has been rather candid with the news media; pressures always operate to cause a President to be less than candid with the media, but Carter resisted these rather well during his first year as President. He is still learning about the Presidency, but he has been given the benefit of the doubt rather frequently by the media. This will end, but probably by then Carter will be showing better mastery of his almost impossible job.

Press Secretary Jody Powell of the Carter Administration has not had an easy job, as the relationship between President Carter and the media has not been a smooth one since Carter's first few months as President. Powell has had credibility because of his closeness to the President, but this very fact has caused the media to be suspicious of his stance as a friend of the media. After all the press secretary is the President's man and not the media's man.

---

[32]This account is based on a personal interview with Barry Jagoda, Special Assistant to President for Mass Media and Public Affairs, in his Washington office September 1, 1977.

Regarding this relationship, in September 1977, Newsweek correspondents David M. Alpern, Lucy Howard, Eleanor Clift and Thomas M. DeFrank in Washington, commented, in part:

"He came to the White House like a Southern breeze, a press secretary who could make fun of reporters, himself--even the President on occasion--and still get the job done. After eight years of bitterness and distrust in the Ziegler-Nessen press operations, many correspondents believed Jody Powell to be the most promising Presidential spokesman in years. But in recent weeks, Bert Lance's tangled affairs have given Powell his first real test under fire, and the press secretary has lost some of his professional cool and credibility. At one recent press briefing, John Osborne of the New Republic told him publicly what many White House reporters had begun saying in private. 'You and your people,' warned the courtly veteran correspondent, 'are just about ready to go over the wall on this Lance thing.'

"The Lance case has forced both Powell and the press to face some facts of life. As Powell's good-old-boy banter gave way to nasty cracks, angry phone calls and sharp confrontations, members of the media were reminded again that the press secretary works for the President and not for them. But while Powell's line clearly reflected the attitude of the Oval Office, it was regularly undercut by new and embarrassing facts. 'Sometimes the rhetoric gets a little overblown on both sides,' Powell conceded last week. 'But sometimes overblown rhetoric is the only way to make the point.' . . ."[33]

White House Press Office: Gerald R. Ford, Jerald ter Horst and Ronald Nessen

The relationship between President Ford and his two press secretaries, Jerald F. terHorst and Ronald Nessen, was rather good, although terHorst resigned as a matter of conscience when Ford pardoned former President Richard Nixon. Nessen had somewhat better access to the President than terHorst, partly as a re-

---

[33]See "Jody Faces Life", in Newsweek, September 19, 1977, pp. 119, 120.

sult of the pardon episode by his own testimony[34] but
Nessen developed the reputation of being thin-skinned
in his relations with the working press. Since former
President Ford is writing his memoirs for publication
in 1979 and Nessen has gone back to active journalism
and lecturing, not much documentation is available for
this period. However, such material will be available
in due course at the Gerald R. Ford Presidential
Library at the University of Michigan in Ann Arbor.
Future scholars of the Presidency will doubtless consult it.

White House Press Office: Richard Nixon, Ronald
Ziegler and Gerald Warren

        The Presidency of Richard Nixon found the press
secretary's position filled by Ronald Ziegler until
Ziegler lost most of his credibility with the news
media when he was obliged to state that his Watergate
denials were "inoperative". Ziegler then succeeded
Herbert G. Klein as White House director of communications, and Gerald Warren acted as Nixon's press secretary until the resignation in August 1974. Ziegler is
now an engineer, but his pre-White House background
was with the J. Walter Thompson Advertising Agency.
He also once served as a tour guide in Disneyland in
Anaheim, Calif.[35]

White House Press Office: Lyndon B. Johnson, George
Reedy, Bill Moyers and George Christian

        Of the massive material on Lyndon Johnson's
several press secretaries including George Reedy, Bill

---

[34]For Nessen's view of his job as press secretary, see Hoyt Purvis, ed., The Presidency and the
Press (Austin, Texas: Lyndon B. Johnson School of Public Affairs, University of Texas at Austin, 1976), pp.
21, 22, 25, 35, 36, 39-41, 45, 46, 48, 55, 56, 74-77,
79, 80, 82-85.
        [35]Ziegler's comments at LBJ symposium. Note
also that a dissertation is being written about Ziegler's work as White House Press Secretary under Nixon.
Also see William E. Porter, Assault on the Media (Ann
Arbor, Mich.: University of Michigan Press, 1976), considered one of the better sources on Nixon's "warfare"
with the news media.

Moyers and George Christian, there is a great deal of interesting information regarding the lengths to which the White House and the networks went in getting adequate microphone equipment and color lighting equipment for the White House.

That is too detailed for this book, but the most interesting finding in the open files of the LBJ Library on press operations was the details of the briefing system which LBJ used for the media contacts made by all members of his staff. Each staff member was required to report to the President through the press secretary all contacts made with media people, including what was told to the media and what media persons told the White House staff. Some excerpts are given to illustrate the system.

Memorandum for George Christian   May 25, 1967

I had lunch today with Al Otten of the Wall Street Journal.

The primary subjects covered by our conversation were the House action on the Education Bill yesterday, problems in the cities, Republican philosophy, and 1968 presidential politics. In general Otten gave me a great many more of his views than I gave of mine.

On the House fight yesterday he wanted to know why we did not put greater effort into defeating the Green amendments. I told him I thought we had planned this thing precisely right. That the Quie amendments are by far the more destructive; that if we had diluted our efforts we might have lost everything; that we are in a position to recoup from the Senate which has an impeccable record in educational matters; and that, in substance I believe we came out of the fight yesterday with a fairly good piece of legislation. . . .

He asked me how I thought the President would do in 1968. I said that I thought that things were going well for the President and that I thought he would win even if the Vietnam situation remained the same in 1968 as it is now. He asked me my opinion of the various Republican contenders and I told him Rockefeller was most attractive to me, but would not be nominated; I did not think Romney had staying power; that I thought Reagan was just this side of the line of being a kook, and that I thought Nixon would be the nominee.

Sherwin J. Markman

Memorandum to Tom Johnson   May 17, 1967

From: Ben Wattenberg

I had lunch yesterday with Saul Friedman of Knight newspapers, who covers specifically for the Detroit <u>Free</u> <u>Press</u>. Accordingly, he has been following Romney closely and has travelled with him extensively in recent months. . . .

From his background, then, he has an interesting overview of the 1968 campaign.

He thinks that Romney, not Nixon, will get the nomination; and he feels that Romney, not Nixon, would be a much more difficult candidate for Lyndon Johnson to run against. He is not wildly ecstatic about Romney as an intellect, but by no means does he view him as a jerk, which some of the reporters do.

He recounted for me Romney's extremely impressive record as Governor, and his sensational vote-getting prowess--60% of the vote last November, bringing in with him Senator Griffin and five additional Republican Congressmen.

He sees a Johnson-Romney campaign in 1968 as a close horse race, if the Vietnam situation is more less as it is today. The President, he feels, will be much stronger if Viet Nam is settled by then. That is the key to the whole election, he says: Viet Nam.

THE WHITE HOUSE
WASHINGTON
MEMORANDUM FOR THE PRESIDENT   May 11, 1967

FROM: George Christian

Press Contacts:

Drew Pearson--Delivered the attached
letter (not in file). He told me he has been
on the road again, and does not think things
look good politically. He said that in Michigan, he got the impression you would carry
Detroit but lose the state if the election
were held today.

He made some suggestions: television interviews as occasional substitutes for televised
news conferences (he doesn't think TV news
conferences project you as well as interviews);
he believes we must offset the anti-Texan sentiment by occasionally poking some fun at
Texans in minor speeches ("The President still
needs to come across more human" he says.)

Pearson also put in another bid for the
interview with the editors of Stern. He said
the President had told him that I object very
strongly to exclusive interviews, which I confirmed. He says, however, that the President
gave an interview to Stern's opposition paper
back during the Salinger days, and this would
balance it out. I told him we would think
about it. (Stern was a German publication.)

Rowland Evans--Said he had heard that Senator Birch Bayh saw the President last night.
He wanted to know if the President had convinced Bayh to pull off from Poats. (a nominee
for a federal post) I told him I didn't know
anything about it. Evans is very pro-Poats
and thinks that Bayh's opposition is uncon-
scionable.

Martin Agronsky, CBS--Called to ask me to
lunch sometime soon.

Holmes Alexander--Came by to inform me
that a group is planning a pro-Vietnam parade
in New York Saturday. He said they had asked
him to get some support from the President.
I think it is questionable as to whether we
ought to get into any of these things, since
it would leave the impression of government
sponsorship.

April 20, 1967   6:00 p.m.

FOR THE PRESIDENT

FROM: George Christian

SUBJECT: Press Contacts

Walter Cronkite--I had lunch with him and Bill Small of CBS, in which these main points were discussed:

1) The political conventions--Cronkite thinks both parties are going to have severe racial disorders at the 1968 conventions. He thinks, about half seriously, that the Democrats could solve a lot of problems by having a very short convention.

2) National Reconciliation--We agreed that this is one of the most important developments in Vietnam. I discussed the building of a political system there, told him about William L. White's letter to (Ambassador) Lodge, and told him that one of the real results of the Guam conference was to have the generals know first hand the importance the President attaches to pacification, land reform, etc.

3) Strikes--Cronkite expressed the opinion that the American public has a growing revulsion against strikes.

Chalmers Roberts--Called to suggest that the President see the Right Reverend Richard Ambrose Reeves, Former Bishop of Johannesburg, who is one of several preachers who were recently in Hanoi. Roberts said Reeves is going to England tomorrow, that he is not a peace nut, but that he interviewed Ho and' other North Vietnamese leaders and seems to have real insight into what is going on there. Roberts was distressed because the State Department "foisted him off" on an assistant desk officer. I indicated to Roberts that time was too short to arrange anything.

THE WHITE HOUSE
WASHINGTON

March 14, 1967

MEMORANDUM FOR GEORGE CHRISTIAN:

Today the following persons called me:

    Elizabeth Drew
    Phil Potter, Baltimore Sun
    Robert Spivak.

I have not returned these calls.

                    W. MARVIN WATSON

MEMORANDUM FOR THE PRESIDENT   March 8, 1967

FROM: George Christian

SUBJECT: Press Contacts

1) Martin Agronsky of NBC--he is an old friend;
I ate lunch with him and he told me of his
travels around the country on the lecture
circuit. He says that the Administration
is not getting its point over to the people
on the Vietnam war. He does not understand
why we haven't made it clear exactly what
attempts we have made to reach the negoti-
ating stage. He said he has not always
agreed with the President on Vietnam policy,
but believes the vast majority of the people
would back the Administration to the hilt if
they had a clearer understanding of our
goals. He said we are getting murdered by
those who question our goals. . . .

4) Ted Knapp--talked to me last night about the
Andy Glass story in the Washington Post. I
told him I'd talked to three people who met
with Senator Kennedy on February 6 and that
their recollections did not accord with
Glass' account. I told him the discussion
centered around the Senator's impressions
of his trip to Europe and his discussion
with the French, that there were certainly
no threats or anything else similar to the
Glass story, according to those who were
there.

5) Andy Glass--called in to in effect apologize for his story. He said Carroll had
given him a memo on my comments on it.
Glass said he felt "pure in heart" because "I like you guys and I am not trying
to start up a feud in the Democratic
party." He said there is gossip all over
town about the points he mentioned, and he
considered his sources to be so good that
he went ahead on it. I conceded that the
memories of the President, Kosygin and
Rostow would indicate the stories were
wrong.

He also read me a paragraph of Bob Novak's
column which will appear in the morning,
in which Novak said the President told Kennedy he would never meet with him again.
He said this was undoubtedly false, and I
agreed. He said Novak is also printing a
story that five senators sat on Kennedy's
airplane and discussed their election
troubles because of the President's unpopularity. He said he had heard this
same report a week or so ago, had checked
three of the Senators who were supposed to
be there, and all of them denied it had
ever happened.

MEMORANDUM FOR GEORGE CHRISTIAN February 23, 1967

FROM: Tom Johnson

SUBJECT: Press Contacts

CASSIE MACKIN: She said she had been all over
the White House talking to various staff assistants and "Nothing is doing." She is looking for
a feature story of some type. I suggested she
might be interested in doing something on the
educational background of the staff in that no
attention has been given to the credentials
that the Special Assistants hold and the
achievements that each of them has accumulated
over the years. She was not interested, saying,
"There is no news in good news."

MAX FRANKEL: He wants to do a story based on a
week of following the President around from the

time he gets up in the morning until he goes
to bed at night. I told him I didn't think
this would be possible but it would be considered if he put it in writing. He did so.
A copy is attached. Generally I think it
would be a good idea. Max is quite pro-John-
son right now. No story of this type has
been done for a long time. With the messages
going up at such a rapid pace, the story would
show the President's very deep involvement in
this.

KAREN KLINEFELTER: She is doing a biographi-
cal story on the President and wanted to know
what honorary degrees he has received. I gave
her a list of these. She also is interested
in some information on Mr. Robert M. Jackson.
I gave her what I knew about the President's
relationship with him. It was scanty, and
followed exactly what the President told me
about this over the telephone this afternoon. . . .

FOR GEORGE CHRISTIAN   February 20, 1967

FROM: Tom Johnson

Press Contacts:

. . .

4. Maurice Johnson of UPI Photos: I asked
him again about better control of the photographers by the White House News Photographers
Association. I told him the photographers
are unnecessarily noisy during ceremonies,
often knock over ashtrays, and often take very
unusual and frequently distasteful pictures of
the First Family. He agreed, recommended that
George and I meet with the regular cameramen,
and discuss the matter. He is an excellent man
to work with. I believe through his cooperation we will solve at least some of these problems.[36]

---

[36]From files in the Lyndon Baines Johnson
Library, Austin, Texas, compiled in September 1977.

The excerpts from these reports indicate the extreme amount of detail that President Johnson wished to have about his staff's contacts with the news media. The reports often indicated feedback from the media about conditions in the country, as well as White House reaction to media requests for stories, information and other favors. In general, the memoranda support the view long held that Johnson had a strong and continuing interest in his own media coverage and had almost too strong a concern with it, perhaps to the detriment of his own policies and perhaps his own image. It ought to be pointed out that this was only natural, because of his own involvement with the media in his private life. (The Johnson family long owned a controlling interest in an Austin television outlet.)

White House Press Office: John F. Kennedy and Pierre Salinger

President Kennedy was served by Pierre Salinger who was press secretary during JFK's entire term from January 20, 1961, to November 22, 1963, and stayed for a brief period with President Johnson until Reedy and later Moyers and Christian served LBJ as press secretary. Salinger has related his experiences in With Kennedy, a book published in 1966 but he has not yet granted an oral history interview as Johnson's former press secretaries, Christian and Reedy, have. Moyers is working for CBS now and also does not have such an interview on record; he has opened some but not all of his White House papers from the press office.

Two documents from the Central Files of the Oval Office during the Kennedy Administration illustrate some of the press contacts of the Kennedy White House. On September 16, 1963, Arthur Sylvester of the Pentagon, who served as Assistant Secretary of Defense for Public Affairs, sent a memo to Salinger about alleged pressure on editors of Stars and Stripes, the servicemen's periodical, regarding racial stories. It should be noted that 1963 was the year of the Birmingham riots, the University of Alabama confrontation between Governor George C. Wallace and Robert F. Kennedy's Justice Department, and President Kennedy's decision to send strong civil rights legislation to Congress (covering equal accommodations in public places, school desegregation, voting rights, and equal employment rights or affirmative action). Sylvester's

303

memo to Salinger, a part of the record of the White House of the Kennedy years now opened to scholars, stated:

We are looking into the allegations made by the two editors of the European edition of Stars & Stripes in their letters to you concerning pressure from a senior military officer "not to use anything that in any ways (sic) shows the Negro as being heroic in the effort to gain civil rights."

As initial inquiries through the Army Chief of Information and CINCEUR PIO have been unproductive, I have taken this up with the Under Secretary of the Army, Steve Ailes, and the Army General Counsel, Joe Califano. (Note: Califano in 1977 was Secretary of Health, Education and Welfare.) They both realize the seriousness of the situation if there is any truth to the story and have asked the Army Chief of Staff, General Wheeler, to investigate the matter in depth. General Wheeler has ordered a formal investigation by the U.S. Army Europe Inspector General. I believe this should do the trick and will put a stop to any "pressuring" if it exists.

I will keep you informed as we get more information about this matter. Incidentally, General Wheeler is directing his people in Europe to insure that there be absolutely no recriminative action taken against the editors or any other personnel who speak out frankly during the investigation.

This memo was received September 24, 1963, and placed in the Central Files with a notation that nothing else was sent to the Central Files as of September 30, 1963.

Another example of White House press activities during the Kennedy years can be found in a memo from Time-Life Broadcast sent to the White House on June 17, 1963. This memo suggested national leaders to make one-minute appeals for reason in an upcoming period of racial tension. Thirty one-minute spots were desired for radio or television. The only name stricken from the list (probably by the White House although there

is no evidence either way) was that of Representative
Adam Clayton Powell, a controversial congressman who
was also black.

Representatives proposed to the White House by
Time-Life Broadcast were President and Mrs. Kennedy,
Vice President Lyndon B. Johnson, a Southern and a
Northern Senator, the Rev. Dr. Martin Luther King, Roy
Wilkins of the NAACP, Jackie Robinson, Joe Louis,
Willie Mays and Althea Gibson, Bob Hope, Lena Horne,
Leontyne Price, Marian Anderson, Louis Armstrong,
Harry Belafonte, James Baldwin, Langston Hughes, Walter
Reuther, George Meany, Henry Ford II, the president of
the National Association of Manufacturers (NAM), the
president of the U.S. Chamber of Commerce, Roger Blough
(of U.S. Steel), the Rev. Dr. Billy Graham, Francis
Cardinal Spellman, Richard Cardinal Cushing, Bishop
Fulton J. Sheen, Dr. Henry Van Dusen (a Protestant
clergyman), the president of the National Council of
Churches, and a leading Rabbi. The memo was received
June 20, 1963, and placed in the White House Central
Files without any notation as to what action was taken
by the White House or Time-Life Broadcast. Presumably
the plan was adopted.

As testified to by such varied individuals as
Arthur Krock[37] and Benjamin Bradlee, executive editor
of the Washington Post,[38] Kennedy had mostly excellent
media relations during his tenure. Kennedy had been a
journalist himself for a short time and was known as
the author of two books, Why England Slept, his senior
thesis at Harvard which was published with the assistance of Henry R. Luce, and Profiles in Courage,
written while JFK was a Senator.

Gilbert Harrison, former editor of The New
Republic, stated in an interview that President Kennedy tried to woo the people he considered his critics,
such as Henry Luce, publisher of Time. Harrison said,
"He cared what they said about him", and recalled a
visit to Saigon in which he was told by an Embassy
political officer about a visit to Saigon by Kennedy
when JFK was a congressman. Young JFK wanted to talk

---

[37]See Arthur Krock, Memoirs (New York: Funk &
Wagnalls, 1968).

[38]Benjamin Bradlee, Conversations With Kennedy
(New York: Pocket Books, 1976).

to the journalists and was particularly interested in meeting and talking with the Saigon AP correspondent. Asked about contacts with Pierre E. G. Salinger, the Kennedy press secretary from 1961 to 1963, Harrison recalled a controversy with Salinger just after the assassination about a piece in The New Republic written by the French correspondent, Jean Daniel, who had interviewed Fidel Castro and thought he had arranged an interview with JFK just prior to the assassination. Harrison, incidentally, had introduced Daniel to Kennedy when the latter was in Congress.[39]

Edward P. Morgan of ABC stated in an interview that he never succeeded in getting a personal interview with Kennedy but he judged Salinger to be an effective press secretary and "very shrewd". Morgan thought both Salinger and Klein were competent in their work for Kennedy and Nixon respectively.[40]

Peter Lisagor, the late correspondent for the Chicago Daily News, stated in an interview given for the Kennedy Library oral history project, that he felt Kennedy's practice of televising his news conferences caused a kind of "artificiality of the theatrical press conference", and he said that President Johnson retreated from this. Lisagor was with Kennedy during the Vienna summit with Khrushchev in 1961, and as a pool reporter he recalls hearing Kennedy tell Bill Lawrence of ABC News, "You can describe my mood as somber."[41]

The late Henry R. Luce of Time told an oral history interviewer that he was impressed with Kennedy's reading habits. He found Kennedy reading a book about President McKinley during the Wisconsin primary campaign, and later while visiting JFK at the White House found the President had been reading a book which was a novel written by the 19th Century

---

[39]From Oral History Interview, Gilbert Harrison, John F. Kennedy Library, Waltham, Massachusetts.

[40]From Oral History Interview, Edward P. Morgan, John F. Kennedy Library, Waltham, Massachusetts.

[41]From Oral History Interview, the late Peter Lisagor, John F. Kennedy Library.

British Prime Minister, Benjamin Disraeli.[42]

E. William Henry, JFK's second chairman of the FCC after the resignation of Newton Minow from that post, recalled his first meeting with Kennedy, and also his views of Kennedy's ideas about telecommunications policy. Henry stated, "He (JFK) lived up to his publicity. He was charming, quick, bright, interested, gracious and obviously a man who was not only capable of doing the job but looking forward to it with great enthusiasm. I did notice quite a change in the President between that night--the night before the Inauguration when he was bubbling with enthusiasm and looked like a very young man--and the time when I saw him some two years later, having spent two years in the White House and having absorbed its cares and burdens. He was very definitely a changed man. . . . His appearance and his manner was changed in that he had obviously aged and he was obviously more deliberate. . . . (About the FCC), there was plenty of controversy going on. Minow came in on the crest of the Kennedy wave and did a superb job of capitalizing on the impact that that wave made nationwide. . . ."[43]

President Dwight D. Eisenhower had a somewhat distant relationship with the media according to most accounts, but it was a good one from Eisenhower's viewpoint in that the media did not probe deeply beneath the hero's mantle in the same way they did during the Nixon Administration. Some news people feel that both Eisenhower and Kennedy escaped close scrutiny from the media unlike Johnson and Nixon, and have suggested that both Presidents might have benefited from such close scrutiny. At any rate, interviews with Robert J. Donovan, author of Eisenhower: the Inside Story and a recent book on the Truman Administration, and with James C. Hagerty throw much light on Eisenhower's press relations. Excerpts from the diary of Hagerty, now open to scholars, also show much about how Hagerty handled Eisenhower's press relations.

Donovan's most interesting contact with the Eisenhower White House came as a result of his "selec-

---

[42]From Oral History Interview, the late Henry R. Luce, John F. Kennedy Library.
[43]From Oral History Interview, E. William Henry, John F. Kennedy Library.

tion" by the White House to write his book about
Eisenhower's first term. He stated that he was con-
tacted by Sherman Adams, given access to much important material, and given a free hand in writing the
book. The volume was a best seller. Donovan felt
Eisenhower always had formal, arms-length relations
with the news media, was never as accessible as JFK
or LBJ. "Eisenhower retained the old formality
towards the press. In many ways . . . there were
changes in press relations under Eisenhower, but reporters didn't get to see Eisenhower. It was a more
unusual thing to ask to see him, and I suppose I could
have, but in those days it would have been such an
extraordinary event that I would have found myself
obliged to reflect largely his views in the book,
which I didn't want to do in that manner . . ."
After the publication of the book, Donovan found his
relations with Eisenhower "extremely formal . . . but
friendly".[44] Donovan's interview gives an interesting
view of the evolution of the White House news conference, which has already been discussed in detail in
this book and previously in Cornwell's work.

The author had the good fortune to talk with
James C. Hagerty on one occasion when Hagerty was an
executive for the American Broadcasting Companies.
Hagerty gave the impression on this meeting of being a
thoroughly professional newsman. He was respected by
all his peers, and his reputation remains high, as the
comments from the Carter White House press aide indicate. Hagerty's diary, kept during 1954 and 1955,
will be examined closely in this chapter, but before
doing that it is useful to summarize some of the matters contained in his oral history interview for
Columbia University's Oral History Project, on file at
the Dwight D. Eisenhower Library in Abilene, Kansas.

Hagerty, a native of Plattsburgh, New York, was
the son of a New York _Times_ reporter, so he got his
newspaper background by osmosis. His father was a
political writer for the old New York _Herald_ and later
for the New York _Times_. Hagerty said, "I can remember
as a youngster being down at Oyster Bay during the
summer when Teddy Roosevelt was there, and Dad was
assigned to cover him. Mother and the family went

---

[44]From Oral History Interview, Robert J. Donovan, Dwight D. Eisenhower Library, Abilene, Kansas;

iown to spend the time with Dad, when he was down
there on summer assignments." Hagerty majored in
politics and economics at Columbia, and worked for the
Times and the old City News Association. On gradu-
ating, he joined the Times staff and worked as a legislative correspondent in Albany; he was there for eight
or nine years as a political reporter. When Thomas E.
Dewey was elected Governor, Hagerty joined Dewey and
then in 1952 he joined Eisenhower before the presidential campaign. Hagerty spent 17 years in government, nine with Dewey and eight with Eisenhower. At
his first meeting with "Ike", he was introduced by
Dewey. He recalls that President Truman clearly made
one overture to Eisenhower about supporting Eisenhower
for the Presidency as a Democrat. He was told about
this meeting by Eisenhower. Other matters recalled by
Hagerty include his first time to brief Eisenhower,
the Governors' Conference of 1952 at which a strategy
was worked out for the Republican Convention against
Taft in Chicago, the selection of Nixon and Eisenhower's meeting with Taft in Chicago, the Eisenhower
decision to go to Korea and the trip to Korea, the
Nixon fund scandal, TV press conferences and radio tap-
ing. Hagerty recalled coverage of the 1953 Eisenhower
inauguration. He said that in 1968 President Johnson,
who occasionally consulted Eisenhower, wanted the
former President to visit the Far East on his behalf,
but Eisenhower wasn't well enough. Hagerty also recalled the Kennedy-Nixon TV debates of 1960, the press
arrangements for Eisenhower's meeting with Khrushchev,
and preparations for Eisenhower's visit to the USSR,
which never took place. Hagerty also discussed the
briefing process in the Eisenhower White House, and the
first filming of a White House press conference, which
he pioneered for Eisenhower.[45]

Some excerpts from Hagerty's diary for 1954 and
1955 are instructive. These are selected at random
from the material now available at the Eisenhower
Library and indicate the thoroughness and relative
formality of the White House briefing system under
Eisenhower (in contrast to the Carter method):

---

[45]From The Reminiscences of James C. Hagerty,
in the Oral History Collection of Columbia University
(Eisenhower Administration Project), on file in Dwight
D. Eisenhower Library, Abilene, Kansas.

Monday, January 4, 1954--Busy day--meeting
with Cabinet and GOP leaders on message in
Cabinet room starting 8:30 A.M., lasting 'til
1 P.M.--reviewed message--all seemed to go all
right. Dan Reed (New York Republican congressman) objected to tax sections, left to work
out with (Treasury Secretary George) Humphrey.

TV-Radio chat--9:30-9:45 P.M.--Montgomery
handling, tho Cabot (Henry Cabot Lodge, former
Senator) tried to get in way--messed up talk,
insisting on changing single words to $2 ones--
bit discussion on "no depression"--Cabot argues
not politically wise--won out over my &
Hoover's (?) objections--Dave Lawrence panned
points Cabot put in following day--saying not
simple English--couldn't agree more.

Dress rehearsal 3 P.M.--Pres. using tele-
prompter, not cards, went fine--talked him
into doing some that night.

Used makeup for night--CBS gal did good
job--so did Pres.--after speech McCann, Montgomery, Cabot, Mayme and self waited upstairs--
she in fine spirits--talked about campaign,
conventions--said he made up mind to run because found Taft wing of GOP and Truman
inane (?) pettiness--said man who put most
pressure on him was Jim Duff (former Senator
from Pennsylvania).

Thursday, April 1, 1954--In at 7 A.M.--all
hell broke loose last night and this A.M. on
H-bomb release. Drew Pearson's column
described in detail words and N.Y. Times then
broke their story--AP, UP & INS followed (In
checking later found that Pearson's story had
moved into offices 2 days before. Am sure
newspapers getting columns deliberately kept
quiet and were determined to break story anyway) Radio, TV and photos moved stuff at
7 A.M., after getting okay from Civil Defense
after I called them.--When told Pres. about
it, he, like I, was mad at Pearson--"maybe
you have to talk to his man, but as far as
I'm concerned I wouldn't let him cover anybody in government--and if anyone was caught
talking to him or his men, I'd fire them on
the spot."--

Indochina situation getting really bad.
French want more help from us, but want it
at their terms--refuse to let us train locals
or send in American troops on long term basis--
fear that would hurt what they call "French
prestige"--at luncheon at W. H. with Pres.,
Rob Hornell and Walker Stone, Pres. expounded
on problem--said U.S. might have to make decision to send in squadrons from 2 aircraft
carriers off coast to bomb Reds at Dienbien-
phu--" of course, if we did, we'd have to drop
(?) it forever"--French very difficult to
handle--almost impossible.

Called in Radio-TV network spokesmen in
P.M. and requested time Monday for Pres.--
Fri. for (Attorney General Herbert) Brownell.

Friday, April 16--As usual, Republican
leaders in Senate sold us down the river on
EDC assurance story. Saltonstall and Wiley
said that they had not been informed on
statement. Dulles told me later he had personally cleared statement with Saltonstall
and Wiley and produced the original draft
with changes made on it in their own hand-
writing. Clearance was made in March, and
both Saltonstall and Wiley's only defense was
"we forgot it." Democrats taking same line
for political purposes despite the fact that
they also were told about it in March. Congressional Republicans worried more about
winning an election than saving the world
and winning the peace--interested only in
being reelected, not realizing that by actions they are helping to defeat themselves.

Other announcements during the day but
nothing important.

In afternoon started to get queries on
off-the-record talk Nixon made to newspaper
editors in Washington. Nixon, in answer to
hypothetical questions said that he did not
believe French would fold up in Indochina,
but if they did, we would have to hold Indochina because of its vital importance to
free world. Also quoted as saying that Oppen-
heimer was loyal American. Checked with Nixon
to see if this were right, and he said it was

311

but that he was answering hypothetical questions. Played dumb on this in answer to all
queries. Think it was foolish for Dick to
answer as he did but will make the best of it.

Marv Arrowsmith (AP correspondent) and I
went to dinner at General Blanchard's home at
Camp Gordon--Nice evening!

Saturday, April 17--. . . Talked to President in the morning about Nixon speech, and
he asked me to get in touch with Bedell Smith
and have State Department put out statement
on hypothetical question without cutting
ground from under Nixon.

Released exchange of messages between the
President and Bao Dai (Emperor of South Vietnam) and (French Premier) Rene Coty on fighting at Dienbienphu. . . .

State Department called me while at dinner
and read text of statement which in effect
pointed out that Nixon was answering hypothetical question but that United States
never expected French to pull out of Indochina. They issued their statement Saturday
night for Sunday morning papers.

Monday, May 10, 1954--. . . Just then I
got called out of the meeting (with President
Eisenhower) by telephone call from Foster
Dulles about Times story from Geneva that the
Russians had turned down the President's
atomic proposal. Dulles suspected a British
leak on this one and recommended that White
House answers be limited to the statement he
made with Molotov on May 1st that we had the
Soviet note and that we were studying it here
in this country--Still slight hope that Soviets
who are insisting on limitation of atomic
weapons will be forced to change their mind by
public opinion and support President's plan--
Doubtful but no use giving them an excuse by
issuing statement from here on exchange at
this time.

Lunch with Walter Winchell. Am sure Winchell came to see me as emissary of McCarthy
group. Wanted to get me to say it was a good

idea to call off McCarthy-Army hearings and
to recommend that they be taken off television.
Told him could not give such a word--that we
would not interfere with Senate proceedings.
Stevens and Army insistent on getting McCarthy
on stand and I agree. Winchell seemed a little
disappointed at my reaction, but hope we don't
fall for this one. It will be duck soup for
the Democrats if we do.

First day back after week off--Usual hectic
welcome!

Monday, June 7, 1954: At Waldorf-Astoria,
New York City, overnight.

Spent the day talking to radio and tele-
vision presidents on the President's orders.
He wanted me to give them advance notice that
we would be asking for time during June and
July to carry the need for the passage of the
Eisenhower program to the American people.

My first visit at 11:00 A.M. was to CBS.
Talked with Frank Stanton and Bill Paley.
Told them quite frankly the following (which
I repeated to all the others during the day):

I said that the President had made up his
mind to bring the legislative program to the
attention of the American people in June and
July in order to put pressure on Congress to
pass it. Told them that I was calling on
them at the personal direction of the President who wanted them to know in advance what
we were thinking about. I said that we would
expect to use the President alone and with
Cabinet officers during the next two months.
Pointed out specifically three things to them:

1. That we would try not to interfere too
   much with the big commercial shows of
   the networks;

2. That we would try to be as non-partisan
   as possible to avoid their getting requests for equal time from the Democratic Party or from people like Wayne
   Morse or Joe McCarthy. In reference to
   McCarthy, I told them I did not think

313

any of the President's talks could be
construed as an attack on McCarthy
and permit him to ask for time.

3. That we would not propose a series of
talks for any set weekly period but
that we would do it on a "play by ear"
basis from time to time.

Paley and Stanton, who are good friends,
were considerably interested and very helpful.
In brief, this is what they told me.

They urged that in their opinion the President would have to kick off this drive with
something dramatic. Both urged that he
address Congress in Joint Session on "the un-
finished business of the Congress." They were
sure that that would be covered by all networks
without any question. They were not so sure of
whether we could get all networks to carry
Cabinet members even though they might appear
with the President.

As an alternative they strongly urged
Cabinet members to appear on panel programs,
to arrange regional and local broadcasts if
they were speaking in various sections of the
country. They also recommended that we send
everyone possible in the Administration out in
the field to talk the program. As far as the
President is concerned, they were both unani-
mous in their feeling that the first kickoff
speech should be done before a live audience
so that the applause could be heard by those
who were watching it in their homes. This
would have a good psychological advantage and
would be much better than a quiet studio
speech.

Had lunch with Toots Shor at his restaurant
and learned one important item. He told me
that McCarthy was in telephone consultation
every day with Dick Berlin and that Berlin
was running McCarthy's publicity and was the
brains behind McCarthy's handling of himself
and his witnesses at the hearings. Have suspected this for a long time but this is the
first time I have had proof. Dick apparently
has been shooting his mouth off about this,

314

and Toots gets around.

After lunch at 2:00 I saw Robert Sarnoff and Bill Weaver of NBC. Their reaction, in brief, was pretty much the same as CBS officials although they seemed more concerned about requests they might have for equal time. That is understandable since NBC has always been weak-kneed on that sort of thing. General Sarnoff was in Canada so I did not see him. His son, Robert, appeared to be more interested in whether we could not get the President on color television than anything else, but Weaver caught on fast. Weaver, strangely enough, thought a Joint Session would be a dramatic way to kick off the drive.

. . . Joined Bob Kittman, President of ABC, at the Stork Club of all places. Had his General Manager with him, and we discussed at great length the whole subject. Bob was more concerned about the political implications, but since he is a good reporter that was only natural. He raised one simple point: "Are you starting the campaign this early and won't that be the impression everybody will get?" He did not expect me to answer it and I made no attempt to do so. He said he would go along and cooperate to the fullest extent.

As a result of these conversations here are the impressions I get:

1. There would be no difficulty with radio and we would get delayed broadcasts throughout the night.

2. We probably would have some difficulty getting all television networks to carry us live. Both CBS and NBC people "mentioned" the possibility of CBS and NBC taking turns. Sure ABC and Dumont, however, will carry live.

3. Networks afraid of flood of requests for equal time and expense it would entail. . . .

Wednesday, July 14, 1954: . . . At the
press conference briefing with the President
we discussed the following:

1. Bedell Smith's Return to Geneva and
   the Dulles trip to Paris--It was
   agreed that the President merely say
   that an announcement was expected
   soon and let it go at that.

2. Syngman Rhee's visit with the President at the White House on July 26th--
   We had a mimeographed announcement on
   the visit of President Rhee and the
   President agreed to announce that at
   the start of the conference.

3. The Tax Bill--We had a short summary
   of the tax bill, giving its more important features which the President
   agreed to read at the opening of the
   press conference. I told him that I
   did not think the people of the country
   realized the many good features of the
   bill for the average person. I said
   that the Democrats had made much of the
   fact that this was a "rich man's bill"
   and had completely overlooked the advantages of the bill for child care,
   retired people and widows, parents of
   children who work part-time, people
   with sick and accident insurance,
   people with medical bills, farmers doing soil and water conservation work
   and taxpayers with non-relative de-
   pendents. The President agreed to
   this and thought it was a good idea.

4. The President's proposal made by the
   Vice President at the Governors Conference for a $50 billion highway plan.

5. Politics, including Meek in Illinois,
   Dewey in New York, Curtis vs Crosby
   in Nebraska. On these the President
   said he would not get into this subject and he was not engaged in primaries.

Other topics we quickly ran over were:

1. Civil Service increases in pay.

2. Soviet atom power plant--In that con-
    nection, the President said he would
    tell the newspapermen he had not given
    up on his UN atomic proposal and he
    was determined to carry it through
    whether the Soviets agreed or not.

3. Legislation--Farm Bill, Anti-Red Pro-
    gram, Hawaii, adjournment date.

4. Health Reinsurance--On this President
    said he was going to pull out all the
    stops, get indignant and lambast those
    who voted against.

5. AEC-TVA.

6. Summer plans for Denver.

The press conference went over very well
and we subsequently released for direct
quotes the President's remarks on the Tax
Bill and the Health Reinsurance Program. . . .

Tuesday, July 24, 1954: In at the White
House at 7:15 A.M. The President called me
up to his bedroom at 7:30. He said that he
wanted me to stay with him throughout the
morning so that he would have a record of
any conversations that took place. He asked
me also to sit in on the Korean-American talks
with the same thing in mind. . . .

After the President dressed we went out
into the living room section of the second
floor and I had an opportunity to discuss
quite a few things with him.

1. Denver--I suggested to the President that
it might be a good idea to have prepared now
statements on important legislation which he
could sign in Denver. These statements would
be newsworthy and would emphasize the fact
that he had merely changed his White House
operations from Washington to Denver and it
would take the edge off the so-called "vacation" stories. He agreed to this and told
me to follow through and get it done. He

317

also agreed that he would make short statements on legislation for the newsreel and TV
newsreel cameras that would be covering us
in Denver and would permit radio to take
tapes of these statements.

2. My work--The President said that he knew
I was up to my ears with the mechanics of my
job and suggested that I give consideration
to another man coming into my department to
help Murray handle these mechanics. Such a
move, to be made in September, would permit
me to pay more attention to policy decisions
and ideas. I told the President that it would
be somewhat difficult to work it out exactly,
that part of my job of necessity required me
to spend many hours of each day with the
newspapermen so that they wouldn't go off
half-cocked on stories about the Administration. He agreed with this but also said that
he hoped I could get freer so that I could
start fires rather than have to put them out
all the time.

3. 1956--For the first time the President
virtually told me that he would run again in
'56. He put it this way: "A lot of people
are urging me to run again for another term.
They say that I should never discuss this or
give any indication of which way I am going
to decide until the very last moment in 1956.
I suppose they're right. But when the time
comes to make this decision, I will make it
by myself after consultation with a few
people in the White House, including your-
self, Jerry Persons and Sherm Adams. Right
now I kind of think that the answer will be
that I will run for another term, but I am
telling everyone that they better not speculate on this and let me make the decision.
After all, it is my life and it will have to
be my decision."

4. Tension--The President told me that he
was beginning for the first time to feel the
tension of his office. He thought that that
was only natural because of the closing weeks
of the Congressional session plus the very
heavy burden of international decisions which
he has had to make these days. "It's not the ꞌ

job particularly that bothers me or the title.
It's the multiplicity of petty problems that
many people bring to me. The selfishness of
the members of Congress is incredible and the
manner in which they try to put me on the spot
and want me to decide questions that never
should be brought to me are just about driving
me nuts." . . .

Tuesday, December 7, 1954: In at 8:15.

Saw the President in the morning and he decided to have a press conference tomorrow
morning at 10:30.

I reminded him that tomorrow was the anniversary of his "Atoms for Peace" UN speech and
that I had asked the Department of State to
get up a paper which would outline the progress
that this nation has made with other nations
and in the United Nations in carrying through
on the proposal. . . .

The inevitable happened this afternoon.
McCarthy broke with the President in a speech
before a hearing of his Committee in which he
made a statement in typical McCarthy fashion
blaming the President for congratulating
(Senators) Watkins and Flanders and holding up
the work of the investigation of communism,
while at the same time urging patience and
niceties toward the Chinese Communists who
were torturing American prisoners. McCarthy
accused the President of "weakness and supine-
ness" in ferreting out Communists here and
said that he had been asked if he were going
to apologize to the Senate for activities
which led to his censure. Instead, McCarthy
said he wanted to apologize to the American
people for campaigning for the President in
1952 on the grounds that the President would
be tough on Communists here at home.

When the story broke on the ticker, I
first called Brownell, told him of it and
recommended that we bring up to date the
President's June 2nd statement in which he
pointed out the record of the Department of
Justice and the FBI in dealing with Communists
here at home and also deliberately pointed out

319

that the constant surveillance of communism
is a 24-hour-a-day, 7-days-a-week, 52-weeks-
a-year job. Brownell thought that this would
be a good answer, and I then went in to show
the President the AP and UP ticker stories.

The President was alone in his office at
the time and was reading the Encyclopaedia
Britannica. I asked him if he was reading
the Federalist Papers and he said no he was
looking up some information he wanted on the
origin of the Jewish race. He said he was
interested in finding out more about their
history, that he had a breathing spell and
was just reading about them.

I said I regretted that I would have to
disturb his afternoon but that McCarthy had
just let go with the expected blast against
him. . . .

The President put down the Encyclopaedia
and carefully read the news stories. Then
without any show of anger whatsoever he
turned to me and said, "Jim, this is what
we've been expecting and I am not at all
sorry to see it come. I rather suspected
that when I had Watkins in on Saturday, Mc-
Carthy would see in that visit an invitation
to him to use it as a personal attack upon
himself. But that's all right with me. I
never had any use for him, as you know, and
I am just as glad that he has made this statement now rather than waiting for a later time
to do it. How do you suggest we handle this
right now?"

I brought in with me a copy of the June
2nd statement and told him of my conversation
with Brownell. . . . I recommended that he
allow me to call in the newspapermen and tell
them that as far as McCarthy's statement was
concerned, the White House had this to say:
On the international situation, I would refer
them to the President's press conference of
last Thursday. On the charge of weakness
against communism at home, I would refer them
to the June 2nd statement which the President
had made. . . . I urged that I be permitted
to do this so that an answer from us would

appear in the same stories as the McCarthy
attack and so that we would not be forced
into a position at the press conference tomorrow of waiting 24 hours before answering
him.

The President took off his glasses and bit
the earpiece of them as he thought this out.
He said then: "Go ahead, Jim. You put it
out in your name." Then, getting up he
started to walk back and forth behind me.
As he did so, he started to talk. He said
that as far as he was concerned, he was
finished trying to work with the radical Right
Wing of the Republican Party and that he would
fight them from now on. "I've had just enough
from the McCarthys, the Welkers, the Malones
and people like that. This party of ours has
got to realize that they won't exist unless
they become a party of progressive moderates--
unless they can prove to the American people
that they are a middle-of-the-road party and
turn their backs on the extremes of the Left
and particularly the extremes of the Right.
If there is one thing that I am going to try
to do during the next two years. . . ." (I
interrupted at this point to say "Don't you
mean the next six years, Mr. President?" He
laughed and said, "Right now, I'm speaking of
the next two years. You and I will talk about
the next four years one of these days.")
"These next two years I have just one purpose,
outside of the job of keeping this world at
peace, and that is to build up a strong progressive Republican Party in this country . . .
If the Right Wing wants a fight, they're going
to get it. . . ."

The President then chuckled to himself and
said, "Jim, you've heard this speech many
times before, but I just wanted to get it off
my chest today. Thanks for listening. Now go
out and make your announcement." . . .

Wednesday, January 12, 1955: . . . In the
briefing conference with the President I ran
over rapidly the Dulles suggestions (Hagerty
frequently conferred with Dulles on foreign
policy matters before Ike's news conferences,
the Diary indicates) and he accepted all of

them. He said that on both the Churchill and
Nehru visit he would say that he would be willing to meet anytime they wanted to see him.
He also said he would be very strong on the
Bricker Amendment should it come up at the
press conference and make it clear that he
was not giving in one iota. (None of these
questions came up at the conference, much to
our surprise.) . . .

Adams and some of the staff members asked
me just as the President's briefing was over
and we were leaving the room to go to the
press conference if we could not arrange to
get some of these press conferences on television or at least before cameras. After the
press conference I told the President I
thought it would be useful to get some camera
work in the press conference similar to the
way we make recordings--that is, that the
White House says what is and what is not to
be used. At 2:30 I had a meeting with the
industry representatives. We are going to
try to work out a system where we use four
cameras--2 sixteen mm. and 2 35 mm. We will
try to line it up so we can use it at the
press conference next week. . . .

Thursday, February 3, 1955: In New York
in the morning. . . . Back at the White House
at 3:30.

Visited in New York in the morning with
Frank Stanton of CBS, General Sarnoff of NBC,
John Daley and Bob Kintner of ABC. Dropped
in to see them to find out how they thought
the televising of the press conferences was
going. Their reactions were all very favorable, although Frank Stanton raised a point
that may come up in the future. He said that
CBS had not decided completely whether to run
a special show each Wednesday night on the
press conference. They had given a half hour
on network, both radio and television, the
first time, but had only given radio network
last night and had stuck to film clips from
the press conference on their television
news shows. He said the reason for this was
that they projected the cost of doing this
on a regular basis every Wednesday and had

322

estimated that it would cost CBS-TV $500,000
a year to give a public service half hour
each Wednesday without sponsorship. He asked
me if I had ever considered letting them
sponsor such a program and I told him I had,
but that the answer had to be in the negative.
He said he was sure that would be my answer
and that was why his people would have to
study this matter a little longer. "It may
be that we will ask you to let us do it occasionally, once a month or every two weeks."
I told him that if that were the situation,
they would have to make the request to me,
that I would not put the White House in the
position of ordering it without an industry
request.

Sarnoff raised nothing of importance except to say that he thought it was a very
good start and that the reaction they had
received throughout the country was very
favorable. Kintner and Daly took just the
opposite viewpoint from CBS. They said they
were planning to have a half hour network
show every Wednesday night from 10:00 until
10:30 and said they hoped I would release
enough for them to fill a half hour show with
both the actual film and commentary. They
said if I could release 15 or 20 minutes each
time, that would take care of it. . . .

Monday, March 28, 1955: . . . Had Bill
Lawrence of the New York Times in today to
raise hell about a Times Review of the Week
piece last Sunday which said among other
things that "anger by the Democrats over the
release of the Yalta papers was a result of
the way the Department (meaning the State Department) a day before giving the text to the
New York Times had tried to send confidential
copies to Senator George and others on the
Hill." I told Lawrence that I thought this
was one hell of a way to run a railroad and
that to this day I did not know how they got
their report, but if they did get it from
the State Department and publicly admitted
it, that was one sure way of not getting anything in the future.

Bill was actually flabbergasted to read

323

the Review of the Week piece and he called
Scotty Reston immediately. Reston had been
away for the weekend and had not seen the
article and was as amazed at it as Bill.
Lawrence said he had called Sulzberger directly and Sulzberger had Lester Markel,
the editor of the Sunday Times, call him
back. Markel said that it was just a mistake
and that it had slipped through. I am sure
that both Reston and Lawrence are telling me
the truth on this and that it was an error.

We agreed we should not do anything about
it now, but I warned both Reston and Lawrence
that if the issue was raised in Congress, we
would have to deny it and that I fully expected them to deny it also. They agreed to
do so. . . .

Augusta, Georgia, April 12-April 20: . . .
1. The President is going to use the AP
Luncheon in New York City next Monday to make
a strong plea for his Reciprocal Trade Program. He is going to characterize it as the
very keystone of his whole policy to bring
peace to the world and prosperity at home.
. . . The President is going to say that he
wants this program, that he is going to fight
for it and that "he will not support those
who do not support him". That is all he is
going to say on the support question at that
time. He is going to throw out this idea
briefly, anticipating the second step which
will be:

2. At the next press conference the
President wants a question asked as to what
he meant at the AP luncheon by saying he
would not support those who did not support
the Reciprocal Trade Program. In answer to
that question he is going to make quite a
strong answer, outlining the things that we
have been trying to do for the two years we
have been in office and then he will let
the real story out of the bag . . . He is
going to use the Reciprocal Trade Bill as a
yardstick for personal support of himself.
. . .

The President is quite insistent on this

and thinks that the time has come for him to separate (as he puts it) "the men from the boys" within the Party. Having completely made up his mind on what he is going to do, I think he is going to get quite a kick out of it. . . .[46]

Here is Hagerty's account of events related to Eisenhower's heart attack and convalescence in 1955:

Saturday, September 24, 1955, was a cold rainy day in Washington. But I was enjoying it. I was on vacation--the first one I had had in several years. The President was in Denver; he had just returned from a fishing trip in the Rocky Mountains. Murray Snyder, the Assistant Press Secretary, was with him. Everything was quiet.

I had returned home in the mid-afternoon from Columbia Country Club, where I had been soundly beaten in the second round of the second flight of the Club championship. On arriving home I had glanced at the early edition of the afternoon paper, the Washington Star, and had read with mild interest a story from Denver which reported that the President had not gone to his office that morning, but was remaining at his Denver residence--the home of Mrs. Eisenhower's mother, Mrs. Elivera Doud. The story said that the President had had a mild stomach upset and wouldn't be in to work that day. I remember remarking to my wife, Marge, that it was too bad the President had an upset stomach, but that he probably got it by eating something too fast, before he rushed out to play a round of golf. Then I went into the downstairs den and laid down for a nap.

At five o'clock (2 P.M. Denver time), I was startled out of a sound sleep by the incessant ringing of the White House phone on the desk. As I jumped up and rushed over

---

[46] James C. Hagerty Diary, 1954-55, in James C. Hagerty Papers, Dwight D. Eisenhower Library, Abilene, Kansas.

to pick up the receiver, I knew something
was wrong. (By prearranged agreement, the
White House telephone operators only jingled
my home phone once on routine calls; con-
tinual ringing meant important, very important, business.)

As I picked up the receiver, the operator
said: "It's Mr. Snyder calling you from
Denver. He says it's urgent."

The next voice I heard was Murray's. It
was strained and choked with emotion.

"Jim, Dr. Snyder has just told me that
the President has had a heart attack and
that he has taken him to Fitzsimmons Army
Hospital."

At Murray's words, I think my own heart
skipped at least a couple of beats. Several
immediate questions tumbled out of me.

"How bad is it? When did it happen?
Does anyone here in Washington know?"

Murray replied that he did not know any
of the details as yet, that the doctor had
just phoned him. He said that no one in
Washington knew about it; that it was up to
me to notify the Administration people.

I asked him when he was going to make the
public announcement, and he answered that he
had put in a telephone call to the Brown
Palace Hotel (where the newsmen stayed)
notifying them to come immediately to the
White House Press Room at Lowry Air Force
Base.

"I think you have about a half-hour jump
on them, but as soon as they get here, I'm
going to put it out," Murray warned. "Jim,
I intend to play this straight and give the
fellows everything as fast as I can get it.
Okay?"

"I couldn't agree more, Murray. Play it
your way and give them everything you can.
We've got a hell of a responsibility on our

shoulders now. I'll catch a plane out as
soon as I can. I'll call the Vice President
and the Cabinet and let them know, but I'll
tell them to leave you alone; you're going
to be busy as soon as you make the first
announcement. I'll call you back at 3
o'clock your time. Good luck."

I hung up the phone and for a few seconds
felt as if I'd been slugged. The President
of the United States has had a heart attack,
I kept thinking to myself. What will happen
to him and to the country? What a shock
this is going to be to the world. But then
I knew I had a job to do--and only less than
a half-hour to do it in before the news broke.

I picked up the phone and got the White
House operator back. I asked her how many
operators were on duty. She said that there
were only herself and one other operator--
the normal complement for a quiet Saturday
afternoon.

"You better get everyone in," I told
her. "Mr. Snyder has just told me that the
President has had a heart attack and has been
taken to a hospital."

"My God," the operator gasped, "that's
terrible. What can I do for you now?"

"Get me the Vice President wherever he
is and after that get me Jerry Persons," I
said. (Sherman Adams, the Assistant to the
President, was in Europe on vacation and
Major General Wilton B. Persons, USA (Retired), was the ranking White House officer
that day.)

As the telephone operator was getting the
Vice President, I called out to my wife, told
her what had happened, and without a word she
started packing a bag for me. . . . At the
same time, I started writing out on a scratch
pad things I would have to do. The list has
long since been lost--I'll never remember
what happened to it, but here (are) some of
the things I wrote down in a few minutes it
took to get the Vice President:

"Notify VP--find out where he will be.

"Persons--between us call all Cabinet members.

"Call Air Force for plane.

"Send cable to Adams.

"Find out next call to Denver about notifying President's family."

The White House operator broke in on my hasty thoughts--I had kept the telephone receiver cupped to my ear with my shoulder as I jotted down the notes.

"Here's the Vice President," she said.

"Hello, Jim," the Vice President said. "What's up?"

"Dick, I've got some bad news. Sit down. I've just had a call from Murray Snyder in Denver. The President has had a heart attack--"

"Oh, my God," the Vice President interrupted. "When, how bad is it--"

"I don't know, Dick," I replied. "Murray just had time to tell me what I've told you. It happened sometime today and Dr. Snyder has taken (him) to the Army Hospital at Denver. Murray is going to announce it within the half-hour. I wanted you to know it right away. I've got a call in for Jerry Persons and between us we'll call the members of the Cabinet. I'm going out to Denver as soon as I can get a plane. I'm going to call Murray back in an hour and get more details and, of course, I'll keep in constant touch with you--both while I'm here and when I get to Denver."

"Please keep me fully informed," the Vice President responded. "You know, Jim, maybe this won't be serious. I know many people who have had heart attacks and have had complete recoveries. We all need the

328

President. I'm sure he'll be all right.--"

The operator broke in at (this) point and
said: "Mr. Hagerty, I've got Mr. Persons on
the line but Mr. Snyder is calling in again
from Denver."

I told her to ask Mr. Persons to stand
by and to put Mr. Snyder on immediately and
told the Vice President: "Murray's calling
from Denver. I'll take him and come right
back to you." The Vice President said that
he would remain on the White House line and
I cut in to Murray.

Murray said, "Jim, Dr. Snyder just called
me from the hospital. Here is the bulletin
I'm going to put out."

"Read it slowly so I can take it down.
The Vice President is on the other line and
I want to read it to him," I said.

"All right, here it is: The President
has just had a mild anterior coronary throm-
bosis. He has just been taken to Fitzsimmons
General Hospital. He was taken to the hospital in his own car. That's the end of the
bulletin," Murray reported.

"Anything else, Murray? Any other details?"

"Well, not much at this time. It's getting hectic out here, as you can imagine.
But Dr. Snyder did tell me that it was a
mild attack, not a critical one. And the
President was taken to the hospital in his
own car. That's a good sign--they didn't
think it necessary to use an ambulance. They
also took an electro-cardiogram at Mrs. Doud's
house. It showed an attack, but again a mild
one. That's about all I know now."

"Thanks, Murray, I'll call you later.
How much time have I still got," I asked.

"About twenty minutes, I would guess," he
replied. "So long."

As Murray hung up, the operator connected me immediately with the Vice President and I read the bulletin to him and told him what Murray had reported to me. I told him I had better get to work with Mr. Persons in notifying the Cabinet members. He agreed and said he would remain at home and for me to call him back just as soon as I got any further reports. I said that I would call him back within the next half-hour, if only to give him a report of notifications to the Cabinet.

I then got Jerry Persons on the phone, broke the news quickly and abruptly to him. He was as shocked as I was--but we both realized that we had an important job to do and couldn't take the time to express our own personal feelings to each other. We knew how each other felt--we didn't have to say anything to each other.

We quickly ran down the list of Cabinet members, with Jerry agreeing to take the bulk of them. He realized that I had other matters to attend to, like making arrangements for a plane and--once the news broke-- of myriads of press calls that would be flooding into the White House. I was assigned to call the Secretary of State and the Secretary of the Treasury. Jerry recommended that I call General Thomas White, then vice chief of staff of the Air Force, and make arrangements for a plane. We agreed to get in touch with each other again within the hour. I told Jerry that I would draft a short cable to Sherman Adams and give it to the Secretary of State to relay to Adams overseas through State Department channels.

I then asked the telephone operator to get me the Secretary of State, John Foster Dulles. She connected me with him at his Washington residence and I told him the news and gave him the same reports I had given the Vice President. Mr. Dulles' reaction was the same as the Vice President('s). He was deeply shocked.

"Jim, this is terrible news," he said. "It is terrible news for the President's family and for the country. But it is equally terrible for the free world. The President is looked upon as the leader of the free world. It will come as a great shock to our friends and to all free nations."

But, then, as did the Vice President, the Secretary of State repeated almost word for word the hope that the President's attack was not critical and, like the Vice President, said that he personally knew many friends who had had a heart attack and who had recovered and continued to perform their duties.

I told the Secretary that I was going out to Denver and that Mr. Persons would be the White House staff officer through whom I would clear and that Mr. Persons would remain in touch with him. I told him also that I would report to the Vice President. The Secretary said he thought that this was a fine arrangement.

"Always remember", he added, "that the President, in his wisdom, has set up a fine Cabinet and staff system to take care of any emergencies."

I couldn't get the Secretary of the Treasury right away--his home phone didn't answer, so I had the operator place a call to run down General White. As she started to do this, she reported that Mrs. Ann Whitman, the President's personal secretary, was calling from Denver. As Ann came on the line, she was crying, but like the wonderful person she is, stopped it when she began to tell me of certain things Dr. Snyder and Mrs. Eisenhower wished me to do. She said that Mrs. Eisenhower would call John--their son-- but that she would appreciate it if I would notify the President's brothers and arrange with them a system of keeping them up-to-date daily on the President's condition. She also told me that Dr. Snyder wanted Dr. Thomas W. Mattingly, head of the Cardiological Division at Walter Reed Army Medical Center in Washing-

ton, to come out to Denver as soon as possible. Col. Mattingly, who had yearly par-
ticipated in physical examinations given to
the President over the last ten years, was to
bring the records of those examinations with
him, Ann added.

I said I would call General Leonard D.
Heaton, Commanding Officer at Walter Reed,
and make these arrangements and would bring
Dr. Mattingly out with me. I asked Ann how
much time I had before Murray made his announcement, and she replied that Murray had
just told her that he was going down to the
press room in a few minutes.

"At the most, you have five minutes, and
at the least about two," she said.

I told Ann I would see her as soon as I
could get out to Denver and then asked the
operator to add General Heaton to my growing
list of calls--calls that I was now quite
certain I wouldn't be able to make before
the news broke.

I then called to my wife and asked her to
bring in a portable radio, which I turned on,
set it at the National Broadcasting Company's
Washington station. I knew that Ray Scherer,
NBC's White House correspondent, who was in
Denver, would break in on the network just as
soon as Murray's press conference was over
and that it would be the quickest way to know
when the news would be announced to the world.
I asked Marge how she was getting on with my
packing and she told me to go right ahead with
my work, that my bag would be ready whenever I
wanted it.

I told the operator to drop all the calls
she was working on and to get me Dr. Milton
Eisenhower, the President's youngest brother,
who was then serving as President of Pennsylvania State University. Milton lived nearest
to Washington of all the brothers--Edgar, the
oldest, lived in Tacoma, Washington; Arthur,
in Kansas City; and Earl, in La Grange, Illinois. I figured with the limited time I had
left before the public announcement, it would

332

be right to get through to at least one of the family and set up the reporting system requested by Mrs. Eisenhower. As luck would have it, I got through almost immediately to Milton.

I know that my voice was choked up when I told him the news. But Milton, as always, was kind and considerate. I gave him all the reports that I had to date and he then suggested that in order to take some of the load of phone calls off my back he would call his brothers. He said that he would work out with the family the person I was to call. He said that he would suggest that one of the brothers be designated to receive any and all reports, and that that brother would be then responsible (for) relaying the information to the others. I told him that I would be at Denver sometime that night and would call him after I had a chance to talk to the doctors on the case.

Milton then made one suggestion that later turned out to be one of the wisest steps taken during the whole history of the President's attack. He pointed out that Fitzsimmons was an Army Hospital that Dr. Snyder, Dr. Mattingly, and the Fitzsimmons doctors were all Army medical men. Good men, that was sure, but still Army officers. He suggested that public confidence probably would be greatly increased in the handling of the President's illness if a leading civilian heart specialist was called in immediately. I told him that I thought that this was a very wise suggestion and that I would pass it on immediately.

(Actually, many other persons, including Dr. Snyder and the Fitzsimmons doctors, came to this same conclusion at almost exactly the same time, as I later found out, but Dr. Milton Eisenhower was the first one I had had a chance to talk to during the hectic 30 minutes since Murray Snyder had first called from Denver with the news of the President's

333

attack.)[47]

The Hagerty account of the Eisenhower heart
attack shows two things: (1) the behind-the-scenes
work the press secretary must do in an emergency, and
(2) the degree to which Hagerty as a trusted press
secretary was also an important advisor to Eisenhower.
Eisenhower reportedly looked to Hagerty for advice on
policy, much as President Carter does with Jody
Powell.

What Is the Prospect for This Linkage In the Future?

The question which naturally follows this discussion is: What is the prospect for this linkage
between President, public and the mass media in the
future? Before looking at the prospects under President Carter, for purposes of contrast one may speculate briefly on what the linkage might have been had
either Ford or Reagan, the other two principal candidates, won the Presidency instead of Jimmy Carter.

If the Ford Administration had been given another term from 1977 through 1981, it seems possible
that the President's image with the public and the
news media would have firmed up and that the fluctuations in his popularity that were so noticeable during
the campaign might have finally come to an end. This
would have depended on his ability to unite the Republican party behind him and also on his ability to win
the support of independent voters and conservative
Democrats, something he found it hard to do during the
actual campaign. Still, it probably would have represented a continuation of a stalemated situation in
which Ford and the Congress would have continued to
contend over vetoes of new legislative initiatives
until the election of a Democratic President or a more
conservative Congress had resolved the conflict.

If Ronald Reagan had won the Republican nomination and the presidential election, which at one time
seemed at least a possibility, he would have projected
a conservative image, but the test of policy-making

---

[47]Special entry in James C. Hagerty Diary,
1954-55, in James C. Hagerty Papers, Dwight D. Eisenhower Library, Abilene, Kansas.

might have caused him to move in a more moderate direction. Thus he might have had the same problem with Republican conservatives which Ford had during his administration. Reagan would have probably enjoyed good media treatment for awhile because of his flair for the dramatic, but if he took a strong ideological stance he would have probably attracted press criticism. Altogether, he could have been expected to be about as conservative as Ford but probably not much more so, because the public did not want an ultra-conservative President.

The actual outcome was the election of Jimmy Carter. While President Carter has only recently taken over the reins of government, it is possible to determine the outlines of his relationship with the news media and the public. Mr. Carter is a moderate or centrist President, which is apparently what the public determined it wanted for the present juncture in history. The President was viewed by the voting public as somehow more liberal than Gerald Ford but as more conservative than Morris Udall or George McGovern, and this put him in the center of the political spectrum. He also projected a reassuring image as to his personal morality and ethics. The public's perception of Carter was inevitably affected by the mass media's perception of him, but he showed a degree of flexibility which was an indication that he would make a strong effort to keep in tune with public opinion.

The outlook for President Carter is for a modest degree of public popularity and for a reasonably good working relationship with the news media--in short, a continuation of the "return to normal" which began under the Ford Administration. But under Carter the conservative drift will probably not go any further, even if Carter does not prove to be more than occasionally liberal.

The prospect for the relationship among White House, media and public under some other President is difficult to imagine, but we can theoretically suggest that it would have been different under a more conservative President than either Ford or Carter, or under a more liberal President than either man. The more extreme the views of an elected President, the more likely he is to have difficulty with an essentially moderate majority of the public. The media tend to accept liberal ideas more readily than the general public, which is more moderate, but neither is

really truly strongly conservative. The basic underlying attitude about ideology is one factor determining this relationship, but since the Watergate scandal
it is also heavily affected by the way in which the
public views the integrity, the trustworthiness and the
moral character of its President and those around him.
If any President can pass this test, the public might
be willing to accept a different ideology and perhaps
the media would too.

The general prospect for the linkage relationship between the Presidency and the mass media (and the
linkage relationship between the Presidency and the
public) is that it will be subject to continuing fluc-
tuation, perhaps more subject to events than to the
impress of the personality of any particular President
or his ideology. Elections may be determined by foreign policy developments or turns in the economy, and
in the long run these are the kinds of factors that
influence the triangular relationship among the Presidency, the public, and the mass media.

Thus putting the relationship in some kind of
historical perspective, one can say that FDR, Kennedy
and Eisenhower had a relatively high degree of public
popularity, while Truman, Johnson and Nixon (as well
as Ford) all came into office with a reasonable degree
of popularity, which to some extent was diminished by
the force of events. In terms of the relationship of
each man to the news media, FDR, Kennedy, Eisenhower
and Ford seemed to have the best relationship, while
Truman, Johnson and Nixon had more problems, especially
the latter two. Truman had a strong following among
the working press, but his following did dwindle toward
the end of his term. In each case events like Korea,
Vietnam and Watergate probably had a good deal to do
with affecting the nature of this relationship.

One may ask how Ford's management of media
relations has affected the prospect for this relationship. Even though Ford at times had an uneven relationship with the mass media, it has probably improved
the prospect for this relationship because Ford was
able to reassure both the public and the news media
that it was possible to accept the President's word
and that he could be a credible political figure, a
notion that had been discounted rather severely under
Nixon and Johnson.

In concluding this chapter, I'll draw some

336

general conclusions about the linkage of the Presidency and the mass media. The institution of the Presidency is charged with the task of governing and policy making, while the institution of the mass media is charged with the task of informing the public. When the two are able to work in parallel directions, it seems that the working relationship can be a harmonious one. When the two are working at cross purposes, the relation can be a very discordant one. It has been the case since 1965 that in two administrations the relation has been discordant and in a third the relationship has been an uneasy one. Perhaps during the Carter Administration, the President will be able to restore a harmonious relationship even as he seeks to restore a harmonious relationship with the public at large. But the task will be a difficult one, if only because the depth of public disillusionment (and thus the cynicism in the mass media) has grown to considerable proportions.

So much for the linkages between these institutions. In the next chapter, I'll turn my attention to the impact of the linkages between the Presidency and the mass media on the political system in which both institutions operate.

CHAPTER SIX

IMPACT OF PRESIDENCY-MEDIA LINKAGES ON THE

POLITICAL SYSTEM

. . . The record of the Watergate coverage
shows no hounding of the President. Quite the
contrary. The press did not speak as a chorus
with one voice. The President had his own de-
fenders; equally important, his noncampaign's
non-communications in 1972 initially came
across louder than the message of Watergate.
Ultimately, it was not the "power" of the
press but the substance of the evidence--in
the Senate documents, in the House Committee's
39 volumes of information, and in the President's own behavior--that was decisive. The
message, not the medium, was the message. . . .

. . . Like most institutions in American
society, the press shared in the general decline in public confidence registered in the
Louis Harris polls from the mid-1960s on.
Typically, the majority of the public tends
to treat the press--quite properly, in my
opinion--as just one more of the goods and
services of society; this sensible majority
makes judgments mainly on a case-by-case
basis. . . . Rabbi Korff, the Nixon loyalist
and a mythmaker past the bitter end, announced
he would lead a crusade against the "big media".
He found few followers and quickly passed from
public sight. The sensible majority--sharing
neither the Rabbi's devil theories nor the
press's professional hypochondria with its
own well-being--had moved on to other
matters of immediate concern, such as food
prices and mortgage money. . . .

> --Edwin Diamond, The Tin Kazoo: Television,
> Politics, and the News (Cambridge, Mass.:
> MIT Press, 1975), pp. 218-220

. . . How do members of the Washington
community assess a President's prestige with
the American public? They talk to one another
and to taxi drivers. They read the columnists

and polls and news reports. They sample the
opinions of their visitors and friends. They
travel in the country and they listen as they
go. Above all, they watch Congress. Generally speaking, only national party politicians,
legislative leaders, congressmen in unsafe
seats, and lobbyists in trouble wet their
fingers every day to gauge winds blowing
toward the White House from the public. Most
others, and especially most bureaucrats, concentrate on the winds blowing from the
Capitol. . . .

> --Richard E. Neustadt, _Presidential Power:_
> _The Politics of Leadership, With Reflec-_
> _tions on Johnson and Nixon_ (New York:
> John Wiley & Sons, 1976), p. 157

* * * *

Impact of Linkages on Executive-Legislative Relations

In the preceding chapter, various types of linkages between the Presidency and the mass media were
discussed in a general fashion. In this chapter I
wish to examine the impact of Presidency-media linkages on the larger political system of which the
Presidency is a part.

The impact of linkages will be discussed both in
terms of problems arising from linkages and benefits
derived from linkages. The problems will be discussed
first.

One problem arising from linkage with the mass
media is the issue of "leaks" from Congress. When
"leaks" occur in which a congressman or a member of his
staff gives information to the mass media, the result
may or may not be damaging to the Administration in
power. But one thing is certain; when "leaks" occur
on Capitol Hill, the White House has little if any
control over the information, and that is one reason
Presidents have sometimes been reluctant to disclose
sensitive information (concerning intelligence, for
example) to congressional committees. This has sometimes brought the White House into conflict with members of Congress. This is particularly true of a
policy area in which presidential and congressional

339

powers may overlap.

During the controversy over the Watergate scandal, much dispute occurred about information on the White House tapes which President Nixon was willing to turn over to the federal courts and Judge Sirica, but which he did not wish to turn over to congressional committees. Much of the information was eventually disclosed, but this result came about largely because of public pressure and the courts' attitude, rather than through successful efforts by congressional committee chairmen and the leadership to pry it loose. But this is one illustration of problems which arise from "leaks" from Congress.

Since the institution of the "leak" of information to the mass media is well established in Washington, it should be clear that not all "leaks" come from Capitol Hill, but rather that much information favorable to it is leaked by the Administration. Thus Administration leaks' impact on the political system should be examined too. In general, such leaks tend to disclose information favorable to the Administration while congressional leaks may disclose information damaging to the Administration. This may be true even when the same party controls both the Presidency and Congress. When it is true, it is largely because of the built-in institutional conflict in the checks and balances system of the American national government.

One recent example of a "leak" from an official Administration source was the disclosure to an author named John Newhouse of the background and details of negotiations with the Soviet Union over the SALT (Strategic Arms Limitation Talks) agreements. This information was later published in a book entitled Cold Dawn, which put Secretary of State Henry Kissinger and the Administration in a favorable light.[1] On the other hand, several recent books about the CIA were published without the co-operation of the agency (most of them by former agents), and in at least one case the CIA went into the federal courts in a successful

---

[1] John Newhouse, Cold Dawn (New York: Holt, Rinehart, and Winston, 1973).

effort to have the material censored prior to publication.[2]

In examining problems arising from linkage, one must also look at the impact on public opinion as it affects legislation. Leakage of information which causes public opinion to react positively or negatively to various Administration proposals, for example, is quite likely to have an impact on legislative decisions in Congress.

One good example which might be cited of this is the controversy over defense spending and the antiballistic missile (ABM) which occurred in 1969.[3] Prior to that time, defense spending had gone on relatively unquestioned. But opposition to the war in Vietnam, and the increasing desire of many citizens to spend federal funds on other projects such as aid to blighted urban areas, brought about opposition to such projects. The Administration leaked information putting the new project in a favorable light, and its congressional opponents (particularly Senator Edward Kennedy, D-Mass.) leaked information showing the proposed project in an unfavorable light.

In this instance, the leaked information may have impacted on public opinion considerably, although some surveys showed a large segment of the public was unfamiliar with the issue. The active portion of the public was informed on this issue, however, and the pressure mounted on Congress and on the Nixon Admini-

---

[2]See Victor Marchetti and John D. Marks, The CIA and the Cult of Intelligence (New York: Alfred A. Knopf, 1974) and Philip Agee, Inside the Company: CIA Diary (New York: Bantam Books, 1976). The first book was censored by the courts at the request of the CIA, and the author of the second was deported from Britain at the request of the CIA. For another book which stirred a controversy over leaks, see Matti Golan, The Secret Conversations of Henry Kissinger (New York: Bantam Books, 1976).

[3]See Robert W. Russell, "The ABM in American Defense Policy", in William.C. Spragens and Robert W. Russell, eds., Conflict and Crisis in American Politics (Dubuque, Iowa: Kendall/Hunt Publishing Co., 1970), pp. 31-42.

stration ultimately resulted in a considerable cutting back of the project, even though technically the Administration won a close victory in the congressional vote on it as the funds in dispute were appropriated. But the impact of leaked information is made clear by this example.

Linkage problems arise as public opinion is affected by controversies about confirmation of the President's major appointees. Most recently, this has occurred in the case of Griffin Bell, President Carter's choice for Attorney General. Bell's chances of confirmation were damaged but not fatally, by information leaked by the NAACP and other opponents of his nomination. In earlier instances, Nixon nominees such as Harrold Carswell and Clement Haynsworth for the Supreme Court were rejected because of adverse public reaction to the information that was leaked by opponents of the nominations. As for Haynsworth it was disclosed that he had issued court opinions in cases involving a possible conflict of interest. Although he was generally considered a capable jurist, this fact brought his ethics into question and eventually undermined his chances. In the Carswell case, research by Columbia University law students determined that he had a very high rate of reversal by the higher courts on his decisions. This fact was widely publicized, as was the fact that a number of deans of law schools around the country opposed him as being unqualified for the Supreme Court bench. Thus again leaked information had an impact on public opinion, which in turn had an impact on the reaction to public opinion in Congress, where the final decision had to be made--in this case in the U.S. Senate.[4]

The Presidency also has linkages through the mass media with the public. This fact plus the negative impact which sometimes occurs as a result of congressional reaction to White House "leaks" and related controversies, often causes the President to "go over the heads of Congress" to the public. Some examples of this can be found during the Nixon Administration, when during the confirmation fight over the Carswell and Haynsworth appointments to the Supreme

---

[4]See Richard Harris, _Decision_ (New York: E. P. Dutton & Co., 1971), a case study of the Haynsworth and Carswell nomination controversies.

Court, President Nixon went on television to urge public support for his position. To some extent, Nixon
also used this technique to build up public support
for his position on the war in Vietnam. This was when
his position was not receiving very strong support
from a Congress divided between hard-liners and advocates of peace negotiations.

So far I've been talking mostly about negative
results of linkage between the Presidency and the public and the Presidency and the mass media. But there
are also some benefits to the political system, as the
examples cited below will demonstrate.

One benefit to the political system which results from the kinds of linkages I've just described
is the greater level of public knowledge of the
issues. Public knowledge of the issues means that the
President through the media can provide greater information to the mass public because of the White
House press office's efforts to put out information
about the President's program, his positions, and
other material relevant to current issues. This is
usually done, of course, so as to put the President
and his views in the best possible light. But the important thing is that it _is_ done, and to the extent
that it is done it prevents the lowering of a veil of
secrecy over the White House--secrecy which is always
a danger for the President, because public ignorance
or misinformation about the President and his Administration may cause distrust or lack of credibility.
The public may come to feel the President is keeping
it in the dark or even misinforming it; alternatively,
if the White House follows an open information policy,
telling the good along with the bad, the public is
more apt to feel that the President and his press
aides are "leveling", telling it the truth. The direct result of this kind of openness is an increase in
the public's information about and knowledge of the
President's views, White House happenings, and policy
directions the President is contemplating. This kind
of information benefits not only the public, but also
the mass media disseminating it, and also other
elected officials such as those in Congress.

Another benefit to the political system arising
from these kinds of linkages is closely related to
greater public knowledge of the issues. This benefit
consists of the greater public awareness of the
issues. A subtle but important distinction is made

here between public knowledge and public awareness of
the issues. The public may have much knowledge in the
form of facts and information, but it may still be unaware of the importance or significance of a specific
issue. This is where public awareness becomes important. The public should not only know more about an
issue, but it should also know why that issue is important and significant. This kind of public awareness grows out of the linkage between the Presidency
and the mass media; it provides an extra dimension of
understanding for the average citizen. For example,
the President can communicate through one linkage device, the news conference, after which mass media disseminate information about a new legislative proposal
(Medicare in 1965, Social Security in 1935, or current
proposals for revision of the tax laws).[5] Through this
means the public's information and knowledge of the
issue is increased. But the same kind of linkage can
also disseminate the President's views of why this
issue is important; it can thereby create a greater
public awareness. Both these factors may benefit a
President seeking the adoption of a particular program. But more importantly it is of benefit to the
functioning of the entire political system of which
the Presidency is but one part.

Beyond public knowledge and awareness of current issues, other benefits to the system arise from
linkage. The mass media and the public can team up to
oppose corruption in the executive branch. This would
not be possible without some kind of linkage of the
kind just described. Various examples can be given,
but the most obvious recent example of executive
branch corruption is the Watergate scandal. The scandal would never have been brought to the public's
attention if it had not been for the alertness of the
mass media, specifically the doggedness of Woodward
and Bernstein, the Washington Post reporters chiefly
responsible for digging out the details of the scandal. The existence of the White House tapes and the
co-operation of Judge Sirica did play an important
part in the revelations, but surely the role of the
media was a central one. Again when the cover-up
appeared to be succeeding and the "Saturday Night

---

[5]Elmer E. Cornwell Jr., Presidential Leadership
of Public Opinion (Bloomington, Ind.: Indiana University Press, 1965).

344

Massacre"occurred in October 1973, it was the outcry
from the media and the public which brought on the impeachment proceedings which eventually brought about
the end of the Nixon Administration's tenure.[6]

Just as the mass media and public can team up
to oppose corruption in the executive branch, so they
can also team up to oppose corruption in the legislative branch. Some recent examples of this include the
sex scandal involving former Representative Wayne
Hays, chairman of several powerful committees in the
House, and the scandal involving former Representative
Wilbur Mills, who had been chairman of the House Ways
and Means Committee. It was largely the publicity
provided by the mass media, as well as the negative
public reaction, which eventually forced both men involved in these respective scandals to retire from
public life.[7] When a scandal occurs in the legislative branch, the executive branch is sometimes eager
to help the mass media bring out the facts for the
public. When the scandal is in the executive branch,
the legislative branch may aid and abet the expose.
So it can be seen that the kind of linkage that occurs
when the public learns about abuses can be beneficial
in helping to develop a demand from the public for reform in government.

---

[6]See Carl Bernstein and Bob Woodward, All the
President's Men (New York: Simon and Schuster, 1974);
Woodward and Bernstein, The Final Days (New York:
Simon and Schuster, 1976); Frank Mankiewicz, U.S. v.
Richard M. Nixon: The Final Crisis (New York: Quad-
rangle, 1975); Lewis Chester, Cal McCrystal, Stephen
Aris and William Shawcross, Watergate (New York: Bal-
lantine Books, 1973); Mary McCarthy, The Mask of State:
Watergate Portraits (New York: Harcourt Brace Jovano-
vich Harvest Book, 1974), and Theodore H. White,
Breach of Faith: The Fall of Richard Nixon (New York:
Dell, 1975). For a different viewpoint about the
media's role in Nixon's downfall, see Bruce Herschen-
sohn, The Gods of Antenna (New Rochelle, N.Y.: Arlington House, 1976). For still another view, see John
Dean, Blind Ambition: The White House Years (New York:
Simon and Schuster, 1976).

[7]See Milton C. Cummings Jr. and David Wise,
Democracy Under Pressure, Third Edition (New York: Harcourt Brace Jovanovich, 1977), pp. 435, 436 for an account of the Wayne Hays affair and another Capitol Hill
scandal, the Tongsun Park-Korean lobby investigation.

The media, the public and one branch of government can combine against another branch when a clear breach of law or ethics has occurred. This can again be illustrated by the case of the Watergate scandal. When the mass media began to discover the facts and the public had become aroused, the courts as a part of the entire judicial system played a significant part in seeing that the wrongdoers were brought to justice and that corrective action was taken. It may even be true that when scandals such as those of Wayne Hays and Wilbur Mills embarrass one branch of government, such as the Congress, other members will also join in efforts to bring about cleanup and reform. Various abuses of power by committee chairmen in Congress have doubtless contributed to the reform movement there.

Some examples can be cited of both problems and benefits arising from linkages before moving on to the next section. The one problem I would like to consider briefly is the kind of problem arising from such "leaks" as those of the Pentagon Papers and various intelligence secrets. It turned out that much of the information in the Pentagon Papers had been previously published in fragmented form; there was actually relatively little that was new in them. What was different when the Pentagon Papers were published was that for the first time official evidence was provided for a pattern of behavior in Vietnam which the public may not have been aware of. Obviously, the taxpaying public is entitled to know a great deal, but the thing which concerned public officials more than the release of the Pentagon Papers themselves was the fact that a precedent may have been set for much more damaging disclosures in the future. The problem grew in large measure of course out of the inadequacies of a classification system which put entirely too many public documents in the secret or highly classified category, when there was no need for this. The Pentagon Papers case was a reaction. But despite a widespread public feeling that disclosures of the papers was not only appropriate, but even overdue, one can acknowledge that some circumstances could arise when such unauthorized disclosure of classified documents could be damaging to the national interest. Some of the more obvious examples would be disclosure of sensitive intelligence secrets, such as letting the Soviet Union know how much intelligence we have on their missile systems or something similar.[8] Perhaps another example might be disclosure of the contingency plans for wars or major international emergencies, which if incorrectly reported in the news media, might cause widespread and unnecessary public alarm.

Examples of benefits have been mentioned briefly above, but it should be emphasized that sensitization of the public to such matters through the news media may have helped to create public attitudes which would lead to prevention of future Watergates or similar scandals, or perhaps to prevention of future Wayne Hays-Wilbur Mills type cases. This point probably does not have to be elaborated on, but it is an important one nonetheless.

Impact of Linkages on Executive-Bureaucracy Relationship

If we examine the impact of linkages on the relationship between the executive leadership at the White House and Cabinet level and the bureaucracy which this leadership is responsible for supervising, several problems can be identified which arise from such linkages. One of these would be the effect of "leaks" from the bureaucracy itself. During the Nixon Administration, the President and his aides felt, rightly or wrongly, that many people in the bureaucracy were holdovers from previous Democratic administrations and were therefore not to be trusted. Nixon had plans for eliminating some of these bureaucrats from the government, but in addition his administration had plans to neutralize their influence by putting a White House "agent" in each executive branch department or agency in a key role. This plan was never fully developed but is interesting for its implications. To some extent Nixon's suspicions may have been correct but this has probably been true when other changes in the party in power have occurred, so the most note-

---

[8]See Neil Sheehan, et al., The Pentagon Papers (New York: Bantam Books, 1971), and Sanford Unger, The Papers and the Papers (New York: E. P. Dutton and Co., 1972). Also see David Halberstam, The Best and the Brightest (Greenwich, Conn.: Fawcett Crest Books, 1973), especially pp. 327, 343, 432, 441, 450, 498, 600, 769, 797.

worthy thing about the Nixon Administration's attitude to the whole situation was its paranoid aspect.

The "leak" game is one which can be played in two directions. If one begins with the assumption that the White House establishment and the bureaucracy are at odds with one another, then leaks from the White House against the bureaucracy should be just as important as those from the bureaucracy directed against White House staffers, or the President. To some extent this kind of conflict often occurs in various institutional settings between those with temporary tenure and those with ongoing tenure. It is a normal type of conflict, but it can usually be controlled. The main limitation of White House "leaks", as the Nixon people eventually found out, is whether they are credible to the public and the news media or not.

The problems go beyond executive relations with the bureaucracy, however. Another kind of problem arising from linkage is the effect of linkage on public opinion. This in turn has an impact on bureaucratic decisions. In the field of domestic policy decision-making, the environmental area could be cited to illustrate this point. Bureaucratic decisions are made which could cause damage to the environment--e.g., the decision, to delay the air pollution standards for the auto industry--but if the White House has through its leaks developed a linkage which can convince the public that such steps are necessary, the needed actions may be decided on any way, despite opposition within the bureaucracy. The public may view the executive leadership and the bureaucracy as working together, when in fact the two are in conflict; this impression by the public may be the result of some kind of linkage.

Another problem arising from linkage where executive leadership conflict with the bureaucracy is concerned, is the tendency of bureaucrats to "go public" in order to save their pet programs when they are threatened by the Administration. A good example of this is the information "leaked" by the Pentagon when a new Administration is considering the elimination of research and development on a new weapons system which may cost billions of dollars. The bureaucrats in the Pentagon see the failure to fund the system as a threat to their own agencies and administrative units, and they therefore may try to influence the decision

348

by leaking information helpful to themselves. The controversies over the B-1 bomber, the Navy's cruise missile and the new MX missile are examples of this kind of situation.

Nevertheless, benefits to the system do arise from linkage which affects executive-bureaucracy relationships. The greatest of these benefits may be the greater level of public awareness of the bureaucracy's problems. Although "bureaucracy" may be a dirty word in this day of zero-based budgeting,[9] much of the public is unaware of the real problems faced by civil servants in the bureaucracy. But a controversy over an issue such as a new weapons system may make it clearer to the public that many dedicated people work in the bureaucracy, that the fault may be more with the system than with the individuals in it.

Some good effects have occurred within the bureaucracy as the result of the work of various public interest lobbying groups. One of the best known of these is Common Cause, founded by John Gardner, a former HEW Secretary in the Johnson Administration. Common Cause has concentrated on procedural reforms in government such as opposing the seniority rule in Congress. The Common Cause organization has been a useful outlet for government employees and others who cannot engage actively in partisan politics, because it has provided a channel for their reform impulses. However, it has avoided some relatively non-partisan issues because it appeared to be afraid to tackle them. One of them was the Nixon impeachment issue,[10] on which Common Cause never did take a stand. This indicates some weaknesses in the organization, but on balance it has probably accomplished a good deal of lasting worth.

---

[9]Zero-based budgeting requires justification of expenditures from a "zero base" at regular intervals (annually, every other year, etc.). The program, if unjustified, would be budgeted at "zero", or eliminated.

[10]The original split over the Nixon articles of impeachment in the House Judiciary Committee in 1974 followed ideological (liberal-conservative) lines rather than partisan lines. Some Republicans voted for the articles of impeachment, and ultimately after the "smoking-gun" evidence, all Republicans on the committee supported them just prior to Nixon's resignation.

Another much publicized public interest group is Ralph Nader's Public Citizen organization. Public Citizen has been issue oriented and it has worked especially hard on environmental issues as they have come up in the Congress.

In all this discussion, not much has been said about the need to protect the legitimate needs of the bureaucracy against political or partisan encroachment. The original purpose of the Pendleton Act of 1883 which established the federal civil service system was to remove the "spoils system" from appointments to federal office at the level of the average bureaucrat. The system has worked reasonably well, although considerable room for improvement remains. The concern currently is with entrenchment of inefficient bureaucracies at increasing cost to the taxpayers, but this problem may be somewhat exaggerated. The problem really may lie with a system which rewards administrators who have the largest budgets and the greatest number of employees working under them. Professionalism and the need to keep partisan politics out of the bureaucracy remain significant concerns, and the best way the public can be made more aware of this is through more sensitive reporting of the bureaucracy's workings through the news media. This is sometimes made difficult because of unnecessary secrecy imposed within the bureaucracy, another problem which must be dealt with.

Examples can be given of problems in the executive-bureaucracy relationship which get complicated by media coverage. Consider the Federal Bureau of Investigation for a moment. In Victor Navasky's book, Kennedy Justice, some good illustrations are given of the conflict which occurred between the Kennedy Administration, particularly Attorney General Robert Kennedy, and the FBI, particularly Director J. Edgar Hoover, in the implementation of civil rights policy. The coverage of these conflicts in the news media exposes them to the public, and this inevitably increases the power stakes involved in the conflicts and makes them more difficult to resolve.[11]

---

[11]See Victor Navasky, Kennedy Justice (New York: Atheneum, 1971).

350

Other examples of problems in the executive-bureaucracy relationship that are caused and complicated by media coverage include the case of the Central Intelligence Agency. The CIA obviously relies on secrecy to carry out its functions, whether these include intelligence gathering or the carrying out of so-called "black operations". Thus any publicity is likely to compromise its work. The recent leakages and disclosures of CIA agents' names obviously put them in some peril; the CIA station chief in Athens was murdered after his name was disclosed.

Some general conclusions can be drawn about the impact of linkages on executive-bureaucracy relationships. First, both problems and benefits to the system develop out of linkage in this relationship. The administration in power can benefit itself and sometimes the public by disclosures about the bureaucracy, but at the same time it should do this so as not to exacerbate the conflict between the executive leadership and the bureaucracy itself. One should always remember that the bureaucracy will outlast the temporary leadership of any administration in power, which includes people in such posts as CIA director and FBI director. Therefore, the bureaucracy may follow a tactic of ignoring directives from the top as much as it dares and for as long as it dares--a kind of delaying tactic. But one concludes that it is possible for linkage to promote a more harmonious relationship in this area.

Impact of Linkages on Executive-Judicial Relationship

When one examines linkages occurring with news media coverage in executive-judicial relations, it is apparent that one obvious distinction can be made. This is that the federal judiciary, in particular the United States Supreme Court, has more of a "shielded" nature than the so-called "political branches", Congress and the Presidency.

An illustrative example of this protected or "shielded" nature of the judiciary can be given. In April 1977, a report was circulated through the media that a five-to-three vote had been taken within the Court that an appeal from the Watergate defendants, John Mitchell and H. R. Haldeman, should not be heard. The report indicated that Chief Justice Burger had delayed announcement of the decision in an effort to persuade a majority to allow the appeal. At the time the report was circulated, the media stated that it was believed that the rumor represented the first time the confidentiality of the Supreme Court's conference was known to have been breached by a "leak".

Institutionally, the Supreme Court has a degree of insulation from the day-to-day workings of the political arena, but it does not work in a vacuum. During the 1930's, when advanced social reform legislation was being adopted in Congress--sometimes at a pace faster than desired even by the Roosevelt Administration--the Court for several years struck down innovative New Deal legislation. But after the President offered his Supreme Court "packing" plan to Congress in 1937 (even though the President did not get any of his program passed except for provisions allowing justices to retire at age 70), the Court did "bend" somewhat and the "swing" justices began to uphold the Administration viewpoint more frequently, as for example in the legal area of wages and hours legislation affecting women and children.[12]

Another example can be cited in the Warren Court decisions during the 1960's extending protection to the rights of the accused in criminal cases. Such decisions as those in the Miranda and Escobedo cases, extending pre-trial rights of defendants to be informed of the nature of charges against them, drew criticism from both the police and the public in the late 1960's as urban rioting and other law-enforcement problems made the public more conscious of such social issues as society's right to protection against abuse by criminals.[13] Ultimately, when the Nixon appointees joined the court the nature of the decisions reflected this public concern. The Burger Court began to give more scope to law enforcement officials and it modified some of the more far-reaching civil liberties decisions of the Warren era.[14] But it took time for the justices

---

[12]See C. Herman Pritchett, The American Constitution (New York: McGraw-Hill Book Co., 1977), pp. 530-534.

[13]See Pritchett, op. cit., pp. 454-458.

[14]See Pritchett, op. cit., p. 458 for references to Michigan v. Mosley (1975) and United States v. Mandujano (1976).

to catch up with public opinion, to the extent that their opinions reflect tides of opinion in a rather crude way.

Where do the news media enter the picture? It could be suggested that by the manner in which they put these controversies on the public agenda and by the way in which criticism of the Court was headlined and discussed on television, the media sensitized the justices to the public criticism.

Another aspect of executive-judicial relations related to media coverage is that of judicial appointments. The Constitution prescribes that the President makes judicial appointments, normally with privately made suggestions from members of the bar, congressmen, judges and other community leaders. Unlike the lower-court appointive process where the President usually follows the advice of senators and congressmen, the selection of Supreme Court justices usually involves numerous considerations of policy expectations, regional, inter-party and intra-party politics. The political considerations are a normal and healthy part of the process. But sometimes the press learns about such appointments through "leaks" and sometimes it does not.[15]

The most recent appointment to the high court at this writing was that of Justice John Paul Stevens by President Ford in 1975. This was a closely guarded secret, and the announcement caught many by surprise, although there had been speculation in the press and by broadcasters. There was a great deal of interest in the appointment because of the conservative jurists selected by President Nixon during his tenure. As it turned out, Ford's choice appeared to be more moderate than those of Nixon but not really a liberal. It ought to be added here that it is hard to classify Supreme Court justices according to ideology because of their independence once appointed, but certain general trends and tendencies can be detected where jurists are appointed from the lower courts.[16]

---

[15]David J. Danielski, A Supreme Court Justice Is Appointed (New York: Random House, 1964).

[16]See Glendon Schubert, The Judicial Mind: Attitudes and Ideologies of Supreme Court Justices, 1946-1963 (Evanston, Ill.: Northwestern University Press, 1965).

The four Nixon appointees included Chief Justice Warren Burger, Associate Justices Harry Blackmun, William Rehnquist and Lewis Powell Jr. All were conservative choices, with Burger's appointment coming in 1969, that of Blackmun in 1970, and Powell's and Rehnquist's in 1971. Blackmun and Burger voted together so frequently in their early years on the court together that they were sometimes popularly referred to as "the Minnesota twins". But in terms of publicity, the men who received the most attention in the news media were probably none of these appointees. Rather the most publicized men were Judge Clement Haynsworth of South Carolina and Judge Harrold Carswell of Florida, Nixon choices for associate justice who were rejected by the Senate. Haynsworth generated attention in the news media because of charges that a conflict of interest had occurred when he ruled in cases involving the Vend-a-Matic and Brunswick companies, whose shares he had held. He was not charged with making any illegal profit but the whole controversy indicated a kind of insensitivity to moral matters which was damaging to Haynsworth. The media gave a great deal of coverage to Haynsworth because of this controversy, as well as because of the opposition to Haynsworth by organized labor and civil rights groups. The Senate ultimately rejected this nomination.

The next nomination to stir controversy was that of Carswell. He was serving as a judge of the Fifth Circuit Court of Appeals after a previous period when he had served as a federal district judge by appointment of President Eisenhower. Soon his segregationist views as voiced in 1948 began to come out. Then it was learned he belonged to a country club which had purchased property with a restrictive covenant deed. But perhaps the most damaging thing brought out about Carswell was the finding of some Columbia University law students that he had one of the highest reversal rates of any judge in the federal system. Since Carswell was already opposed by organized labor and civil rights groups, too, as Haynsworth had been before him, he too lost in his confirmation battle. When Rehnquist and Powell were appointed they were relatively non-controversial because both men had high prestige in the legal profession.17

Prior to the controversy over the Carswell and Haynsworth appointments there was a previous clash relating to the effort of President Lyndon B. Johnson, who in 1968 was a "lame duck", to appoint' Abe Fortas, a sitting associate justice, as chief justice at the time of Chief Justice Earl Warren's impending retirement. In rejecting the Fortas appointment, the Senate also declined to act favorably on the nomination of Homer Thornberry as associate justice.18

In the coverage of these events, the controversy between the executive and legislative branches over judicial appointments generated sufficient heat to warrant extensive attention from the news media.

Another way in which media coverage has an impact on executive-judicial relations concerns the President's reactions to Supreme Court opinions. The press of his day conveyed to the public the disappointed reaction of President Theodore Roosevelt to the opinion of Associate Justice Oliver Wendell Holmes in the Northern Securities case, and from that time to the present Presidents have sometimes been surprised

---

[17]See the following: Reg Murphy and Hal Gulliver, The Southern Strategy (New York: Charles Scribner's Sons, 1971), especially Chapter 6, "The Court of Last Resort", pp. 131-155; Richard Harris, Decision (New York: E. P. Dutton & Co., 1971), a case study of the Carswell nomination controversy; Jonathan Schell, The Time of Illusion (New York: Alfred A. Knopf, 1976), pp. 80-83, 184-187, a summary of the Haynsworth and Carswell controversies and the denouement of the story with the Rehnquist and Powell confirmations; Elizabeth Drew, Washington Journal: The Events of 1973-1974 (New York: Vintage Books, 1976), pp. 77, 180, 304, references to the relationship of President Nixon with the judiciary as a result of the controversies; William Safire, Before the Fall (Garden City, N.Y.: Doubleday & Co., 1975), pp. 267-269, a Nixon speech writer's viewpoint of the controversy.

[18]See Lyndon B. Johnson, The Vantage Point: Perspectives of the Presidency 1963-1969 (New York: Holt, Rinehart & Winston, 1971), pp. 543-547, the former President's account of the controversy, written during his retirement at the LBJ Ranch; Jerald F. terHorst, Gerald Ford and the Future of the Presidency (New York: The Third Press, 1974), pp. 119-126, an account of the Douglas impeachment controversy:

355

at court opinions and this attitude may have leaked
into speculative stories in the media. The memoirs of
the late Chief Justice Earl Warren state that his part
in the 1954 Supreme Court opinion in the controversial case of Brown v. Board of Education of Topeka resulted in an extremely cool relationship between himself and President Eisenhower.[19]

Other examples could be cited, but when Presidents' reactions to Supreme Court rulings are specu-
lated about in the news media, the Court's judicial
role constrains it. Justices feel the necessity for
impartiality and remain aloof from the situation.
Presidents, who have more freedom of action, have
usually chosen to make their displeasure about decisions known through leaks rather than public comment.

Impact on Executive-Public Relationship

The impact of news media coverage on executive
relations with the public is normally one of indirect
linkage. The process is one in which the public
forms images of the President through news coverage.
Such events as President Carter's inaugural walk down
Pennsylvania Avenue,[20] the early publicity about
President Ford's habit of toasting his own English
muffins, the homey features about LBJ and the ranch,
are all examples of this kind of image formation.
Apart from this symbolism,[21] columnists and correspondents also disseminate to the public their impressions about the incumbent President's decisiveness or
indecisiveness and other characteristics of his
leadership.

In addition to this indirect linkage, direct
linkage occurs through formal television addresses
such as all recent Presidents have made, "fireside
chats" such as the well-remembered 1977 one in which

[19]Earl Warren, The Memoirs of Earl Warren
(Garden City, N.Y.: Doubleday, 1977).

[20]See Robert Shogan, Promises to Keep: Carter's
First 100 Days (New York: Thomas Y. Crowell, 1977),
pp. 96-109.

[21]Shogan, op. cit., pp. 109-133.

President Carter wore his cardigan, televised interviews done on an informal basis such as a couple of
quick questions at a Rose Garden ceremony, and also
news conferences. Some question may exist as to how
direct or indirect the news conference format is, but
clearly where the President alone is communicating,
the event can be described as a "direct" one.

As for the nature of linkage between the President and the public, there are two types of linkage.
The first of these is political linkage and the second
is communications linkage.

The President's political linkage in his role
as party leader occurs through the electoral process.
Normally when a regularly elected President goes
through the process of building a nationwide coalition
of constituencies, running in the primaries, achieving
the nomination at his party's convention, and mounting
a successful race in the fall election campaign, he is
developing the political dimension of his linkage
with the public. This type of linkage is oriented
toward personal contact.

The President's communications linkage with the
public also occurs through the use of the news media.
At campaign time this includes television, newspapers,
radio and magazines (even such campaign staples as
billboards, bumper stickers and buttons), but the most
important aspects of the communications linkage occur
in the use of the mass media. Television operates to
help the public develop impressions, but the print
media function so as to allow the public--especially
opinion leaders--to develop an issue perception about
a President in his role as a candidate.

The media can modify public images of the
President at various phases of his incumbency, or even
when a potential President is still in the closing
phases of a successful campaign. An example of this
can be seen in 1968 when Richard Nixon was erasing the
"loser's image" carried over from his losses in 1960
and 1962 (he was defeated for governor of California
by Edmund G. (Pat) Brown in the latter year). He
played the piano and sang songs and projected a more
relaxed attitude than he had had in the 1950's as

Vice President.[22]

Public perceptions of a President seem to reflect the ability of the media to "make" or "break"
him. Media people argue that they only report what
happens, but the fact that they are looking for the
newsworthy and that most Presidents go through a cycle
of image-making which includes both a buildup stage
and a debunking stage have much to do with public perceptions.

The same media that aided Nixon in gaining
office through the reporting of the 1968 Chicago convention riots--inadvertent through this aid may have
been--helped to "do him in" at the time of Watergate.
The experience of both Johnson and Nixon indicates
that looked at over a longer period of time than just
one campaign, a kind of rough impartiality can be seen
in the effects of the news media coverage as it relates to incumbents as well as to presidential candidates.[23]

It is not empirically possible to describe
exactly how the linkage function occurs, but examples
can be cited from three recent administrations as to
whether linkage had a positive or negative impact. At
the time of the Cuban missile crisis the media coverage probably was helpful to President Kennedy. Prior
to his television address, there was some voluntary
withholding of information by the media but from the
President's viewpoint, no matter how many statements
were made by Senator Homer Capehart (Republican-Indi-
ana) and the Cuban exiles, he did not feel in a position to make an official statement until he had
photographic evidence of the missile emplacements in
hand. This was delayed for a time by weather conditions, and meantime the media had no choice but to
publish accounts of allegations made about the build-

---

[22]See Theodore H. White, The Making of the
President 1968 (New York: Pocket Books, 1970).

[23]For a discussion of bias in presidential
election coverage by the media, see Edith Efron, The
News Twisters (Los Angeles: Nash Publishing Corp.,
1971), and Edward Jay Epstein, News From Nowhere (New
York: Random House, 1973).

ing crisis.[24] Public opinion polls indicated a rallying to the President, a phenomenon noted also when
Eisenhower dealt with the Suez crisis of 1956 and more
recently in 1977 when President Carter announced his
initial energy program.

An example of how this process can operate in a
negative fashion is the development of the "credibility gap" of President Johnson during 1966 and 1967.
The early Great Society period had brought him a good
deal of favorable media coverage, growing out of his
legislative achievements. But when the media's attention turned to Vietnam, the secretive nature of Johnson's approach to this subject tended to plant feelings
of deception with the media and thus eventually with
the public.

The same kind of erosion of public support
occurred again with Richard Nixon. He had built up a
good deal of public support through the period up to
the Vietnam truce in 1973, but that was the high point
of his support. After more and more revelations about
the Watergate scandal came into public knowledge,
Nixon slipped more and more in the polls until just
prior to his resignation his popularity index was
something around 26 per cent, comparable to that of
President Truman during the Korean war.[25]

To summarize with general conclusions about
media linkage and its impact on the executive-public
relationship, one can observe that (1) fluctuations are
quite likely to occur over the four or eight years of
an incumbency, and (2) the media contribute to but are
not the only factor in the public's fickleness toward
Presidents during their tenure.

Result of Impact on Policy-Making Process

Since the communications process is a dynamic
one, in which diffusion of information and opinion are

---

[24]See Robert F. Kennedy, Thirteen Days: A
Memoir of the Cuban Missile Crisis (New York: W. W.
Norton & Co., 1969).

[25]See Theodore H. White, Breach of Faith: The
Fall of Richard Nixon (New York: Dell Publishing Co.,
1975).

complemented by public reaction in reverse communication and feedback, one must analyze the effect of public feedback on Presidential policy positions.

Again the relationship is one difficult to pin down, but it is clear that in a democratic system, the White House does react to public input. One example of this would be the statement by the Carter White House that public reaction to the 1977 energy package would be considered. Another example is the gradual response of the Johnson Administration to public concern with the issue of the war in Vietnam. By early 1968, pressures were building for the White House to respond to the public clamor for negotiations to end American involvement in the war. While there was little movement in the negotiations, the Johnson Administration did respond to the extent that negotiations were set in motion in May of the same year, following the President's March 31 speech in which he announced the truce initiative and his own withdrawal as a candidate for re-election.

Public response to policy pronouncements from official Washington is not limited to the White House, of course. Public reaction is registered also on Capitol Hill. It may be somewhat more difficult to determine congressional policy positions prior to enactment of legislation, but public reaction is monitored very carefully on Capitol Hill. Such legislative moves as the Cooper-Church Amendment and the McGovern-Hatfield Amendment, designed to bring about American withdrawal in Vietnam, came as a result of public pressures.

The two-way communications linkage also affects public opinion to the extent that certain parameters or boundary lines are imposed on both the President and Congress in compromising disputes. There are solutions within the bounds of what the public will accept, and there are solutions that are simply infeasible because they are beyond what the public will accept. Boundary lines of what the public will accept may not always be the determining factor as well. A good illustration of this can be found in the policy field of gun control. Despite the passage of a watered down Gun Control Act of 1968, much pressure by gun control activists for tighter controls has been countered by an effective anti-gun control campaign by the National Rifle Association, which is tightly organized and able to mount stiff lobbying efforts. Thus public opinion polls favoring the imposition of gun control do not really mean that much freedom of action for congressmen, because the smaller but vocal opposition has such intense feelings on the matter. All this conditions the opinion climate in which the White House is obliged to work.

Gun control is an example of an issue on which a small proportion of the population holds a strong opinion, but occasionally an issue comes along on which most of the general public holds intense opinions. One example of this can be found in opinions on both sides of the issue of Vietnam withdrawal in the period immediately after the 1968 Tet offensive. Still another example is the feeling about the Watergate scandal immediately after the "Saturday Night Massacre" of 1973, which prompted an outpouring of letters and telegrams to officials in Congress and ultimately triggered the impeachment investigation of 1974.

This prompts some general conclusions about the impact of political communication on the policy-making process. A safe sort of general rule to follow is that intensity of feeling on controversial issues is likely to make a difference in official response. It is almost certain to be taken into account when there is a dominant opinion, and will be considered strongly when even a relatively small group feels keenly about an issue. Where this kind of sentiment does not exist on an issue, both the President and Congress can feel more free to shape policy. Even here, a cautionary note must be added. This is that events can sometimes awaken public interest in a particular issue; what has been relatively quiescent as an issue may change to an issue fraught with public concern. So it is necessary for public officials, including the President, to be aware of the fact that they have a relatively limited amount of political capital to spend in achievement of earnestly desired goals. This is why Presidents usually seek to develop major initiatives in the first year of an administration, a time when their popularity is likely to be at the highest point of the four-year cycle.[26]

---

[26]See Stephen Hess, <u>Organizing the Presidency</u> (Washington: Brookings Institution, 1976).

Result of Impact on Functioning of Electoral Process

The policy-making process does not operate in a vacuum, because the two-way communication that has just been described also has its effect through the electoral process. This may be somewhat more indirect than the immediate impact on policy-making, but it is important nonetheless.

One factor here is how linkage affects the public's perceptions of a President. Examples can be cited from administrations beginning with Franklin Roosevelt. His popularity had its ups and downs; it hit its peak about the time of the second election in 1936 and it was relatively high during his first term. However, with the onset of the war and the aging of his administration there was a long-term decline following the third-term election in 1940. Even between the second and third elections his popularity dipped somewhat because of such things as the ill-advised primary "purge" attempt of 1938 and the 1937 Supreme Court "packing" proposal.

During the Truman Administration, a period of seven years and approximately nine months, the President's popularity dipped from a high of around 71 per cent at the time of V-E Day and V-J Day in 1945 to a low of less than 30 per cent at the depth of his unpopularity during the Korean War in 1952. Correctly assessing this, Truman decided not to be a candidate in 1952, even though provisions of the Twenty-second Amendment banning third-term candidacies specifically exempted him.

Because of his relative inaction during his eight-year term, Eisenhower maintained a high degree of popularity from the beginning of his first term in 1953 up until 1958, when economic distress began to deflate his popularity. Ike's popularity did not dip to the extent that Truman's did, however, because Truman endorsed some controversial policy initiatives (civil rights, health care legislation) in addition to losing popularity because of the Korean War.

The 1963 assassination has somewhat obscured the fact that President Kennedy's relatively high popularity with the general public had not translated into a solid program of legislative achievement during the 1961-1963 period. At the time of his death, Kennedy was in the process of attempting to build addi-

362

tional public support for a re-election effort in
1964.

President Johnson began with high public support because of the sympathy factor following the
assassination. He maintained this kind of support
through 1965, the year of the most productive period
for the Great Society. But LBJ's popularity began to
wane because of his Vietnam policy and by the end of
his term in 1969, the cycle was on a downswing.

With Nixon, the early popularity curve was not
quite so high as that of some of his predecessors.
He hit his peak at the time of the 1973 Vietnam truce
but his support had dwindled to a low point in 1974
at the time of resignation.

Result of Impact on Policy-Making Process

Public reaction to policy initiatives of Presidents and congressmen can be described as a "feedback
loop" in the two-way communications process which
affects policy-making processes. Presidents consider
public reactions to their policies in many ways; one
can analyze cases where public reactions do not cause
them to change their policies, and cases where public
reactions do bring about policy changes.

A good example of an instance where the public
reaction did not bring presidential policy changes can
be found in the Johnson Administration prior to March
1968, when the President was adamant about his policies in Vietnam despite mounting public and congressional pressure for a change. The President was
simply convinced that his policy was "right"; he did
not finally change course until a request for further
escalation early in 1968 from General William Westmore-
land and the Joint Chiefs of Staff forced him to
realize that to continue on his previous course would
be counter-productive. One of those who is supposed
to have helped convince him on this point was his Secretary of Defense, Clark Clifford, whom he appointed
when Robert MacNamara left the Cabinet.[27]

---

[27]See Townsend Hoopes, The Limits of Intervention (New York: David McKay Co., 1969).

A second example of an instance where public reaction was uninfluential in fixing presidential policy was in the Cambodian incursion in 1970. President Nixon was determined to follow a policy of interdicting Communist supplies and so he ordered troops into Cambodia in the spring. Massive demonstrations and domestic unrest failed to deter him from action in this direction because he felt had a majority of public opinion behind him.

In each example cited, public and congressional reaction was eventually taken into account. But a clearer example of a decision made by President Nixon which ran counter to widespread criticism may have been the Christmas 1972 decision on the bombing of Hanoi. Whatever the reason, the truce was signed near the end of January 1973.[28]

An example of an ambiguous shift in policy which may have resulted as much from changing circumstances as from shifting public opinion, was the policy reversal by President Carter in April 1977 on a proposal for a $50 tax rebate as part of his economic stimulus package. The President had strongly advocated this earlier in the year, but the inflation indicators began to move up rapidly and he became sufficiently concerned about this to drop the rebate plan. There had been lukewarm reactions in the business community--indeed widespread opposition--and many Democrats in Congress had obviously endorsed the plan primarily because a new President of their own party had asked for it.

Still another example of a presidential policy shift, in direct response to public sentiment, would be the endorsement by the Kennedy Administration of a strong civil rights package after the Birmingham riots and the George Wallace "stand in the schoolhouse door" at the University of Alabama in June 1963. The Administration, while considered privately to favor stronger civil rights measures, had endorsed only a very mild piece of legislation even after the first "sit-ins" and "Freedom Rides" had occurred between 1960 and 1962. Kennedy did not want to endanger other important goals

---

[28]See R. Gordon Hoxie, Command Decision and the Presidency (New York: Readers Digest Press, 1977), p. 318.

such as the adoption of a new reciprocal trade policy with foreign nations by pushing so rapidly on civil rights legislation as to endanger the other measures. When public opinion became aroused on it, he moved quickly however, as he obviously felt he could not afford to lose public support by inaction.[29]

Still another bargaining situation can be used to illustrate public reaction and how it brings presidential response. President Carter in March and April 1977 had talked of reductions or cuts in some 30 water projects for dams, irrigation facilities and the like. Reaction from various constituencies made it advisable for him to back away from his early position and he wound up only cutting or removing some 17 of the projects from his budget proposal to Congress. Some of these were later restored.

In the Nixon and Ford Administrations, continuing Democratic control in Congress and reforms which weakened the hold of the conservative coalition there made for a good deal of conflict. This was accompanied by bitterness during the Nixon era. While this was muted during the Ford years, there were still numerous vetoes. Ford was perhaps a bit less activist and strident in his conservatism than Nixon and was probably a bit more pragmatic about using the veto for bargaining. But by the end of the Ford era, Congress had become less quiescent. This was so to the point that by 1977 a public opinion poll conducted for CBS and the New York *Times* indicated that the public had become more used to looking for policy initiatives from Congress and no longer tended to look to the White House for all such initiatives. This may have accounted for some of Carter's early and continuing problems with Congress.[30]

Within the boundaries of what the public is willing to permit or what the public expects, there is

---

[29]See Bruce Miroff, Pragmatic Illusions: The Presidential Politics of John F. Kennedy (New York: David McKay Co., 1976), Chapter Six, "'Listen, Mr. Kennedy': The Civil Rights Struggle", pp. 223-270. Also see Carl M. Brauer, John F. Kennedy and the Second Reconstruction (New York: Columbia University Press, 1977), especially pp. 61-88, 230-320.

[30]See Shogan, op. cit., pp. 204-215.

still a good deal of room for the President and Congress to work out compromises. That was the outcome
of the controversy between Carter and Congress over the
water projects in 1977, but Carter did damage his relationships with Congress by the rather abrupt manner
in which the word was first disclosed. The influential Representative Morris Udall (Democrat-Arizona)
learned about it from the press. Still, the legislators are probably more tolerant of such behavior in a
new President still learning the ropes than would be
the case near the end of a term.[31]

Examples can be given of issues on which the
public feels strongly and on which it eventually got a
presidential response. Two examples which come most
readily to mind are the issue of Vietnam during the
Tet offensive of early 1968, when it appeared that public opinion was moving toward favoring a withdrawal,
and the concern with Watergate and the impeachment investigation after the "Saturday Night Massacre" of
October 1973.

Examples of situations where the public seems
almost indifferent include the issue of gun control,
discussed above (except in periods immediately after
assassinations or assassination attempts), and the
issue of hunger in other countries.

As for general conclusions about the impact of
public reaction on the policy-making process, I find
that (1) the public fixes the boundary lines of political discourse and solutions are normally worked out
within the boundary lines of what it will accept; (2)
the intensity factor of how strongly people feel about
current issues has a great deal to do with the success
or failure of policy initiatives, and (3) the institutional rivalry between the executive and legislative
branches is an intervening variable which will work on
the outcome of policy controversies equally as much as
public feedback to messages coming from the President
and Congress.

Result of Impact on Functioning of Electoral Process

Public perceptions of current issues and participants in them result in another kind of "feedback

---

[31]See Shogan, ibid., pp. 212-215.

loop" in political communication. That is to be found not in the policy process, but instead in the electoral process.

The communications linkage has an obvious effect on public perceptions of the President. Whether deliberately or accidentally, the mass media conveyed the image of President Kennedy as a vigorous, active young leader; that of President Johnson as an earthy wheeler-dealer; that of President Nixon as a kind of recluse with a permanent inferiority complex; that of President Ford as a kind of "regular guy" who toasted his own English muffins, but also as a kind of bumbler who stumbled and fell down on the ski slopes or alighting from a plane, and that of President Carter as a smiling, Bible-carrying man whose views on political issues were somewhat ambiguous. The ambiguity surrounding Carter's image might probably be dispelled by his eventually having to take stands on many controversial issues, but he appeared to have a shrewd ability to position himself on many issues by taking a moderate, centrist attitude.

Linkage also affects public perceptions of a President's opponents during a campaign. One very interesting turnabout in this kind of image-making occurred in the 1972 campaign. George McGovern was the wonder-worker during the primary season, but then attacks by Hubert Humphrey and other foreign policy hard-liners and McGovern's own ineptness in dealing with the Eagleton controversy and other campaign developments, even the selection of a second running-mate, damaged him greatly in the eyes of the public. It is a real question as to how much of this was done by the candidate himself and how much by the news media. Much the same kind of thing happened to Barry Goldwater in the 1964 campaign in which he opposed President Lyndon Johnson.

It is an interesting phenomenon to observe how linkage affects public perceptions and awareness of new political figures at the presidential level. To cite an example from much earlier history, Abraham Lincoln no doubt benefited from his "Cooper Union Speech" in New York prior to his 1860 nomination; somewhat like Carter, he followed a policy of studied ambiguity during much of the campaign. His emergence really began with the Lincoln-Douglas debates of 1858, however. Or to examine the emergence of FDR, he had been a vice presidential candidate in 1920 and

governor of New York State for two terms. Nothing in
his 1932 campaign led anyone to expect anything unortho-
dox; he even promised a balanced budget, but he got a
tremendous bit of exposure with his 1928 nominating
speech for Al Smith.[32] Dwight Eisenhower needed no
such buildup; he received it during World War II, much
as Herbert Hoover had become well known during World
War I. Harry Truman became known through the work of
his defense profiteering investigating committee in
the Senate. JFK was given his first real exposure at
the 1956 Democratic convention as a contender for the
vice presidential nomination, although he got some
attention when he defeated Lodge for the Senate in
1952. But the thing which really gave him huge national exposure and was the decisive factor in his
emergence was doubtless the television debates with
Richard Nixon in 1960. Lyndon Johnson had become well
known as a Senate majority leader in the 1950's, so
much so that many said that his vice presidency represented an "eclipse", and in the case of Richard Nixon
a kind of re-emergence, or in Jules Witcover's words,
a political "resurrection" took place.[33] Gerald Ford
came into the public eye first as minority leader in
the House of Representatives. Lacking this kind of
Washington experience, Jimmy Carter brought about his
emergence through gruelling participation in a round
of 30 state primaries. The way in which these events
were filtered through to the public through the mass
media certainly affected the public's perception of
these men. But in each case there was some input on
the part of the candidate himself.

Case study examples can be given of the impact
of linkage in election campaigns. The three most recent presidential years will be analyzed.

In 1968, Hubert Humphrey came through to the
public, fairly or not, as wishy-washy. He had trouble
deciding whether he would run for the Presidency after
the Johnson withdrawal and the Robert Kennedy assassination. Once he achieved the nomination in Chicago

---

[32]See Kenneth S. Davis, FDR: The Beckoning of
Destiny, 1882-1928: A History (New York: G. P. Putnam's Sons, 1972).

[33]See Jules Witcover, The Resurrection of
Richard Nixon (New York: G. P. Putnam's Sons, 1970).

amid the shambles of the convention riots, he began a campaign almost from scratch with the President sulking on the sidelines and many early supporters of Kennedy and McCarthy sitting on their hands. When he finally moved slightly from the Administration's position on Vietnam policy with his Salt Lake City speech in October 1968, he began to get some grudging support from the party's left, but he also succeeded in irritating the President. The blame for the defeat was not entirely his, but Humphrey might have done better and given the public a more positive image with more decisive action earlier in his campaign.

George Wallace in 1968 was probably at the peak of his popularity, although in the pre-Maryland primaries in 1972 he was running strongly. But Wallace was apparently more able to capitalize on his strength as a third-party candidate, and he was drawing as high as 15 to 20 per cent in some of the polls with his statements on "law and order" and hard-line views on foreign policy. Wallace's tactical blunder which probably badly damaged his image was the selection of General Curtis LeMay as a running mate; this hurt him, but perhaps not so much as the counter-campaign that organized labor conducted on Humphrey's behalf to deflate Wallace's claim to be the "friend of the little man". Probably a crucial factor in the decline of Wallace late in the campaign was the realization of many voters that one of the major party candidates was the likely winner.

Richard Nixon in 1968 managed to project the appeal of a "comeback" candidate and parlay this along with dissatisfaction with Democratic conduct of foreign policy into a tight election victory. Although Nixon was noted for a long-running feud with the news media, it was probably ironically his relatively good press in 1968 which helped lead to his victory. Two decisions made about his campaign strategy also contributed to this result. One was to say as little as possible about Vietnam and to finesse the issue. He did this by saying that he did not want to interfere with the Johnson Administration's conduct of the truce negotiations in Paris. The second decision that paid off was to run a tightly-controlled media campaign. Except for an appearance on "Meet the Press" late in the campaign, the media exposure which Nixon received on television was only on his own sponsored paid programs. In these he effectively used the "Hillsboro format" with a friendly audience which to all appearances was a group from the general public.[34]

If one considers the hapless fate of Senator
George McGovern in 1972, it is necessary to consider
that he was in a sense a prophet introducing issues
for which the public was not yet ready. Also he was
very open about allowing the media to cover every aspect of his campaign, while his opposition was relatively secretive and also had the advantage of being
able to use "surrogates" to campaign for the President.
Thus he was at a disadvantage; to this can be added
the tactical blunders of the Eagleton fiasco and the
$1,000 statement on economic policy. Considering all
this, is it any wonder that in 1976 Jimmy Carter was
willing to take criticism for being "fuzzy on the
issues"? He had before him the example of what happened to his predecessor who was frank and forthright.

McGovern's opponent in 1972, President Richard
Nixon, began positioning himself to influence the public through the media with two important moves in the
summer of 1971. He announced the imposition of price
and wage controls, and he also announced plans for a
summit visit to Peking. Thus he was able to take advantage of foreign policy maneuvering in both Peking
and Moscow at the time of the Democratic primary season in 1972.

Two prime examples of skillful use of television
in the 1976 primary season can be cited. The first
was the skill with which former Georgia Governor Jimmy
Carter exploited favorable media coverage of the Iowa
precinct caucuses preceding the New Hampshire primary.
Carter led Birch Bayh, Sargent Shriver and Fred Harris
in Iowa and in New Hampshire ran ahead of these
more liberal candidates as well as Representative
Morris Udall of Arizona. Although the 30 primaries
during the season included some which brought setbacks
for Carter, particularly his losses to Senator Henry
Jackson in Massachusetts, to Senator Frank Church in
Nebraska and Oregon, and to Governor Jerry Brown in
California, his overall record in the primaries re-
flected his effective use of media. When he carried
Ohio on the same day he lost California to Brown and

---

[34]See Dan Nimmo, The Political Persuaders: The
Techniques of Modern Election Campaigns (Englewood
Cliffs, N.J.: Prentice-Hall, 1970), pp. 142, 143, 153.

pro-Humphrey and pro-Brown delegates did well in New Jersey, it was clear that nationally Carter had the best chance for the nomination. Soon thereafter endorsements from key leaders like the late Mayor Richard J. Daley of Chicago, Governor George Wallace of Alabama, and Senator Edward M. Kennedy of Massachusetts made a first-ballot nomination all but a foregone conclusion. This was of course in marked contrast to 1968 and 1972, when rioting in the streets of Chicago and divisive floor fights in Miami Beach respectively were carried on national television for all to see.

The second example of effective use of television with somewhat limited political resources was the decision by former Governor Ronald Reagan of California, reportedly on the advice of his wife Nancy, to go on live television to promote his candidacy against President Gerald Ford after Ford had done well in early primaries. Reagan ran strongly in North Carolina, Texas, and Indiana and made a strong contest in Kansas City, ultimately falling short of defeating Ford by less than 150 votes. It is true that Ford, while he was a sitting President, had never developed a national constituency in winning a presidential election, but after his succession following the Nixon resignation in 1974 he had been developing his national constituency during the primary season. Some felt that in the race against Carter, Ford employed his most effective strategy by playing the presidential role to the utmost while Carter was using more time stumping. Ford did quite well under the circumstances, since he had to carry at least some of the burden of the Watergate scandals in which he was not personally involved. This became unavoidable to him when he concluded that he could not move ahead with his job as President without pardoning Richard Nixon, and this action in September 1974 which may have improved his intra-party position was probably costly to him in terms of Independent and Democratic support.[35]

But the main event in the fall campaign, however much criticized by the public and the networks was the series of presidential debates carried in Sep-

---

[35]See Jules Witcover, Marathon: The Pursuit of the Presidency 1972-1976 (New York: Viking Press, 1977), pp. 90, 391, 392, 395.

tember and October. (CBS announced that it considered the ground rules for the first debate a violation of its editorial prerogative, but carried it anyway.) President Ford took advantage of initial ner-
vousness on Carter's part in the first debate and was
felt by a plurality of voters to be the winner. In
the second debate, however, Carter was more aggressive
and hard-hitting, and Ford got the worst of it with an
ill-considered remark on the territorial integrity of
Soviet satellite nations in Eastern Europe. To most
observers, the third debate was a draw. But as in
1960, when a lesser known candidate faced a well known
candidate, a draw could be seen as an advantage to the
"new face". This proved to be the case with Carter as
it was with Kennedy in 1960. Carter won in the popular vote with a margin of approximately 51 to 48 per
cent (Senator Eugene McCarthy, an Independent, received the lion's share of the remaining 1 per cent of
the vote). In comparison, Kennedy's share of the 1960
vote was 49.9 to 49.7 per cent for Nixon. The debates were generally considered to have been less crucial in 1976 than in 1960, because of the greater
sophistication of the television audience. But no one
denied that they played a role in the campaign.

One additional comment should be made about the
1976 campaign. It was the first presidential campaign
conducted under the guidelines of the 1974 amendment
to the 1971 Fair Campaign Practices Act. According to
these guidelines, when each candidate agreed to accept federal funding they agreed to a $22 million
limit on campaign spending. The greatest portion of
this money went for television and a lesser amount for
other media.

In general it could be said that the mass media,
especially television, represent a crucial factor in
the campaign situation. This is despite the apparent
validity of Klapper's "nexus" hypothesis, which stated
that the media function amid a multiplicity of variables in which all combine to produce reactions among
the public attending to the media.36

36See Joseph T. Klapper, The Effects of Mass
Communication (New York: The Free Press of Glencoe,
1961).

Conclusions About Impact of These Linkages

In modern mass societies, the communications linkage between leaders and the public is important in all types of systems. It becomes crucial, however, in a system which uses as its norms the democratic standard of a relatively high degree of public participation. With this in mind, what can one conclude about the whole network of linkages analyzed in the context of the total political system?

Executive-legislative relations are critically affected by the public linkage with leaders because inevitably Presidents and members of the Congress vie for public support of differing approaches to domestic legislation and foreign policy matters. The intensity factor and the element of degree of public attention to an issue are important features of this aspect of linkage.

In the executive-bureaucracy relationship, linkage is also important. The critical distinction between any administration in power and the ongoing bureaucracy is the transitory nature of the former and the relative permanence of the latter. The bureaucracy changes incrementally as a rule and it is the exception rather than the rule in modern government when any administration truly gets a handle on the bureaucracy. A significant element in this whole relationship (both in foreign and domestic policy-making) is the timing of "leaks" and disclosures. This can normally be analyzed in the framework of whether the administration or the ongoing bureaucracy has the most to gain from disclosure or withholding of information.[37]

In the executive-judicial relationship, the executive normally gets more attention in the news media and the judiciary gets more shielding. But this is a relative thing, as indicated by an April 1977 column by Jack Anderson voicing criticism of Chief

---

[37]See, for example, Thomas M. Franck and Edward Weisband, eds., Secrecy and Foreign Policy (New York: Oxford University Press, 1974), especially Thomas L. Hughes, "The Power to Speak and the Power to Listen: Reflections on Bureaucratic Politics and a Recommendation on Information Flows", pp. 13-41.

Justice Warren Burger's refusal to disqualify himself
from considering former Attorney General
John Mitchell's appeal from his 1975 Watergate conviction. Anderson pointed out that Associate Justice
William Rehnquist, like Burger a friend of Mitchell,
had disqualified himself. But the independence of the
Court permitted Burger to take this position despite
media criticism.

The executive-public relationship is obviously
affected by the use of the media. Approaches used by
President Carter in cultivating this public interaction, in addition to the standard device of the traditional televised news conference, have included the
"phone-in" experiment with Walter Cronkite, the "fireside chat" in which the President spoke informally on
television wearing a cardigan, and the "media blitz"
which accompanied his proposal of an energy package of
legislation to the Congress. Generally the public is
fickle but usually understanding of Presidents having
difficulty. There are limits to its tolerance, however, as proved by the events between 1972 and 1974,
including the various investigations of the Watergate
break-in and the ultimate resignation of President
Nixon. Interestingly, although he was the first President to resign, President Nixon was not the first to
consider doing so. A staunch devotee of the British
parliamentary system, President Woodrow Wilson considered a similar move after the Republican off-year
election victory in 1918. But he was dissuaded by advisers who felt that such a step was contrary to
American tradition.

Insofar as the linkage impact on the executive
is concerned, it is obvious that the President operates as one part of a systemic whole. The relationship between President and public cannot be understood
outside the dynamic interrelationship among the Presidency, Congress, the judiciary, the bureaucracy and
the public.

A final question must be asked. Is the impact
of media linkage overestimated or underestimated?
This is not the kind of question which can be answered
in a simplistic fashion. The best that can be done
here is to set forth arguments on both sides.

Instances where media influence seemed not to
have a decisive impact can be cited. President Franklin D. Roosevelt was opposed by a wide majority of the

nation's newspapers in each of his campaigns. Yet he was elected each time. President Nixon was roundly criticized by more television network commentators than those who defended him; yet he won in a landslide victory in 1972. The situation with network commentators may be offset somewhat, however, by small cities' dailies, many of which gave Presidents Nixon and Ford good treatment in display of news even where they may not have editorialized in their favor. And of course it is generally known that editorial pages are not the most widely read part of newspapers today, as countless readership surveys have confirmed.

Other instances can be cited where the impact of the media may have been underestimated. Perhaps the two presidential television debate series, separated in time by 16 years, may be the most frequently cited example. Even here, the best empirical studies leave a good deal to conjecture because of problems of interpretation and methodology. The evidence is still out on the Carter era, but many critics already feel that since the beginning of the electronic communications era, Carter's mastery of the use of the media is on a par with that of FDR and JFK. Time will tell, and it may be easier to make comparisons between Carter and Roosevelt than between Carter and Kennedy, if Carter serves two full terms and longer-term comparisons can then be made.

Ultimately, it is left to each person's own best judgment. The evidence is conflicting. It is safe to say, however, that modern mass media remain an important influence on the average citizen's life, whether their impact is overestimated or underestimated.

CHAPTER SEVEN

PROSPECTS FOR THE FUTURE OF THE PRESIDENCY-

MEDIA RELATIONSHIP

The Wired Nation looks splendid in prospect,
and there can be little doubt that broadband
networks of some sort will come about in cities.
But the economics of a national rewiring are
far less understood than the technology. To
wire all of New York City would cost approximately $1 billion. To wire all the United
States would, according to one estimate of the
Sloan Commission on Cable Communications, cost
$1.3 trillion. While there has been consider-
able progress in transmitting wide bandwidths,
the equivalent of thirty-eight television
channels, over short distances through the air,
a truly comprehensive national cable television
system would probably have to rely on communications satellites. . . .

>   --Brenda Maddox, in Beyond Babel: New
>   Directions in Communications (Boston:
>   Beacon Press, 1974), p. 164

If our civilization should ever end, future
historians will not find the weapons of its
destruction among the fallen pillars of the
White House or the Capitol or the Supreme
Court. They will need to search for the
suppliers of prejudice that armed the millions
of fallen antennas resting on the rubble of
rooftops.

>   --Bruce Herschensohn, The Gods of Antenna
>   (New Rochelle, N.Y.: Arlington House,
>   1976), p. 145.

Cable television . . . makes feasible a
national government information channel. It
might provide information about social security benefits, home loans, or other government
programs. It could make it possible to file a
tax return, apply for veteran's benefits, or
vote direct from the home. . . .

Other technological developments can be
expected. A number of companies already produce videocassettes and videocassette players
and recorders. . . . In the next decade, these
devices will become inexpensive. Political
parties can produce videotape programs and
circulate them to homes and local meetings.
Congressional hearings and debates could be
videotaped. . . .

>   --Newton Minow, et al., Presidential Tele-
>   vision (New York: Basic Books, 1973),
>   pp. 165, 166

* * * *

Possible Technological Development in Broadcasting

Considering the present state of relationships
between the Presidency and the news media and how this
affects the public, I'll speculate about prospects for
the future of this relationship.

While the style of White House communications
with the public through the news media may be affected
by technological advancements, there will probably be
less change in the way in which the President and his
White House staff communicate with the public than in
the way in which the public responds. This is because
new developments may make it possible for citizens to
have a greater input into governmental decision-making.
The maximum possible exposure for Presidential statements is already possible.

In this chapter, I'll examine some prospective
changes, beginning with possible political effects of
anticipated technological development in broadcasting.

Some effects of technical improvements have
already been experienced. President Carter's news
conferences can now be viewed live on color television,
while in the Eisenhower era black-and-white television
transmitted edited film clips of White House news conferences; in the Kennedy era live coverage of news
conferences was begun, but that too was in black-and-
white. The vividness of color adds to the impact of
the coverage but the questions and answers aren't
really affected.

377

Network broadcasting of color television coverage of White House news conferences and videotaped excerpts from them has expanded notably since 1951, when President Truman's signing of the Japanese peace treaty in San Francisco was the first such event televised live on black-and-white nationwide transmission.

A technological change which widened the impact of immediate live television was the introduction of satellite transmissions. Thus when Presidents Nixon and Ford visited Peking and when President Carter visited London and Geneva, satellites made it possible to view the summit visits live rather than seeing the events by videotape or film hours later. This merely added to the instant character of broadcasting rather than content of the coverage, but it did add to the illusion of seeing history being made live.

Other technological advances already achieved have included the spread of cablevision to many areas where over-the-air broadcasting was the sole means of televised communication only a few years before.

What effects will the spread of cablevision have on coverage of White House-related events? It probably means that audiences will be enlarged, but in a day when a large proportion of viewers stick with their soap operas at 2:30 in the afternoon rather than choosing the Presidential news conferences (they can do this if they have non-network channels available) this may simply mean that access to White House news coverage is more readily available to those who have a real interest in it; it may not mean a larger audience or a wider impact. As videocassette improvements occur and such systems become feasible in taped and disc form, it will be more possible for viewers to watch Presidents and Vice Presidents, their top staff aides and key Cabinet members at a more convenient time without interfering with other viewing habits. Again this may be merely a more convenient thing for viewers but it may not increase the size of the audience. The videocassette can be set to record programs from live TV for up to four hours while the family is away from the household, asleep, or even elsewhere in the home watching other programming. The playback can then occur at the viewer's choice.

Two-way cablevision is another possible technological development now feasible, although for economic reasons it may not come at an early time. This would make possible (when 50 to 100 channels are available) individuals' response to statements of public officials. It seems to have more immediate and direct likelihood for usage for local government officials, but it could certainly further polling activities for Presidents and other national officials when and if two-way facilities ever become widespread.

Pay television may be more widely used to allow entertainment, sports and other programming to be brought into homes or to allow motel guests to watch adult films, but this too is a technology which could be used imaginatively. A benefit performance under these circumstances need not be limited to a pre-Inaugural gala but could include fund-raising devices involving the audience as well.

Other refinements of existing modes of broadcasting can be expected to change the packaging of what the public sees, but it may change the contents of the package remarkably little.

Possible Technological Development in Print Media

Like the broadcasting portion of communications, the print media have not been standing still in recent decades and can be expected to continue to make advances. Some effects of technological improvements have already occurred in recent years and can be identified briefly.

Improved photo technology has made possible improvement in the quality of wirephotos published in newspapers, more widespread use of color photography for reproduction in the press, and in general a broader use of pictorial coverage has resulted.

Electronic copy-editing is a process which may add speed to the process of handling of news stories once the copy leaves the hands of the reporter, but it is doubtful that the content of the stories will change.

A more significant effect on newspapers, magazines and other printed periodicals in recent years has probably been the indirect impact of television. With the public in effect able to gain headline and superficial coverage through the electronic media, newspapers and other print media have been obliged to search for the "meaning of the news", to publish more analysis and probe in greater depth for a perspective on White House-related events. John Osborne's White House analysis for the New Republic certainly provides this kind of interpretation, and daily newspaper coverage has gone much more into investigative reporting.

More use of color is being seen in newspapers and especially in magazines. Newsweek recently introduced "run-of-paper" color which enables it to present more graphic layouts of color photography surrounding great events involving Presidents and other notables.

Taking a more speculative look at the future, the 1980's and 1990's are expected to bring such developments as the capability for facsimile newspapers received instantaneously in subscribers' homes, instantaneous two-way communications between readers and editors, possible facsimile delivery of magazines, and similar types of new departures. Since today's "near saturation" communications situation has not prevented widespread public apathy toward Presidents and government officials, one cannot be sanguine about the likelihood that such innovations will really increase the public's interest in or knowledge about what its President is doing.

Underlying these surface questions is a more meaningful one: Will future changes in the nature of the news media bring merely more of the same or will they bring different directions in the Presidency-media relationship? An answer to this calls for conjecture in the ways in which Presidents and their advisers will seek to make use of innovative techniques. Skill in such things as the town-meeting and phone-in techniques that President Carter has used indicates a flair for public relations, but even if he and future Presidents make use of facsimile, two-way communications or other technologies, will this really change the underlying nature of the Presidency-media relationship?

It seems more likely that institutional changes in the Presidency itself are going to be the sources of changes in this relationship rather than changes in media technology. So let's turn in that direction in the next phase of this analysis.

Possibilities for Institutional Reform in the Presidency

Whether the events of Watergate were interpreted as a systemic breakdown or an aberration in the functioning of the White House, much attention was drawn in the mid-1970's to the question of institutional reform in the Presidency. Here are a few of the possibilities mentioned when such reform is discussed nowadays.

Much concern was voiced with checking the "runaway" or Imperial Presidency. All the old checks had apparently been undermined and even the informal ones such as party influence and public opinion had been weakened. The trend was noted as early as the Roosevelt years but appeared to pick up momentum during the forty years or so from the time of Roosevelt's inauguration to Nixon's resignation.[1]

Insofar as changes in the institutional structure of the Presidency were concerned, shifts of power toward the White House staff became marked as Presidents especially since Kennedy's time tried to develop new and more effective co-ordinating machinery inside the White House. This had the effect of downgrading Cabinet officials (whose influence was already on the wane) and of enhancing such White House staff members as the director of the Office of Management and Budget (whose position during the final part of Nixon's term was finally made subject to Senate confirmation).[2]

---

[1]See, for example, James MacGregor Burns, _Presidential Government: The Crucible of Leadership_ (Boston: Houghton, Mifflin Co., 1966); Arthur M. Schlesinger Jr., _The Imperial Presidency_ (Boston: Houghton, Mifflin Co., 1973); Theodore C. Sorensen, _Decision-Making in the White House_ (New York: Columbia University Press, 1963); Theodore C. Sorensen, _Watchmen in the Night_ (Cambridge, Mass.: MIT Press, 1975); Jonathan Schell, _The Time of Illusion_ (New York: Vintage Books, 1975).

[2]See Joseph A. Califano, _A Presidential Nation_ (New York: W. W. Norton & Co., 1975); George Reedy, _Twilight of the Presidency_ (Cleveland: World Publishing Co., 1970); Thomas E. Cronin, _State of the Presidency_ (Boston: Little, Brown, 1975); Douglass Cater,

With the mushrooming of the White House staff
(in fairness it should be said that the increased co-
ordinating function would have caused part of this in
any event), some changes in personnel selection also
occurred. The staff aides had been drawn from legal
and journalistic backgrounds in Roosevelt's time but
recruiters were casting their nets more widely by the
Nixon era and it was known that the Nixon White House
included a number of persons with media backgrounds
but largely from the world of advertising--a contrast
to the aides in previous Democratic administrations
who had been correspondents or persons from Capitol
Hill staffs who had been concerned with media and public relations.

What form should institutional reform in the
Presidency take? There is no real consensus on this
question and discussion of reform sometimes gets side-
tracked into controversy about who has been most able
to reduce the size of the White House staff, as
occurred at a Princeton meeting in 1975 which was
attended by Arthur Schlesinger Jr. and Donald Rumsfeld.

Some suggestions have been made, however, to
make the Presidency more responsive to the public and
to attempt to develop safeguards to prevent abuse of
power. Some of the proposals have dealt with the selection and recruitment process of Presidents themselves. The Fair Election Practices Act of 1971, as
amended in 1974, puts strict limitations on campaign
contribution procedures. Federal financing of presidential campaigns on a matching-fund basis, although
not mandatory, was accepted by the Ford and Carter campaigns in 1976. There was, however, criticism of the
law's existing structure as being unduly restrictive
on minor party candidates. Full disclosure provisions
and greater attention to campaign ethics have changed
things somewhat.

Other reforms have been made by the parties in
nominating practices, with Democratic reforms including more timely selection of delegates, efforts to secure fair representation for women, youth and minori-

Power in Washington (New York: Vintage Books, 1964);
David Wise, The Politics of Lying (New York: Random
House, 1974); Garry Wills, Nixon Agonistes (New York:
Signet Books, 1970).

ties, and broadening of representation on the National Committee. Republicans have also adopted incremental reforms, although less sweeping ones.[3]

The other principal area for reform suggestions lies in the operation of the White House itself. Ironically, though his motives may have been to increase his own partisan control of the policy-making process, a beginning was made on this between 1971 and 1973 by Richard Nixon.

The Nixon proposals presented to Congress in 1971 called for a streamlining of Cabinet machinery with departments outside State, Defense and Treasury to be re-organized into departments of Community Development, Natural Resources, Human Resources, and Economic Development. Despairing of early congressional action on these functional departments, early in 1973 President Nixon announced he had asked his Secretary of Agriculture and his Secretaries-designate of Health, Education and Welfare (HEW) and Housing and Urban Development (HUD) to act as Counsellors for Natural Resources, Human Resources, and Community Development respectively. After the Watergate scandal broke, these appointments were dropped.[4]

---

[3] For detailed discussions of reform in the parties, see: Chapter Seven, "Reform of the National Nominating Convention System" by the author, in William C. Spragens and Robert W. Russell, eds., Conflict and Crisis in American Politics (Dubuque, Iowa: Kendall/Hunt Publishing Co., 1970), pp. 85-97; Austin Ranney, Curing the Mischiefs of Faction: Party Reform in America (Berkeley: University of California Press, 1975); Alexander M. Bickel, The New Age of Political Reform: The Electoral College, the Convention, and the Party System (New York: Harper & Row, 1968); Chapter One, "Party Reform: A Movement Comes to Life", in John S. Saloma III and Frederick H. Sontag, Parties: The Real Opportunity for Effective Citizen Politics (New York: Vintage Books, 1973), pp. 13-49.

[4] See "Government Reorganization", Nixon: The Second Year of His Presidency (Washington: Congressional Quarterly, 1971), pp. 1-3; "Government Reorganization", Nixon: The Third Year of His Presidency (Washington: Congressional Quarterly, 1972), pp. 72A-79A) (this contains the full proposal for the four new

President Carter, who in his campaign stressed
the need for government reorganization and restructuring, called in the early days of his Administration
for a Department of Energy. He got this effective in
October 1977 and was given re-organization powers somewhat modified but similar to those of his predecessors.
According to one account, "Carter requested not only a
renewal of the reorganization act (which expired in
April 1973) but a broadening of the executive authority as well. His proposal retained the one-house veto
and the 60-day review period in the House and Senate,
but added new provisions not included in the act when
it expired. Carter asked for a four-year extension of
the authority, the power to amend a reorganization
plan within 30 days of its submission to Congress, the
authority to submit more than one plan every 30 days,
elimination of the requirement that each plan deal
with only one 'logically consistent subject', and an
emphasis in each plan on the identification of anticipated management improvements rather than expected
cost-saving."[5]

In addition to the restructuring of the White
House staff and executive branch departments and agencies, various proposals have been made for some type
of plural executive. One such idea was put forward by
former Vice President Nelson Rockefeller during his

---

functional departments); "Executive Reorganization",
Nixon: The Fourth Year of His Presidency (Washington:
Congressional Quarterly, 1973), pp. 56A-59A); "Gov-
ernment Reorganization", Nixon: The Fifth Year of His
Presidency (Washington: Congressional Quarterly, 1974),
pp. 95A-96A; Richard Nathan, The Plot That Failed (New
York: John Wiley & Sons, 1976), and Walter F. Mondale,
The Accountability of Power (New York: Basic Books,
1975).

[5]See "Carter's Early Initiatives: Government
Reorganization", President Carter (Washington: Congressional Quarterly, 1977), pp. 50, 51, including a
discussion of the proposal for energy agency reorganization. See also discussion of executive branch structure from Roosevelt through Nixon in Stephen Hess,
Organizing the Presidency (Washington: Brookings Institution, 1976); see also Robert Shogan, Promises to
Keep: Carter's First 100 Days (New York: Thomas Y.
Crowell Co., 1977), pp. 147, 148, 161, 167, 241, 244,
283.

tenure as New York governor. This would have provided for a Vice President for Foreign and Defense Affairs and a Vice President for Domestic Affairs, each of whom would have helped the President to co-ordinate White House administration. The Nixon arrangement with four counselors appears to be a variation of this.

Something discussed during the campaign of 1976 was the idea of revitalizing and restoring the Cabinet system and downgrading the importance of the White House staff. There appear to be limits to this kind of reform, given the need for co-ordination which the staff performs for the President today. But President Carter moved somewhat in this direction by giving (for example) Secretary of State Cyrus Vance more authority than that accorded Zbigniew Brzezinski, White House national security affairs adviser. This situation was the opposite of that in the first Nixon term when Henry Kissinger as security advisor apparently had more authority on major issues than did Secretary of State William Rogers. The ideal of such a system would be to return the Cabinet to its Truman-era importance, but there are real doubts whether this can ever be done.[6]

It does seem possible that some checks can be placed on the influence of the White House staff, and that a restructuring of the executive departments that makes more sense may be possible. Major restructuring of executive branch departments, however, probably awaits restructuring of congressional committees. Some of this was done in the Senate with the Stevenson reforms approved in 1977, but for the present reforms may lie primarily within the realm of White House reform. Even this may prove more difficult than some

---

[6]See Robert McNamara, The Essence of Security: Reflections in Office (New York: Harper & Row, 1968); Dean Acheson, Fragments of My Fleece (New York: W. W. Norton & Co., 1971); John Morton Blum, From the Morgenthau Diaries: Years of War 1941-1945 (Boston: Houghton Mifflin Co., 1967); Harold L. Ickes, The Secret Diary of Harold L. Ickes, Volume II, The Inside Struggle (New York: Simon and Schuster, 1954).

had anticipated.7

White House reform can be contrasted with executive branch reform in that it is concerned with the President's immediate staff, the personnel in the White House Office, and the Executive Office of the President. Departmental matters would not be encompassed in the scope of such reform; if White House reform is effectively put into practice, the odds may improve later for a more sweeping executive branch reform. But the problem remains complex.

Interview Data from Washington Interviews on Reform

During the fall of 1974, shortly after the Nixon resignation, the author undertook exploratory interviews about attitudes on White House and executive branch reform by seeking responses from a sample drawn from members of the U.S. Senate, Senate staffs and party officials.

The research proposed to consider executive branch reform, and more specifically that of the White House staff, in the systemic context of which the White House and its mini-bureaucracy are a part.8 The veto function of the Congress in the modern operation of national government (as exemplified in the previous

---

[7]Robert Cunningham of the Carter White House Reorganization Task Force stated that the Carter Administration as of October 1977 had reduced the White House staff from the Ford final figure of 480 down to about 430. After transferring the Office of Drug Abuse and Office of Telecommunications Policy into line departments, Cunningham predicted the Carter White House staff would be at the level of 350 by February 1978. (Presentation at Eighth Annual National Leadership Symposium, Center for the Study of the Presidency, Marist College, Poughkeepsie, New York, October 1977).

[8]See my article, "Outsiders' Views of White House Reform", in Presidential Studies Quarterly, Volume VII, Nos. 2 and 3, Spring-Summer 1977, pp. 153-159. I am indebted to R. Gordon Hoxie, president of The Center for the Study of the Presidency, for permission to reprint some of this material.

discussion of the mechanics of executive branch reorganization in legislation empowering Nixon and Carter to undertake such reforms) makes it important to understand how the White House is viewed on Capitol Hill. The effective functioning of the White House staff is measurable in part by the perceptions that specialists on the Hill have about the White House staff performance.[9]

In the interviews, respondents were first asked: "Do you believe structural reform of the Executive Branch will accomplish more than more careful selection of personnel?"

Here is a sampling of the responses on this question:

"You have to do both. There's some structural reform that was needed. Nixon was abominable in the selection of atrociously bad people. Structural reform is needed in the Executive Branch for Cabinet affairs and budget especially. Generally you need to have closer or more screening of people the President selected. Congress does not need a veto power on the process, but the White House itself could benefit by

---

[9]Although proposed prior to the Senate Select Subcommittee investigation chaired by Senator Sam Ervin (D-N.C.), proposals made by John S. Saloma III and Frederick H. Sontag, Parties: The Real Opportunity for Effective Citizen Politics (New York: Vintage Books, 1973) are relevant to this discussion. Saloma and Sontag proposed that convention nominations for President and Vice President be made with emphasis on the ability to govern (p. 75), and that increased citizen participation and public education throughout the convention process should be encouraged by the parties in co-operation with candidates, citizen groups and the media (p. 86). A thorough discussion of presidential accountability may be found in Theodore C. Sorensen, Watchmen in the Night: Presidential Accountability After Watergate (Cambridge, Mass.: MIT Press, 1975) and Walter F. Mondale, The Accountability of Power (New York: Basic Books, 1975). See also Part Two, "The State of the Presidency as an Institution", in Paul J. Halpern, ed., Why Watergate? (Pacific Palisades, Calif.: Palisades Publishers, 1975), pp. 85-149.

scrutinizing of would-be appointees by an ad hoc committee. Government consultants should serve on this
committee to disclose interests and background of
would-be appointees."

"No. I think careful selection of people is
the most important thing. This is not to say that rational structures cannot help in most important ways.
Bad people can abuse the best structure. Good people
can make a bad system work. When I was in the Executive Branch I saw a rational system being abused.
There has to be a willingness to use the structure as
well."

"No. I think no matter what the structure is,
the human factor always plays a huge part. The Mafia
has got a good structure."

"My senator probably feels that while both are
important, structural reform is very important. Unlike some persons who have said that personnel is more
important than reform, he feels that decision-making
would be better channeled this way (with structural
reform)."

"It's very difficult to choose between the two.
Far more intense and systematic congressional over-
sight is the most important thing. The kind of thing
Schlesinger is writing about in The Imperial Presidency is a structural problem that may have a structural answer. (Here the respondent cited the experience of Egil Krogh in the Watergate case.) If the
President were forced to deal directly with Cabinet
officers, that would help."

"Is there a need for reform? I don't think
it's terribly pressing. The structure of the office
is logical. The President's staff is structured by
law. That's inflexible. Cabinet members are appointed with confirmation, but the actual staff people
are not confirmable. Any statutory positions on the
White House staff should be subject to confirmation.
This applies to such positions as Executive Secretary
of the National Security Council and Director of the
Domestic Council. That's the area for structural reform. For example, in the previous administration,
John Ehrlichman should have been confirmed and asked
to testify."

"The basic need is strong personnel. I don't care what the structure is. It won't go anywhere unless you have strong people."

"We're supposed to be fairly careful in selecting personnel. One would think you're getting just about as careful selection as you can. . . ."

Respondents were next asked whether they felt the type of scandals which occurred in the Nixon Administration, including the Maryland kickback scandal, could have happened in any other administration. These were the opinions expressed:

"The same kind of scandals have already happened once (in 1924). We had a Congress which lent itself to greater scrutiny of the Nixon Administration than has been true in the past. There was an adversary atmosphere. There was poor judgment of people. The President reflected poor judgment. History's judgment of Harding is a parallel. The option is always there."

"It's quite obvious. The Senator believes that these actions could have occurred in another Administration. It's quite unfortunate. These kinds of things have been going on since the 1920's. Most important, the flagrancy and even more detestable exploitation in the situation are against the best interest of the nation and this is what makes them so injurious to the political process."

"I would doubt it."

"The diligence of the press uncovered these scandals. I doubt that it's ever been carried on to this degree in the history of the Republic."

"Yes, they could have happened in earlier times."

"No, with a strong caveat (the Maryland case was different from Watergate). The quid is not as close to the quo as that. It was a matter of ends and motive. There is a difference in kind. It seems unlikely to me that it could have happened. I can't see it happening in any other administration; the LBJ staff was not comparable. It was very aberrational. I would consider it extraordinary and unlikely."

"It depends on how you define the Nixon-Agnew type of scandals. If you're referring to the obstruction of justice, I would say yes. If you refer to the misuse of executive agencies by the administration, I would have to say that this is less likely. It is not possible to have a Watergate situation in any administration. Even Ford is subject to the abilities of those he hires."

"This follows from the first question (the selection of personnel). They probably could happen. It depends on the kind of people involved and their attitude toward such affairs. The scandals are of two obviously different types. The Agnew scandal is a more common kind of payoff scandal. Either you could have seen occur."

"Certainly the scope of abuse has never been greater than in the Nixon period. It never could have happened in earlier administrations. . . ."

"I think that any type of scandalous situation is a function of the people that are involved in it. The system (in which they work) may make it harder or easier to take place. Only in the most restricted circumstances would it be possible for things like that to happen. It was Nixon's nature to encourage this. Nixon was a supply officer in World War II. You can see it build up to a Grant or Harding type of situation. I think there is a difference between the Nixon and Agnew scandals. I suppose one is sort of a venal crime and the other is a crime that's definitely more serious. Subverting the democratic system and ideals of this country, that's infinitely worse than the other. You can't make the punishment for the first worse than the other. In the old days we had 'The Man Without a country'. Part of the problem lies in the kind of attitude that's allowed things like that to take place and people like that to get elected to office. It gets down to the materialistic nature of the country. I don't think Nixon would care and the people wouldn't either. Kickbacks, using the government to make money on, is something that detracts from the country. It has a material measurable impact on the country. . . ."

The next question asked was whether the respondent could suggest a means for the public to avoid electing men tending toward criminal behavior to elective office in the future. The responses were as follows:

"I don't know if there's an answer to that question. The public should require candidates to make a disclosure. Nixon could have disclosed all his assets and that would have had an effect in 1972. There are a lot of good values we need to get back to. Our young people should try to make us live up to our ideals--as close to the ideals I was taught as possible. We should try to ventilate our system. I don't know what will happen if we don't reinstitute personal morality. This is a level of consciousness we need to explore, including new weapons to war on poverty. If the people of the country are not basically moral, government and business won't be."

"This is a very complicated question. A lot of axioms apply. A greater sense of public awareness is needed, and this is part of the answer. This would develop conditions in which you are less likely to elect Watergate type people. Part of the problem is that our people know through direct experience less and less. The country is growing and our country is becoming less democratic. This is the area of our greatest concern. Mathematically, there has been a loss of democracy."

"I'm going to be candid and point to James David Barber's thesis that the President has to be a man of character. The public has to be more careful in its analysis of the character of men running for office. The press has a more serious obligation than it has always performed in the past. The press has to be more careful not to give the public hasty and superficial impressions of men running for public office."

"I don't know if there's any one way. We have to pressure the parties and candidates to try to avoid future campaigns that resemble the Nixon 'Selling of the President' in which you don't get a glimpse of the real man. I would be in favor of the repeal of Section 315 of the Federal Communications Act. We need more openness, without perhaps going so far as having a Clark Kent panel of psychologists to screen the candidates."

"For the near term, until we forget about it, there's going to be an awful lot closer scrutiny of people's finance which is very important. People with something to hide will be more reluctant to run. Disclosure laws can be tightened."

391

I next asked what the respondents thought of a proposal to make White House staff members subject to election by the people instead of appointed by the President. Responses were as follows:

"In 1968 we had a Republican executive and a Democratic Congress and also in 1972. Unless you ran them all on the same ticket, a President might wind up with a good part of his staff from the opposition party. This came up with Ford's hearing for confirmation (as Vice President). Compatibility is a factor. The role of the staff has to be looked at carefully. A degree of accountability is a factor, and there may be over-concern with the public image."

"The question is rather tangential to that of what sort of procedures will be followed in the workings of the White House staff. The Senator, like President Ford, considers that the Executive Office has grown too greatly. We should consider returning authority to the Cabinet departments. The size to which the White House staff had grown gives it too monarchical and imperial a position."

"Any person should have his own personnel. This is true of mayors, governors, Senators, and Presidents."

"I would be opposed to that."

"The idea is just dreadful. It's just insane."

"It's a form of Parliamentary system. Instead we ought to strengthen the Cabinet. Traditionally it has been responsible to a diversity of constituencies as well as to the President. Organizational constituencies can get their opinions expressed to the President. I don't think that the public would be helped by starting to elect staff."

"I think the President inevitably has to choose his own personal staff. He has to have people he trusts who will go with him."

"The elective idea is terrible. Instead, anyone in public office (elective, appointive, civil service) should be willing to make full disclosure. Monitoring by interview should be required, and background disclosure should be submitted. All the background and

public statements of proposed appointees should be
provided (in the screening process)."

Still another question asked of the group of
respondents was: What in your opinion is the greatest
or most useful reform which could be made in the
Executive Branch? In the White House staff?

The responses were as follows:

"Use Cabinet officers and their corresponding
bureaucracies on decisions that affect those areas.
That would be the greatest reform they could use. The
President should be dependent on those Cabinet officers. There shouldn't be a bureaucracy and staff dup-
licating the bureaucracies outside the White House."

"The most useful reform would be to have someone who understood constitutional imbalances and
acted to do something about it. This is true of both.
They should focus attention toward the way their power
should be used. Power that is shared has to be used
constitutionally in accord with a long history of submission to the Constitution."

"The most useful reform would be to create a
permanent special prosecutor or an _independent_ special
prosecutor with authority to investigate the Executive
Branch. Such a prosecutor couldn't be appointed without the support of Congress. The appointment of
Jaworsky is a good model."

"If you're going to have any sort of accountability, it must be Cabinet officers and White House
staff. This is not a productive period for Cabinets.
Cabinet members represent contact points for a variety
of interest groups. The staff doesn't like to have
anybody create a threat to the President."

"We would favor increasing the authority and
power of the Cabinet and thereby decreasing the power
and authority of the White House staff."

The next question asked was: What can Congress
do through the legislative route to promote reform of
the Executive Branch?

"Just about all the Executive Branch is responsible to the Congress. If Congress wanted to, we could
have a real strong influence over the Executive Branch.

The Nixon reform to streamline the Executive Branch (the proposal for four super-departments) would have had to get Senate approval. The Department of Agriculture and the Department of the Interior are examples of Departments with client groups that have to be taken into consideration."

"Congress really can't do much more than it already has to promote greater responsibility. Congress must reform itself. The Senate has proposed a review of its committee structure and seniority system. Once this is done, Congress will be in a better position to promote reform within the White House staff." (Note: Some of these reforms had occurred by 1978.)

"Something along the lines of Nixon's reform of the Executive Branch would be useful. The Executive Branch has got to initiate the idea. It must come from their end. Congressional initiative is darn near impossible."

"Congress can create such agencies or abolish them as they see fit. There is too much concentration of power. The White House staff is too large, too remote, too irresponsible to the people."

"Some of the things the Senator has talked about include a question and report period--a kind of variation of the parliamentary question hour. A resolution was introduced to this effect. It might force Presidents to name Cabinet officers who can stand up to Presidential questioning. If they had to come to Congress, they couldn't be like (former Secretary of State) Rogers and defend policies they had an indirect effect on. A bill to create the office of congressional legal counsel was endorsed by the staff of the Watergate committee. The Executive Branch must be more responsible to Congress than in the past. There are problems with both these bills, but the Executive Branch is becoming more responsible."

"Congress should eliminate emergency laws Presidents have used. . . ."

To summarize the responses, it seems clear that a reaction has developed to the long-term aggrandizement of power on the part of the White House at the expense of Congress and the Cabinet departments. This trend, evident since 1933, has occurred through administrations of both parties and it is largely a response to objective demands placed on the governing system. It is partly through the accident of the current party realignment, reflected in a large independent voting bloc which has placed opposing viewpoints in the executive and legislative branches, that Congress is becoming less quiescent. But the class of 1975 in Congress certainly did not represent the beginning of efforts to reform the executive; clashes between the executive and legislative branches were common in Roosevelt's time and have only varied in intensity since then.

The pressures of forty years and public impatience to do something about pressing domestic problems have contributed to the enlargement of the Presidency, which as Cronin so aptly put it has "swollen" in response to these needs. It is now being recognized that the system can go out of kilter if the "swelling" is allowed to continue too long unchecked. But as some interviewees pointed out, part of this swelling has been the result of congressional and popular inertia.

It should be further remembered that the democratic system was not designed for efficiency, but rather for the optimum amount of input from the public which the system serves. Personnel, structures and legislation are all means to an end--serving the public interest as temporary majorities shift.

Likely Relationship Between Technological Development and Institutional Reform

In considering the likely relationship between technological development in the mass media and institutional reform in the Presidency one must first ask: Is there any apparent relationship between the two?

Since technological development of the media may extend the number of citizens whom the President can reach, thereby increasing the potential exposure of his ideas, one could conclude that there is a relationship between technological improvement and the nature of the presidential institution, indirect though such a relationship might be.

To illustrate, with technological advancements in communications such as the potential development of a nationwide cablevision network and an international

395

satellite system (whose beginnings we have already seen with Intelsat), the President's ability to communicate with his publics (in the United States, in allied nations and around the world) is enhanced. This may not necessarily cause an institutional restructuring of the Presidency. But if it makes it more possible to increase public awareness and to promote an "open Presidency", the potential is there for restructuring and changing the nature of the Presidency.

Remember also that the Presidency functions in the context of the other variables such as the incumbent's leadership style, the political context in which he relates to the Congress and the public, and the general opinion climate of any given time.

A follow-up question to be asked once some kind of relationship is established, is: If so, what kind of relationship can be projected? The leadership style of any President may cause more changes in the actual operation of the Presidency than restructuring and institutional reforms of that type. But Nixon did put a finger on one difficult problem when he designed an effort to gain more responsiveness in the bureaucracy with the "super-Cabinet" model. It seems more likely that communications improvements and advancements will affect the Presidency's relationship with the public than with the inner workings of the bureaucracy. The kind of restructuring Nixon attempted probably wouldn't be affected that much by technological advances. Carter has already proposed a new Department of Energy which came into effect in October 1977; he is also seeking other shifts such as the Califano restructuring of HEW, an entire program of welfare reform, the health care program and other new proposals.

But it seems likely that any President's ability to exploit the potential for greater communication is likely to weigh more heavily than technological improvements in communication, no matter how solid these gains may be. The minicam or microcam technology may make it possible to transmit television pictures of presidential activity no matter where he goes, but does that really change the relationship between the President and the public? This would lead one to expect that a minimal or incremental change in relationship is about the most that can be expected. The public should not expect great changes as a result of technological advancement.

In looking at this idea, one concludes that total change is unlikely on the basis of communications advancements, but that incremental change may be expected. The degree of shift in relationship may be quite limited, however, because of the overshadowing of technology by such factors as changes in presidential leadership style from one administration to another, the dynamics of the presidential relationship to the bureaucracy, to Congress and to the public, and related political factors.

Where Is the Presidency Heading in Terms of Democratic Ideals?

The Presidency is in a time of reassessment as 1980 approaches, but it seems the experience with Ford and Carter shows we probably can't expect any early resumption of the trend toward an Imperial Presidency. This is solely intuitive conjecture, but it appears that the trauma of Watergate and the presence in the voting population of the generation which experienced this crisis will leave its mark on the Presidency for the next five or six administrations, much as the Depression and various wars have left their mark. Even though Watergate may be considered an aberration it was still a watershed.

The Imperial Presidency trend was probably caused in part by a long period, really from the end of World War II until the Vietnam truce in 1973, in which almost excessive attention was paid to foreign policy by Presidents. The experience with Carter indicates that the most domestically oriented president-- in this case one with a background as Governor, the first such chief executive since FDR--will find foreign policy matters very attractive to deal with because of the relative freedom of decision-making in that sphere. Welfare reform, energy packages require great negotiation and conciliation with Congress.

Reform of the Presidency is nonetheless possible. This is related to hopes for democratic ideals, because responsiveness to the public is the core of democratic expectations. The good fortune that both Ford and Carter had to work at building up a national constituency has helped to improve these relations, but there may be a "lost generation" with cynical tendencies because of the Nixon-era experiences. So the outlook for reform is mixed. It has outer limits.

397

Has Television Helped or Hindered Development of the Presidency as a More Responsive Office?

Has television been a help or a hindrance to the process of developing more responsiveness to the public in the Presidency? It's possible to present evidence supporting arguments on both sides of this issue.

Clearly by making instantaneous communication more widely possible, television has enhanced the potential for making the Presidency more responsive. This is because it has made possible new formats of communication. The willingness of Presidents to use these new possibilities limits the potential somewhat, however.

Also television has made possible the development of institutions that come into conflict with the Presidency in some instances. The suspicion of the networks and of broadcasting in general which was reflected in the orchestrated Agnew attacks on "querulous criticism" of a small group of network newscasters indicates how this kind of institutional conflict can develop. Agnew, however, never bothered to attack friendly communications channels such as newspapers which gave support to Administration policies. Most government officials, and especially the President, are almost certain to be unsatisfied with coverage of public affairs whether on television or in other media.

Thus we find some support for the view that television has helped the President to communicate with the public, especially when he goes directly to the public to present his unvarnished views.

But I find support for the view that Presidents consider television something of an impediment when the reporting of correspondents and the analysis of commentators intervenes. It has been both a blessing and a curse, from the viewpoint of the men in the Oval Office.

Conclusions About the Future of the Presidency-Media Relationship

Considering prospects for the future of the Presidency-media relationship, let's first examine the ideal situation from the public's viewpoint. This is the circumstance in which both the Presidency and the news media will act as a check on each other. The White House will question coverage which is patently unfair or one-sided and will attempt to keep the media on their toes (sometimes competition does more than the White House; that was true of TV networks regarding the Woodward-Bernstein coverage of Watergate, as they were late in realizing the significance of the story). Presidents with a constituency which is sympathetic can expect support in seeking to avoid the cheap shot and unfair type of coverage. But let them lose their popularity and they are not in a good vantage point in the constant tug-of-war with the media.

As for the media, they provide a necessary check on the Presidency and may especially exploit "leaks" of information to help sensitize the public to the existence of significant issues. The media did this admirably in the handling of the "Pentagon Papers", and usually have been quick to point out the shortcomings of administrations of both parties. Such instances as the Credit Mobilier scandal of the 1870's and Teapot Dome in the 1920's can be cited from the more distant past. In recent times, newspapers, radio, and television all helped to expose the "five per cent" scandals of the late Truman era, the Sherman Adams scandal of the Eisenhower period, the Billy Sol Estes scandals in the Agriculture Department during Kennedy's time, the Bobby Baker case during LBJ's tenure, all the numerous scandals handled under the generic title of "Watergate" (including the dirty tricks, tax manipulations, etc.) in Nixon's time.

Two dangers are possible in the situation, and these are domination of the media by the Presidency or domination of the Presidency by the media. Complete domination is unlikely by either, but let's explore each of these dangers briefly.

Domination of the media by the Presidency may seem unlikely in the wake of Watergate, but it could occur in the future. This is because the Presidency maintains control of much of the flow of news through scheduling of news conferences, classification of various documents and other devices. It may not abuse this power, but the possibility of deception is always present. One example of this can be found in the secret bombing of Cambodia, which was kept covered up as far as the American people were concerned, possibly

long after espionage agents from the opposing bloc
were informed about it.

Some would argue that the media came perilously
close to "hounding" a President out of office in the
final days of the second Nixon Administration. Although public confidence had been lost by the choice
of courses of action by the Administration before this
occurred, the Nixon experience ought to alert the public to the dangers of dominance of the Presidency by
the media. This is only likely to happen in the case
of a weak President, unable to inspire public confidence, but even though it may be a lesser danger than
White House domination of the media, it ought not to
be totally forgotten.

The modern separation of powers may focus more
on the White House relationship with the media, rather
than on the White House relationship with the rest of
the political and governmental system.[11] The informal
aspects of White House interaction with other institutions have changed to become almost more significant
than the formal relationships with other governmental
branches because of the increased possibility for public awareness of issues.

Some general conclusions can be stated about
the future of the linkage between the Presidency and
the media. First of all, there is a built in co-
operation and competition present. Each needs the
other, but the different viewpoints of each institution mean the relationship will be an uneasy one. The
public may turn first to one, then the other, as the
dynamics of power and influence change, but the ambiguity of this love-hate relationship (or conflict-
co-operation if one prefers) seems destined to continue into the indefinite future.

A second expectation is that the public will be
quite permissive with future White House occupants,
except in cases where much is seen to be at stake.
This attitude of the public is likely to give both the
Presidency and the media a good deal of flexibility in
their relations, and this seems to be a healthy thing.

---

[11]For a discussion of such informal checks on
the Presidency, see James MacGregor Burns, Presidential
Government (Boston: Houghton Mifflin Co., 1965).

Finally, the Presidency and the media are almost certain to depend on the public as a referee in their competition. This seems to grow out of the democratic culture we have developed. This state of affairs will serve the public interest in the long run.

INDEX OF NAMES

Fall, Bernard B., 7
Fenno, Richard F. Jr., 157
Fillmore, Millard, 163
Flanders, Ralph, 319
Ford, Betty, 265
Ford, Gerald R., 3, 7, 12-13, 21, 27, 31, 33, 35, 45,
    56-57, 61, 68, 74, 80-85, 87, 95, 100, 106, 114,
    116, 123, 128, 133-141, 139n, 144, 147, 149, 152-
    156, 158, 160, 167-168, 170-171, 174, 180, 187, 224,
    231, 235, 238, 247-249, 251-252, 257, 259-260, 262,
    265-266, 268-269, 279-286, 294, 334-336, 353, 355n,
    356, 365, 367-368, 371-372, 375, 378, 390, 392, 397
Ford, Henry II, 305
Fortas, Abe, 60, 170, 355
Franck, Thomas M., 373n
Frankel, Max, 301
Franklin, Benjamin, 182
Friedheim, Jerry, 256
Friedman, Milton, 194
Friedman, Saul, 297
Friendly, Fred, 32, 220n
Fritchey, Clayton, 231
Fulbright, J. William, 6, 7, 19, 31-32

Gallup, George, 49, 195
Gardner, John, 349
Garfield, James A., 164
Garroway, Dave, 211
Gawthrop, Louis C., 149n, 158n
George, Walter, 323
Gibson, Althea, 305
Glass, Andy, 300-301
Golan, Matti, 341n
Goldberg, Arthur, 170
Golden, Harry, 182
Goldman, Eric F., 127n, 277, 277n
Goldwater, Barry, 124, 126, 367
Goodman, Mark, 196
Goodwin, Richard, 258
Graber, Doris A., 273n
Graham, Billy, 305
Graham, Fred, 177
Graham, Katharine, 185, 194, 220
Grant, Peter, 202
Grant, Ulysses, 164, 390
Granum, Rex, 284
Greeley, Horace, 42
Green, Dwight, 188
Grier, Anne, 177
Griffin, Robert, 168, 297

Grossman, Michael B., 291n
Gruening, Ernest, 76
Gulliver, Hal, 186, 355n
Guthman, Edwin, 56n

Haas, Karl, 202
Hackes, Peter, 239
Hadden, Britt, 193
Hadley, Arthur T., 49n
Hagerty, James C., 14, 73, 81, 147, 238, 249-254, 256-257, 286, 287n, 290, 290n, 307-309, 309n, 317-318, 320-334, 334n
Halberstam, David, 7, 18, 207n, 211, 347n
Haldeman, H. R., 16-17, 129, 146, 150, 157, 174, 256, 258, 351
Halpern, Paul J., 387n
Hamilton, Alexander, 41, 273
Harding, Warren, 64, 106, 164, 175, 274, 389-390
Hare, Ernie, 206
Harriman, Averell, 108, 110, 153
Harrington, Michael, 197
Harris, Fred, 370
Harris, Louis, 49, 195, 338
Harris, Richard, 342, 355n
Harrison, Benjamin, 164
Harrison, Gilbert, 305-306, 306n
Harrison, William Henry, 163
Hart, Gary, 40n, 52n
Hart, John, 212, 239
Hart, Philip, 168
Hartman, David, 217
Hayes, Rutherford B., 164
Haynsworth, Clement, 196, 342, 354-355
Hays, Wayne, 185, 199, 345-347, 345n
Hearst, Patty, 196
Hearst, William Randolph, 231
Heaton, Leonard D., 332
Henry, E. William, 307, 307n
Herschensohn, Bruce, 22n, 345n, 376
Hersh, Seymour, 179, 184
Hershowitz, Mickey, 183
Hess, Stephen, 78, 133n, 361n, 384n
Hickel, Wally, 157
Hilsman, Roger, 123n
Hiss, Alger, 26, 68, 77, 278
Hitler, Adolf, 107, 207
Ho Chi Minh, 299
Holland, Bob, 196
Holmes, Oliver Wendell, 170
Hoopes, Townsend, 363

Hoover, Herbert, 64, 106, 123, 143, 149, 163-164, 274-276, 368
Hoover, J. Edgar, 350
Hope, Bob, 205, 305
Hopkins, Harry L., 108, 108n, 110, 153
Horne, Lena, 305
Howard, Lucy, 294
Howe, Louis, 249
Hoxie, R. Gordon, 364n, 386n
Hughes, Emmett, 258
Hughes, Howard, 10
Hughes, Langston, 305
Hughes, Thomas L., 373n
Hull, Cordell, 110
Hulteng, John L., 241n, 243n
Humphrey, George M., 310
Humphrey, Hubert H., 8, 55, 91, 103, 126, 179, 189, 193, 278, 367-369, 371

Ickes, Harold, 156, 385n

Jackson, Andrew, 41, 101, 105, 161-165, 273
Jackson, Henry (Scoop), 85-86, 140, 370
Jagoda, Barry, 283-292, 293n
James, Dorothy Buckton, 96n
Jameson, Bob, 239
Jarrell, Tom, 239
Jaworsky, Leon, 393
Jefferson, Thomas, 41, 100, 162, 273, 273n
Jenkins, Walter, 183
Johnson, Andrew, 161, 161n, 163-164
Johnson, Lady Bird, 285
Johnson, Lyndon B., 6-7, 11-12, 16, 18, 23-26, 28, 31-32, 35, 44-45, 53, 55, 63, 74-76, 82, 87, 89-90, 100, 103, 105, 112, 114, 118-127, 127n, 134, 139, 147, 153, 155, 179, 216, 225, 243, 249, 251-252, 254-256, 258, 262, 265, 269, 275, 277, 277n, 279-280, 287, 291n, 296-297, 301-303, 305-309, 336, 339, 349, 355-356, 355n, 358-360, 363, 367-369, 389, 399
Johnson, Maurice, 302
Johnson, Tom, 297, 301-302
Jones, Billy, 206
Jordan, Hamilton, 16, 146, 250, 259

Kalber, Floyd, 203, 211, 239
Kaltenborn, H. V., 43, 205, 207
Katzenbach, Nicholas, 9
Kearns, Doris, 7, 56n, 76n, 77n, 127n, 173, 173n
Kefauver, Estes, 48, 103
Kennedy, Edward, 86, 131, 197, 341, 371

McNamara, Robert S., 7, 119, 363, 385n
McNamee, Graham, 207
Meany, George, 86, 305
Meir, Golda, 130
Meredith, James, 120
Metz, Robert, 7, 211
Mickelson, Sid, 207, 243
Mills, Wilbur, 185, 196, 345-347
Minow, Newton N., 45n, 307, 377
Miroff, Bruce, 74, 365n
Mitchell, John, 19, 58, 133, 157, 351, 374
Mitchell, Lee N., 45n
Mitchell, Martha, 196
Moley, Raymond, 194
Mollenhoff, Clark, 81n, 189
Molotov, V. M., 312
Mondale, Walter F., 287, 384n, 387n
Monroe, Bill, 239
Monroe, James, 162, 273n
Montgomery, Robert, 310
Morgan, Edward P., 306
Morgenthau, Henry, 385n
Morse, Wayne, 6, 76, 313
Morton, Bruce, 239
Morton, Rogers, 81-82
Moyers, Bill, 12, 13n, 14, 18, 75, 81, 147, 190, 194,
    213, 216, 249, 255-258, 255n, 296, 303
Moynihan, Daniel P., 259
Mudd, Roger, 212, 239
Murdoch, Rupert, 231
Murphy, Reg, 355n
Murrow, Edward R., 43, 207, 211-212, 255n
Murrow, Janet, 255n
Muskie, Edmund, 91

Nader, Ralph, 350
Nathan, Richard, 384n
Navasky, Victor, 350, 350n
Nehru, Jawaharlal, 322
Nessen, Ron, 3, 13, 81, 147, 238, 249, 251, 257, 257n,
    261, 261n, 284, 294
Neustadt, Richard E., 29, 60n, 123n, 291, 291n, 339
Newhouse, John, 20, 340, 340n
Nie, Norman H., 242n
Nimmo, Dan, 45n, 291n, 370n
Nixon, Pat, 194, 266

Pritchett, C. Herman, 352n
Pulitzer, Joseph, 188

Quinn, Sally, 185

Rabin, Yitzhak, 130
Ranney, Austin, 383n
Rather, Dan, 177, 183, 212, 216, 239, 251, 262, 265, 279
Ray, Elizabeth, 199
Reagan, Nancy, 371
Reagan, Ronald, 3, 27, 46, 58, 82-84, 91, 125, 134-135, 137, 139, 141-144, 154, 156, 160, 261, 281, 334-335, 371
Reasoner, Harry, 192, 212, 239
Rebozo, Bebe, 190, 266
Reed, Dan, 310
Reedy, George, 14, 75, 147, 249, 254-256, 255n, 258, 303, 381
Reeves, Richard A., 299
Rehnquist, William, 169, 354, 374
Reston, James (Scotty), 184, 231, 234
Reuther, Walter, 305
Rhee, Syngman, 316
Rice, Grantland, 207
Riegel, Donald, 168
Roberts, Chalmers, 299
Robinson, Jackie, 305
Rockefeller, Nelson, 33, 129, 281, 296, 384
Rodino, Peter, 33, 128, 174
Rogers, William, 130, 385, 394
Romney, George, 157, 296-297
Roosevelt, Eleanor, 66, 276
Roosevelt, Elliott, 67n, 108n
Roosevelt, Franklin D., 17, 35, 59-60, 64-65, 69, 87, 95-96, 101, 104n, 105-113, 106n, 109n, 118, 122, 125, 138, 149-150, 150n, 153-155, 157, 161-166, 166n, 172, 176, 186, 188, 249, 258, 275-276, 292n, 336, 352, 362, 367, 368n, 374-375, 381-382, 384n, 395
Roosevelt, Theodore, 64, 101-102, 154, 161, 163-165, 170, 274-275, 308, 355
Roper, Burns, 195
Rosenblum, Victor G., 221
Rosenman, Samuel, 258
Ross, Charles, 147, 249
Rossiter, Clinton, 169n
Rostow, Walt W., 153, 301
Rourke, Francis E., 291n
Rudd, Hughes, 207, 239

ABOUT THE AUTHOR

WILLIAM C. SPRAGENS, Associate Professor of Political Science at Bowling Green State University, Bowling Green, Ohio, since 1969, is the co-author of Conflict and Crisis in American Politics (with Robert W. Russell) (Dubuque, Iowa: Kendall/Hunt Publishing Co., 1970). He has also contributed to the following books: Marius Livingston, ed., International Violence and Terrorism (Westport, Conn.: Greenwood Press, 1977); Joseph S. Roucek and Thomas Kiernan, eds., The Negro Impact on Western Civilization (New York: Philosophical Library, 1970), and Joseph S. Roucek, ed., The Slow Learner (New York: Philosophical Library, 1969). He has contributed articles or book reviews to the following publications: Journal of Politics, Presidential Studies Quarterly, Western Political Quarterly, Political Science Quarterly, Il Politico, DEA News of the American Political Science Association, Wisconsin Review, and Journal of Negro History. Prior to receiving the Ph.D. in political science at Michigan State University in 1966, Professor Spragens was a working editor and reporter, having worked on the Lexington (Ky.) Herald, Owensboro (Ky.) Messenger & Inquirer, Dayton Journal Herald, and Fort Wayne (Ind.) Journal-Gazette. He has previously served in the Political Science departments at the University of Tennessee-Knoxville; Millikin University, Decatur, Ill., and Wisconsin State University-Oshkosh. He is currently working on a project related to presidential press secretaries, a project on media habits of voters in presidential elections, and a textbook on American foreign policy. He has been honored as a Falk Fellow, a Ford Foundation legislative intern in Michigan, a life fellow of the Institute for International Sociological Research, and a life member of Delta Tau Kappa, international social science honorary. He has been listed in such reference works as International Authors and Writers Who's Who, Dictionary of International Biography, Community Leaders and Noteworthy Americans, Who's Who in the Midwest, and American Men and Women of Science. In 1976 he was chosen as a participant in a Symposium on International Violence and Terrorism at Glassboro State College, Glassboro, N. J.